Using Alpha Four™

SHERRY J. MARTIN

EDITH G. JENKINS,
CONTRIBUTING AUTHOR

FOREWORD BY SELWYN RABINS
CO-CHAIRMAN, ALPHA SOFTWARE

D1213961

Publisher: Lloyd J. Short

Associate Publisher: Rick Ranucci

Acquisitions Editor: Chris Katsaropoulos

Product Development Manager: Thomas H. Bennett

Book Designer: Scott Cook

Production Team: Christine Cook, Keith Davenport, Brook Farling, Kate Godfrey, Carla Hall-Batton, Bob LaRoche, Laurie Lee, Loren Malloy, Caroline Roop, Linda Seifert, John Sleeva, Lisa Wilson, Allan Wimmer, Phil Worthington

CREDITS

Product Director
Walter R. Bruce III

Production Editor
H. Leigh Davis

Editors
Jo Anna Arnott
Kellie Currie

Technical Editor
James Francis Xavier Little, Jr.

Composed in Cheltenham and MCPdigital by Que Corporation

DEDICATION

To Jay
—*S.J.M.*

SHERRY J. MARTIN

Sherry Martin is the president of Computers Without Fear, Inc., a computer instruction and consulting firm, for network installations and hardware and software sales and training. CWF has offices in Boston and Cape Cod. Sherry has a bachelor's degree from Smith College and a master's degree in education from Boston University. Formerly a real estate broker and the editor of a weekly newspaper, she has been a photographer and reporter for the Boston *Herald-Traveler* and the Boston *Globe*. Sherry also has lectured and taught in many local schools and universities.

Sherry has been the leader of the Boston Computer Society's Alpha Four Users Groups for two years. She also is a contributing author for the Pinnacle Publishing, Inc., newsletter *Alpha Forum*.

EDITH G. JENKINS, Contributing Author

Edith Jenkins also lives in the Boston area. She is a graduate of Bennington College with a degree in economics. Edith is currently employed as a technical support person at Alpha Software. For two years, she was an applications developer and consultant with Computers Without Fear in Boston. During this time, much of the thinking and some of the writing for this book was done.

TRADEMARK ACKNOWLEDGMENTS

Thanks to all the professionals at Que Corporation whose help and guidance made this book possible. A special thanks goes to Rick Ranucci for taking a chance on the project; to Tim Stanley for getting me started; to Walt Bruce for keeping me on course; and to Leigh Davis for pulling the pieces together at the end.

My gratitude to all the friends and family who have put up with the trials of producing this book. To Bob Keddy, and Francie Peake before him; and the Alpha Four Technical Support Department, Laura, Pete, and Jim Little, for sticking with it. To Chris McDonald; my staff, Chris K., Chris B., Linda, George, Nancy, and Mercedes. To Pam for her gentle comments and to Jim Goff for being there.

To the members of the Boston Computer Society's Alpha Four User Groups, Boston and Cape Cod—too many to name them all, but special thanks to Bill, Diane, Jim, Joel, Tom, Dennis, and Joe, for suggestions, contributions, and patience.

—S.J.M.

We at Alpha Software are delighted that *Using Alpha Four* is being written by Sherry J. Martin, a long-time friend of Alpha products, and being produced by Que Corporation, an acknowledged leader in fine computer publications.

Sherry's knowledge of this Alpha Four and her understanding of the users of Alpha Four come from her experiences as a teacher, as an applications developer, and as the leader of the first Alpha Four Users Group, sponsored by the Boston Computer Society. Therefore, *Using Alpha Four* contains real-life examples to assist in problem-solving for beginners as well as advanced users.

Alpha Four Version 2 is greatly expanded in function and scope over ALPHA/*three* and Alpha Four Version 1. Still, Version 2 is a natural outgrowth of the earlier software. Users of ALPHA/*three* and all versions of Alpha Four can benefit from this book because the basic functions and comfortable menu-driven interface is recognizable to all who have worked with the products.

Selwyn Rabins, Co-chairman
Alpha Software Corporation, Burlington, Massachusetts

CONTENTS AT A GLANCE

Introduction 1

I Alpha Four Basic Techniques

Quick Start 1: A Typical Alpha Four Session 11
1 Navigating Alpha Four 35
2 Defining and Creating Your First Database 53
3 Entering Data 69
4 Indexing, Sorting, Searching, and Updating Records 111
5 Creating Field Rules To Control Data Entry 143
6 Creating Reports 159
7 Developing Strategies for Special Reporting 185

II Intermediate Alpha Four

Quick Start 2: Understanding the Relational Skills
of Alpha Four 227
8 Using Sets 245
9 Moving Your Data and Files 259
10 Using Alpha Four Tips, Tricks, and Techniques 289

III Advanced Alpha Four

Quick Start 3: Creating Applications and Scripts 307
11 Creating Applications 331
12 Creating Scripts 355
13 Using Expressions and Functions 393
14 Documenting Your Work 417

Appendix A Other Resources for Help 433
Appendix B Installation Procedures 435
Appendix C Using the Network 439
Appendix D Problem-Solving Sample Expressions 445
Appendix E Favorite Expressions from Alpha Four Techs 453
Appendix F Error Codes in Alpha Four 455

Index 459

Introduction 1

What Is Alpha Four? 2
    Features for Beginners 2
    Features for Current Users of Version 1 3
    New Features in Version 2 3
What Hardware Configuration Do You Need? 5
Who Should Read This Book? 5
How This Book Is Organized 6
Starting Alpha Four 8

1 Alpha Four Basic Techniques

Quick Start 1: A Typical Alpha Four Session 11

Using Alpha Four 12
Starting Alpha Four 13
Creating the INVENTRY Database 14
Entering Data into the First Record 17
Making Easy Calculations with Field Rules 18
Checking the Rules 22
Producing Results 23
Organizing Your Data 24
Choosing Your Output 25
Customizing Your Data-Entry and View Screens 27
Using a Second Kind of Calculated Field 29
Reporting on Your Data 30
Summary 33

1 Navigating Alpha Four 35

Knowing When You Need Alpha Four 35
Defining a Database 37
    Development of Databases 38
    Development of Alpha 38

Taking a Short Tour of Alpha Four 40
    Main Menu 40
    Keystroke Conventions 41
    Screens and Windows 46
    Default Screen Settings 48
    Protection Options 51
    Help 52
Summary 52

2 Defining and Creating Your First Database 53

Understanding Database Terminology 54
Listing Objectives for Your Database 55
Putting Information Down on Paper 57
    Ask the Right Questions 57
    Map Out the Fields 59
Defining Your Data Needs 60
Field Naming Rules 63
Creating the File 65
Entering Records 66
Summary 68

3 Entering Data 69

Using the Default Input Form 70
    Entering Data in View Mode 71
    Entering Data into Character Fields 72
    Entering Data into Numeric Fields 72
    Entering Data into Date Fields 73
    Entering Data into Logical Fields 73
    Entering Data into Memo Fields 73
Using the Default Browse Table 74
    Entering Data in Browse Mode 75
    Editing and Changing Data in View
        or Browse Mode 75
    Using Alternative Techniques for Data Entry 75
Defining New Input Forms 76
Defining New Browse Tables 79
    Customizing an Input Form 82
    Practical Uses for Calculated Fields 83
        Using a Calculated Field 84
        Creating a Calculated Field 85
    Moving and Deleting Text and Fields 87
    Using Lines and Boxes as a Highlight 88

Using Special Forms 88
   Enhanced Data Entry 89
   Security for Sensitive Data 89
Using Browse Tables for Multiple Records on View ...89
   Making Browse Tables Work for You 90
   Using Color in Browse Tables 92
   Another Example Using Color Expressions 94
   Long Text Fields in Browse Tables 95
   Using Browse Tables for Data Entry 96
   Using Browse Tables in Sets 97
Using Range and Index Commands 97
   Finding Records 98
   Using Range Commands with Filters 98
   Using the Locate (Search for) Command 98
   Using Search and Replace 99
   Using Delete and Undelete Records 101
   Marking a Record for Deletion 102
Backing Up Your Data 103
Packing the Database 104
   Using an Alternative to Packing 105
   Using Pack Step-by-Step 106
Summary 106

4 Indexing, Sorting, Searching, and Updating Records 111

Understanding How Indexes Work 112
   Speeding Up Your Work 113
   Designing the Index 113
   Creating an Index 114
   Indexing Options 114
   Understanding the Power of an Index 115
Creating an Index 117
   Using an Index To Tie Databases Together 118
   Reconfiguring Your Database 120
Understanding Subgrouping 121
   Using Set Pieces 121
   Using Indexes To Eliminate Duplicates 124
   Setting Up a Unique Index 125
   Removing Duplicates in Existing Databases 126
   Understanding How Index Files Work 126
   Detaching Indexes 128
   Updating, Attaching, and Detaching Indexes 129

Understanding Searches 130
  Understanding the Difference
    between Range and Search 131
  Making a Filter Active 132
  Making a Filter Inactive 133
Defining Searches..133
  Using Expressions To Refine Data Retrieval 133
  Defining the Difference between .AND.
    and .OR. 134
Creating Indexes and Summary Databases 135
Creating a Summary Database 136
  Performing Sample Searches 138
  Mastering Global Update 138
  Changing the Case in a Range of Records 138
  Updating a Field 139
  Performing Sample Global Updates 140
Summary 141

5 Creating Field Rules To Control Data Entry....................**143**

Writing Field Rules 144
Selecting User-Entered and Calculated Data Fields ...144
Understanding User-Entered Field Rules 146
  CASE CONVERT 146
  TEMPLATE 147
  MASK 148
  ALLOW EXCEPTIONS 148
  DEFAULT MODE 148
  INCREMENT 149
  REQUIRED 150
  SKIP ENTRY 150
  PROMPT 150
Creating Lookups by Using Tables or Databases 151
  Creating a Lookup Table 151
  Creating a Lookup Database 152
Exploring Lookups 154
Summary 157

6 Creating Reports..**159**

Using the Report Writer 160
  Defining Your Goal 161
  Using Input Forms 161
  Using Browse Tables 162

Using Mailing Labels and Letters 162
Using Columnar Reports 162
Using Quick Setup versus Custom Report 164
Exploring Sections 168
Creating a Database from a Report 168
Using a Page Header 170
Using Titles 171
Using Details 172
Using Page Footers 173
Using a Summary Section 173
Using Formatting Options 175
Length versus Window 175
Justification 176
Data 176
Format 176
Applying Basic Formatting Options 178
Making Lines Disappear 179
Formatting Memo Fields 179
Formatting Numeric Fields 180
Formatting Date Fields 181
Saving and Previewing Your Report 182
Printing Your Report 182
Defining a Printer Driver 183
Summary 184

7 Developing Strategies for Special Reporting 185

Using Advanced Reporting Techniques 186
Organizing Your Data 189
Creating an Index 191
Using Special Reporting Techniques 193
Borrowing a Format 194
Using Save To Create a Support File 194
Refining Your Reports with Ranges and Filters 194
Creating Calculated and Summary Databases 195
Using Calculated versus Summary Fields 196
Placing Fields in Custom Reports 197
Averaging with Zeros 198
Defining Mailing Labels 199
Making Mailing Labels 199
Using Pre-defined Label Definitions 200
Individualizing Your Label for Your Needs 202
Printing Multiple Copies of Labels 202
Placing Fields on Your Label 202
Improving the Look of Your Label 203

Adding Special Emphasis to Mail Labels 204
Formatting Options on Labels 206
Using Special Formatting for Labels 206
Using SYSTEM Fields on Labels 207
Using Subgroups 208
Defining Ranges and Printers 208
Using Memo Fields in Reports 209
Indexing a Record 210
Lettering Your Database 214
Creating a Letter 214
Controlling Page Layout 216
Using Conditional Expressions 217
Using a Word Processor 218
Using Alternatives to Reports
To Summarize the Data 219
Using Other Kinds of Summarized Reports 219
Using Field Statistics 219
Using Summary Databases 221
Summary 223

II Intermediate Alpha Four

Quick Start 2: Understanding the Relational Skills
of Alpha Four 227

Defining a Relational Database 227
Preparing for Sets 228
Creating a Sample Set 228
Fine-Tuning with Link Parameters 233
Zooming around Your Files 234
Managing Your Desktop 235
Understanding Zoom and Switch 236
Controlling Output from Sets 237
Enhancing Reports in Sets 237
Useful Samples of Linked Databases 240
Posting Invoice Totals to Customer Files 240
Summary 243

8 Using Sets 245

Forging Links 246
Creating Forms and Browse Tables in Sets 247
Entering Data in a Set 249
Linking Parameters 250

Creating a Set 251
   Choosing Sets versus Lookup Databases 251
   Creating Field Rules in a Set 252
   Determining Field Origin 252
      Creating an Index 253
      Defining a Global Update 253
      Creating Field Rules 253
   Retrieving the Linked Data 254
   Using Colorful Math 255
Copying a Set 256
Summary 258

9 Moving Your Data and Files 259

Copying a File 260
Understanding the Relational Commands 262
Posting Data from One File to Another 265
   Understanding How Posting Works 265
   Marking Posted Records 269
Distinguishing between Post and Append 269
Splicing and Dicing with Subtract, Join,
   and Intersect 271
   Extracting Nonmatching Records
      with Subtract 272
   Creating a Third File from Two Files
      with Join Database 273
   Intersecting Data Files 276
Performing Crosstab Functions 277
Summarizing the Effects of Relational Commands 282
Putting Yourself into the Import/Export Business 284
   Understanding ASCII 284
   Importing and Exporting 285
   Dealing with Spreadsheets 286
   Talking to WordPerfect 286
Summary 287

10 Using Alpha Four Tips, Tricks, and Techniques 289

Get the Right Hardware 290
Get the Right Software 290
Write Down Your Procedures 291
Learn This Program Well 291
Learn Applications and Scripts 291

Using Shortcuts 292
    Changing Data in Records by Using
       a Calculated Field 292
    Creating an Automatic Lookup
       on More Than One Category 292
    Changing the Colors of the Entire Screen 293
       Version 1 293
       Version 2 295
    Using Colors for Help 296
    Using Alt-F5 and Alt-F6 To Cut and Paste 297
Organizing Records 297
Using Pseudo Fields To Prevent Unauthorized
    Data Changes 298
Personalizing Your Work 299
Creating Scripts for Shortcuts 300
Creating Field Rules 300
Making Records Easy To Find 301
Using Subgrouping 301
Summary 303

III Advanced Alpha Four

Quick Start 3: Creating Applications and Scripts 307

Understanding an Application 308
Creating Applications 309
    Creating a Sample Application 311
    Creating a Macro in the Application Editor 314
Understanding Scripts versus Applications 315
Creating Scripts 316
    Creating a Dialog Script 316
    Creating a Keystroke Script 318
Using New Tools 319
Specializing File Names 320
Managing a Desktop 321
Processing a Desktop 322
Understanding Variables 323
    Defining and Using Variables 324
    Creating a Variable 325
    Viewing the Variables 326
Using Triggers 326
Passing Data between Files with Triggers 327
Summary 328

11 Creating Applications **331**

Learning the Art of Menu Building 332
Planning Your Menu System 335
Defining the Structure 335
Designing the Application 337
Creating a Sample Application 339
    Creating the Menu 340
    Dressing Up Your Banner 341
        Drawing a Line 342
        Drawing a Box 342
    Creating Template Screens 342
    Changing Your Banner 343
Adding the Details to Your Menus 344
    Spacing and Styling Your Menus 344
    Adding Menu Items 345
        Adding a Help Line 346
        Adding the Action 346
    Helping the File 347
Creating the Macro 347
Including Help Screens in Your Application 350
Calling and Going to Other Applications 350
    Calling and Going to a Subapplication 351
    Asking for an Application 351
Giving Yourself a Master Class 352
Summary 354

12 Creating Scripts **355**

Setting Up for Scripts 356
Defining Special Purpose Scripts 356
Choosing Script Location 357
Playing Scripts from a Tools Menu 358
Using Script Variables 359
    Understanding System Variables 360
    Defining System Variables by Programming 360
    Setting Variables within a Script 360
    Using Tools Scripts 361
    Carrying Data between Records 363
    Summarizing the Operation 363
Understanding Trigger Scripts 365
Planning Your Application 367
    Setting Defaults 367
    Identifying the Startup Directory 368
    Starting from a Different Directory 368

Alternative Starting Procedures 369
Initializing the Application 369
Automating Scripts with !s 370
Saving Variables between Sessions 371
Locating the Defaults 371
Understanding .UDNs 372
Passing around the Scripts 373
Using Scripts for Accounts Receivable 374
Adding Scripting Power to Sets Management 374
Using Field Statistics Variables 375
Polishing Your Performance 376
Solving Real Problems with Scripts 377
Setting a Filter Using a Variable 378
Unsettable Variables 378
Script Commands Directory 378
New Script Commands 392
Summary 392

13 Using Expressions and Functions **393**

Learning Syntax Rules 394
Where To Use Expressions 394
Syntax Rules for Functions 394
Using Expressions for Data Entry 395
Using the Clipboard 395
Using Operators 395
Using Pattern Matching 396
Stepping through an Expression 397
Solving Problems Encountered with Expressions 398
Demystifying IF Statements 400
Using Dates 401
Using Automatic Dating 402
Using Dates in Field Rules 402
Using Global Update with Dates 402
Using Indexes, Searches,
and Filters with Dates 402
Alpha Four Functions List 403
Summary 416

14 Documenting Your Work **417**

Using the Runtime Version 418
Installing the Runtime Product 418

Using A4DOC 420
    Using A4DOC To Document a SET 420
    Using A4DOC for Script Documentation 422
Editing Scripts with SCRIPTED.EXE 424
Stripping the Desktop 427
Creating a Library of Scripts with A4LIB.EXE 428
Running A4LIB.EXE 428
Prototyping with Alpha Four 429
Making Your Own Library 430
Using Pictures in Documentation 431
Summary 431

A Other Resources for Help **433**

B Installation Procedures **435**

C Using the Network **439**

Installing Alpha Four on a Network 439
    Counting Users 440
    Using Password-Protection 440
Network Limitations 441
Default Settings on the Network 441
Private Directories 442
Using Scripts on a Network 442
Sharing with DOS 442

D Problem-Solving Sample Expressions **445**

Expressions for Personal Names and Prefixes 445
Tips and Traps for Mailing Lists 448
Menus for a Sample Application 450

E Favorite Expressions from Alpha Four Techs **453**

F Error Codes in Alpha Four **455**

Index **459**

Introduction

Welcome to *Using Alpha Four*. With this book as your guide, you are about to become a talented Alpha Four user. Alpha Four has been designed with the beginner as well as the advanced user in mind. The designers know that when it comes to putting your own business into a computerized form, the line between beginner and expert can be very small.

What the authors of the software know about your business is very little. What they *do* know is that if you give a person who knows his or her business well a software package that works the way people think it should, success is assured.

Success, in this case, means your success and that of the Alpha Software products. As this book goes to publication, a new version of Alpha Four has just been released. Version 2 has new capabilities that enhance the use of the original package, adding multi-user capability, a scripting language, and a great number of refinements to the original Alpha Four. Fortunately, only in rare instances does Version 2 change the way the earlier versions function. A special Version 2 icon in *Using Alpha Four* (see margin) indicates procedures and information that are different from the preceding version. In each case, the difference is noted and explained in notes throughout the book for users of both versions.

NOTE   This book reflects changes through Alpha Four Version 2 in-line Release 2.00.04.

This book is written with the beginner and the expert in mind. It is for users of Alpha Software products including ALPHA/*three* and Database Manager II, because many of the functions in Alpha Four, Version 2, retain a family resemblance to the earlier versions.

Alpha Four is for any computer user who knows that it is time to automate his or her operations—when it becomes necessary to translate the operations that any user undertakes on a regular basis to analyze, regulate, document, implement, augment, or automate the work. I have worked with Alpha Four users whose businesses are so diverse that it would take the Yellow Pages to describe them. The interesting thing is how many similarities—rather than differences—there are among supposedly varying operations.

What Is Alpha Four?

Alpha Four is a *relational database* software system for IBM compatible microcomputers. Alpha Four was first released in 1989, an outgrowth of the earlier ALPHA/*three*, which was non-relational, or a so-called *flat file database*.

Because Alpha Four is a relational database with compatibility with all Xbase files—dBASE, FoxPro, Clipper, and others—you can exchange data among these programs and even import and export files between Lotus 1-2-3, WordPerfect, and other DOS-based software.

Technical support is available to registered users through the Alpha Software Hotline (617) 272-3680. Upgrade information is available from the main number (617) 229-2924. Registered users also can obtain help by calling the Alpha Software Bulletin Board (617) 229-2915, the Tech support FAX number (617) 273-1507, or the Computers Without Fear Bulletin Board at (508) 540-8777.

Features for Beginners

The new user of Alpha Four has a large variety of support mechanisms, including the tutorial and reference manuals supplied by the company, audio and video tapes, and an increasing number of users groups that are springing up around this country and Canada. Alpha Four Version 1 has been published in German and other languages are planned.

So why do you need a book on Alpha Four? In a new software environment, beginners generally find that it is easier to work through small problems with examples and exercises, engage in a discussion of new ideas, and follow a program that has been designed for learning. While also serving as a reference, this book presents the needed material in a different way from the Reference Manual; this book offers the facts in a less formal manner. With this book at your side, and in conjunction with the Alpha Four Reference Manual, you should be able to perform mighty tasks with your database.

Features for Current Users of Version 1

Current users of the previous version will find a minimum of new learning involved initially with conversion of files to Version 2. A recent study of registered users showed that for a great many of them, Alpha Four was the first software they were obliged to learn on their own. These people were attempting to answer several large questions at once: *How does this box with the screen on top work? What does DOS mean? And what is a database, anyway?* The memory of the whole experience may obscure the fact that Alpha Four itself is easy to learn, if you have the right tools.

Using Alpha Four is not intended to teach you how to use a computer nor to teach any great amount about the use of the disk operating system. It is intended to get you up and running in a minimum amount of time, with as little pain as possible. This book will help you become functional with database management.

New Features in Version 2

Although the basic operations are largely the same between Versions 1 and 2, a number of enhancements are worth highlighting (see table I.1).

Table I.1 New features in Version 2

Category	Enhancement
Sign on	Automatic script path and desktop loading
Network capability	Compatible with all major network software
	Complete record locking
User interface	Pop-up windows for prompts
	Dialog boxes
Forms	25 screens per form
	Definable access limitations
	Form and table level security
Searches	Soundex *sounds like* searches
Applications	New functions
	New macro editor
	Block cut and paste

continues

Table I.1 Continued

Category	Enhancement
Macros	Increased to 3,000 characters each
Scripts	36 script commands
Functions	Many new functions
Memory variables	Accessible and manageable
Cross tabulation	Creates summarized file on key fields
Shell to DOS	Runs other DOS programs
Telephone dialer	Can be built into applications
	Remembers local area code
Indexes	15 instead of 7 allowed
	Identification with attached file
	Selective (filtered) index
	Indexing speed dramatically improved
Desktop	Saved definition for files open
Append	Improved control with new options
Color palette	Saved color palette
	Adjustable color scheme
Find command	Contains a history feature
Printer control	Postscript printer drivers available during installation
Windows compatible	PIF file comes with installation
Capacities	EMS and XMS recognized
Case sensitivity	dBASE III and dBASE IV compatible
Parameters database	Designed to pass data to and from external software
Memory management	Reduced use of RAM, no more out of memory errors

There are more complete explanations of the each new feature in later chapters throughout the book.

What Hardware Configuration Do You Need?

As a stand-alone system, Alpha Four requires one floppy drive and a hard drive with at least 4M of space for installation of the program and tutorial files. In this configuration, DOS 3.1 or above is desirable.

Alpha Four requires a personal computer with at least 512K RAM, although 640K is recommended. Extended (XMS) and expanded (EMS) memory are recognized by the software and will improve its performance.

Alpha Four Version 2 is designed to work best with a hard disk with no less than 5M of available space before the program files are installed.

To operate Alpha Four on a local area network, the network software must be Novell NetWare or NetBios-compatible. The software also must support the record and file locking protocols of DOS 3.1. If you are operating with diskless workstations on the network, Alpha Four will run.

Video monitors supported include monochrome, Hercules, CGA, EGA, and VGA.

Although a printer is not required for using Alpha Four, it is recommended. All output can be sent to the screen or to a disk file. More than 200 printer drivers are available for installation with Alpha Four. The list includes dot matrix, laser, and PostScript printers.

Who Should Read This Book?

Using Alpha Four is being published by Que Corporation because a book about Alpha Four was the most frequently requested title in 1991. As winner of *PC World's* coveted Editor's Choice award in December, 1991, as well as numerous prestigious designations, Alpha Four is emerging from the pack of *No Programming Required* software as a leader in the end-user responsive databases.

If you think that you need a database, you should consider Alpha Four. This book can help you make the decision concerning whether Alpha Four will suit your needs. If you are new to database management, this book helps you get a head start on using the more complex functions.

This book makes no assumptions about the level of experience you bring to learning Alpha Four. A new user should begin at the beginning of the book and create the files described and follow through with the exercises outlined. More experienced users can skim the early sections to discover changes from Version 1 to 2 and go on to the intermediate section, which discusses sets and relational commands, and to the advanced section, which focuses on applications, scripts, expressions, and special operations.

How This Book Is Organized

This book is divided into four major parts: Part I, "Alpha Four Basic Techniques"; Part II, "Intermediate Alpha Four"; Part III, "Advanced Alpha Four"; and Appendixes A through F, which cover a variety of technical tips, error messages, and sample applications. The three Quick Starts help you explore the operations in each section with a short tutorial—just to break the ice.

Part I, "Alpha Four Basic Techniques," shows you how a database is designed and created. You will learn how to analyze the data you want to track and how to organize that data into logical groupings. You will create a database, enter data, design input forms, create field rules, work with indexes, and learn to design and print a simple report.

Quick Start 1, "A Typical Alpha Four Session," helps you start the program and walks you through the process of creating a database, entering data, making field rules, and printing reports.

Chapter 1, "Navigating Alpha Four," gives a bit of history on Alpha Software product development and explores the question of who uses Alpha Four and why. This chapter indicates the menuing system, keystroke conventions, and help techniques. The definitions of database terminology are here.

Chapter 2, "Defining and Creating Your First Database," examines the issues of field types and capabilities and the rules for naming fields.

Chapter 3, "Entering Data," presents the basic functions of entering and editing data, developing an input form and browse table, applying formatting to the data seen on the screen, deleting and undeleting records, and packing the database.

Chapter 4, "Indexing, Sorting, Searching, and Updating Records," examines the importance of indexes and range settings in Alpha Four. This chapter also explores the technique of creating searches and producing a summary database and performing a global update.

Chapter 5, "Creating Field Rules To Control Data Entry," goes into detail about controlling data-entry procedures with a series of field rules that apply formatting, allow calculations, and provide look-up capability.

Chapter 6, "Creating Reports," shows you how to use the report writer in Alpha Four. This chapter explains about calculated fields and various kinds of formatting applicable to reports.

Chapter 7, "Developing Strategies for Special Reporting," offers special techniques for creating great reports.

When you have learned the basics of Alpha Four with a single file, you are ready to explore the possibilities of linking files for viewing and using related data in Part II, "Intermediate Alpha Four."

Quick Start 2, "Understanding the Relational Skills of Alpha Four," shows you how to design a set that makes fields in separate databases available for viewing and reporting.

Chapter 8, "Using Sets," illustrates each phase of combining related files and shows you how to make scripts work within sets.

Chapter 9, "Moving Your Data and Files," gets into step-by-step instructions on posting data from one file to another as well as building new files based on existing files. Here you will also explore importing and exporting data to and from other DOS applications.

Chapter 10, "Using Alpha Four Tips, Tricks, and Techniques," is the place to look for techniques that have been developed over time while using Alpha Four.

Part III, "Advanced Alpha Four," examines the real power of Alpha Four. This section is designed to assist the would-be developer create applications that are elegant and functional.

Quick Start 3, "Creating Applications and Scripts," works through several sample scripts, the creation of a small menu-driven application, and the use of expressions and other functions having to do with creating a special purpose application. This is a quick session using the basic principles for developing applications, scripts, and expressions.

Chapter 11, "Creating Applications," shows how the various parts of Alpha Four are combined to create a working system.

Chapter 12, "Creating Scripts," shows how scripts can enhance your use of Alpha Four from start-up to shut-down.

Chapter 13, "Using Expressions and Functions," gives the details of expressions, commands, and functions, with examples of their use.

Chapter 14, "Documenting Your Work," illustrates an often-neglected aspect of creating applications for others to use.

Using Alpha Four also contains six appendixes: Appendix A, "Other Resources for Help"; Appendix B, "Installation Procedures"; Appendix C, "Using the Network"; Appendix D, "Problem-Solving Sample Expressions"; Appendix E, "Favorite Expressions from Alpha Four Techs"; and Appendix F, "Error Codes in Alpha Four."

Starting Alpha Four

This book is based on Version 2 of the software, introduced in early 1992. All files developed for earlier versions of this software are compatible. Therefore, the files and applications you developed and stored in an earlier version of Alpha Four can be retrieved and converted to be used with Version 2.

The conversion process is menu-driven and complete with minor exceptions, which are noted in Appendix B. However, if you are using Version 1, you should be comfortable with this book because most of the techniques and the menus are the same in Version 2 as in Version 1. Where Version 2 has significantly changed the procedures, we have pointed out the differences in the text and included the Version 2 icon.

Alpha Four Basic Techniques

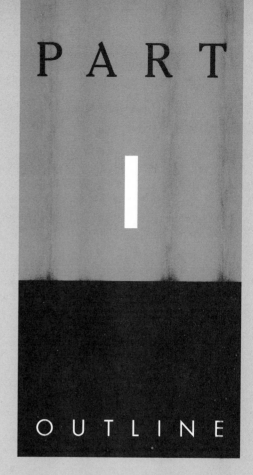

PART

1

OUTLINE

QS1. A Typical Alpha Four Session

1. Navigating Alpha Four

2. Defining and Creating Your First Database

3. Entering Data

4. Indexing, Sorting, Searching, and Updating Records

5. Creating Field Rules To Control Data Entry

6. Creating Reports

7. Developing Strategies for Special Reporting

A Typical Alpha Four Session

There is nothing—absolutely nothing—half so much worth doing as simply messing about in boats...or with boats...In or out of 'em, it doesn't matter.
    Kenneth Grahame, The Wind in the Willows

This Quick Start is the first of three tutorials presented in this book. Each Quick Start introduces a major section of the book and gives you a head start on using Alpha Four. The Quick Starts take you step-by-step through simple examples of the techniques and concepts that are examined in greater depth in the chapters in that section.

Each chapter has three functions. The first is to act as a reference tool and explain in detail the use of the various features of Alpha Four. The second is to present examples of these features and lead you through the development of an application. The third is to offer hands-on exercises, where appropriate, and help you work through real database activities. You learn to examine the separate parts; then you put them together in a working package.

The Quick Start is a preview that enables you to begin using Alpha Four immediately. This book encourages experimentation, because exploring the capabilities of the software and your hardware is wise before you commit live data to the rigors of on-the-job testing.

Quick Start 1 begins where you begin, with the Alpha Four start-up. In Part I, you create several simple databases: an inventory list, invoices, and a customer database. These tasks will be followed in Part II by more sample files to keep other kinds of records: CHECKS, PAYMENTS (deposits), LEDGER (a listing of all activities in the bank account), TENANTS and RENTPAID to monitor a rental business, and CONTACTS, to track notes of conversations and meetings. These files represent sketches rather than the whole picture. They are intended to illustrate methods of using a database—not to advise the design of a business system.

The book follows the story line of a small business—a boatyard on the coast of Maine. As owner of the boatyard, you can develop the appropriate files and reports regarding customers (OWNERS); employees; suppliers (VENDORS); parts lists or INVENTORY of items for sale; invoices; checks written and returned from the bank; a CONTACT file to track conversations, meetings, and special instructions from boat owners for the care of their vessels (time calculations); and the development of an application to assist the office help in using the program.

This material involves all aspects of using Alpha Four and highlights the important distinctions between Versions 1 and 2. Therefore, the book can serve as a reference manual and a tutorial. The basic functions of ALPHA/*three* and Version 1 of Alpha Four are described for users of the earlier version of Alpha software.

Before you begin using Alpha Four, you must install the software on your computer. The complete description of installation is found in Appendix B. The installation procedure creates several subdirectories that contain demonstration files to be used with the tutorial book that comes with the software. Because this material is excellent, you should perform the Alpha Four tutorial and the step-by-step instructions given in this Quick Start.

Using Alpha Four

This book is based on Version 2 of Alpha Four. If you have created applications in an earlier version, you should convert them by using A4CVT.EXE, a conversion program found in the directory where you install Alpha Four. The term *compatible* indicates that *Program A* can read and work with the files created by *Program B*. Because Alpha Four files are *downwardly compatible*, you can use your earlier work in Version 2.

The conversion process is menu-driven. A few minor changes may be necessary. For example, if you are using the **Choose database/set** command in an application in Alpha Four Version 1, the syntax of the command has changed slightly. Adapting to this change is a small price to pay for the command that enhances this choice.

Alpha Four works best with a fixed disk with at least 5M of available space before the program files are installed. This chapter assumes that you have Alpha Four Version 2 installed on your computer. If you have not installed Alpha Four Version 2, refer to Appendix B for step-by-step assistance with installation and system-configuration.

Starting Alpha Four

Your computer should be displaying an on-screen prompt that looks like one of the following:

```
C:\>

C>

D:\ALPHA4V2\>
```

In the first and second cases, you are at the root directory of your first hard disk, known as the C drive. In the third case, your computer has two hard disks (or more) or one large hard disk with several partitions. The computer is logged on to the D drive and the subdirectory that was created when Alpha Four was installed. If you are still at the root directory, completing the following steps takes you into the Alpha Four program:

1. Type **CD** and the name of your subdirectory.

2. Type **A4**.

   These commands can be entered in upper- or lowercase letters. Each line ends when you hit the Enter key. The first Alpha Four screen is shown in figure QS1.1.

   The opening screen will be replaced quickly if you do nothing. Alpha Four automatically finds the last database file in use and returns to that database if no other instruction is given.

3. Type **A4** from the directory where the software is installed. The program automatically accesses the AVMOVIES database, which is one of the demonstration files provided with Alpha Four. During installation, a file is created that instructs Alpha Four to find this file. After you create your own file, Alpha Four will return to your file, the most recent one used.

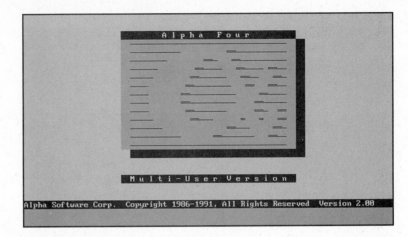

FIG. QS1.1

The Alpha Four opening screen.

4. For simplicity, wait at this screen while Alpha Four makes the choice for you. The menu screen, which appears by default, is shown in figure QS1.2.

```
Current database : C:AVMOVIES            Records in database : 51
Primary index    : by Record Number


                    Alpha Four Main Menu
         ►View/enter records          Database/set design

          Print                       Layouts

          Search lists                Applications

          Indexes/ranges              Utilities

          Global update/delete        Other

          Choose database/set         Quit


 View, change, enter or delete records
  Help   AltF1Quick record   AltF2Quick play  AltF3Script menu  AltF5DOS access
```

FIG. QS1.2

The Alpha Four Main Menu shows the primary functions of the program.

Creating the INVENTRY Database

The file already active and named at the top of the screen is the last file that Alpha Four was using. You can start to create your own database by performing the following steps:

1. Use the arrow key to move the highlight bar to **D**atabase/set design and press the Enter key; or press **D** to make the selection in one keystroke.

2. Select **C**reate new database.

3. As shown in figure QS1.3, type **INVENTRY** at the blinking cursor and press the Enter key. (A file name in DOS can be only eight letters long, so users must take some liberties with proper spelling.)

On the next screen, you can enter a database description, such as *Boatyard's File*. When you are finished, press F10 (Continue).

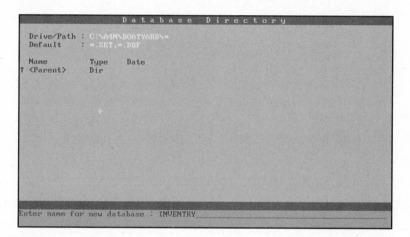

The design of the INVENTRY database is simple. When you reach this point, the program waits for you to enter the names and types of fields and their lengths as shown in the following table. Perform the following steps:

1. In the first column, Field Name, type **ITEM_NO**. The underline character separates the two parts of the word for visual separation. No spaces can be used in a field name.

2. Press the Enter key to move to the column title Field Type. The default value is Character. The prompt line at the bottom of the screen indicates other choices: Numeric, Date, Logical, and Memo.

3. Enter the fields with their types and lengths as shown in the following table:

Field Name	Field Type	Field length	Decimal Place
ITEM_NO	Character	4	
PART_NO	Character	6	
DESCRIPT	Character	30	
ARR_DATE	Date	8	
UNITS	Character	25	
PRICE	Numeric	10	2
QTY	Numeric	6	0
TOTAL	Numeric	10	2

4. The final step to creating your first database is saving the file on the disk. Alpha Four uses the F10 key as the Save key. F10 also is considered the Continue or Go Ahead Key. By pressing F10, you return to the Main Menu. Your database is ready to receive data.

5. From the Main Menu, select **View/Enter** records, the top-left menu choice. Because no records are in the database to view, Alpha Four shows an empty record and waits for you to press **E** to Enter data. Figure QS1.4 shows the default data-entry screen with data.

NOTE Version 1 automatically activates the Enter Mode when you press View and no records exist.

```
1    ITEM_NO   : 0008
2    PART_NO   : 13328
3    DESCRIPT  : Teak Oil
4    ARR_DATE  : 02/01/1993
5    UNITS     : Pint
6    PRICE     :        15.00
7    QTY       :
8    TOTAL     :         0.00




ENTER                        Record : 20
Change    F10 Continue   Esc Exit without saving
```

FIG. QS1.4

The default data-entry screen with data.

Entering Data into the First Record

In this section, you enter the data for several records so that you have some material with which to work. In later chapters, you learn to Append records to this file from an external database mailed by or downloaded from the vendor. A PARTS database will update the prices for records existing in INVENTRY.

To create the first record, perform the following steps:

1. ITEM_NO field: Type **0001** in the first field and press Enter. This number represents the first of many items that you order for your boatyard and will become the tracking number for this item.

2. PART_NO field: Type **13325** in the next field. Press Enter again to move to the next field.

3. DESCRIPT field: Type **20' mast, maple**. You can erase a mistake by using the Backspace key. To correct a field already entered, press the up-arrow key and retype the entry.

4. ARR_DATE field: Type **040192**. The date field accepts data the easiest way. Do not enter a — (dash) or a / (slash) to separate the characters. Simply type the two digit day and month numbers and two or four digits for the year. If you choose to enter **92** for the year, Alpha Four will convert this to 1992. The shortcut Alt-D enters today's date, as the computer is set. Press Enter or down arrow to go to next field.

5. UNITS field: Type **each**. This is a character field designed to contain definitions, such as *each, carton, dozen,* or *ton.*

6. PRICE field: Type **345.00**. When entering numbers, although they represent currency, do not use commas or dollar signs. These are not *legal* numeric characters. Currency symbols (or ¥, £, or $) and commas are applied with formatting commands, which are discussed in the sections on customizing the screens and reports. Decimal points are automatically entered by the definition of the field type. You don't need to enter the zeros after the decimal point.

7. QTY field: Type **1**. Numeric fields, such as quantity, do not need decimal points. Enter the data as a simple number.

8. TOTAL field: Type **345**. After you enter the last field, TOTAL, press Enter, Alpha Four starts to save your record automatically. If you press Enter a second time, the record is saved and a new blank record form appears.

A little practice in entering records makes this process easier. If you were running a small boatyard in Maine, what would you want to stock in the spring? Enter a few records of those imaginary items, just to get the hang of entering data. After pressing F10 to continue, the menu at the bottom of the screen indicates that you can select Change Enter Next Record, F10 Continue, or Esc Exit without saving.

The following data contains two more examples to enter:

0002	0003
DG-70	RO-112
Jam Cleats, 6"	5/8" nylon line
04/03/92	04/04/92
Each	FT
25.00	.84
10	100
250.00	84.00

The preceding calculations are simple, but if you needed to enter a greater amount of this kind of data, these data-entry procedures would slow to a tedious pace. Alpha offers a solution by using *field rules*. By designing a rule that multiplies the PRICE by the QTY, a TOTAL results. Press F10 to continue and select M for Main Menu.

Making Easy Calculations with Field Rules

After returning to the Main Menu from the data-entry screen, you can create field rules to solve the problem of calculating the PRICE by QTY and other items as needed. Field rules are designed to perform calculations, to apply formatting (caps, lowercase, etc.) to individual fields, to provide a measure of error checking, and to define lookup procedures for automatic data entry.

To create field rules, from the Main Menu, perform the following steps:

1. Select **D**atabase/set design, **F**ield rules, **C**reate/edit. The next screen that appears is shown in figure QS1.5. This screen shows two windows: upper and lower. The cursor is highlighting the first field in the database. To affect this field, you must press the Enter key or F9 to select this field and to jump into the lower window.

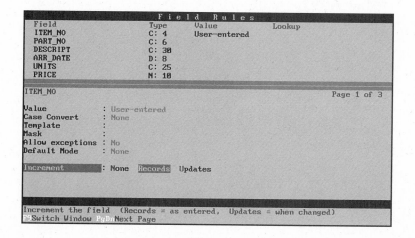

```
                       F i e l d   R u l e s
   Field                   Type    Value          Lookup
   ITEM_NO                  C: 4    User-entered
   PART_NO                  C: 6
   DESCRIPT                 C: 30
   ARR_DATE                 D: 8
   UNITS                    C: 25
   PRICE                    N: 10

 ITEM_NO                                              Page 1 of 3

 Value              : User-entered
 Case Convert       : None
 Template           :
 Mask               :
 Allow exceptions   : No
 Default Mode       : None

 Increment          : None


 F10 Continue   F9 Define Rule   F8 Delete Rule
```

FIG. QS1.5

The two-window screen of Field Rules shows the field names in the top window.

Little needs to be done with a field, such as ITEM_NO, in terms of formatting. However, one annoying chore of data entry can be dealt with here. At the bottom of the screen is a choice called **Increment**. The option here enables you to define the field as automatically creating its own data by incrementing from the previous record. Of course, one record must be entered to start the process. Then, the field will add one to the previous record's number. This is still a character field. If your record starts with a character plus a *number*, Alpha Four will understand. In other words, A-345 will be followed by A-346, and B999 will be followed by C000.

2. To create this field rule, use the down-arrow key to highlight Increment where None shows. Select Records at Increment, as shown in figure QS1.6. Press F9 to return to the upper window.

```
                       F i e l d   R u l e s
   Field                   Type    Value          Lookup
   ITEM_NO                  C: 4    User-entered
   PART_NO                  C: 6
   DESCRIPT                 C: 30
   ARR_DATE                 D: 8
   UNITS                    C: 25
   PRICE                    N: 10

 ITEM_NO                                              Page 1 of 3

 Value              : User-entered
 Case Convert       : None
 Template           :
 Mask               :
 Allow exceptions   : No
 Default Mode       : None

 Increment          : None  Records  Updates


 Increment the field  (Records = as entered, Updates = when changed)
 F9 Switch Window  PgDn Next Page
```

FIG. QS1.6

In the lower window of Field Rules, create a rule to create incrementing numbers in the ITEM_NO field.

Many options exist in field rules for changing the way data is entered, calculated, and retrieved. The options are discussed in detail in later chapters of this book, particularly in Chapter 5. The next task is to enter a calculation for PRICE by QTY just to get you started thinking about other kinds of automatic entry you want Alpha Four to perform for you.

A calculated field can contain an extremely complex formula. In this case, you will be creating a calculation for the TOTAL field:

1. Highlight the TOTAL field in the top window, and press Enter. Notice that other options disappear when you move the cursor to the lower window and change Value from User-entered to Calculated and press Enter. Also notice that new choices appear at the bottom of the screen.

2. Select F2 to access field choices from the current database. In the case of this simple formula, it would be just as easy to type PRICE times QUANTITY as it is to use the F2 key to point to your selection.

   Or would it? How did you name that field? QUANTITY or QTY? You should use the *point-and-shoot* method of selecting fields, by using the arrow keys to move the highlight to *point* at your selection and pressing Enter to choose or *shoot* it.

   When you press F2, a box appears and shows the name of the current database, INVENTRY. The SYSTEM database also is shown in this box. Twenty-two fields stored by the system are accessible here. Press Enter on INVENTRY to select database. You work with these fields in the discussion of expressions and functions in Chapter 13.

3. Highlight the word PRICE and press Enter. This action places the first field on the Expression line.

   The first field to be entered into the calculation is PRICE. This field name must be followed by a function. The functions are available when you press F3.

4. Press F3 and move the highlight down to multiply. Press Enter to select this function.

   Typing the asterisk (*) to represent multiplication would really be easier. However, because functions become progressively more complicated, using the automatic formatting help with the F3 key assures you success. Choose F3 and press PgDn several times to view the numerous choices available here. Six screens are available to review. Esc will pull you out of this menu. Enter the asterisk any way that you choose. Then add the last field, QTY, by pressing F2 to use the pop-up window for field choice. Once again, point-and-shoot your selection.

If this were a longer, more complex formula, you might require more space in which to type and view your work. Press F6 to open an *Expression Window*. Then press F7 (Evaluate) to watch the computer calculate your records to see whether the results are correct. If you press F6 before selecting the second part of your equation, you get an error. Choose F6 before starting the equation or after completion.

5. Repeat the field selection process in Step 2 to choose QTY.

6. Press F7 (Evaluate) to test whether your expression works properly.

You cannot leave the calculation line unless the formula you design is correct in spelling and syntax. Error messages will appear, depending upon the type of problem Alpha Four encounters in trying to use your formula. Error messages are listed and described in Appendix F.

When your formula looks like the example in figure QS1.7, press F9 to move to the upper window.

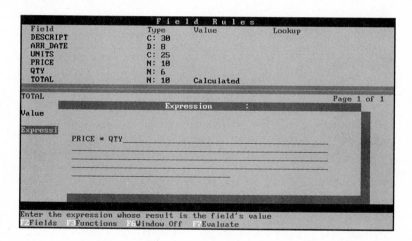

FIG. QS1.7

The Expression window PRICE * QTY.

One more automatic calculation will help here. In the ARR_DATE field, the default Expression to produce today's date is DATE( ) (see fig. QS1.8).

To save the field rules, your highlight must be in the upper window. Press F9 to switch between the top and bottom windows. From the top window, press F10 to continue or save the Field Rules. This action will return you to the Main Menu.

```
                         F i e l d   R u l e s
   Field                  Type      Value          Lookup
   ITEM_NO                C: 4      User-entered
   PART_NO                C: 6
   DESCRIPT               C: 30
   ARR_DATE               D: 8
   UNITS                  C: 25
   PRICE                  N: 10

 ARR_DATE                                            Page 1 of 3

 Value              : User-entered
 Range Check        : No


 Default Mode       : None  Value  Expression
 Default            : DATE()
 Increment          : None

 Select the method for supplying the default value
   Switch Window  PgDn Next Page
```

FIG. QS1.8

Create a default expression in the date field.

Checking the Rules

The effect of writing these field rules can be seen in the next record you enter. The next ITEM_NO will pick up from your last one and the TOTAL field will calculate PRICE times QTY as the rule dictates. Existing records, those created before the field rules were designed, will not be changed by these new elements. However, the calculation of PRICE times QTY will occur as soon as each record is updated or changed. In the case of a database with numerous records that are not active all the time, this could be a problem. You can solve this updating problem by performing the following steps:

1. From the Main Menu, select **D**atabase/set design, **F**ield rules, **R**e-evaluate. This action forces a recalculation of all records you request.

2. Press Enter to accept Yes to mark for deletion records that do not meet the field rules. Marking the records does not actually delete them.

   Alpha Four asks whether to mark records that cannot be evaluated properly. The default answer here is Yes. The records that failed to operate properly in the reevaluation will be give a small *deleted* mark that looks like ♦ (diamond). This mark does not indicate that the record will go away. It simply marks the record for further attention. The techniques associated with delete marks will be considered in several sections of this book. The Pack command actually erases the marked records (see Chapter 3).

This action will produce the Range Settings screen, shown in QS1.9. This screen appears in numerous locations throughout Alpha Four. It enables you to choose the order and range of records to be processed. In this case, you press F10 to continue and leave the choices on the Range Settings screen as they are.

3. Press F10 to continue.

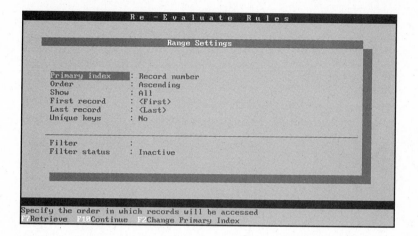

The Range Settings screen is important to many Alpha Four functions.

Alpha Four shows you how many records were revaluated and how many were marked. Press F10 to continue. After you perform the revaluation function, your records will be properly computed in the TOTAL field.

Producing Results

From the Main Menu, select **V** to view the newly reevaluated records. You also can see these records in the **B**rowse format by pressing **B** for browse from the Main Menu or from View. Browse shows as many records as will fit on the screen but only as many fields as will fit across the 80 column screen. By moving the cursor from left to right across the screen, you will first see the screen shown in figure QS1.10.

The fields at the end of the records will appear as you continue to press the right arrow key (see fig. QS1.11). The TOTAL field should be properly calculated.

```
ITEM  PART_N  DESCRIPT               ARR_DATE   UNITS       PRICE      QTY
0001  13328   Teak Oil               02/13/1992 Pint         15.00      10
0002  34525   Non-skid strips        11/02/1991 yd.           0.50     150
0003  653D    Trailer Balls, 1 7/8" Zi 09/19/1991 each         8.00      10
0004  5435.1  Seat Cushions, 24"     10/20/1991 each         19.95       5
0005  445     Maple oars, 8'         01/07/1992 pr.          53.70       4
0006  DG-78   Jam Cleats, 6"         12/27/1991 each         24.00      15
0007  CH7141  Halyard Stoppers, single 12/27/1991 25          75.00       5
2000  543     White deck paint       01/27/1992 pint         16.13       2
2001  DR-650  Zippy Clene, vinyl clean 02/02/1991 case, per     3.45      10
2003  AB-25   Mooring Anchor, 25#, up 10/02/1991 each         83.45       5
2004  RO-723  3-strand spun dacron lin 05/17/1991 1200 ft.    192.00       5
2005  342     Large Sponge           09/12/1991 each          4.50      25
2006  FF-234  Propane stove tanks    02/14/1990 refill        2.25      20
2007  CO-410  Galvanized Anchor chain, 09/15/1991 per ft.      2.45     500
2008  EB7644  Life preserver, adult  07/01/1991 each         18.95      10
2009  1603    Red lead paint, antifoul 06/02/1991 gal.        12.95      50
2010  EGH-01  Monourethane Coatings  02/02/1990 gal.         16.45      25
2011  RO-112  5/8" nylon line        10/19/1991 ft.           0.84      25
2012  FE8789  Fender, inflatable     04/20/1991 each         24.95      15

BROWSE                      Record : 13                               A
  ↑ ↓  Change Enter View Find Index MainMenu Options Tools
```

FIG. QS1.10

In Browse mode, use the right- and left-arrow keys to scroll.

```
DESCRIPT              ARR_DATE   UNITS       PRICE      QTY     TOTAL
Teak Oil             02/13/1992 Pint         15.00      10    150.00
Non-skid strips      11/02/1991 yd.           0.50     150     75.00
Trailer Balls, 1 7/8" Zi 09/19/1991 each       8.00      10     80.00
Seat Cushions, 24"   10/20/1991 each         19.95       5     99.75
Maple oars, 8'       01/07/1992 pr.          53.70       4    199.80
Jam Cleats, 6"       12/27/1991 each         24.00      15    360.00
Halyard Stoppers, single 12/27/1991 25        75.00       5    375.00
White deck paint     01/27/1992 pint         16.13       2     30.00
Zippy Clene, vinyl clean 02/02/1991 case, per  3.45      10     34.50
Mooring Anchor, 25#, up 10/02/1991 each       83.45       5    417.25
3-strand spun dacron lin 05/17/1991 1200 ft. 192.00       5    960.00
Large Sponge         09/12/1991 each          4.50      25    112.50
Propane stove tanks  02/14/1990 refill        2.25      20     45.00
Galvanized Anchor chain, 09/15/1989 per ft.    2.45     500   1225.00
Life preserver, adult 07/01/1991 each        18.95      10    189.50
Red lead paint, antifoul 06/02/1991 gal.     12.95      50    647.50
Monourethane Coatings 02/02/1990 gal.        16.45      25    411.25
5/8" nylon line      10/19/1991 ft.           0.84      25     21.00
Fender, inflatable   04/20/1991 each         24.95      15    374.25

BROWSE                      Record : 13                               A
  ↑ ↓  Change Enter View Find Index MainMenu Options Tools
```

FIG. QS1.11

Use the arrow keys to scroll to the end of the table.

Organizing Your Data

You will not always examine or use your records in the same order as they are entered. You need to find other ways that the data can be arranged to work best for your application. For optimum data organization, you may want to create several indexes to view the data and locate specific records.

For example, you may want to examine your entire INVENTRY list for its current dollar value but only for items in current inventory with a total value greater than $50. To show this list, you need an index on TOTAL, a search on TOTAL greater than 50, and a report that prints the results.

The first step is to create the index. From the Main Menu, select **In-dexes/ranges**, **C**reate an index, and type **INV_TOT** for the index name. Choose **T**able Mode, and select the TOTAL field by using the F2 (Fieldnames) key. Press F10 (Continue) twice. Alpha Four creates the index file, which gives you a way to see your records in a specified order.

The second step is to create a search for records with totals greater than $50. Select **S**earch lists, **O**ne-time search, **T**able Mode, press F2 (Fields) to select the database (INVENTRY), and highlight the field TOTAL. The next column is highlighted and asks for an operator. Press F2 (Operators) to see the available choices, and select >, the greater than sign. Then type **50** into the field that asks: Search For What? Press F10 (Continue). The Range Setting screen appears and shows that the Primary index is INV_TOT. The primary index tells you that the *found* records will appear in order from the lowest to the highest. Press F10 to continue.

From the Main Menu, press **B** for Browse to examine the list of records that match the criterion of a number greater than 50 in the TOTAL field. Check whether the records are listed from the lowest to the highest in the expected order. If you press **R** for Range, the Range Setting screen appears. You can reverse the list by changing the Order from **A**scending to **D**escending.

Indexing is examined in depth in conjunction with searches and ranges in Chapter 4.

Choosing Your Output

Draw a *picture* on paper of every conceivable type of output you will require from the database—from labels to invoices. These sketches will help you track the forms as they begin to multiply. The exercise also helps you understand the difference between reports, forms, browse tables, mail labels, and letters. Although the differences may seem clear to you, you should consider the following points.

By using forms you can perform the following tasks:

- Show one record at a time (as many fields as a page can contain)
- Design a fill-in-the-blanks output
- Create calculated fields
- Show boxes, lines, and colors to define areas of the screen
- Use block move/delete/copy
- Print headers on each page

- Print page number and record number on each form
- Adjust top and bottom margins
- Set to specific range and printer
- Use a default setup and the borrow feature
- Restrict access to change, delete, edit, etc.

By using input forms you *cannot* perform the following tasks:

- View more than one record at a time on-screen
- Limit the View mode to a specific index or range

Forms are used for viewing and for printing. Version 2 contains 25 screens. Version 1 has 10 screens.

By using Browse tables you can perform the following tasks:

- View 20 records simultaneously in spreadsheet format
- Create calculated fields
- Use all formatting and color definitions
- Reorder and resize the columns for better presentation
- Restrict access to change, delete, edit, etc.

Using Browse is good for a quick visual check to edit large amounts of similar data fast. The switch between Browse and View modes is fast. Browse is less effective for printing than a report and considerably less flexible.

By using browse tables you *cannot* perform the following tasks:

- Make adjustments in field names, except to truncate them by reducing the width of the window
- Use boxes to emphasize text
- Make a physical cross-reference between records in the same file

By using reports you can perform the following steps:

- Define calculated fields
- Show multiple records on one page
- Set to specific index, range, and printer
- Subgroup the record to create subtotals on the groups
- Summarize the data for a group of records
- Draw horizontal and vertical lines to separate data elements

- Use headers and footers for reports, pages, and subgroups
- Define a specific record count per page
- Adjust all margins
- Use a quick setup with default titles
- Borrow from a previously created report in another file
- Add or remove any section of the report form

By using reports you *cannot* perform the following steps:

- Draw a box
- Do a block move, delete, or copy
- Print data from more than one record in a single row

Using mail labels, you can perform the following steps:

- Send the output from different records to be printed side by side, from one to six across the page
- Set to specific index, range, and printer
- Borrow from previously created mail label in another file
- Use pre-defined sizes to fit commercially printed label stock
- Define the number of copies to be printed as more than one

By using letters, you can perform the following steps:

- Create a prompted input at the time of printing
- Define all margins
- Select boilerplate text to print based on conditional statements in the text
- Do a block move, delete, and insert
- Print from any database that contains appropriate fields

Customizing Your Data-Entry and View Screens

The default entry screen is useful for many types of simple data entry. However, there are many reasons for customizing the input form. The most obvious is better visual definition of what data should go where. Less obvious purposes include creating a form to be printed.

Examples of forms to be printed include a receipt for a purchase, a room registration, a contract, or a bid form. Any of these can be designed for printing on a full 8 1/2"-by-11" or 8 1/2"-by-14" page, including calculations based on fields in the database.

In View mode, you can edit the current form by choosing **Option**, **Edit**. The Options screen in Edit mode appears, as shown in figure QS1.12

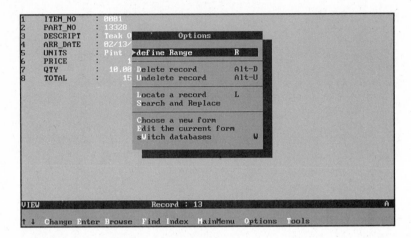

The active edit screen indicates fields as heavy, dashed lines. To make your screen more visually balanced, you can move sections from one place to another. Your cursor is in the top-left corner of the screen. Press the F4 (Block) key to retrieve the Block menu. You select Move by pressing the Enter key. This action enables you to mark an area of the screen to be moved. Use the arrow keys to draw the highlight down to cover the last line and to the right to cover the fields. Press Enter again and move the highlighted section with your arrow keys. Press Enter when you are finished.

Designing an input form is as personal as your signature. Everyone has an idea of how they should look. A good principle to follow is to keep it simple and uncluttered. You can clean up the field names just as you would with a word processor. Drawing a box around certain areas will emphasize their importance or simply make the screen look tidy.

Use the function key options at the bottom of the screen to experiment with your form.

Using a Second Kind of Calculated Field

An important function of the customized input form is showing computed information that is based on data existing in the file or formulas you define. The INVENTRY database does not contain a field to show the percent of markup to the dealer's price you want to add to make a list price for your customers. You can create that field by pressing Alt-C to access the Calculated fields screen. Create your own field name, such as LISTPRICE, in the Name column and write the definition in the Expressions column, such as (PRICE * 1.2), to show a 20 percent markup for the item. The F2 key will produce the list of fields from which to choose, or you can type the expression as shown in figure QS1.13.

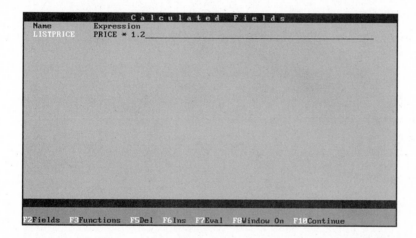

FIG. QS1.13

The Calculated Fields screen on an input form.

Press F10 to save the calculated field and return to the form editor. After the calculated field is created, you can place it on the input form. Place your cursor where you would like the new field to appear. Press Alt-F to retrieve the Databases Box. Notice a third choice now exists, the new Calculated database. This is where the field you just defined will be found. Select Calculated and press Enter to place the field in this position. When the screen pleases you, select F10 to save. You will see the new field has an entry. Because this is a calculated field, it is not stored in the database. It must be re-created for each form or report.

Calculated fields, in combination with field rules, give great power to the data-entry process. In a similar manner, you can have spectacular results designing forms to print single records and reports. A complete discussion of creating data-entry forms and browse tables appears in Chapter 3.

Reporting on Your Data

Reports are generally considered groups of records shown in column format. The individual items of data are shown in the detail section; page headers and footers describe the report; and the summary section is where totals and other calculations are shown. Begin a report from Alpha Four's Main Menu, and perform the following steps.

1. Choose **L**ayout, **R**eports, **C**reate/edit to begin the process.

2. Select a letter to identify the report—any available letter, A through Z.

3. Choose **Q**uick Setup.

4. Type a descriptive name, such as **Inventory summary - 1992** on the Report description line. Move the highlight to the bottom line to change the number to 2 to make the default number of spaces between fields smaller. Don't change any other defaults for now. Press F10 (Continue).

   The report writer in Alpha Four is easy to manage when you get some basic techniques under control. The description of the report, the width, the number of grouping levels are defined on the Quick Report Parameters screen. This screen with many more options is accessible from the report screen as well. For this report, make the default spaces between fields 2. Generally, however, you can accept the default entries on this screen, shown in figure QS1.14.

   The field selection screen appears next. Use the F2 key to fill in the field choices of ITEM_NO, PART_NO, DESCRIPT, ARR_DATE (omit UNITS), PRICE, and QTY. As you select the fields, the length of each is calculated at the bottom of the screen (see fig. QS1.15).

5. Use the arrow keys to move the highlight back to the length definition and reduce the length of DESCRIPT to 15 and PRICE to 9. This will leave room to add the TOTAL field with a length of 10 on the 80-character report.

6. Press F10 (Continue) to design and add more features to this report.

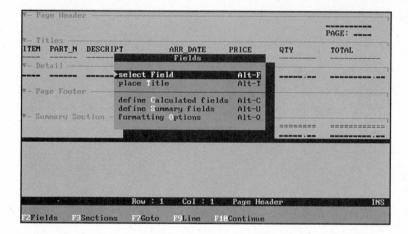

FIG. QS1.14

A report gets its descriptive title on this screen.

FIG. QS1.15

Choose F2 to select the fields pop-up box.

The Report Writer screen can be considered in its several sections. The section called the page header is where the title of the report is entered, just as it might be in a word processor. In any section, fields can be selected to be placed on the field with Alt-F, the shortcut, or F2 (Fields) and Enter. Either of these actions presents the Databases menu. Choose your database, INVENTRY, to find the fields you need for a report on this data by highlighting each one in turn to select it for the report.

When you have chosen all of these fields, press F10. You can clean up the titles to make the report layout look like figure QS1.16.

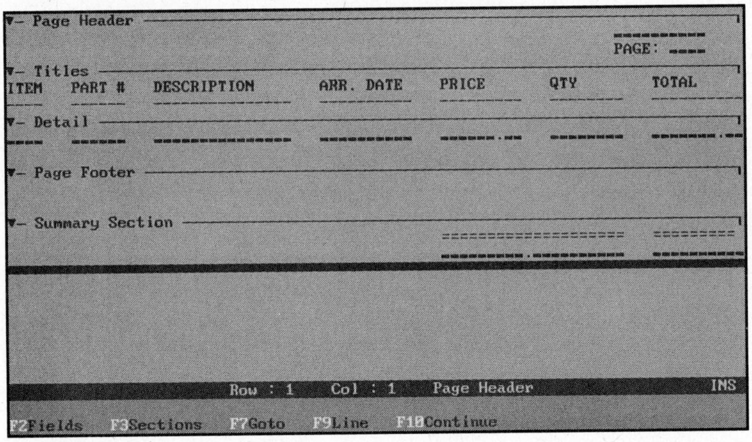

FIG. QS1.16

The Report Design screen.

The results of this report may be seen by pressing F10 and choosing Preview. This is a quick way to know whether your report is going to look right. Press F10 to Save the report and choose Print from the Alpha Four Main Menu to create your report on paper.

The report should resemble figure QS1.17.

12-14-1990
PAGE: 1

ITEM	PART #	DESCRIPTION	INPUT DATE	PRICE	QTY	TOTAL
0001	123456	Oak rudder, 6 ft.	04-03-1992	35.00	4	140.00
0002	F-42	Hemp, 1/2 in.	04-03-1992	45.00	10	450.00
0003	345.4A	Herreshoff Sails,	04-04-1992	245.00	6	1470.00
				$325.00	20	$2060.00

FIG. QS1.17

Preview of your Report.

By selecting the Print menu, you can send your report to the screen, to a printer, or to a file on your disk. Generally, you will select Screen until you know that your report is properly designed.

The reason for sending a report to a file is to send it to a word processor or desktop publishing program for further enhancement. Alpha Four does not recognize fonts in report writing. Use of other report writing programs, such as R & R Report Writer, will resolve this issue if you require more extensive control of your reports. There are many

software packages on the market today that can be used to add pictures, sketches, and scanned logos to your work. The quality of the production will, of course be determined by the type of printer you use. Laser printers are becoming a standard in the business world, but a high quality dot-matrix printer can serve the same purpose at somewhat less cost.

Summary

Alpha Four is the relational database for non-programmers. If you never need to perform an operation that requires designing a set or an application, you still have at your fingertips the menuing system and the intuitive structure that respond directly to the need that you do have. With pop-up boxes and extensive help screens, the defining and designing of your database is as simple as knowing how your own business is run.

The truth is, you can become your own developer with Alpha Four. With the point-and-shoot techniques and other aids to the beginner, anyone who knows what he or she wants to accomplish with the data at hand can manage the business of a database with professional competence.

This completes your Quick Start tour of creating a database, entering data, and using the data. You have learned to enter data, design field rules, create input forms, and design reports with which to bring the data back out to you. All of these basic techniques are used as we progress in learning Alpha Four. Further detail on all of the subjects covered here will be offered in the following chapters of Part 1.

Your business has finally bought another computer to supplement the word processor on the secretary's desk. The boss says, "Get productive and save money. Do the marketing mailings in house." You know it's a database problem. You find an advertisment for Alpha Four. It says it's the relational database for non-programmers, so you buy it. Where do you go from here?

You are in personnel. The headquarters has purchased another company out of state. New employees, new health and insurance benefits, and new tax rules must be added to your system. And, they have lost the only MIS person who could manipulate your program. Looks like you will have to gather the files from the new outfit and tie them in with yours. Is this the time to redo the whole thing? How do you make the next decision?

You are managing a growing business with markets expanding in Europe. Daily currency changes and constant price changes from your dealers are driving you crazy. Proper pricing for the U.S. market will mean life or death to your company. Alpha Four is doing wonders for your golf partner. She says it will do the same for you. What's the next step?

The budget has been slashed for help at church or your college. Your former volunteers are now found on the unemployment lines. If the Donations Program is ignored, things will get worse for everyone. You will have to take charge of the computer. You have been giving the Lotus 1-2-3 spreadsheet a real workout. It has the check register and all the donations information. A friend mentions Alpha Four. Will it solve your problem?

These kinds of problems present themselves regularly in offices, schools, homes, and businesses of every kind, every day. More people are using microcomputers for more everyday functions than ever before, because these computers are cheaper and the cost of office help is rising. Whether the job will be done by you or by your staff, the task must be made easy enough for the *computer illiterates* but powerful enough to keep you clear of hiring a programmer. This book is designed to inform you of the possibilities for improved management of your data.

Data is the lifeblood of modern business. Data-poor businesses simply do not survive in the fiercely competitive marketplaces of the 1990s. This failure applies also to businesses that fail to manage their data properly. Business people who use computers are constantly seeking better ways to gather, manipulate, and report data.

Some users, however, leap into new data-management methods without exploring them fully. Whether the final product is to be a check or a complex analysis with subgroupings and preprocessed records, more

Navigating Alpha Four

Order and simplification are the first steps toward the mastery of a subject—the actual enemy is the unknown.
Thomas Mann, The Magic Mountain

This chapter gets you started with Alpha Four by discussing why people use electronic databases and how they are used to emulate or improve upon a paper-based system; this chapter also offers a short history of database management and of Alpha Software. You learn to navigate the menus and discover the basic keystrokes and concepts that carry you where you need to go. This chapter also explores the on-line help system that is built into the program.

Knowing When You Need Alpha Four

Alpha Four is the first relational database powerful enough to become a standard for major corporations and easy enough to serve the needs of the individual business owner or manager without the need for a MIS department or a hired programmer.

Even so, data management can get out of hand. Do any of the following situations sound familiar to you?

can be derived from your data-management system if you know enough about the underlying concepts.

Defining a Database

Computer terms can be confusing to beginning users. With the arrival of so-called integrated software, knowing where the *spreadsheet* stops and the *database manager* begins is difficult. Before launching into creating a database, this chapter defines some terminology. A database or flat file is simply a means of organizing information so that users can easily retrieve, sort, extract, or update it. The register in your check book is actually a manual database.

These days, databases are more likely to reside on computers and to run the full range from client listings for one-person businesses to enormous on-line collections of full-text magazine articles. An electronic database management system is a computer program, such as Alpha Four, that manipulates the data in a database. The software lets users extract, sort, and perform other operations on the contents of the database—the data itself. Each piece of information in a database is stored as a record. Each record is designed around a structure that consists of several or many fields. Fields can be designed to accept characters, numeric data, date information, logical (yes/no) information, and memo fields.

An analogy that works here is a checkbook register in which each check is written on a separate line (record), with its check number, the date, the payee, and the amount. Each of these items is a *field*. A *record* is made up of fields. You will take a closer look at records and their components later in this chapter. A relational database is a file that is linked to another file in such a way that they can appear to be the same file. Only records that share common data in a specific field will appear together.

Medical records showing results of examinations must be attached to only one patient's file. The patient is related to the exam results using a common field, PATIENT_NO. In another example, every invoice is addressed to a single customer. Each invoice can have only one customer, so the invoice and the customer are linked using a customer number field, such as CUST_NO.

A lookup database is one file that provides previously entered data to a newly created or edited record. In Alpha Four, pop-up windows can be created to enable the user to point-and-shoot to select items. The use of field rules allows the user to manage what will happen to the data as it enters the system. You can write a rule to force all CAPS in the STATE

38

field. You can write a rule that multiplies QTY times PRICE. There are many more things that can be done in field rules that will automate and facilitate your data entry.

Development of Databases

Ever since the Phoenicians made lists on clay tablets to describe the inventory of their trading vessels, managers have been tracking business-related information. Of course, more business information must be tracked today, but technology has kept pace with the data explosion. In the late 19th century, Herman Hollerith developed the first recognizable software to accumulate census data for the U.S. government. When big computers became commercially available some 50 years later, the major banks and insurance companies adopted Hollerith's seminal database-management system. Since then, the evolution of business-data management has closely paralleled that of the small computer.

The power of desktop microcomputers has spurred the development of fast, capable, and user-friendly database-management software. Electronic data-management systems, such as Alpha Four, are just outgrowths of the manual systems they have been designed to replace. Because they take advantage of desktop microcomputing power, however, database-management systems expand your problem-solving capabilities well beyond what you can do by hand. As a result, a good data-management system can enhance the style and work flow of your office.

Development of Alpha

Alpha Software is not new to the electronic data-management arena. The company's original database manager for small computers was Database Manager II, produced in 1982. This product gave users something they had not seen before in a data-management program: the capability to retrieve and utilize files from dBASE II and Lotus 1-2-3. With Database Manager II, users could also preview records on the screen before sending reams of paper through slow, noisy printers. Database Manager II users clamored for more features and functions. In response, the company brought out ALPHA/*three*, which took care of many users' database requirements quite nicely. One of ALPHA/*three's* big advantages was its capability to index, as opposed to Database Manager's sorting. ALPHA/*three* also had a slicker, faster interface for

the user. Database Manager II's interface was typical of its time. It presented one option at a time, so the user had to go through many screens to achieve one command.

As personal computers became cheaper and more powerful, however, users came to expect even more from their data-management software. Once again, Alpha Software set out to learn just what those expectations were. The result was powerful, friendly Alpha Four, introduced in March 1989. Alpha Four's major enhancement was its relational capability, including the use of *sets* linking up to 10 databases. The creation of a set enables the user to create multiple forms and reports plus database lookups; these are the great advances of Alpha Four.

Two recent additions to the Alpha family are dbQuick and R P L, a language and development environment. dbQuick4 is a RAM-resident or *terminate, stay resident* (TSR) program. After a TSR program is loaded into memory, it stays tucked away until called on to perform a specific function. dbQuick's main function is to capture a name, record, or other chunk of information from a database and paste it into a word processing document, for example. The program has plenty of other enticing functions, including the capability to use a modem in the computer to dial a phone number.

R P L is designed for programmers who want to create memory-resident programs. This language enables the user to create applications that launch, suspend, and resume other DOS applications so they can share data between them. Release 2.0 of Alpha Four has additional capabilities that are discussed in this book. Release 2.0 is the network-capable version of Alpha Four that runs under the Novell Operating System and all NET BIOS machines. The network version provides record-locking capability to keep two or more users on the network from changing the same record at the same time.

All Alpha Software products have down-the-line compatibility and consistency. Because each new Alpha product builds on its predecessors, you do not have to get used to an entirely new user interface if you come to Alpha Four with experience in using ALPHA/*three* or Database Manager II.

From the beginning, Alpha has put a great deal of care and thought into designing products that you can grasp intuitively and that can help you solve real data-management problems. Of course, that does not mean Alpha Four will automatically drum up the ultimate data-management application for your business.

Like any computer program, Alpha Four is only as capable as the people who use it. This book gives you the jump starts as well as detailed explanations, so that you can make the best possible use of Alpha Four's built-in power and flexibility. Every user has different data-management requirements . . . and different problems.

You can find the answers to your specific questions in the reference material in each chapter. Hands-on practice is offered in the example databases illustrating various features and functions throughout the book. If these sources are not adequate, check out the sample applications that are available when you do a full installation of the program. You also can get these and other applications on disk by writing to Computers Without Fear, Inc., P.O. Box 1027, West Falmouth, MA 02574.

Taking a Short Tour of Alpha Four

Now that you've considered the problem you need to solve with Alpha Four, you're almost ready to start creating a database to do it. Before you enter any data, however, you should get to know Alpha Four a little better. If you already have some experience with Alpha Four, you may want to skip this section.

Main Menu

The Main Menu (see fig. 1.1) of Alpha Four appears when you start the program, unless a special application has been designed to provide a customized menu. In either case, a menu is the first thing you should see.

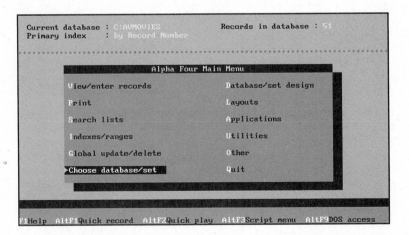

FIG. 1.1

The Alpha Four Main Menu.

The Alpha Four Main Menu contains the following three main parts:

1. The top two lines tell you which file is current, which index is active, and how many records are in the database as a whole or in the current search list.

2. The Main Menu itself indicates selections—consider them doorways—to different activities. The Layout choice enables you to create a report, form, mail label, browse table, or letter. The Print selection, parallel on the Main Menu, sends the reports, forms, tables, and letters defined in Layout, to the printer, to the screen, or to a file.

3. Users of Version 2 have another menu at the bottom of the screen. The Alt-F1 (Quick Record) and Alt-F2 (Quick Play) keys enable you to record a script that will be called UNTITLED. Alt-F1 records UNTITLED; Alt-F2 plays the UNTITLED script. Alt-F3 accesses the Scripts menu, where the script path is identified. Users of all versions can see a line of text at line 23 of the screen, which is called the *prompt line* and gives a brief description of each menu selection that the moving bar highlights.

You can access choices from the Main Menu in two ways. The moving bar selects menu choices. When you move the bar to a menu choice and press Enter, another menu below the Main Menu is revealed. This second level menu may, in turn, have another level below that. The Esc key works two ways. On certain menus, Esc will bring you up one level, on others, Esc will bring you back immediately to the Main Menu.

The second way in which Alpha Four enables you to select an item from the menu is by choosing the bright capitalized letter, such as the **U** in **U**tilities or the **P** in save and **P**review.

When you press the highlighted letter, you do not need to press the Enter key. Boldface type in this book and a bright letter for the active initial of the command on-screen are used to highlight keys that you press to execute a command.

Keystroke Conventions

The function keys work in a special way. *Press F1* means that you should find the F1 key on your keyboard and press it once. Likewise, *press Alt-F3* means that you should find the Alt key—an extended keyboard may have one on each side of the space bar—and hold it down while pressing the F3 key (see fig. 1.2).

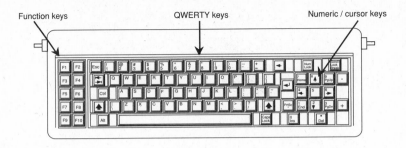

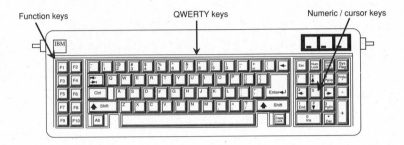

FIG. 1.2

The IBM PC
keyboard (top),
the IBM AT
Computer
keyboard
(center), and the
IBM Enhanced
keyboard
(bottom).

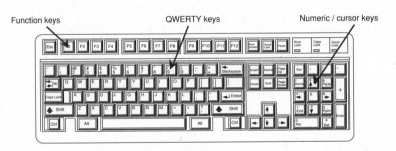

Alpha Four contains a number of shortcut keys to help you speed
through your work. You can use F1 and Alt-F10 in almost any situation.
Others are specific to certain locations. These shortcut keys can be
seen on a number of menus following the main screen. You perform the
following keystrokes, instead of callling up the menu:

Function Key	Action Performed
F1	All help screens, context-sensitive
Alt-F1	Quick record, a temporary macro
Alt-F2	Plays Quick macro

Function Key	Action Performed
Alt-F3	Brings up the complete Scripts menu
Alt-F4	Brings up the Play Scripts menu
Alt-F9	Suspends Alpha Four, exits to DOS
Alt-F10	Returns to the Main Menu from almost any location

NOTE Your work will not be saved before you return to the Main Menu by using Alt-F10, which is a CANCEL command. Any work that has not been saved will be lost.

From the Main Menu:

F2	Database Format/Set Tree: Press F2 to display all fields, their type and width, and the length of the entire record. If in a set, this key will show the structure (tree) of the set. (Also available in View and Browse.)
F3	Status: Shows information about the database/set, file sharing mode; status of memory usage; presence of extended and expanded memory; number of network users (if a multi-user version), current desktop loaded; current path, records on file, system date and time, selected mode, selected browse, selected range, and selected printer. (Also available in View and Browse.)
E	Accesses Enter mode (not shown on menu)
B	Accesses Browse mode (not shown on menu)
W	Accesses open databases (not shown on menu)

In View and Browse modes:

F2	Database Format/Set Tree (see above)
F3	Status Screen (see above)
Alt-D	Marks the current record for deletion
Alt-U	Unmarks the current record
Alt-M	Accesses the Memo Editor
L	Locate: Allows the user to search for records containing certain information

continues

In View and Browse modes:

R	Defines a Range setting screen
F	Finds a record using the primary index
0-9	Auto-Hop through the records. 0 will hop through the records quickly, 1 allows one second between each record, 2 allows two seconds between records, etc.
I	Selects the Primary Index

In Enter mode:

Alt-R	Copies all fields from the record last on the screen into all fields in the current record
Alt-F	Copies contents of a specific field from the last record on the screen into the corresponding field in the present record
Alt-M	Enables access to the Memo Editor when the cursor is highlighting a memo field
Alt-D	Places the DOS system date in the field
Alt-C	Recalculates all calculated Fields

Layouts (In Create/Edit mode of all layouts except letters):

Alt-F	Selects a Field to display on the Layout
Alt-C	Defines a Calculated Field
Alt-O	Formatting Options Screen
Alt-I	Inserts a Line above the current cursor position
Alt-D	Deletes the line at the current cursor position
+	Increases the display length of the field currently under the cursor position. Available on the layout screen only, use the dark (gray) + key
-	Decreases the display length of the field currently under the cursor position. Available on the layout screen only, use the dark (gray) - key
Alt-S	Saves the Layout

In report design:

Alt-T	Selects a Field name to display on the Report as a title
Alt-A	Adds a line to the end of the section
Alt-U	Defines a Summary Field
Alt-P	Saves and Previews the report to the screen (Version 1.1 and above only)

In form design:

Alt-T	Selects Field to display on the Form with its title
Alt-M	Moves a block of text and/or fields

In Browse table design:

Alt-Z	Sizes a Field—Increase/decrease length of field
Alt-M	Moves a Field

In mail label design:

Alt-T	Selects a Field to display on the Label with its title
Alt-P	Saves and Previews the Mail Label to the screen (Version 1.1 and above only)

In letter design:

Alt-D	Deletes a block
Alt-C	Copies a block
Alt-I	Inserts a block
Alt-F	Selects a Field to display on the Letter

To design applications:

Alt-I	Inserts a Menu Item
Alt-M	Moves a Menu Item
Alt-D	Deletes a Menu Item
Alt-S	Saves the Application

The application painter:

Alt-M	Moves a block
Alt-D	Deletes a block
Alt-C	Copies a block
Alt-L	Toggles text\color link

Copying and pasting:

Alt-I	Inserts a block
Alt-C	Copies a block
Alt-F5	Copies the expression or field value into the memory buffer
Alt-F6	Pastes the expression or field value from the memory buffer

Alpha Four is not case-sensitive, so you don't have to worry about using upper- or lowercase letters in keystrokes. The highlight is a bright bar on your menu or screen. It is moved with the arrow keys, left, right, up, and down. It is sometimes considered a cursor, but generally a cursor is just a small blinking bar like ▌ or small box such as ■. When the cursor is a bar, your typing will overwrite existing text. When it is a box, your typing will push existing text ahead of itself on the screen. The Ins and Del keys change the cursor from the ▌ to the ■ and back again. This should not be confused with the Backspace key, which is at the top of the keyboard above the Enter key.

The Enter key is the most important key on the board. Therefore, it is usually the largest one. On some computers it even says Enter on it. Others simply indicate a left-facing arrow with a hook on the end. A menu in a software program is like a menu in a restaurant. You can point at your choice and the waiter will nod and bring your supper. You can point at an item with your highlight and hit the Enter key. The program understands and executes your command.

Screens and Windows

You can use two ways to gain access to the commands on Alpha Four's Main Menu and submenus. You can use the arrow keys to move the highlighted bar through the choices, and then press Enter when the desired option is highlighted. Or, you can press the letter on the keyboard that corresponds to the highlighted letter in the option you wish to select. This letter is usually the first letter of the option. For example, you can press **Q** to choose **Q**uit from the Main Menu and execute the command. You do not need to press Enter after selecting the letter because the initial is designed to act by itself as an instruction to the computer.

Some Main Menu options bring you to Alpha Four submenus, of which there are two varieties: those at the bottom of the screen you are using and those similar to the Main Menu, where choices appear in a column down the center of the screen. Depending on the situation, choices (menu selections) also appear in pop-up boxes that sometimes appear to overlap.

Submenu screens also show a prompt line on the next-to-bottom line to inform the user about the options available or actions that can be taken from the current position of the highlight. Choosing **V** from the Main Menu places you in **V**iew/Enter Mode, which also has a menu at the bottom of the screen (as shown in figure 1.3). Although this one-line menu looks different from the Main Menu, you use the same techniques to select options from it as from the Main Menu. During many Alpha Four operations, you can gain access to items or screens that do not appear on a menu display. For example, to see the Range Settings pop-up menu (see fig. 1.4), you can press **R** from the View or Browse mode and see more menu choices.

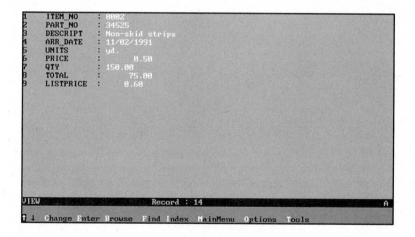

FIG. 1.3

The View/Enter screen has a menu line across the bottom of the screen.

The box shown in figure 1.4 represents another kind of menu and offers choices that define which records can be viewed. As you work with Alpha Four, you'll find that you can use these pop-up menus as shortcuts in laying out entry screens or reports.

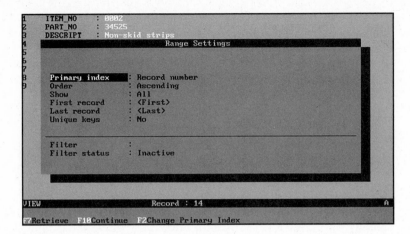

FIG. 1.4

The Range
Settings screen.

In these situations, you move the highlight bar up and down and then press Enter to choose an item from the menu. An option called *Window On* appears on many Alpha Four menus—the Range Setting screen, for example—at the *Filter* line. When a choice is available to you, it appears on the menu line. You can use this window to enter longer phrases or expressions that do not fit in the area initially provided.

To activate a window, press F6. The window or *expression box* that pops up contains several lines on which you can type your phrase or equation. To remove the window from the screen, press F6, which now says Window off, again or press the Esc key. Move the highlight from the top line of the Range Settings screen to the line that says Filter. Notice that the F6 choice appears as your cursor arrives at this line. When you choose F6, another window appears on top of the first to indicate that the first operation will be affected by what you do in the second window. If still another menu lies behind your current one, yet another window will pop up in front, as shown in figure 1.5.

If you get stuck, remember that help is just a keystroke away. Alpha Four has *context-sensitive help screens*. When you press F1, you will see a help screen that describes your current Alpha Four situation. The prompt line at the bottom of the help screen describes all the choices that appear on Alpha Four menus, except for functions and fields. Press Esc to get out of Range screen.

Default Screen Settings

Many database programs assume complete control over a large number of functions that relate to specific systems. The default settings screen in Alpha Four is designed to give you complete control over 16 elements of your work that range from the format of currency symbols to the mechanisms for storing data and showing the Help line. Many of these choices are self-explanatory. Others are worthy of consideration to discover how your work patterns can be improved or enhanced by their settings.

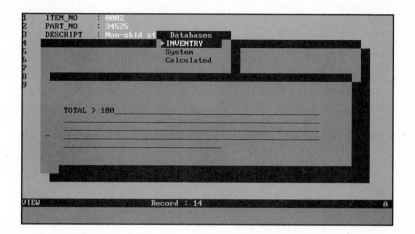

FIG. 1.5

Press F2 to make this Database box appear over the Filter window and above the Range Settings screen.

Several items on the Default Setting screen in figure 1.6. are related to the language spoken by the user. Others relate to conditions on the computer or the network system. These should be considered with care in order to optimize the use of your system. The default screen settings are listed in table 1.1.

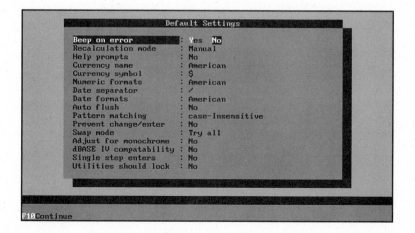

FIG. 1.6

The Default Settings screen, showing common settings.

Table 1.1 Default Screen Settings

Setting	Function
Currency name	Enables the user to define what word will be used during the extended format for money. For example, 'Dollars' or 'ECU'.
Currency symbol	User entered symbol, $, F, C, £, E
Numeric formats	American and European numeric formats exchange the use of the comma and period.
Date separator	Choice of / or -
Date formats	American (MM/DD/YYYY), European (DD/MM/YYYY)
Auto flush	Forces the software to save each record to the disk as it is written—flushes the memory. May be turned off to save data entry time. (Similar time factor to recalculation)
Pattern matching	Forces matching to both length and case; to case only; or not case-sensitive.
Prevent change/enter	Locks many functions when set to Yes. See list below.
Swap mode	Informs the software to use disk space, EMS, XMS, or to try all options from memory usage.
Adjust for monochrome	Removes references to available colors if Yes.
dBASE IV compatibility	Adjusts for dBASE compatible memo fields and numeric format.
Single step enters	By selecting Yes, you force the program to return to View or Browse mode after each record is entered. User must select Enter command to continue to enter next record. This is useful to activate a trigger script based on the Save Record trigger.
Utilities should lock	A network facility, this setting prevents record changes or entry when these utilities are being executed by another user in the same database: Append, Post, Join, Subtract, Intersect, Export, and Global update.

Protection Options

You can restrict access or prevent changes to the database in several places. The Default Setting Screen initiates global restrictions, which are detailed below.

The default setting for Prevent change/enter is extremely powerful. If set to Yes, the option enables the following functions:

- In View and Browse modes, the user cannot change, enter, delete, undelete records. The user can edit and choose new input forms and browse tables.

- All print commands are allowed.

- On the Index menu, the user can choose a new primary index and create/edit a range setting. The user cannot create, erase, update, attach, or detach an index, nor erase a range.

- On the Database/set design menu, this command will prevent the user from creating or modifying a set, creating, reconfiguring, or erasing a database, creating or changing field rules, or changing the name or description of a database. It will permit the user to create a duplicate database.

- On the Applications menu, the user can create, alter, and erase an application.

- On the Utilities menu, the user can use the following commands: Copy, Summarize, Import, Export, and all relational commands except Post. Cross Tabulation is permitted. The user is not permitted to use the commands Append, Pack, or Zap.

- On the Other menu, nothing is restricted.

Other places where passwords and restrictions to access can be defined include the following:

- Password protection of menus on applications at the Application Parameters screen and at each menu choice.

- Prevent/Allow Alterations for Reports, Labels, Forms, Browses, Ranges, and Searches on the Applications menu.

- Restrict access from View and Browse mode on the View and Browse edit screens.

- Password protection against changing a database name or description on the Database/Set Options screen.

Help

The goal of this book is to augment the resources Alpha Software currently has in place to assist its users. When you need help, you should use whatever is available. Fortunately, there is a growing amount of support available for Alpha Four users. The first place to look for answers to your Alpha Four questions is the index of this book. This book is intended to supplement the Alpha Four Reference Manual.

You may also find answers in the Alpha Reference Manual and Tutorial. Moreover, Alpha Software maintains an electronic bulletin board for anyone with a modem and an interest in Alpha Four problem solving. When you upload questions or files to the bulletin board, you can expect an intelligent response from the Alpha Technical Support Team within a short time.

As a last resort, you can call the Alpha Technical Support Team directly. They are willing to assist on truly technical matters but cannot assist you in designing your applications. In instances where the program simply will not perform as you expect and you have reached a dead end, the techs will help willingly. For later reference, the telephone number for the Alpha Software bulletin board is (617) 229-2915. The Technical Support Team phone number is (617) 272-3680.

Summary

In this chapter you have learned a bit of the background of Alpha Four and the historical conditions that brought you to use an electronic database. This chapter covered some of the basic language needed to deal with this world of information management, and you examined the first techniques you will need to proceed with creating a database. This will give you the understanding to get moving toward your goal of complete mastery of your own business data accumulation and reporting needs.

Defining and Creating Your First Database

I've got a little list—I've got a little list.
W. S. Gilbert, The Mikado

This chapter helps you develop an understanding of designing a database with Alpha Four. This basic understanding is needed as a foundation for all other activities in this book. The first part of this chapter gives the rules for creating a database, shows the steps required for this operation, and can be used as a reference for creating a database.

The second part of this chapter explains the theory of the design, creation, and use of a *flat file*, which is a file that is not linked in a relationship with another file. This section also delves into some of the principles of database design.

The third part of this chapter offers a sample database for hands-on practice. Later in the book, these files—or databases—will be linked into a relational *set* so that you can see data from more than one database in your forms, browse tables, and reports.

Understanding Database Terminology

The first rule of defining a database is to identify the specific purpose of your database by answering the question, "What is being tracked?" The answer to this question will help you define the several separate files you may need to design to accomplish your purpose. An analysis of the paper-based databases involved in your area of concern can help you visualize the functions that your electronic database should perform (see fig. 2.1).

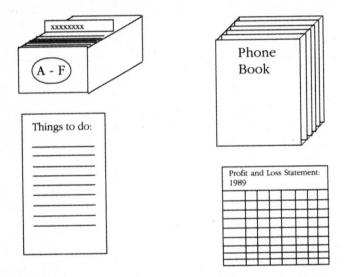

FIG. 2.1

Common paper-based databases.

Alpha Four uses the dBASE tradition of referring to a collection of related data as a file or database. Other database software publishers have used the term *table* to describe the same thing. Two other terms used in classical database terminology are *entity* and *attribute*. An entity is the item being tracked, such as customers, students, or invoices. Each entity is described by its own attributes. For example, the first name of a customer is specific to the entity in that record. One record is a collection of fields that contains the descriptions or attributes of that entity.

A database (file or table) can have many records; each record can contain as many as 128 fields to describe a specific record; each field is defined as a specific type (character, numeric, date, logical, memo) and given a certain length in which the data must fit.

Listing Objectives for Your Database

Some users plunge into database design as soon as they install Alpha Four. The trouble with database applications developed on the fly is that they tend to miss more often than they hit. Usually, these databases can meet a business's needs for only a short while. When the business grows or changes, the user is often stuck with a messy, time-consuming redesign project.

You may believe that getting your Alpha Four database application in gear quickly is imperative. However, you will save yourself substantial long-term grief if you plan the database before typing a single keystroke. Discovering what you expect from the database is the key to good database design. You should frame your objectives accurately and clearly from the outset. You will find that the correct design comes more easily if you ask the following questions:

1. What information do I want to track and where is it found?
2. How do I want to categorize the information?
3. How do I want to sort the information?
4. What type of output is required: forms, reports, mail labels, etc.?

Asking and writing down your questions first is critical if you want to design a database that is functional and appropriate to the needs of your business. One of this book's primary goals is to teach you how to break down those needs and then use Alpha Four to meet them.

Suppose that you want to create a computerized check register for your small business. Remember that an electronic database is simply an extension of its manual counterpart. Therefore, the initial functions of an on-line database closely parallel the operations performed manually.

As you begin examining the kinds of databases that you want to automate, you can understand your role as the designer, who is the person in the middle, literally and figuratively (see fig. 2.2).

Your on-line check register should work the same way as your current bookkeeping ledger. The key here is to focus on the process rather than the specifics of your data-management software. You might want to have the database contain the following kind of information:

- A list of your checks, printed in numerical order
- An alphabetical list of your payees

■ A list of separate personal or business expenses

■ Subtotals by category (Office Supplies) or by individual payees (The Beeper Co., Inc.)

■ A mailing list for sending promotional information or holiday greetings

■ A record of sales taxes paid

■ A list of donations to local charities

■ Special employee tax information

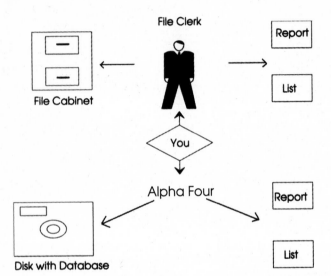

FIG. 2.2

The role of the database designer.

With such a database, you can easily find and review the checks for insurance bills, employee health expenses, uniforms, equipment depreciation, and other categories at tax time. After your basic check register database is up and running, you can expand its functions to provide more sophisticated analyses. Computerizing the process enables you to add other dimensions, such as automatic calculating and manipulating data to produce reports with minimal effort.

Good electronic database design begins with a pencil and paper. Just as an architect must draft a detailed plan before constructing a building, you must compile lists and sketch forms and reports before you can create a database with Alpha Four. Your advance work may take some time but will pay off in a smoothly functioning database that does not need to be revamped every week.

When you have tested your first version for a while and can see that certain items should be changed, you can fine-tune the original database design, add or remove fields, change calculations in field rules, and reorganize indexes to make the work more effective. The changes are relatively easy to make in Alpha Four—at least in the beginning stages of your work. As you get further into developing applications, changes become more complicated to implement, although the software itself can track a great many changes, such as adding or removing fields if a backup copy of the file structure is kept before structure changes are made.

Putting Information Down on Paper

The trick to successful database design is to zero in on your database needs. Sometimes this stage comes before you know exactly what an electronic database can do for you. A systematic approach can help you isolate problems before they become real headaches. This book's approach to database design has five simple steps, the first three of which are discussed in this chapter. Indexes and forms are considered in the following two chapters.

1. Ask the right questions.

2. Map out the fields.

3. Create the database.

4. Map out the indexes.

5. Design the forms.

Ask the Right Questions

The first question to ask is, "Why do I need this particular database?" The goal is to avoid creating a database that looks great but fails to perform the desired function.

Do you want the computer database to replace a complex, long-established manual system with reams of office forms and file drawers bursting with manila folders? Are you simply creating an on-line version of your address book? Or are you trying to develop a database to handle a new project that is itself still in the planning stages?

After you have the primary rationale for your database, you can develop a strategy for implementing it. A good database always springs from a well-conceived plan. When I work with a client to build a database, I begin by spending an amount of time appropriate to the scope of the project discussing what the client wants the database to do. I usually perform the following exercise to help my clients evaluate their data-management needs and expectations:

■ Examine any existing reports—*any* report, from the most complicated balance sheet to the simplest mailing label—that you expect the use of your database to automate. This examination begins to show you the fields you will need to create.

■ Describe your computational needs: counting this, averaging that, calculating the number of days between important dates, and determining estimates for pricing or billing.

■ Describe in writing or sketch how you would like the data to appear on-screen during the entry process and how the screen should look when someone is entering, editing, or simply examining the data.

■ Make sketches by hand of the new reports you need, including tables, mailing labels, and form letters.

■ Examine and describe the kind of information you need to determine the length of each piece of information. (This exercise is a preliminary for setting up your database fields.)

■ Review the work to ensure that everything you need is included and that everything you think you want is really needed.

During this stage of analysis, consider the following two important rules for database management:

1. Always categorize the data in logical groups. A list of inventory items should contain fields for a part number, a description, price, quantity, and so on. A customer file should have specific fields about names, business and/or home addresses, business and/or home telephone numbers, and other categories to suit your needs.

2. Never enter duplicate data in more than one field or in more than one database, unless it is to be used to link two or more databases in a logical combination or *set*. For example, if you create an ORDERS database to record items purchased from your inventory by your customers, the ORDERS database exists to record the transaction. The link in ORDERS to the customer database is through a CUST_ID field, which matches a CUST_ID field in the customer file. The item to be ordered is linked to the ORDERS database through an ITEM_ID field found in ORDERS and INVENTRY. This kind of duplication, of course, is required for the linking process.

Thoughtful participation in the exercise and consideration of the rules above will tell you a lot about your database requirements. Be careful, however: *What you do at this point can profoundly affect the rest of the database design process.* The good news is that you usually can easily change a database design in Alpha Four even after records have been entered. Remember to put all your thoughts in writing, and be specific.

Map Out the Fields

Creating fields in an Alpha Four database is a fairly simple and straightforward matter. Resist the temptation to dive into the process, however, until you have actually defined your fields, which is the information you want to include in each database record.

Alpha Four enables six field types for different types of data. Each field must have its type and length defined as it is created. Certain types of fields have a predefined length that cannot be changed by the user.

1. A *character field* accepts any character or symbol available on the keyboard. You can set a character field to be as long as 254 characters. This kind of field is sometimes referred to as *alphanumeric*.

2. A *numeric field* accepts only valid numbers and a decimal point. You define the number of places on both sides of the decimal point. The length can be 1 to 19 spaces. The decimal places can be 0 to 15 places but no more than the field length minus 2.

3. A *date field* accepts valid data characters in the MM/DD/YY format. The length of a date field is 8 characters.

4. A *logical field* accepts only four characters in upper- or lowercase: T (for true), F (for false), Y (for yes), or N (for no). The length is 1 character. It also accepts a blank space that is treated as neither true nor false.

5. A *memo field* accepts any character and is unformatted. A memo field may appear on-screen during data input or may consist merely of the message MEMO. Although memo fields are very flexible, you should be aware of alternatives to using them. The default length is 10 characters during the creation of the database. The actual length can be determined for each form or report in which the field is used.

6. *Calculated fields* are not an official type of field but are listed here and described further in Chapter 3 to help prevent confusion.

   While working with Alpha Four, you frequently will run across the need for calculated fields. Because you do not define calculated fields when you create a database, however, they are not considered a formal field type.

Defining Your Data Needs

If you ran a boatyard, you would get off on the right foot by analyzing the data you would require to operate successfully as a business. Take a closer look at some of the information that you want to track. You will need to know the name of the owner of each boat, the boat's name and overall length, any balance on the account, and the date that it will be launched.

You might visualize writing the information for each boat on a single 3"-by-5-" index card. Figure 2.3 shows two examples of paper-based employee and customer information cards.

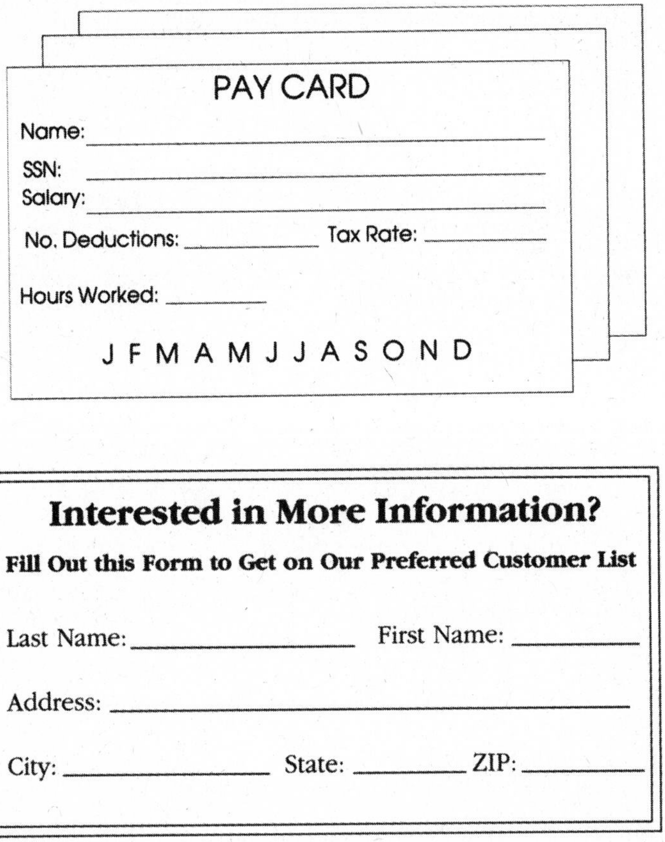

PAY CARD

Name: _____

SSN: _____
Salary: _____

No. Deductions: _____ Tax Rate: _____

Hours Worked: _____

J F M A M J J A S O N D

Interested in More Information?

Fill Out this Form to Get on Our Preferred Customer List

Last Name: _____ First Name: _____

Address: _____

City: _____ State: _____ ZIP: _____

FIG. 2.3

Traditional paper-based data-entry forms.

Consider one owner's information to be one record. In this database, a *record* is a collection of information about one owner and his or her boat. In a payroll database, a record may contain all the relevant information about one employee. You define a record by telling the computer which pieces of information compose that record. For this file, each boat is tracked with the following information:

Owner	Name	Length	Balance	Launch Date
Fenton	Wind Song	48 ft	234.75	05/28/92
Stanton	Blue Chip	64 ft	334.50	06/02/92
Smith	Sea Maid	20 ft	150.25	06/02/92

Each of these pieces of information is called a *field*. So far, the database has five fields: Owner, Name, Length, Balance, and Launch Date. The words OWNER, YACHTNAME, LENGTH, BALANCE, and LAUNCHDATE are the *field names*.

The job of designing a database begins with defining the necessary fields. During that step, or maybe a half-step later, you must decide what type of information each field will hold. For instance, the LAUNCHDATE field will store dates. The LENGTH and BALANCE fields will store numbers. The OWNER and YACHTNAME fields hold words, phrases, letters, and perhaps characters that look like numbers. As you explore Alpha Four's capabilities, you will learn how to facilitate the data-entry process by using field rules to provide entry shortcuts and guidance.

In Alpha Four, you can choose from two ways to create a new database:

1. When you type **A4** from DOS or otherwise access your program, the Main Menu is the first thing you see. Select **D**atabase/set design, **C**reate a new database, and type a valid DOS filename of eight characters or less. Alpha Four adds the three letter extension .DBF.

2. Create a new database from the Database Directory, shown in figure 2.4. Press F5 (Create), and type a valid DOS filename as above. Press the Enter key.

On the screen that appears after you name the database, enter a description of the database you are about to create; this step is optional but recommended for convenience. In Version 2, this screen holds the option for adding a password to this database, which is examined in Chapter 10.

You must consider one last issue before you begin to type away on your new database: the structure of the data itself. Consider the following preliminary notes for the fields for the owner's name and address file:

Field Name	Field Type	Kind of data
OWNER	Character	40 alphanumeric characters
YACHTNAME	Character	25 alphanumeric characters
LENGTH	Numeric	Numbers between 15 & 65 ft.
LAUNCHDATE	Date	8 (06/14/93)
TOTAL	Numeric	Dollars between 0 & 10,000.00

```
                    D a t a b a s e     D i r e c t o r y
   Drive/Path : C:\BOATYARD\*
   Default    : *.SET,*.DBF

   Name       Type    Date
 ↑ CONTAC     SET     02/02/1992
   CONTEST    SET     02/01/1992
   INVO       SET     01/31/1992
   INVOICES   SET     02/28/1992
   INV_NOLN   SET     12/22/1991
   OWN_INV    SET     12/22/1991
   PAYMENT    SET     12/22/1991
   WORDSET    SET     12/01/1991
   ADD_WARN   DBF     02/11/1992
   AVMOVIES   DBF     01/20/1992
   BILLS      DBF     02/24/1992
   CHECKS     DBF     03/07/1992
   CONTACT    DBF     02/07/1992
   INVENTRY   DBF     02/17/1992
 ↓ INVOICE    DBF     02/28/1992

   Enter name of the database/set : C:\BOATYARD\CONTAC.SET
   F3 Import F4 History on F6 Refresh F5 Create Db F8 Detail on F9 DOS
```

FIG. 2.4

The database directory shows you the names of existing files to prevent duplication of names.

A potential problem is indicated here. Will you want to send letters and use mailing labels to correspond with customers? To anticipate these needs, you can separate the owners' first and last names into two fields. In this way, you can find a customer by searching on the LASTNAME field, to print mailing labels in alphabetical order, or to create the following heading for a form letter:

Ms. Anne J. Stanton
235 Arrowhead Rd.
Crabapple Cove, ME 04992

Dear Anne:

You can create this heading only if you place first names in a FIRSTNAME field and last names in a LASTNAME field. Because owners' titles (Mr./Ms./Mrs./Dr.) also should be available, you can create a third field called PREFIX. For further standardization, you could add MIDDLE and SUFFIX, but they are not needed here.

Many database users need to sort mailing lists by state or by ZIP code. When you start to set up your database, you should create separate CITY, STATE, and ZIP fields for addresses.

The following are two prime examples of how you can prevent hassles by building your database with a thorough understanding of your expectations. By separating FIRSTNAME and LASTNAME fields, you can get rid of that computer-generated form-letter look. Your letters will be much more polished and professional. In addition, sorting by ZIP code can save you money by making you eligible for presorted mailing rates.

Field Naming Rules

When giving names to fields, you must follow these rules:

- Field names must be no more than 10 characters long and must begin with a character, A through Z, but can contain numbers 0 through 9.

- Field names cannot contain any spaces.

- The underscore (_) is the only acceptable character for dividing parts of field names (ZIP_CODE).

Table 2.1 includes all the fields used in the boatyard example in this book:

Table 2.1 Field Definitions for the OWNERS Database

Field Name	Field Type	Length	Decimals
OWNER_ID	Character	4	
PREFIX	Character	8	
FIRSTNAME	Character	15	
MIDDLE	Character	8	
LASTNAME	Character	20	
ADDRESS1	Character	30	
ADDRESS2	Character	20	
CITY	Character	15	

continues

Table 2.1 Continued

Field Name	Field Type	Length	Decimals
STATE	Character	2	
ZIP_CODE	Character	10	
HOME_PHONE	Character	13	
YACHTNAME	Character	20	
LOA	Numeric	4	1
DINGHY	Logical	1	
LAUNCHDATE	Date	8	
COMMENTS	Memo	10	
CUR_BILAMT	Numeric	7	2
CUR_BILDAT	Date	8	
LASTPAYAMT	Numeric	7	2
LASTPAYDAT	Date	8	
BALANCE	Numeric	7	2

The first field in the table is a unique owner identifier. Anticipating a day when the boatyard might have two owners with the same first and last names, this field provides an easy way to refer to owners and their data without confusion. You can devote a four-character field to owner ID numbers.

You may wonder why ZIP_CODE is a character field when ZIP codes in the United States range from five to nine numbers. Actually, Alpha Four database designers have a compelling reason to put ZIP codes in character rather than numeric fields: Because numeric fields are used in calculations, commas may be added and initial zeros dropped. Further, the result of entering **02140-1806**, a legitimate Boston area ZIP code, is 334. The software will not enable you to enter two numbers with a minus between them, so you must make this a character field.

Also, numeric fields do not allow for the parentheses you may need to include in telephone numbers with area codes, Social Security numbers, and Insurance Claim Codes. In any field of this kind, the input looks like a number, but the data act like characters.

The LOA (length over all) field represents the overall length of each vessel. This numeric field covers a range of boat lengths from 15 to 65 feet. A more precise LOA record could be recorded by using one decimal place. Therefore, the field length is 4 with 1 decimal place, as shown in table 2.1.

DINGHY is a logical field that indicates whether each customer will be storing a dinghy or rowboat with his or her main vessel. As mentioned earlier, logical fields accept only True/False and Yes/No input. Alpha Four itself creates the field with one character when you give the designation L for logical in the field type.

LAUNCHDATE is the date that the boat is returned to the harbor, usually after winter storage. The Alpha Four program knows that this kind of field requires eight characters, but there are two choices of valid date entry formats. You can enter the date with or without the full year: DD/MM/YY or DD/MM/YYYY. In either case, Alpha Four shows the result as 01/01/199x, whatever year your computer system indicates. On an input form, the field length must be at least 10 characters—longer if you wish to take advantage of the extended date format. During data entry, Alpha Four verifies the date and issues an alert if there is a problem.

Creating the File

Now you can call up Alpha Four and enter the field information you have so carefully designed by using the field list shown in table 2.1.

To create the sample database, perform the following steps:

1. From the Main Menu, select **Database/set design, Create a new** database.

2. Type the name **OWNERS**. Alpha Four will add the three letter extension .DBF. Press the Enter key.

3. Type in the description of the file. Give the file a name that will distinguish it from other files. Press F10 (Continue).

4. Type in the names, field types, and lengths listed in table 2.1.

5. When all the fields are defined properly, press F10 (Continue).

Enter the first field name, **OWNER_ID**. Alpha Four field names must be no more than 10 characters long, and they cannot include spaces or begin with a number. If you wish to have a visual delimiter to make a field name easier to read, use the underscore (_), as in OWNER_ID. Press Enter to advance to the Field Type column.

The default entry here is Character. You can accept this default, press the first letter of a valid field type, or hit the space bar to scroll through the offerings.

The valid field types, displayed at the bottom of the screen, are Character, Numeric, Date, Logical, and Memo. Because you want OWNER_ID to be a character field, enter **C**. The cursor moves to the fourth column and prompts you for the length of the field; enter **5**. Because character fields do not contain decimals, Alpha Four does not offer this choice here. Enter the remaining fields shown in table 2.1.

Use the arrow keys to move the cursor around the Create Database screen. You can place the cursor at any field to change its name, type, length, or number of decimal places.

When you have finished setting up the fields, press F10 to save the database structure and return to the Main Menu.

> **NOTE** For further information on the theory of database design, see *Introduction to Databases*, by James J. Townsend, Que Corporation, 1992.

Entering Records

You can now enter records in the OWNERS database. Begin by pressing **V** to select the View/Enter Records option from the Main Menu (see fig. 2.5). Notice that the word ENTER is in the lower-left corner of the screen. The fields you created appear on the default input form, ready to receive data.

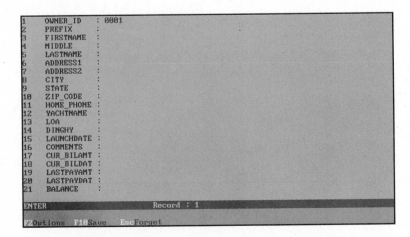

FIG. 2.5

Entering data for the first record.

Entering and saving records with this form is like creating a 3"-by-5" index card for each owner with a boat in the boatyard. Enter the following record by creating your own address information. When you get to the Memo field, enter the Memo Editor by pressing Alt-M. Write a phrase or two, then press F10 to save the memo. The last five fields will be filled in later by using the Post command described in Chapter 9.

Following is some sample data about one owner and his vessel. Use this data to help yourself get started on entering your first record.

Client:	1001
Owner:	Mr. Alfred H. Fenton
Yacht Name:	Wind Song
Dinghy:	Yes
Length:	48.0
Launch Date:	04-01-1992

After you have entered the preceding data, press the Enter key through the last five fields to move to the end of the record. These last five fields are intended to receive posted data, so they are not filled in here. Alpha Four displays a menu with the following options:

`Change; Enter next record; F10 Continue; Esc Exit without saving`

To add another record, press the Enter key. If you would like to edit the record currently on the screen, type **C** for Change. F10 saves the current record, takes you out of Enter mode, and returns you to View mode, which is designated by the word VIEW in the lower-left corner.

NOTE To switch from View to Enter modes, you type **E** instead of pressing the Enter key. In most other circumstances, you start Alpha Four processes by highlighting the choice with the menu bar and pressing Enter.

To see how it all works, practice entering records for several customers of our Boats and Storage, Inc. The following is more sample data with which you can create sample records.

Client:	102	Name:	Captain David Jones
Yacht Name:	Momma's Hopes	Dinghy:	No
Length:	64.0		
Launch Date:	04-01-1993		

Client:	103	Name:	Ms. Anne J. Stanton
Yacht Name:	Blue Chip	Dinghy:	Yes
Length:	28.0		
Launch Date:	06-01-1993		

Client:	104	Name:	Dr. F. Eugene Garland
Yacht Name:	When Free	Dinghy:	Yes
Length:	64.0		
Launch Date:	05-10-1993		

Client:	105	Name:	Mr. John Smith
Yacht Name:	Sweet Sister	Dinghy:	No
Length:	55.0		
Launch Date:	03-30-1993		

Client:	106	Name:	Mr. John L. Smith
Yacht Name:	Sea Maid	Dinghy:	Yes
Length:	20.0		
Launch Date:	06-15-1993		

After entering the data one record at a time, you can make the records appear in table or spreadsheet format by typing **B** to select the **B**rowse option. You can select Browse when you are in View mode or at the Main Menu. (Although the Browse option does not actually appear on the Main Menu, the option is available.) Browse mode displays up to 20 records on one screen. By using the arrow keys, you can scroll through the data to see records that are not currently visible on the screen.

Entering records in the Browse mode is not customary. There are no points of reference, no labeling except the field name at the top of the screen. Both field rules and formatting applies, but the Enter function is less than satisfying as you can only see the fields that fit across the 80 character screen.

In the next chapter, you explore ways you can customize browse tables and input forms for better data viewing. Many functions are available to simplify data entry and viewing.

Summary

This chapter presents a path for good database design by creating on paper the plan for the sample database. The chapter examined the rules for good design and guided you to start construction on a complete database file to track the boats and boat owners, which are considered customers in many businesses, in the boatyard.

Entering Data

The world is so full of a number of things,
I'm sure we should all be as happy as kings.
                    Robert Louis Stevenson, Happy Thoughts

The difference between a field and the data that is entered into the field is a distinction that requires some thought for the beginner. Entering and editing data is the second step in using an electronic database after the first step of creating the file structure. If you have been following this book's examples, then you have mastered the first step and begun the second step of entering data into the default entry or input form.

This chapter takes you step-by-step through the process of entering data in the default view screen and in the default browse table. After reading this chapter, you should be able to enter and edit data in an existing form and browse table. You usually use the View mode to enter and view data and Browse to view and edit specific fields. The View mode enables you to see your material in context with other data in the same record, and Browse enables you to see many records in context with related records—as many as 21 simultaneously.

As you move through the process of entering and editing data, you will discover ways to manipulate data to make it more useful to you. You may want to see all of your fields on a single screen, rather than running onto several screens, as they must if you have more fields than can fit on the original default screen's 21 lines. You may want to draw a box around specific data to highlight or emphasize that portion of the data entry. You may want to remove certain fields containing sensitive data from a screen used by data-entry people who are not authorized to view the data. Such matters are discussed in the "Customizing an Input Form" section of this chapter.

This chapter considers the ways data is entered into a file in Alpha Four, then the chapter explores the various choices on the **O**ptions menu in the **V**iew form and **B**rowse table—creating and designing an input form or browse table that better suits your needs. The chapter also includes a discussion of selecting a limited range of records, marking records for deletion, and using the Locate and the Search and Replace commands. To round out the discussion, you learn to Pack the database and Copy the database, which is an alternative to Pack.

Using the Default Input Form

You see the default input form the first time you press **V**iew or **E**nter on the Main Menu after you have created a new database. The form shows the first 21 fields or less by their number and field name along the left side of the screen (see fig. 3.1). If more than 21 fields exist, they are seen on the next screens, up to the maximum of 128 fields.

The status line indicates the mode in which you are working. In View mode, you can change to the Change or to Enter modes. Use the up- and down-arrow keys to move between records. Use the right- and left-arrow keys to move across the menu at the bottom of the screen; or select a menu choice by selecting the initial letter of the command. The menu has the following options:

↑↓ **C**hange **E**nter **B**rowse **F**ind **I**ndex **M**ainMenu **O**ptions **T**ools

```
1   OWNER_ID    : 0106
2   PREFIX      : Mr.
3   FIRSTNAME   : John
4   MIDDLE      : L.
5   LASTNAME    : Smith
6   ADDRESS1    : 15 Valley View Rd.
7   ADDRESS2    :
8   CITY        : York
9   STATE       : ME
10  ZIP_CODE    : 03909-
11  HOME_PHONE  : 332-1469
12  YACHTNAME   : Sea Maid
13  LOA         : 20.0
14  DINGHY      : n
15  LAUNCH      :
16  COMMENTS    : ...Memo...
17  CUR_BILAMT  :      1077.50
18  CUR_BILDAT  : 11/27/1991
19  LASTPAYAMT  :
20  LASTPAYDAT  : 11/27/1992
21  BALANCE     :      1077.50

VIEW    Memo              Record : 6                    Page : 1          A
↑ ↓  Change Enter Browse  Find Index MainMenu Options Tools
```

Entering Data in View Mode

After you define your database, as described in Quick Start 1 and in Chapter 2, the next step is to enter data into some records. From the Main Menu, you can move the highlight to the View/enter choice and press the Enter key, or press **E**. The **E** is not shown on the menu but is one of Alpha Four's numerous shortcut keys.

When you press **E** to enter your first record, Alpha Four offers you the default entry screen with all of your fields listed down the left side of the screen with the number of the field and the field name listed next to the blank space where your entry should be typed. You can type your entry in the customary fashion using the Backspace key to erase mistakes in the same line.

If you find a field for which you have no data, simply press the Enter key to pass to the next field. If you find the required data before you reach the end of the record, you can use the up-arrow key to return to the empty field and fill it with the proper entry. When you reach the last field and press Enter, or before the last field if you press F10 (Save), you still have the option to change the entry by pressing **C**hange or quit this form and exit without saving by pressing the Escape key. Press F10 (Continue) again to confirm the saving operation. If your cursor has reached the last field on the form, the program is ready to save the record. Press the Enter key one more time to save the record and start another entry.

When you find a record that contains a mistake, press **C**hange to go to Change mode, then use the arrow key to go to that field and retype the entry. As you type the first character of your new entry, notice that the remainder of the data in the field disappears. You do not need to erase the data, other than by entering the first character. If you want to empty the field entirely, use the space bar as your highlight reaches the field. Pressing the space bar erases all data in the field.

When editing data in a field, you may not want to retype the entire entry, but rather change a word or character some way along in the text. You can use your arrow key to move the cursor to the location of the change and type the change by using the backspace or the delete key to erase errors. Use the Insert key to change to overwrite mode. Overwrite indicates that what you type replaces existing characters. In Insert mode, what you type pushes the existing text ahead as you type in new text. See the section "Editing and Changing Data in View or Browse Mode" later in this chapter.

NOTE When entering a series of records with similar data, you can use the shortcut keys, Alt-F and Alt-R. These commands are dependent on the preceding record for their effect. For example, if you want to enter the same City, State, and ZIP code for several records in a row, you enter the first record manually; then for the next records, you can press Alt-F (Copy Previous **F**ield) to fill in those three fields. If the series is of records that are similar, except for a few entries, then create the record once and create the next similar record using Alt-R (Copy Previous **R**ecord), but remember to change the fields where the data is different between the first and second record.

Entering Data into Character Fields

Character fields accept any characters, numbers, spaces, or other symbols. A character field may be as small as one character and as large as 254 characters. Character fields can accept data from a lookup table or database that is defined in field rules (see Chapter 5). Character fields also can be calculated fields, which also are defined in field rules. These fields accept data from other fields, rather than from user entry. One example is a full name field, which is one long field derived from two or more shorter fields representing a person's name. Numbers can be used in character fields, but you cannot perform mathematical calculations without further manipulation.

Entering Data into Numeric Fields

Numeric fields, whether they are whole numbers, dollar amounts, or percentages, are entered literally. If a number has decimal places, type the integer first, place the decimal point in the proper location, then type the remaining numbers. Depending on how the field was designed, you can enter decimal points. Decimal places must be created as a part of the definition of the field if you expect to be able to see them on the screen. Suppose that you design a number field to have 10 characters and no decimal places. When you enter the number **24.95** in that field, the data will be truncated to read 24—not rounded to 25. Suppose that you design a numeric field to accept two decimal places; when you enter **2495**, the program adds two decimal places and makes the entry 2495.00. If you type **24.95**, the field displays 24.95.

NOTE When you define a numeric field, you can use up to 19 integers and up to 15 decimal places. The decimal places cannot be greater than the field length definition minus two.

Number of decimal places	Example
0	3
1	3.1
2	3.14
4	3.1417
5	3.14999

Entering Data into Date Fields

Date fields are easy to enter—after you get the hang of it. Alpha Four expects you to enter data in the form: DD/MM/YY, where January 1, 1992, is entered **01 01 92**. Alpha Four enters the / or - mark. If you omit the reference to the year, the program inserts the current year in the last four spaces. Dates also have a shortcut key, Alt-D. When you reach a date field in which you want to enter the current (today's) date, simply press Alt-D to see the numbers appear in the field.

Entering Data into Logical Fields

To enter data into a logical field, you are restricted to four choices in two options: T, F, Y, and N; or t, f, y, and n. This field is used as a switch or Yes/No field. Such a field could be used to answer the following question:

```
Include this client in the mailing? (Y/N) __
```

Entering Data into Memo Fields

Memo fields are accessed by pressing Alt-M. You can add or change data in a memo field while entering the record for the first time or later when you edit an existing record. Before the record is finished and saved, when your highlight reaches the Memo field, press Alt-M to access the Memo field editor. Here you see an unformatted space with a few features of a word processor. You can mark a block of text, copy a block of text, and insert a marked block into a new location. You can use these tasks to carry the copied block from one record to another. Use the following shortcut keys:

Alt-D marks and deletes a block of text.

Alt-C marks and copies a block of text.

Alt-I inserts the marked block to a new location.

Memo fields are saved by using F10 (Save). After the memo field has been saved, the text disappears from the screen and leaves only the following notation to tell you that data exists in the memo field:
...Memo...

If this note is not visible on a record, you know that no data is in any memo field on that record.

NOTE   You can display Memo fields on-screen by using the screen edit functions discussed later in this chapter.

Using the Default Browse Table

The default browse table contains every field that was designed as part of the database. The fields are arranged in columnar format in the same order as they are listed in the input form. The difference is that in Browse mode you can see as many as 20 records simultaneously, with the field names at the top of the column, but you can only see as many fields as fit horizontally on a single screen. You can use the down-arrow key or PgDn to view records beyond the first 20. The End key takes you to the last record on the screen, which is record 20 if you are using record number as the index. The Home key takes your cursor back to the top record on the screen.

The status line indicates the mode in which you are working. In Browse mode, you can change to the Change or Enter modes. Use the up- and down-arrow keys to move between records. Use the right- and left-arrow keys to move across the fields, from column to column. The only way to select a menu option is by choosing the initial letter of the command. As in View mode, the Browse mode menu has the following options:

↑↓ **C**hange **E**nter **B**rowse **F**ind **I**ndex **M**ainMenu **O**ptions **T**ools

Entering Data in Browse Mode

Data is entered in a browse table as in an entry form, although the single, horizontal line of fields is uninspiring as a data entry site. You probably will enter new data in View mode, but you probably will edit data in Browse mode, because you can move between records faster and more accurately in Browse mode than in View.

Editing and Changing Data in View or Browse Mode

In View or Browse mode, editing the data is as easy as pressing Change and using the arrow keys to move to the selected field and retyping the data. If the field is long, use the arrow keys to move your cursor to the place for the change. Erase the old data by putting the cursor into overwrite, where new entries erase old text. To change from overwrite to insert mode to enter additional data without erasing the old, press the Insert key on the keyboard.

Check the way the cursor looks when you are in Change or Enter modes. As you press the insert keys, the cursor may change shape, depending on whether you are in Insert or Overwrite mode.

T I P

Using Alternative Techniques for Data Entry

Several Alpha Four techniques, functions, and operations can help you automate your data entry; each method is discussed elsewhere in this book. Alternatives to the standard keyboard user-entry methods of data entry include the following:

1. In Enter mode, depending on the last record shown, perform the following (see the section "Entering Data in View Mode" previously in this chapter):

   Copy previous field, Alt-F.

   Copy previous record, Alt-R.

2. In the following field rules, use an entry provided by the rule (see Chapter 5):

   > Calculated fields
   >
   > Default entries
   >
   > Lookup entries
   >
   > Increment entries

3. With global update, add or change data (see Chapter 4).

4. In an application or script, use menu-prompted user entry: Which month? Which last name? (see Chapter 11).

5. With the relational commands, use data posted from an external database (see Chapter 9).

6. In utilities, have records appended from an external database (see Chapter 9).

Defining New Input Forms

When you need to make changes to your input form, you can approach the issue from two locations in Alpha Four. The first method for changing your input form is to choose the Layouts menu from the Main Menu and select **F**orms and **C**reate/edit a form.

The second way to perform this task is to go to View mode (the default input form appears if this is the first time you have edited the form), select **O**ptions, and **E**dit to see the default edit screen, as shown in figure 3.2.

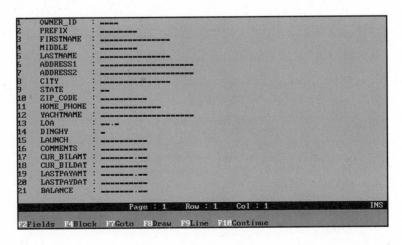

FIG. 3.2

The Edit screen for a default input form.

After you are in Edit mode, the screen in figure 3.2 shows the default input form. The dashed lines represent the length of the field in that location. You can add fields and text to the screen, move portions of the screen, draw lines and boxes to highlight areas, and apply various formatting changes during this procedure.

To edit an input form by using the first of the two methods of defining an input form, perform the following steps:

1. From the Main Menu, select **L**ayouts. Alpha Four displays the **L**ayouts menu. Select **F**orms, **C**reate. Select an unused letter between A and Z.

2. Type a description of the form that will remind you of the purpose of this specific form. Make any necessary changes in the parameters screen, if you will be printing the form.

   For example, you may want to print more than one form per page and change the printer margins. You can make these changes on this screen. Press F10 to continue.

3. A blank screen appears. Place the appropriate text and related fields on the form.

   For example, by using the arrow keys, move the cursor to Row 3, column 8. Select Alt-T to enter a field accompanied by its Title or field name. Press Enter to select the name of your database. Move the highlight to the field you wish to select and press Enter. You can retype the title to give it a cleaner appearance. Instead of ARR_DATE, you can change the title to read Date of arrival or whatever makes sense on your screen.

4. If you need to provide information on this screen that is not user-entered data, you may need a calculated field. To create a calculated field, press Alt-C or F2 (Fields). Type a unique field name on the form that appears. Then, design an expression to appear in that field.

   For example, assume that you are working with a personnel file with a hire date for employees. Create a field to notify you when an employee's review date is scheduled. To create a calculated field for NEXT_REVU, by using the HIRE_DATE field as a base for the expression, create a new calculated field named NEXT_REVU. In the next column, type an expression such as **HIRE_DATE + 120**.

   From the Edit screen, press Alt-C, type **NEXT_REVU**, press F2 to select the HIRE_DATE field, press + (plus), and then type the number of days to be added to the hire date to produce the date of the next review. The screen shows the following:

```
Name        Expression
NEXT_REVU   HIRE_DATE + 120
```

5. After the calculated field has been created, press F10 (Continue) to return to the Edit screen. You must place the newly created field on this screen. Use the arrow keys to move the cursor to the location where you want the field. To place the field, press Alt-F to select the field or Alt-T to select the field with Title, select the Calculated database, highlight the field, and press Enter.

6. After the fields are selected, apply formatting, such as length of field and window, case, justification, through the Formatting Options screen by using Alt-O or F2 (Fields), Formatting Options.

   For example, from the Edit screen, press Alt-O to see Formatting Options. Change the length of a field by changing the number in the **Len** column. Changing the length of the field here does not damage existing data and does not change the structural length of the field. Making a short field longer does not change the actual length of the field. To change the actual field length, you must reconfigure the database (see Chapter 10).

   To change the position of data within the field, change the third column, **Just**, by using **Left**, **Center**, **Right**, or leave it unchanged with **None**. The column headed Fmt has different functions for different field types. Formatting in a character field controls capitalization and applies wordwrap for a field in which the window is shorter than the length. For a numeric field, formatting controls the name and symbol of currency, forces the number to be spelled out, or to be blank if the entry is zero. Date fields have nine variations of formatting. Press F10.

7. Apply distinguishing marks, lines, and boxes by using the F8 (Draw) function. Place the cursor at the point where you want to start to draw a box. Press F8 and select one of the 8 choices, A-H. (The last choice erases an existing line or box.) Use the arrow keys to move to the opposite corner of the box and press Enter. Press F9 (Lines) to see the Line Menu. From this menu, you can add or delete blank lines on the form, center a line of text or left or right justify a line of text, or fill from the cursor position to the end of the line with any character.

8. Move, delete, or copy blocks of text or fields by using the F4 (Block) key.

   For example, to remove the numbers of the fields in the default input form, with the cursor at the top-left corner of the screen, press F4 (Block), and select **Delete**. Use the arrow keys to move down to the last number on the screen and to the right one space. When you press Enter, the numbers disappear.

9. To pre-define the range of records or the index to be used with this form, or to restrict access to certain functions on this form, press the F7 (GoTo) key.

10. Range settings and printer selections can be set during the editing process or later when the form is to be printed. Press F2 to select or create a new range. For more flexibility, select at Print time. On the Range setting line, you can change the setting to a different one than is presently active. If this form is always to be printed in a pre-defined manner, such as with compressed print, select **N**ow for when to specify output device, and select **P**rinter as the output device. When you select Printer, five new lines of choices appear. You can change Compressed Print to Yes to force this choice to be made on the screen, not later when you print the form.

Defining New Browse Tables

Your first look at a browse table may be disappointing. You may find that important fields are off the screen and cannot be seen without many keystrokes with the arrow keys to find them. You may discover that fields longer than 80 characters have forced the records to be separated by one or several blank lines. Or you may want to create a calculated field that reacts with other fields in the database. In any case, editing the browse table is required.

When you need to make changes to your browse table, you can choose two locations from which to approach the issue in Alpha Four. From the Main Menu, choose the Layouts menu and select **B**rowse tables and **C**reate/edit a browse table. Then give the new table any unused letter. Type a descriptive name to remind yourself of the significance of this table, and select the fields.

The second method for editing a browse table is to go into Browse mode (the default table will be seen if this is the first time you have edited the table), select **O**ptions **E**dit to see the default edit screen.

To edit a browse table by using the first of the preceding methods, perform the following steps:

1. Select Layout. Alpha Four displays the **L**ayouts menu. Select **B**rowse tables, **C**reate/edit a browse table. Select an unused letter between A and Z.

2. Type a description that will remind you of the purpose of this specific browse table. Make any necessary changes in the parameters screen, if you will be sending the browse table to a printer.

For example, you may want to pre-define the number of records that will be printed on each page and change the printer margins. If you want to have header information printed at the top of your browse table, change the number of header lines to 1, 2, or 3 and fill in the header information. You also can define the margins and page length. Press F10 to continue.

3. The next screen shows in column format the fields that you can select to go on the browse table. As illustrated in figure 3.3, the fields available include not only your current database but also the system database. If you are working with a set, the fields in the linked databases also are available. The Enter key selects and deselects each field; F6 selects an entire column of fields. If you make a mistake, you can reorder the fields by using F4 (Reorder), or if you really mess things up, you can use F5 (Restart) to clear the field selections and begin again. Press F10 when you have the selection as you like it. Press F10 to Continue.

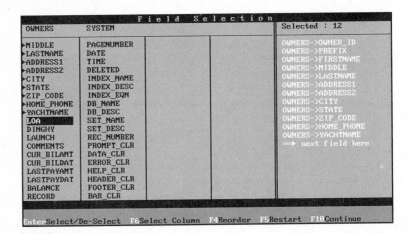

FIG. 3.3

Field Selection screen in Browse format.

NOTE When a field is selected, the ▶ symbol is placed beside the field name in the left column, and the name of the field and the name of its database appear in the right column. The top fields in the system database may be relevant to browse tables.

4. Further editing occurs on the next screen, shown in figure 3.4. Select formatting **O**ptions or press Alt-O to change the length of a field or window, to change justification within a field, to force upper- and lowercase designations, to define wordwrap for longer fields, and to define color selections for each field. The color selection is initiated by using F6 (Set field color). When a color is defined, a check mark ✔ appears on the formatting options

```
OWNERS_ID   : 0106                 HOMEPHONE   : 332-1469
PREFIX      : Mr.
FIRSTNAME   : John
MIDDLE      : L.                   YACHT_NAME  : Sea Maid
LASTNAME    : Smith                LOA         : 20.0
ADDRESS1    : 15 Valley View Rd.   DINGHY      : n
ADDRESS2    :
CITY        : York                 LAUNCH_DATE :
STATE       : ME
ZIP_CODE    : 03909-

                        AMOUNT      DATE
                        1077.50     11/27/1991
                                    11/27/1992
                        1077.50

        COMMENTS   : Hurricane damage. Storage only.


VIEW   Memo                   Record : 6                              A
↑ ↓   Change Enter Browse  Find Index  MainMenu  Options  Tools
```

FIG. 3.4

This form has been redesigned to provide a better grouping of fields.

5. As with an input form, if you need to provide information on this screen that is not user-entered data, you may need a calculated field. To create a calculated field, press Alt-C or F2 (Fields). Type a unique field name on the form that appears. Then, design an expression to appear in that field.

Using the same example, to create a calculated field for NEXT_REVU, using the HIRE_DATE field as a base for the expression, create a new calculated field entitled NEXT_DATE and write an expression such as HIRE_DATE + 120. The steps from the Edit screen are press Alt-C, type NEXT_REVU, press F2 to select the hire data field, type +, and then type the number of days to be added to the hire date to produce the date of the next review. The screen shows the following:

```
Name                      Expression
NEXT_REVU                 HIRE_DATE + 120
```

6. After the calculated field has been created, you must place the field on the screen. Move the cursor to the place where you want the field. To place the field, press Alt-F (to select field) and locate the field on your screen. Select the calculated database, highlight the field name, and press Enter.

7. After the fields are selected, apply formatting, such as length of field and window, case, justification, and so on through the Formatting Options screen by using Alt-O or F2 (Fields), formatting Options.

For example, from the Edit screen, press Alt-O to see Formatting Options. Change the length of a field by changing the number in the Len column. Changing the length of the field here does not damage existing data and does not change the structural length of the field. Making a short field longer does not change the actual

length of the field. To change the actual field length, you must reconfigure the database (see Chapter 10).

To change the position of data within the field, change the third field, Just, using Left, Center, Right, or leave it unchanged with None. The column headed Fmt has different functions for different field types. Formatting in a character field controls capitalization and for a field in which the window is shorter than the length, applies wordwrap. For a numeric field, formatting controls the name and symbol of currency, forces the number to be spelled out, or to be blank if the entry is zero. Date fields have nine variations of formatting.

8. To pre-define the range of records or the index to be used with this browse table, or to restrict access to certain functions, select the F7 (Goto) key. Range settings and printer selections can be set during the editing process or later when the table is to be printed. Press F2 to select or create a new range. For more flexibility, select at Print time. On the Range setting line, you can change the setting to a different one than is presently active. If this table is always to be printed in a pre-defined manner, such as compressed print, select Now for when to specify output device, and select Printer as the output device. When you select Printer, 5 new lines of choices appear. You can change Compressed Print to Yes to force this choice to be made on this screen, not later when you print the table.

Customizing an Input Form

Input forms can be plain and unadorned or they can be complex, multipage printable documents. In either case, several facts must be considered:

1. An input form is independent of the data itself; for example, suppose that you enter five records using the default entry form for a database containing 10 fields, filling every field properly and completely. Then you create a new entry form selecting only three of the fields from your database. The data in the five records is still in the file, but it cannot be seen on the new form. Furthermore, when you create a new record, the missing fields cannot receive data because they are not available using the new form.

2. An input form can exhibit data in a calculated field based on existing fields; on system information such as fields found in the System Database, such as the date, the current index, and others; on a constant value such as a sales tax of .05; or when used in a set, on fields from a related database.

3. Information presented in a calculated field on one input form must be recreated for any additional form, report, mail label, browse table, or letter. The data in a calculated field is not stored anywhere in the database itself. It is calculated at the time of viewing.

4. A calculated field on an input form cannot be used to index the database. The same expression that creates the calculated field, however, generally can be used again to create an index. (See Chapter 4 on indexing.)

Practical Uses for Calculated Fields

To illustrate the differences between calculated fields in an input form and a calculation created in field rules, you can use the OWNERS database created in Chapter 2.

The data entered involves the boat and the owner. The form can take a great leap forward in usefulness if you employ a few calculations. In fact, the form can produce the basics of an invoice with which you can bill the owner for hauling and launching his vessel. Calculations needed to produce an invoice very likely should be stored with each record. These fields store the amount of the sales tax, a sub-total of items, and the grand total of the invoice. If they are designed as calculated fields on the input form, then they must be designed again for each report used in the database. It is generally better that this kind of calculation be done in field rules to become a permanent part of the stored data.

Think of an input form calculated field as one that is especially useful for this form only. Consider the following example: The boat yard must hire a different piece of equipment to haul or launch a boat 48 ft. in length or more. Therefore, as the owner is scanning his records to plan his work, he would find it helpful to have a *flag* emphasize this distinction.

Furthermore, to make the flag stand out, you can make the words highlighted, flashing, or in any available color. The use of color is liberally illustrated in the demonstration files that come with Alpha Four. You can create your own by following the examples later in this chapter.

To edit this input form, choose **O**ptions, **E**dit as shown in figure 3.5.

Notice other capabilities that are available on the Options menu. The commands to Locate a record, Search and Replace, and defining Ranges, and Delete and Undelete records are examined in more detail later in this chapter.

The menu shown on the bottom line of figure 3.6 indicates numerous activities that can be used to enhance the usefulness and visual interest of the input form.

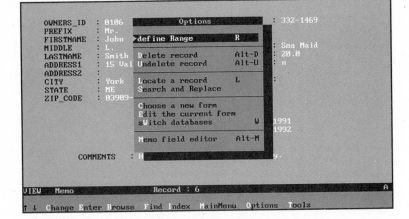

FIG. 3.5

The Options
menu in View
mode.

```
OWNERS_ID   : 0106                    Options              : 332-1469
PREFIX      : Mr.
FIRSTNAME   : John    ▶define Range            R
MIDDLE      : L.                                            : Sea Maid
LASTNAME    : Smith    Delete record          Alt-D        : 20.0
ADDRESS1    : 15 Val   Undelete record        Alt-U        : n
ADDRESS2    :
CITY        : York     Locate a record        L            :
STATE       : ME       Search and Replace
ZIP_CODE    : 03909-
                       Choose a new form
                       Edit the current form
                       sWitch databases       W            1991
                                                           1992
                       Memo field editor      Alt-M

            COMMENTS   : H                                  y.

VIEW   Memo                    Record : 6                              A
↑ ↓  Change Enter Browse  Find Index  MainMenu  Options  Tools
```

FIG. 3.6

The Entry screen
with fields and
text added to
clarify the data
entry process.

```
                    OWNER'S INFORMATION DATA ENTRY FORM
     Owner's ID : 0107              Home Phone  :
     Prefix     : Ms.
     First Name : Carole
     Middle     : F.               Yacht name  : Cheap Shots
     Last Name  : Sloan            LOA         : 34.0
     Address 1  : 33 Bedford Road   Dinghy (Y/N) : y
     Address 2  :
     City       : Acton            Launch Date : 04/01/1992
     State      : ME
     ZIP CODE   :

     ================================================================
                               Amount      Date
          Current Billing Info.:   107.40   12/05/1991
          Current Payment Info.:            12/05/1991
          Current Balance Due  :   107.40        0

          COMMENTS   :

VIEW   Memo                    Record : 7                              A
↑ ↓  Change Enter Browse  Find Index  MainMenu  Options  Tools
```

Using a Calculated Field

Occasionally the entry screen itself can prompt the user with information that is important, based on the results of data that have been entered. A special field can be created to perform this kind of service.

The term *calculated field* has two meanings, both of which are accurate.
The term can refer to an actual field that is part of the database whose
calculations are created by a field rule, or it can refer to the results of
calculations that you can display or print as part of an input form,
browse table or a report. Any confusion here is due to some sloppiness
in database terminology. Occasionally, concepts arrive quicker than
terms. When concepts are similar, terms can get muddled. You will
become familiar with both kinds of calculated fields.

The following are descriptions of two kinds of calculated fields:

1. Initially Alpha Four assumes that all fields are *user-entered*. You type all the information for the field. It is easy, however to change an existing field from a user-entered to a calculated field that uses an Alpha Four expression to produce at least some of its information.

   You perform this task by using Field Rules. An obvious example is the TOTAL field that contains PRICE * QUANTITY as a calculation. A less obvious example is the linking of two character fields, such as FIRSTNAME and LASTNAME, so that they appear as a single field with one space between them. The resulting expression is (FIRSTNAME+" "+LASTNAME) that appears on the screen as John Doe. You will learn more about calculated fields in the sections on field rules in Chapters 5 and 10.

2. The other kind of calculated field is designed on-the-fly during the editing of a report, input form, or browse table. One advantage to using this kind of calculated field is that Alpha Four does not store these calculations as a part of the database, so they do not take up any disk space. One disadvantage is that the calculation must be created for each report, input form, or label to which it applies. A second disadvantage is that the calculation cannot directly become part of an index, which means that records cannot be put in order by that field.

Creating a Calculated Field

To create a calculated field on a form, press F2 to choose the Fields box. Place your highlight on the selection define Calculated field to take the next step.

The screen shown in figure 3.7 indicates where you create your new field. The field you create simply checks another field called LOA and decides whether the vessel is equal to or greater than 48 ft.

The first step in this process is to give the new field a significant name. In this case, it can be the same as the words in the expression. Type **LONG** below the word Name. Next you enter the expression for this field. Below the word Expression, type the following entry exactly as it is written here and end by pressing Enter. Save with F10.

if(LOA>=48, "Long Load"," ")

The following is the translation of the preceding expression to English:

If length over all is greater than or equal to 48, then type the words "Long Load" in this space, if not, type nothing.

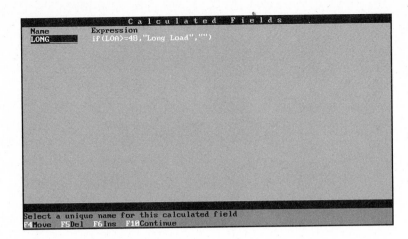

Calculated Fields

Name   Expression
LONG   if(LOA>=48,"Long Load","")

Select a unique name for this calculated field
F4 Move   F5 Del   F6 Ins   F10 Continue

FIG. 3.7

A calculated field designed on-the-fly.

Whatever is enclosed between double quotation marks (" ") is used literally in the field. If the space between the double quotes is empty, the field will be left blank when the expression evaluates the data with the result being false, no, or blank.

An alternative to typing the name of the field (LOA), and frequently a better choice, is to press F2, the Fields key, select the current database name (OWNERS), highlight the field and press Enter. This procedure enters the name with exactly the correct spelling every time.

To place this newly created field on your input form, you must choose it in much the same manner as you would select a field from the active database. Press F2 (Fields) and press Enter to choose select Field (or press Alt-F, the shortcut key) and choose the Calculated database, as shown in figure 3.8. This retrieves a listing of the calculated fields that you have designed for this input form only. Press Enter after selecting the field. Note that the Databases box has three selections: your file, the System database, and the Calculated database after you have created a calculated field (see fig. 3.8).

NOTE The calculated fields defined in this manner must be recreated for use in other forms or reports.

Place the field near the location of the LOA to emphasize the fact that the boat will require special treatment when the boat is hauled from or launched into the harbor.

```
              OWNER'S INFORMATION DATA ENTRY FORM

 Owner's ID  : _____      Databases    Phone    : _____
 Prefix      : _____  ▶OWNERS
 First Name  : _____   System       name    : _____
 Middle      : _____    Calculated             : ___.__  _____
 Last Name   : _____
 Address 1   : _____     (Y/N) : __
 Address 2   : _____
 City        : _____    Launch Date : _____
 State       : __
 ZIP CODE    : _____


 ==============================================================================
                              Amount      Date
        Current Billing  Info.: _____.__   _____
        Current Payment  Info.: _____.__   _____
        Current Balance Due  : _____.__

        COMMENTS    : _____
                      _____


             Page : 1    Row : 1    Col : 1                         INS
```

FIG. 3.8

The Databases
box shows three
choices after
a calculated
field has been
created.

Moving and Deleting Text and Fields

To make room on this input form for more data, mark a group of fields
and field names and move them to a new area of the screen. Place your
cursor on the L of LAUNCH_DATE, and press F4 to select the Block
menu. The shortcut for this procedure is Alt-M. Use the arrow keys to
move the highlight down to cover the area of the screen you want to
move and to the right to cover the first portion of the dashed lines
indicating fields.

When you press Enter here, you can use the arrow keys to move the
highlighted elements of the screen. Place this group of text and fields
on the right side of the screen and align the bottom of the block with
the field DINGHY. Press Enter to complete the move command.

This procedure gives you space at the bottom to make more additions
to the screen. Place the cursor at the top of the screen and choose F9,
the Line key. Now you can insert three lines and type a title at the top
of your screen. Type **MY BOATYARD**, and select F9 again to center the
words in this line.

Use the F4 Block box to delete the field numbers 1-21 if you decide to
move fields out of order. Press the PgDn key to see screen two of your
input form. If you have more than 21 fields on your database, those
numbered 22 and up appear on subsequent input forms. You can use
F4 Block to move the fields on screen two up to screen one, if you prefer to see them all simultaneously. You can delete the field numbers by
selecting the block to be deleted in the same way it was moved.

Using Lines and Boxes as a Highlight

Use the F8 (Draw) key to select the Draw menu and give emphasis to the date and number fields on your screen, such as that shown in figure 3.9. In the Draw menu box, choices A through H produce lines or boxes. The I choice erases other choices.

```
                 OWNER'S INFORMATION DATA ENTRY FORM

       Owner's ID :  _____       Home Phone    : _____
       Prefix     : _____
       First Name : _____     ┌──────────────────────────────────┐
       Middle     : _____           │ Yacht name   : _____ │
       Last Name  : _____     │ LOA          : ___.__  _____ │
       Address 1  : _____  │ Dinghy (Y/N) : __                  │
       Address 2  : _____  │                                    │
       City       : _____     │ Launch Date  : _____       │
       State      : __                  └──────────────────────────────────┘
       ZIP CODE   : _____

       ==========================================================================
                                      Amount      Date
              Current Billing Info.: _____.__   _____
              Current Payment Info.: _____.__   _____
              Current Balance Due  : _____.__

              COMMENTS            : _____
                                    _____

                      Page : 1    Row : 4    Col : 39                    INS
       F2Fields  F4Block  F7Goto  F8Draw  F9Line  F10Continue
```

FIG. 3.9

You can draw a line or a box to enhance the input form.

Input forms can be *painted* by using calculated fields defined by using formatting options. This procedure is discussed at more length in the following section on browse tables. Painting is a somewhat awkward technique but not impossible. In the design of applications in Quick Start III, you will work with designing banners, which can be made very colorful.

Using Special Forms

Although the data entry process for the boatyard is quite uncomplicated and requires only one or two special input forms, other situations can be quite different and require forms to serve a wide variety of functions.

This section explores special input forms by using a modified example from the database files of a rural police department. The town has a variety of personnel using their database, including civilian personnel employed as secretaries and dispatchers. The crime statistics are heavy in traffic violations and alcohol abuse. Citizens require pistol and long gun permits as well as dog licenses. Because this town is near a major city and has two major highways on its borders, police records indicate a good number of arrests for various crimes perpetrated by citizens outside their own community.

Enhanced Data Entry

The dispatcher keeps detailed records on citizens who, for whatever reason, come into contact with the police. These records are helpful in times of crisis and are intended to document people's activities, houses empty during vacations, neighborhood difficulties, territorial disputes, and pet problems. These records are kept confidential, and only personnel who have direct interest deal with the information.

For this reason, the department has different forms designed for special purposes. The database has many fields and is used in a *set* (see Part II), with complaints and reports in a separate file linked by an incremented, unique identification number.

Security for Sensitive Data

In some cases, you may need to secure certain data from the eyes of unauthorized personnel. In the sample police database, for example, information referring to residential property is kept on a single input form with no reference to licenses for dogs or guns. Information about absent owner's requests for house watch are accessible on a form guarded by a password available only to authorized personnel. The principle to be followed in this case is that not all fields need to be seen on every screen.

All of the fields are contained in the same database, but certain fields are viewed only on specific forms. Although the data *exists*, it is not *visible* to unauthorized people. At the least, the data is not available without more time, effort, and knowledge of Alpha Four and the Disk Operating System (DOS) than personnel members usually have. This specialized input form demonstrates the effectiveness of this technique.

Using Browse Tables for Multiple Records on View

Browse tables operate in much the same manner as input forms, except that browse tables can show multiple records in a columnar format rather than a single record. As many as 20 records can be seen simultaneously in Browse mode, but a limited number of fields are visible at any one time. The number of fields visible depends on the width of each. Because the computer screen is usually 80 characters wide, the widest field that may be viewed is 80 characters. You can scroll to the right and left in Browse mode to see more fields. Fields also can be designed to *wordwrap*, show multiple lines in the same field in a single record, as illustrated in figure 3.10.

An effectively designed browse table can serve as a quick report in some applications. Up to 26 browse tables can be defined, as with reports, forms, and other Alpha Four features that are stored by using letters of the alphabet.

		Report of current arrests	
		Prepared by Officer Barletti, 12/21/92	
SERIAL_NO	**ARREST_NO**	**LAST**	**OFFENSES**
90-0003	A90-3	Franklin	Speeding, 45 in 25 mile zone, Winter and School Street. School Zone.
90-0002	A90-2	Hanneberry	B & E, Wilson's Pharmacy, burglar tools in possession, cash and non-prescription drugs in case.
90-0001	A90-1	Jones	OWI/speeding/failure to keep right/ran the light/struck utility pole on corner/ bicyclist thrown onto sidewalk/no serious personal damage/ checked by EMT.
90-0004	A90-4	Wilson	Drunk and disorderly, fighting, foul language.

FIG. 3.10

A sample report as a printed browse table.

Making Browse Tables Work for You

The browse table shown in figure 3.10 is useful because the fields shown are those needed to identify a particular individual by the police department's serial number, by the arrest number, and by the individual's last name. These fields are not shown in the order that an unedited browse table would offer. In fact, before a browse table has been edited, it may be more confusing than constructive and by showing data that is low priority first with important data to the right of the screen.

Figure 3.11 shows an example of a screen that would be difficult to re-late to a specific case or prisoner. Press O for Options to get the pop-up box that enables you to edit this browse table.

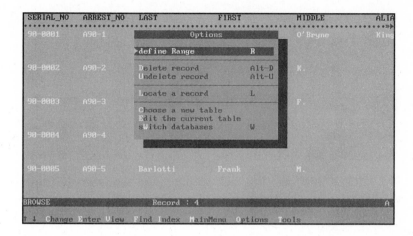

FIG. 3.11

These options are available in Browse mode.

From **B**rowse mode, choose **O**ptions, **E**dit the current table. This com-mand gives you access to editing and formatting functions similar to those in the Edit mode of the View format.

The screen shown in figure 3.12 shows the dashed lines that represent the fields in a browse table in Edit mode.

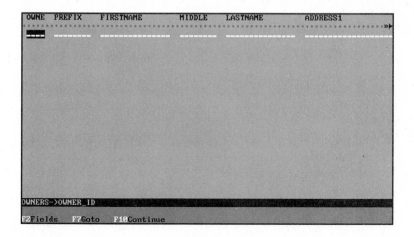

FIG. 3.12

Editing the browse table. Fields show as dashed lines.

From this position, you can add, delete, rearrange, or change the size of fields. Press F2 or Alt-O to access the formatting options available for the fields shown in the browse table (see fig. 3.13).

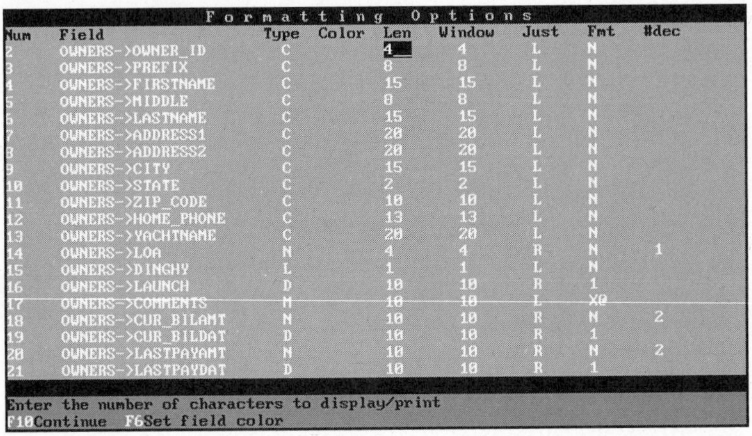

Formatting Options

Num	Field	Type	Color	Len	Window	Just	Fmt	#dec
2	OWNERS->OWNER_ID	C		4	4	L	N	
3	OWNERS->PREFIX	C		8	8	L	N	
4	OWNERS->FIRSTNAME	C		15	15	L	N	
5	OWNERS->MIDDLE	C		8	8	L	N	
6	OWNERS->LASTNAME	C		15	15	L	N	
7	OWNERS->ADDRESS1	C		20	20	L	N	
8	OWNERS->ADDRESS2	C		20	20	L	N	
9	OWNERS->CITY	C		15	15	L	N	
10	OWNERS->STATE	C		2	2	L	N	
11	OWNERS->ZIP_CODE	C		10	10	L	N	
12	OWNERS->HOME_PHONE	C		13	13	L	N	
13	OWNERS->YACHTNAME	C		20	20	L	N	
14	OWNERS->LOA	N		4	4	R	N	1
15	OWNERS->DINGHY	L		1	1	L	N	
16	OWNERS->LAUNCH	D		10	10	R	1	
17	OWNERS->COMMENTS	M		10	10	L	X0	
18	OWNERS->CUR_BILAMT	N		10	10	R	N	2
19	OWNERS->CUR_BILDAT	D		10	10	R	1	
20	OWNERS->LASTPAYAMT	N		10	10	R	N	2
21	OWNERS->LASTPAYDAT	D		10	10	R	1	

Enter the number of characters to display/print
F10Continue F6Set field color

FIG. 3.13

The formatting options available for fields in a browse table.

From here, you can change the length of a field, as shown on the screen in figure 3.13, and you can create a window that is shorter than the length of the field. By placing an X in the Format field, you force the text to wordwrap within that window.

Each column in your browse table can appear in different colors. In fact, each field can be defined by using a conditional statement that will change the color depending on the data entered.

Using Color in Browse Tables

Imagine a gardener who tracks the plantings in her garden. If a plant shows red, yellow, blue, white, or two-tone shades, the name will appear in that color on the screen. The conditional statement could get too long unless a strategy exists. The technique is to have a field in the database that accepts one character. The character indicates the color, R for red, B for blue, and so on.

This technique is particularly effective if the background of the database is defined as white in the configuration screen on the Main Menu. The first step is to set the screen configuration from the Main Menu. Select Other, Configuration, Screen to work with the color settings (see Chapter 10).

The next step to a colorful browse table or view form is to employ the editing techniques provided in Formatting Options.

Choose F2 the Fields key and select Formatting Options, or use the shortcut Alt-O to see the screen in figure 3.14.

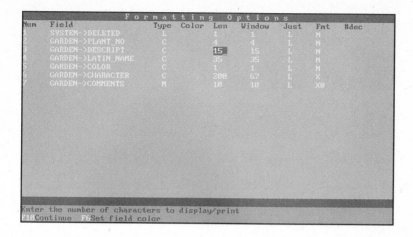

FIG. 3.14

Formatting
options available
in Browse Edit.

The field DESCRIPT for the plant names is defined with a command as
in figure 3.15.

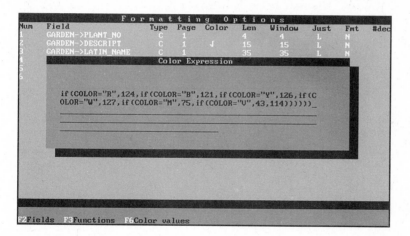

FIG. 3.15

The Color
Expression box
showing a
complex formula
for changing
colors on the
input form.

Place the highlight on the field that is to receive the color expression, and
select F6 to see the color chart. Move the highlight across the three blocks
until the color you like is showing. Press Enter to select the number.

The English translation of this expression is the following:

If the color field = R, then use color # 124, else
if the color field = B, then use color # 121, else
if the color field = Y, then use color # 126, else
if the color field = W, then use color # 127, else
if the color field = M, then use color # 75, else
if the color field = V, then use color # 43, else
use # 114

The preceding is a *nested* IF statement. If the first condition is not met, the expression continues to the second; if that condition is not met, the expression continues until it finds a *true* statement. If no statement is true, then the last *else* says *use this*. The result is a colorful browse table that will look better on your color screen than it does in figure 3.16.

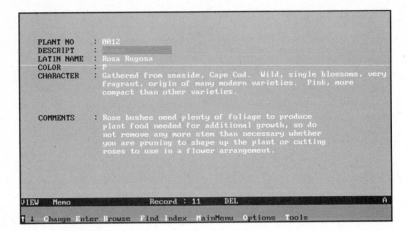

FIG. 3.16

The DESCRIPT field changes color according to the expression defined in field rules.

When you create a color expression in Formatting Options, the   appears on the line where the affected field is listed (refer to figure 3.16).

To make this short example more complete, you should use field rules to design a lookup table to enforce the choices of letters to define the colors chosen (see the section on lookup tables in Chapter 5).

Another Example Using Color Expressions

The gardener's example is used for its dramatically colorful opportunities. Your own database will offer similar chances to highlight certain fields for emphasis. The *blink* choice is effective in some circumstances, especially when a monochrome monitor limits the choices. In another police application, incident reports are recorded on a specific input form that defines the type of incident with letters just as the gardener defined the dominant color of the flowers. In the case of the police department, the letter A was made to blink if the word *accident* appeared in the description of the event.

In this case, the purpose is not cosmetic. It is vital to the officer that the designation of *accident* be noticed by anyone viewing the file.

Long Text Fields in Browse Tables

Using long text fields is important in many database applications. Fields named COMMENTS and NOTES appear in nearly every file. Whatever your application may be—doctor's operating notes, descriptions of telephone conversations, details of accident reports, or sequential notations on purchases—long, relatively unrestricted character fields are useful.

Important differences exist between character fields and memo fields. These differences are largely matters of a technical nature, such as where the data is stored within the file structure itself. Memo fields are held separately and are not a part of the original .DBF file. Therefore, the operation of the file is slowed somewhat by the need to open and close the memo file every time it is used. You should limit your use of memo fields, depending on the number of fields in the database and the amount of calculations going on in the file.

In the GARDEN database, a character field with a length of 200 characters is adequate for a brief description of the plants. Another field of similar length could be added to accommodate planting instructions and a third for propagation issues or purchase and selling information.

Another important distinction between character and memo fields is that the only search that can be defined for a memo field is a query looking for *any occurrence* of a string (series of characters) of data. Such a string might be *sunny* or *shady* to return any record that contains a reference to this string.

By contrast, a character field has a greater range of searching and indexing capabilities. For example, on the screen shown in figure 3.17, the index is designed to alphabetize on the DESCRIPT field that contains the common name of each plant. In fact, the index has two levels, DESCRIPT + COLOR. All petunias will be grouped together, but blue varieties will be listed before pinks and whites. If the index were on the COLOR field, all flowering plants of a certain color would be found together, regardless of their common name.

The value to the index in the **View** and **Browse** mode is that you can quickly find the first occurrence of the record you need by typing in the first few letters of the data you seek. Therefore, by typing **Petu** and so forth at the **F**ind command, you will see the first occurrence of the listing's petunias, in order by color.

In **View** and **Browse**, you can change the order and the range of records without returning to the Main Menu. As seen in figure 3.18, the current index is highlighted when you select Index.

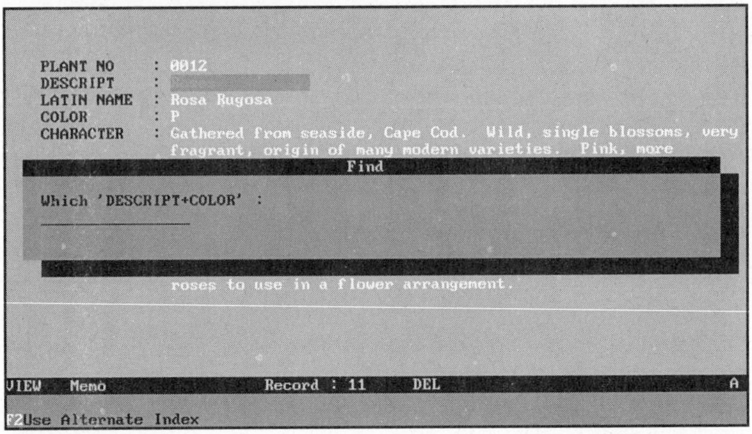

96

FIG. 3.17

The **F**ind command uses the current index to retrieve records.

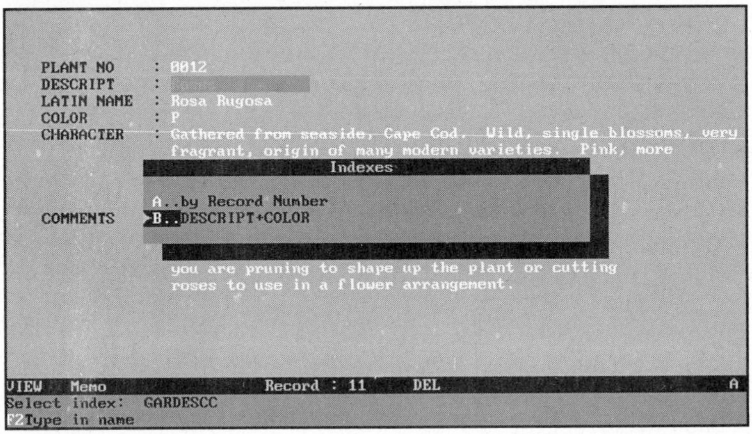

FIG. 3.18

The current index is highlighted when you select **I**ndex from View or Browse mode.

You can select a different index by moving the highlight to a different letter and pressing Enter. Formatting and placement of long fields will be considered again in Chapters 6 and 7, which discuss creating reports in Alpha Four.

Using Browse Tables for Data Entry

You can enter a new record by using the Browse mode, but the usual method is to use View. Entering records using Browse can be frustrating in that your view of the fields is limited to those that fit within your 80-character screen. If the fields are 20 to 30 characters long, only a couple will show on the screen at one time. Of course, if you have many small fields of one or two characters each, then many can be seen at once. Although entering data in Browse mode is tedious, proofreading existing records is much easier in certain cases than it is in View mode. Imagine that you are proofreading a mailing list indexed on a field called CITY. A break in the pattern in the ZIPCODE field will catch your eye more quickly in Browse mode than in View mode. For example:

```
Newton   MA   02166
Newton   MA   02166
Newton   MA   01266
Newton   MA   02166
Newton   MA   02166
Newton   MA   02166
```

In **Browse** mode, you can choose **Change** and move quickly up, down, or across the visible fields and add and correct as you go. Effectively, you have as many records open as are on the screen. Save with F10.

Using Browse Tables in Sets

Because the purpose of a set is to enable you to view fields from two or more linked databases simultaneously, this can occur in a browse table and in View mode. The rules for creating and using sets are found in Part II, Chapters 8 and 10. The important guideline to understand at this point is that you can edit fields in the parent or primary database, but not in the linked databases, although they all appear to be on the same browse screen. If you need to edit a field in a secondary file, you can use the **Z**oom function to access the record directly in the other file.

As in the design of an input form, browse tables also enable you to create a calculated field. These fields can be used in much the same way as calculated fields in View mode.

Using Range and Index Commands

Selecting a specific group or range of records can be done from the **View** or **Browse** mode. You must define the group or range as a specific setting. Press **R** to retrieve the Range setting screen and move the cursor to the appropriate choice. (For more details on Ranges, see Chapter 4 on Indexing.) Any choices on this screen are available in **View** and **Browse**, including any saved ranges. You can retrieve a previously saved range with F7 (Retrieve).

Finding Records

After records are in your database, you must be able to retrieve them. Finding the right records is the issue. The three methods for finding records are the following:

- Use the Find command from View and Browse modes.

- Use a Filter in the Range command to limit the access to just the required records.

- Use a one-time search or a saved search to create a search list containing only the desired records.

Using Range Commands with Filters

To create a quick report, you can decide to restrict the types of records you are seeing on your screen. The Range command enables you to change the index; select All, Deleted, or the Not-deleted records; ascending or descending in order; and to select a range of records according to the index, defined by <First> and <Last> values.

Beyond this, you also can set a Filter to extract just those records that match the desired criteria. Common expressions seen in range filters include the following:

```
STATE = "MA"
TAXABLE=.T.
REVIEW_DATE>{06/01/91}
```

Filters have the agreeable characteristic of being Active or Inactive. After the filter is defined, you can turn it on (Active) or off (Inactive) without disturbing the rest of your range definition. When you exit from the screen shown in figure 3.19, the only records you can view will have the letter R in the COLOR field. All records that do not match this definition will be out of sight until you change the filter.

Figure 3.19 indicates how to set a filter in the Range command. See Chapter 4 for more on indexes, ranges, and filters.

Using the Locate (Search for) Command

Remember that conversation? What did he say about Howie? What was the date of that arrest? Let me look at anything we've got on General Aviation. What can I make that will use up lots of avocados? Whatever the subject, the question may be general to vague, the answer is to peruse the database while the records do the walking. This is the occasion for the Locate command, which is available in View and Browse modes.

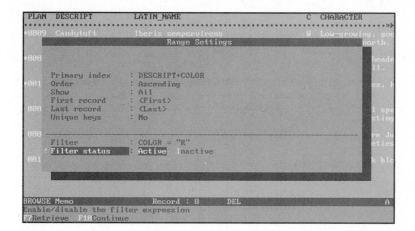

```
 PLAN  DESCRIPT        LATIN_NAME                     C   CHARACTER
 ••••••••••••••••••••••••••••••••••••••••••••••••••••••••••••••••»▶
 •0009  Candytuft        Iberis sempervirens            W   Low-growing, goo
                            Range Settings                        north.
 •000                                                              heade
                                                                   ll.
       Primary index   : DESCRIPT+COLOR
 •001   Order           : Ascending                                es, I
        Show            : All
        First record    : <First>
 000    Last record     : <Last>                                 l spe
        Unique keys     : No                                     sting

 000    ─────────────────────────────────────────────────       re Ju
        Filter          : COLOR = "R"                            eties
        Filter status   : Active  Inactive
 001                                                             k blo



 BROWSE Memo                    Record : 8      DEL                      A
 Enable/disable the filter expression
  F7 Retrieve   F10 Continue
```

FIG. 3.19

Create a range and filter for a browse table or input form.

Locate is different from the Find command discussed previously. Find works upon the indexed field and none other. It is swift to perform its task, but it is not as efficient or precise. Using L enables you to say which field should be examined. Locate usually is used when there is little need for producing the results of this search in hard copy.

Pressing the L in View or Browse produces the following question:

Search for : _____

This question is followed by the screen showing as many of the fields as the screen allows. You can select one, several, or all fields to be searched. The more fields are selected, the longer the search will take. The Enter key selects and deselects each field individually. A field is selected when you see the following mark next to the field name:

After you have chosen one or several fields for the replacement as shown in figure 3.20, press F10 to continue.

Using Search and Replace

Search and replace enables you to discover all records where field DESCRIPT = RED and replace it with BLUE. This option is not available in Browse mode.

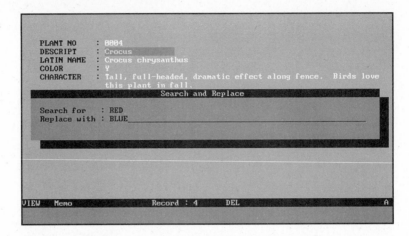

FIG. 3.20

Select the fields carefully in which the Search and Replace command will act.

In Browse, only Search is available. From the View mode, the selection in the Options box includes Search and replace. When you choose Options, Search, the View menu gives you the screen shown in figure 3.21.

FIG. 3.21

Search and Replace is on the Options menu in View mode.

If you were keeping a history of your horticultural efforts, this could be the quickest way to transplant a garden ever devised. You can replace some or all of your petunias with any other plant you like. Actually, the *repotting* can take place in any field you prefer. The next screen shows a list of all the fields in your database. You can perform a global restructuring of your garden plans by using F3 to select all fields (see fig. 3.22.)

Surprising results can occur with Search and Replace commands. This lesson is often learned by the users who experiment with an incomplete understanding of the process, particularly when their understanding of computer use is based on word processing software. Suppose that you are redecorating the homestead and change your mind part way through your instructions to the painters; everywhere you described red, you decide to find and replace with blue.

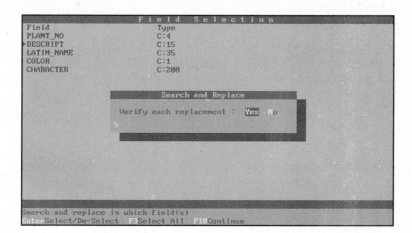

FIG. 3.22

Choose to verify each replacement if there is
any question
of error.

The incautious word processor may find *red* replaced by *blue* inside words like *hereditary* and *redecorate* to create *heblueitary* and *Blueecorated*.

The same can happen in database management. The results could be distressing. At least with a word processor, you can usually stop the process or abandon the file. With a database, the records will be changed as soon as the cursor opens the field.

For that reason, Alpha Four gives you the option of verifying each re-placement. You should accept this offer, at least the first time you try this function. If you select Yes to verify each replacement, Alpha Four will show each found item and slowly blink the replacement on the screen. You may choose to make the replacement, to bypass this oc-currence, quit the find and replace process, or change the original replacement with a different version

Using Delete and Undelete Records

You should understand that when a record is marked for deletion, that record is still in the database and can be considered to be *marked* rather than *deleted*. Removing the record from the file entirely is a separate process. The terminology is confusing. Alpha Software ad-heres strictly to what is called the *dBase standard*, which means that the original database software from Ashton-Tate, called dBaseT, was well known enough that it served to define most of the terminology associated with microcomputer database software.

Another command coming from this tradition is *Pack*. This refers to the actual process of removing a record that has previously been marked for deletion.

Marking a Record for Deletion

The process of marking for deletion, like most computer functions, can be handled in more than one way. Initially, one record at a time, in Browse mode, you can select Alt-D to place the ◆ mark in the first left column on the record. In View mode, Alt-D places the letters DEL at the bottom of the screen.

The screen in figure 3.23 shows that record 11 has been marked for deletion. To remove the deleted mark, select Undelete record from the Options box or use the shortcut Alt-U (see fig. 3.24).

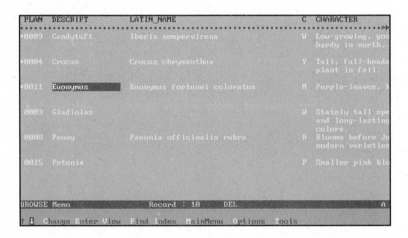

FIG. 3.23

Deleted records marked DEL and also with a ◆ symbol.

When your highlight is on a deleted record in Browse, the letters DEL appear on the bottom line of the screen. The Options box and Alt-U operate in the same manner in Browse as in View modes.

To examine the records that have been marked for deletion, or to eliminate any marked records from view, you can press R from View or Browse and select Deleted or Undeleted from the Range Settings screen, as shown in figure 3.25.

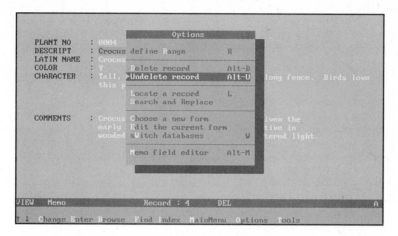

FIG. 3.24

Delete and Undelete commands appear in the Options box.

PLAN DESCRIPT   LATIN_NAME   C CHARACTER
0009 Candytuft   Iberis sempervirens   W Low-growing, goo
                           Range Settings   orth.
000   heade
                                                                  ll.
001 Primary index : DESCRIPT+COLOR
     Order   : Ascending   es, b
     Show   : All Deleted Not-Deleted
     First record   : <First>
000 Last record   : <Last>   l spe
     Unique keys   : No   sting

000 Filter   :   re Ju
     Filter status : Inactive   eties
001   k blo

BROWSE Memo   Record : 10   DEL   A
Access all, deleted or not-deleted records
F7Retrieve F10Continue

FIG. 3.25

Select Deleted or Undeleted records at Show on the Range Settings screen.

Chapter 4 contains a discussion of another method of marking records for deletion by using Global update/delete. This command enables you to work with an entire range of records.

Backing Up Your Data

The only way to retrieve records deleted by using the Pack command is to append them back into your database from a backup file. This can be an arduous test of patience and ingenuity. There are a great number of ways to back up files on a microcomputer. You are certainly playing with a time bomb if you neglect this function.

Although you can spend months or years becoming happily familiar with your computer system and its software and never suffer a loss, the day will come when you will lose data. A printer could jam, a slight power loss could scar your hard disk, a careless moment could irretrievably delete a file. Floppy disks are a tiny expense compared to the hours of work which can disappear in a second.

Backing up procedures can range from tiresome to costly, depending on the method. If the procedure is unreasonably difficult or time-consuming, it is neglected by even the most conscientious computer users. Tape backup systems are costly and drives run in the $200-$500 range, depending on their capacity and speed. Tapes themselves cost between $15 and $35. Software backup programs, such as Fastback, reduce the time, employ floppy disks, and can be automated with a script that can run at the end of a work session, between the last telephone call and the time your coat is buttoned. You should explore a reliable method of backing up your files.

If your database is relatively small, the easiest and most reliable way to back up you work is to copy your file onto a floppy disk. If your files are on your hard disk, perform the following steps:

1. Put a formatted floppy disk in your floppy drive and close the door.

2. Select the database that you intend to back up.

3. From the Main Menu, select **Utilities**, **C**opy database. Alpha Four shows you the database directory screen with your cursor waiting at the bottom for you to type in a file name for the copied file. This is the point at which you are telling the program to copy the file to the floppy disk.

4. Type: **A:\FILENAME** and press the Enter key. The program asks whether you want to copy all fields or selected fields.

5. Choose **A**ll Fields. The range setting screen enables you to select certain records. For a backup, you will probably want to copy all records.

6. Press F10 (Continue).

7. Type a description of the copied file on the Description line.

8. Press F10 again to complete the process.

Packing the Database

After you have decided that your database must be relieved of unwanted or duplicate records, the Pack command is for you. Pack is found under the Utilities choice on the Main Menu. Numerous warnings accompany Pack. You should test Pack on a small, sample database that you create just for the purpose of watching the way it works.

You have one last chance to avoid disaster after you pass the warnings that remind you to back up your data. The next screen offers the opportunity to confirm the removal of each record individually. The top line of this screen says Confirm each removal. If you select Yes, the program pauses at each record marked for deletion until you give it one more go-ahead.

After that, there is no retrieval of records when the Pack command has been completed.

Using an Alternative to Packing

Experts are not immune to deleting records—and even whole databases—that they did not intend to lose. Another safeguard against packing needed records is the Copy command (see Chapter 9) to place only the *deleted* records into a separate file on a floppy disk or a temporary file on your hard disk. If this is done, the deleted records can always be returned to their original form.

Although it may seem to be a round-about way to accomplish the purpose, an alternative to Pack saves time and patience. The technique is to use the Copy command instead of Pack. In other words, create a new database from the old one using Copy with the range set at either the deleted or not-deleted records, depending on how you have used the delete technique.

You also can separate certain records from other records with this technique. Mark for deletion the specific records that will comprise database A. Copy all the deleted records to database A and all nondeleted records to database B. Then you have two databases with no duplications. You should erase the *parent* file of these two offspring.

Appending records is a similar function but must not be confused with Copy. Append does not recognize a range setting. You may create a filter for Append and give the instruction to append only **U**nique; **R**eplace existing and add unique; or replace existing, **M**ark unique, but these are the only ways to limit which records are added to the target database when a file is selected to be appended. The Append command is explored further in Chapter 9.

The purpose for learning this technique is to deal with the case when there are a great many records involved. In this case, Pack may take a long time, particularly on a less powerful PC or XT computer.

Using Pack Step-by-Step

All records marked for deletion are completely, physically removed from the database with the Pack command. To pack your database, start by examining the records marked for deletion. If your file is used by more than one person, it is likely that there are different reasons for which records have been marked. You must check the marked records to see that nothing has been marked that you really do not wish to lose.

With backup disks in hand, proceed to pack the database by performing following steps:

1. From the Main Menu, press **Utilities**, **P**ack. Press F10 (Continue).

2. To the question Confirm each removal: Yes No, you usually will select No, but if you wish to review each record before the deed is done, select Yes here.

3. Press F10 to complete the Pack command.

You can check the deleted records by setting the Range to Deleted. In Browse mode, this shows all deleted records, but the process can be tedious on an older computer. The software is doing a mini-search to comply with the range definition.

In Version 1, if no deleted records are found, Alpha Four informs you:

No valid records found—resetting to show: All, filter:
Inactive.

In Version 2, Alpha Four displays

Record 0

to indicate that no valid records exist.

Summary

In this chapter, you explored the issues of designing input forms and browse tables for a variety of purposes. You employed lines and boxes, calculated fields, and color in the designs. You learned to find records using range commands, the locate function, and to search and replace.

Finally, you have examined the techniques associated with marking records for deletion, backing up the files, and packing the database.

The following sidebars give you concise information for creating/editing an input form and creating/editing a browse table.

Hands On—Create/Edit an Input Form

1. Press **L**ayout, **F**orms, **C**reate.

2. Choose any available letter, A through Z.

3. Give the form a significant description, such as: All Fields, or Use for Address Corrections Only. Press F10.

4. Use the arrow keys to move the cursor to Row 5, Column 15. Press F2 or Alt-T to select field with Title.

5. Press Enter to choose your database.

6. Press Enter to choose the first field.

7. Use the space bar or arrow keys to move the cursor to another location on the screen.

8. Repeat Alt-T and steps 5, 6, and 7 to place all the fields you want to see on the screen.

9. Use F4 or Alt-M to move a field or group of fields around the screen for easier viewing. First *mark*, then use the arrow keys to move the block. Then *drop* the block with the Enter key. (Copy and Delete work the same way.)

10. To highlight an area of the screen, press F8 (Draw), select any line, A to H, and use the arrow keys to draw a line or box. Press the Esc key before Enter to quit if the line or box is in the wrong place. Move the cursor and start again.

11. Press F2, O or Alt-O to change formatting options.

12. To create calculated fields, press F2, C or Alt-C. Put a unique name in the Name field and any valid expression in the Expression field. Press F10 to save.

13. To place the newly created calculated field on the form, press F2 and choose **C**alculated. The new fields are shown in the **C**alculated database. The calculated field can be formatted using Formatting Options.

14. Use F9 (Line) to insert and delete lines, justify text in a line, and fill a line with a character.

15. Press F10(Continue) or Alt-S to save the form.

Use save **A**s to edit an existing form and save with a new letter. This will keep the previous form intact.

T I P

REMINDER Changes on the input form have no effect on existing data. The input form contributes to human understanding, but the computer still sees the data in its raw form. You may wish the date to look like December 24th, 1995, but the machine knows that date is 19951224, entered by you as 12/24/95. The software lets users understand each other.

Hands On—Create/Edit a Browse Table

1. Press **L**ayout, **B**rowse table, **C**reate/edit.

2. Choose any available letter in the alphabet, A through Z.

3. Give the table a significant description, such as: Financial Data Only or Shows expanded memo fields. Press F10.

4. Use the arrow keys to move the cursor to highlight the fields you wish to see. Select from either your database or the SYSTEM database.

5. The Enter key selects and deselects a field.

6. F6 selects a whole column. Choose F4 to reorder the fields. F5 clears choices to start again.

7. Press F10 to Continue.

8. Press F2, F or Alt-F to select more fields, F2, S or Alt-Z to size the fields, and F2, M or Alt-M to change field order.

9. Press F7 (Goto) to select browse **P**arameters, **R**ange and Print Settings, or restrict command **A**ccess. (Ver. 2 only, Restrict Access gives you control of changes to users' activities.)

10. Press F2, O, or Alt-O to change formatting options.

11. To create calculated fields, press F2, C or Alt-C. Put a unique name in the Name field and any valid expression in the Expression field.

12. Press F10 to save.

13. To place newly created calculated fields on the table, press F2 and choose **C**alculated. The new fields are shown in the **C**alculated database. The calculated field can be formatted using formatting **O**ptions.

14. Press F10(Continue) or Alt-S to save the table.

Use save **As** to edit an existing table and save with a new letter. This will keep the previous table intact.

T I P

REMINDER   If a field is too short to accept your formatting changes, the table will show **** in place of the data. Changes on the browse table have no effect on existing data. The table contributes to human understanding, but the computer still sees the data in its raw form.

Indexing, Sorting, Searching, and Updating Records

Alas! how easily things go wrong!
And life is never the same again.
George Macdonald, Phantastes

Indexing is a means for putting your records in some particular order. You don't have to read every word in this book to find out about a particular aspect of using Alpha Four. You can zero in on your topic by looking it up in the index.

Databases also have indexes. Their role is similar to that of book indexes: they tell the database management program where to find each record in relation to other records.

This chapter examines the process of creating indexes and ranges. You learn to attach, detach, and update indexes. You also learn about the idea of subgrouping an index. This chapter discusses methods of adding a necessary field to your database for purposes of indexing and using the *reconfigure database* command. This chapter also explores the techniques of creating searches, summary databases, and global updates based on indexes.

Understanding How Indexes Work

Indexes have two main functions in databases. Indexes enable you to find information much more quickly than is possible in a file without an index, and indexes ensure that the data to be printed in reports arrives at the printer in a specific, predetermined order. At the end of this chapter is an exercise that helps you capture the importance of indexes.

Because indexes are the primary means of arranging information in databases, they can make a big difference in the way you use and gain access to your data. If you want to send out a mailing to the boatyard customers, for instance, it would be helpful to index the OWNERS file by the LASTNAME field to present the owners' last names in alphabetical order. But if you were interested in using the length of each boat to plan storage areas, you might prefer to index the OWNERS file by the LENGTH field, resulting in a list of boats from smallest to largest or from largest to smallest.

In Version 1 of Alpha Four, you can have up to seven active indexes per database. Although any number of indexes can be defined for one database, only seven can be kept active at one time. This was the standard set by the dBASE family of data files in the early development of the format. With pressure from the market and advances in technology, the new standard has become 15 active indexes. Therefore, while only one primary index is functioning to order your records, six (or 14) more constantly are being kept updated by the software.

Indexes are files that contain keys or pointers to each record in the index. Version 2 offers an additional feature: the option of creating a *filter* to exclude records not needed in a particular index.

The importance of this is that the index *sees* only the records that match the criteria in the filter. If you have a database with 500 records of names and addresses, an index on LASTNAME would have pointers to every name. The actual size of the file, if you examined it at the DOS level, could be nearly the size of the .DBF file. With a selective index, the filter can exclude records containing an entry date before 01/01/92, or non-residents of New York state. The size of the resulting index file is smaller, and more important, the speed with which you can find these records is greatly enhanced. Speed becomes increasingly important as the size of the database increases.

Speeding Up Your Work

Building the index file is a combined function of Alpha Four and your computer. To create an index file, you tell Alpha Four which field or fields should be indexed, whether the fields should be in ascending or descending order, and what records should be *filtered* out of the index. Then, Alpha Four tags the records so that the data can be retrieved on command. All this happens at varying rates of speed, depending on several factors.

Alpha Software claims that benchmark tests show that Version 2 can create the index file six times faster than Version 1.1. Earlier versions of the database software, such as ALPHA/*three* and Database Manager II are, indeed, much slower at performing this operation.

Beyond the initial convenience of having the indexing done faster, there are other reasons why this is important to you. With the earlier software, particularly on the earlier hardware, it is not uncommon to run into an `Error Resynching` problem. Generally, you can get rid of this error message by updating the indexes in your database.

If you have many records, if you have many complex indexes, or if your machine is not very powerful, you can have a long wait while the index creation process takes place. With Version 2, the new indexing algorithms built into the program reduce the waiting time considerably. Alpha Four Version 2 also has less difficulty keeping track of the indexes, so the `Error Resynching` message is an uncommon occurrence.

Another rare event, but nonetheless distressing, is the occasional report that a record appears to be *duplicated* by the software. This *error* usually appears in Browse mode as two identical records. When you attempt to mark one of the two records for deletion, a black diamond (marking the records for deletion) appears on both records. Usually, the solution to this problem is to verify that each of the indexes currently attached to the database are appropriate to that database. In other words, an index named LAST.NDX on a last name field in your customer file must never be selected for use in a different file, although a last name field exists in the second file. A new index for the second file must have a different name. When files multiply, particularly in the development stage, this error can occur.

Designing the Index

There are as many ways to design indexes as there are database users and applications. A common practice is to alphabetize a mailing list by the LASTNAME field. You don't have to stop there, however. You can create a more complex index for your mailing list by ZIP_CODE,

LASTNAME, and FIRSTNAME fields. In your reports, you could, for example, create a subgroup of the ZIP_CODE data.

Subgrouping is a way of grouping similar items to compute subtotals or to create more attractive and meaningful reports. Subgrouping is covered later in this chapter and in greater detail in Chapter 7, "Developing Strategies for Special Reporting."

In the next section, you learn how to create an index, how to limit that index, and how to use an index to solve a problem by subgrouping an index.

Creating an Index

To create an index, perform the following steps:

1. From the Main Menu, select **I**ndexes/ranges. Alpha Four presents the Indexes/Ranges menu.

2. Select **C**reate an index and give the index a name that identifies the database with which you are working. For example, if this is a database called OWNERS, and you want to index on last names, you should give the index a name such as OWN_LAST. If you want to index on a STATE field plus last name, give the file a name such as OW_ST_LT, representing OWNER + STATE + LASTNAME.

3. Next, select Table mode. Alpha Four shows the Index Table, which asks for the fields you want in the index. The screen looks like the following:

Level	Field	Direction
1	STATE	Ascending
2	LASTNAME	Ascending Descending

4. Press F10 (Continue). The next screen asks for an Index description that should remind you of the importance of this index. On the second line, the Index expression is shown as Alpha Four has translated it for you. In this case, it should say, STATE + LASTNAME. If you don't enter a description, the index expression is shown as the description.

Indexing Options

In Alpha Four, you can create an index on any character, numeric, or date field.

When creating an index on a character field, you have the following four choices for the order in which you want records to appear, as follows:

Sort Order	Data Appearance
Ascending (A-Z)	0, 01, 1, 11, 123, 2, 3 A, a, B, b,...Y, y, Z, z
Descending (Z-A)	Z, z, Y, y,...B, b, A, a 3, 2, 123, 11, 1, 01, 0
Ascending case-sensitive	A, B, C,...X, Y, Z a, b, c,...x, y, z
Descending case-sensitive	z, y, x,...c, b, a Z, Y, X,...C, B, A

When creating an index on a numeric field, you have the following two options:

Sort Order	Data Appearance
Ascending (0-9)	1, 2, 3, 4,...9, 10, 11, 12
Descending (9-0)	12, 11, 10, 9...4, 3, 2, 1

You have the following two options for indexes created on date fields:

Sort Order	Data Appearance
Ascending	July 14, 1910, to December 1, 1985
Descending	December 1, 1985, to July 14, 1910

Understanding the Power of an Index

To see the benefits of indexing, consider employees in the sample boatyard. Even with a small operation, an employer must keep personnel records. The hire dates of every employee should be noted for salary and performance reviews. During the summer, there is often more than one member of the same family working in the yard. An un-indexed list of their names, first hire dates, and years of employment follows:

ID#	NAME	HIRE DATE	YEARS
1	Tong, Sam	05/15/85	6
2	Tong, Lee	06/01/88	3
3	Makal, Tammi	04/23/90	1
4	Alexander, Zeb	12/01/83	7
5	Gomez, Sally	07/01/89	2
6	Makal, Doug	08/10/90	0
7	Alexander, Michael	05/01/87	4
8	Makal, Francis	04/01/89	2

When indexed by employees' date of hire, the list looks like the following:

ID#	NAME	HIRE DATE	YEARS
4	Alexander, Zeb	12-01-1983	7
1	Tong, Sam	05-15-1985	6
7	Alexander, Michael	05-01-87	4
2	Tong, Lee	06-01-1988	3
8	Makal, Francis	04-01-1989	2
5	Gomez, Sally	07-01-1989	2
3	Makal, Tammi	04-23-1990	1
6	Makal, Doug	08-10-1990	0

When indexed by employees' last names, the list prints as the following:

ID#	NAME	HIRE DATE	YEARS
4	Alexander, Zeb	12-01-1983	7
7	Alexander, Michael	05-01-1987	4
5	Gomez, Sally	07-01-1989	2
6	Makal, Doug	08-10-1990	0
8	Makal, Francis	04-01-1989	2
3	Makal, Tammi	04-23-1990	1
1	Tong, Sam	05-15-1985	6
2	Tong, Lee	06-01-1988	3

Note that the Alexander and Tong brothers' names are not sorted correctly: Zeb comes before Michael, and Sam before Lee. The records have been arranged by only the employees' last names with no consideration for other data.

If you want the list to print with the employees' first names alphabetized after the surname, you can index by both the FIRSTNAME and LASTNAME fields, as the following:

ID#	NAME	HIRE DATE	YEARS
7	Alexander, Michael	05-01-1987	4
4	Alexander, Zeb	12-01-1983	7
5	Gomez, Sally	07-01-1989	2
6	Makal, Doug	08-10-1990	0
8	Makal, Francis	04-01-1989	2
3	Makal, Tammi	04-23-1990	1
2	Tong, Lee	06-01-1988	3
1	Tong, Sam	05-15-1985	6

To obtain this list, you use the index expression LASTNAME + FIRSTNAME. (LASTNAME and FIRSTNAME are, of course, two of the character fields in the example database.) Therefore, this is considered a *compound index*.

These lists are indexed in ascending (A-Z) rather than descending (Z-A) order. When indexed by the YEARS field, however, the list is indexed in descending order. You can anticipate the results of an hire date list in ascending order: It would start with Doug Makal and end with Zeb Alexander.

Creating an Index

Now that you have observed some sample indexes, you can try your hand at creating an index of your own. For practice, go back to the boat owners to create an index on last names.

To create an index, you select the Indexes\ranges choice from the Main Menu. Alpha Four presents the Indexes\ranges menu. Alpha Four lists the existing index names and prompts you for the file name of the index. You should name each index in a way that helps you easily identify the database to which it belongs. Also, the file name that you enter must follow all the DOS file name conventions (8 characters, no spaces, and so on).

To create an index, start from the Main Menu and complete the following steps:

1. Press Indexes\ranges, **C**reate an index, and type the new name **OWNER_ID**. Press Enter.

2. Press Enter again to choose Table mode.

3. Press F2 (Fields) and draw the highlight down to the date field OWNER_ID and press Enter. This is the field with which you can link other records to an individual owner.

4. The screen asks whether the index should be in ascending or descending order. Choose ASCENDING to cause the index to place the lowest number at the top of the list.

5. Type a descriptive name for your index, such as **Identification number of Owners**.

6. The expression should just show the field name OWNER_ID. Press F10 to continue.

NOTE   Version 1 users see A or D instead of ASCENDING or DESCENDING when selecting the direction of an index.

Using an Index To Tie Databases Together

You now have an OWNERS file (created in Chapter 2) with a serviceable index and an inventory file (created in Quick Start 1) that shows the products sold in your establishment. What you need next is a way to tie in the customer (who may or may not be the owner of a boat in your yard) with his or her purchases in an invoice.

You can design an INVOICE database that contains information about each of the following items:

Number	Field	Type	Width	Decimal Place
1	INVOIC_ID	C	4	
2	OWNER_ID	C	4	
3	INV_DATE	D	8	
4	LINE_NO	N	2	0
5	ITEM_NO	C	4	

Number	Field	Type	Width	Decimal Place
6	QTY	N	7	2
7	PRICE	N	7	2
8	POSTED	L	1	
9	TOTAL	N	10	2

This file will contain the *detail portion* of each invoice—information about billable items—linked in a set to the file containing the OWNERS information (if it exists) and the INVENTRY file. The OWNER_ID in the OWNERS database is used as both the link and the look up in the purchaser's name and address while the ITEM_NO is used to link and to look up the inventory item being placed on the invoice. (In Chapter 5, the field rules section illustrates the fine points of enhancing data entry for this procedure; designing sets is discussed in Quick Start 2 and Chapter 8.)

When all these items come together, you can cross-reference the name of the customer who bought the items and the particular invoice to which the detail portion applies. Then, you can create an invoice that looks like figure 4.1.

Blue Water Boatyard, Inc.
Crabapple Cove, ME

November 27, 1991

To: Mr. Alfred H. Fenton
12 Blueberry Island RR 4
Kennebunk, ME 04043

Invoice No.: I002

Line#	Item	Description	Quantity	Price	Units	Ext.Price
1	2001	Non-skid strips	12	0.50	yards	6.00
2	2003	Cotter pins	4	0.50	box	2.00
3	2000	Teak Oil	1	15.00	pint	15.00
			17			$23.00

Terms: 2 % 10 days, net 30 days
No vessel will be launched until balance due is $0.0

FIG. 4.1

Sample invoice for boatyard database.

Reconfiguring Your Database

If you are working with an existing database that you want to revise to work like the ones here, you need to *reconfigure* your database. In the process of reconfiguring a database, the software actually creates a new database using the revised format that you create. Then the program copies the data and other supporting files to the new database and erases the older file.

By using **R**econfigure, you can add, delete, and move existing fields, and you can change field types and lengths. If the action you choose will affect existing data, such as shortening a character field with a length of 20 characters to 10 characters, then the program warns you that the field is being truncated. As long as you are sure that important data will not be lost, you can proceed with the reconfigure.

 CAUTION Data lost through reconfiguration is gone for good unless you have a backup of your file. Be sure to back up your files first.

 NOTE In the process of reconfiguring a database, the software is copying your file. For a brief time, your data is in two places at once and is temporarily using twice as much space on your disk. Be sure that there is enough space on your disk for this procedure to take place. If the program runs out of disk space, you run the risk of losing data and files.

To add a new field to an existing database with **R**econfigure, complete the following steps:

1. From the Alpha Four Main Menu, select **D**atabase/set design.

2. Select **R**econfigure database.

3. Choose **R**econfigure current database.

4. Insert a new field using F6 (Insert) and remove an existing field with F5 (Delete). Press F10 to save the new configuration.

If you are reconfiguring a file containing many thousands of records, particularly if you are working on an older computer, the process could take a long time. Because the process involves making a copy of the original file with changes, and then placing the records into the new file, the amount of time is similar to the amount of time it would take for you to copy the entire database to a new database. There is no range command or filter on a reconfigured database.

Understanding Subgrouping

In Alpha Four, *subgrouping* is the technique needed to calculate subtotals of items in an index, such as those in the INVOICE file. Chapter 7 discusses how to create a printed report with subgroups, but a brief explanation here of how they work will help you plan ahead.

Suppose that you want to obtain a report that breaks down your billing to show the summary of invoices for each client. This means that you need to be able to create a subgroup for each client.

Create the index by using the expression OWNER_ID + INVOICE_NO. Because the index has two fields, you can create a printed report with two types of subtotals, as shown in figure 4.2. Notice on this document that OWNER 102 has four invoices: I001, I003, I008, and I010. Each of the line items is shown in the Item and Quantity columns, and the total for each invoice is calculated. At the end of the table, the total for the specific client is shown before the data on the next client starts to print.

This file is subgrouped twice. The first subgroup is on OWNER_ID and next is on INVOICE_NO. The total shown for subgroup 1, the owner ID, is at the end of that complete grouping. Within subgroup 1, four invoices are listed and totaled in subgroup 2.

The invoices shown in figure 4.2 have been summarized in such a way that the accounting department of your boatyard can clearly see the history of sales for these owners and the total billing for each one. This report is indexed on OWNER_ID and INVOICE_NO, and is subgrouped on the same two fields. This technique can turn scattered data into intelligible information. (See Chapter 7 for more information on advanced reporting techniques.)

Using Set Pieces

The INVOICE detail file contains the line-item information to be printed on the lower half of your invoices. The way the file is constructed, you easily can obtain subtotals for each INVOICE_NO and OWNER_ID. But the information is still incomplete because the file does not provide the invoiced customer's name and address.

You might wonder why not simply plug the client's name and address into each line-item record. With such a file structure, you could print the client's address directly from the first record of the line in the invoice. This approach, however, creates more problems than it solves. Storing every detail in the client's name and address takes up a lot of disk space. Moreover, writing a procedure that prints the name and address information just once, even though it appears in every record, misses the point of having a relational database on your computer.

12/02/1991
Page: 1

	Invoice Date	Line	Item	Quantity	Total Price
Owner: 101					
Invoice No. I002					
	10/10/1991	1	2001	12	6.00
	10/10/1991	2	2003	4	2.00
	10/10/1991	3	2000	1	15.00
				===	=======
Total for invoice: I002				17	23.00
				===	=======
Total for Owner: 101					1723.00
Owner: 102					
Invoice No. I001					
	10/09/1991	1	2007	100	315.00
				===	======
Total for invoice: I001				100	315.00
Invoice No. I003					
	10/10/1991	1	2003	2	1.00
	10/10/1991	2	2000	1	15.00
	10/10/1991	3	2009	3	38.85
				===	======
Total for invoice: I003				6	54.85
Invoice No. I008					
	11/27/1991	1	2005	3	13.50
	11/27/1991	2	2006	2	9.00
				===	======
Total for invoice: I008				5	22.50
Invoice No. I010					
	12/03/1991	1	2008	200	3000.00
	12/03/1991	2	2011	100	1500.00
				===	=======
Total for invoice: I010				300	4500.00
				===	=======
Total for Owner: 102				411	4892.35

continues

FIG. 4.2

List of line items
and invoices.

Owner: 103

Invoice No. I004

11/27/1991	1	2004	300	225.00
11/27/1991	2	2008	3	56.85
11/27/1991	3	2009	5	64.75
11/27/1991	4	2010	1	16.45
11/27/1991	5	2005	2	9.00
			===	======
Total for invoice: I004			311	372.05
			===	======
Total for Owner: 103			311	372.05
			===	======
Total for this report			**739**	**5287.40**

FIG. 4.2

Continued.

Last, but not least, data entry for such a file can be both error-prone and tiresome.

Another idea is to begin a file with the client's name and address, and then include enough fields in the same file for, say, 10 detail items: NAME, ADDRESS, QTY1, ITEM1, COST1, QTY2, ITEM2, COST2...QTY10, ITEM10, COST10. But what if you have more than 10 detail items? Although the 10-item ceiling may be fine for many small businesses, it does limit the functional effectiveness of the billing system.

The recommended method is to keep the original INVOICE file intact and use its OWNER_ID field to "look" into the OWNERS file. As you may recall from Chapter 1, the OWNERS file also has a OWNER_ID field, along with names, addresses, and other pertinent customer information. This is the link or common field.

One of Alpha Four's most useful tools is Set, a means of relating the information in two or more files. To use Set, the files to be linked must share a common field. Because the OWNERS and INVOICE files both have a five-character field called OWNER_ID, the files can be joined in a set.

The concept of sets is introduced now because it is critical that the field shared by the files in the set be part of the indexes for each file. Thus, the OWNER_ID field must appear in the OWNERS file and the INVOICE file and in the index of the OWNERS file. Sets are examined in detail starting in the Quick Start of Part II. The use of sets dramatically increases the flexibility of a database, to the point where it is difficult to consider most applications without this function.

Using Indexes To Eliminate Duplicates

One of the toughest tasks associated with managing a database is cleaning up the duplicate records. If you have received identical catalogs from a mail-order house, you know that databases (especially large ones) are often riddled with duplicate entries. The hard part, of course, is to stamp out the duplicates before mailings reach your customers.

Duplicate records can even be a problem for a small database, such as the boatyard. You may discover that some customers listed in the OWNERS database keep two or more vessels at the boatyard. To solve the problem of having records with the same name and address but different boats, you could take advantage of Alpha Four's set capability. You might begin by designing a file to hold only client personal information—name, address, and phone number. A second file called BOATS can be created to contain one record for each boat plus an owner's ID number to link each boat to the proper owner. With these two files in operation, you do not have to enter a customer's name twice when that customer has two boats. Further, when it comes time to send a mailing to your customers, Alpha Four produces just one letter per boat owner, no matter how many boats the owner has at the boatyard.

You may, however, want to use a flat file and simply watch out for duplicate mailings when the occasion arises. If there are 50 owners in your boatyard, the likelihood of more than a few having large vessels is slim. You may find that it is easier and less complicated to stay with one database, rather than moving into a set. In this manner, if there is more than one record for a single owner, the invoice can be tied to the appropriate vessel with the owner's ID. The database does not care whether there are two records for the same person, as long as there are two identifying numbers with which to collect the data for an invoice.

But because you want to maintain the efficiency of the operation and keep mailing costs down, you must figure out how to prevent the name of a boat owner from showing up twice in a mailing to owners. Indexing is the key to eliminating duplicate entries in Alpha Four.

You can instruct Alpha Four to accept only unique values in an index. If, for example, you build a unique index on the OWNER_ID field, each OWNER_ID entry must be unique. Likewise, if you build a unique index on an index expression, such as LASTNAME + FIRSTNAME + MIDDLE, each customer's full name (the sum of the customer's last name plus first name plus middle initial) must be different from any other customer's full name. Indexes built on fields that hold identifying numbers—Social Security number, part number, vendor number, account number—often are designated as unique.

The capability to use indexes to prevent duplicate entries can be very powerful. Sometimes, however, you might have to allow a certain amount of duplication. For instance, you may need to track a real estate company that is known to have several branch offices within a block of each other. The company name, city, state, and ZIP code may be the same for all the entries, but each branch office must still have its own record in the database. In this situation, it might not be a good idea to have an index that prevents duplicates unless you also designated the street name and number as unique.

Setting Up a Unique Index

For practice, you can select the OWNERS file and set an index on the BOAT_OWN field to be unique by performing the following steps:

1. If the current database is not OWNERS, select **C**hoose database/ set.

2. **O**pen a database option and place the highlight on OWNERS.

3. Press the Enter key to open the database and return to the Main Menu.

4. With OWNERS opened as the current database, select **I**ndexes/ Ranges from the Main Menu.

5. Select the **C**reate an Index option.

6. Type **BOAT_OWN** as the index file name, and choose **E**xpression Mode to create the index.

7. Enter **Boat Owners' Names - Unique** as the index description.

8. With the highlight on Index Expression, press F2 (Fields). Press Enter when the highlight is on the LASTNAME field, and then press F3 to insert a plus sign in the expression. Follow the same steps for the FIRSTNAME and MIDDLE fields. The final result should be the following expression:

   LASTNAME+FIRSTNAME+MIDDLE.

   As you become more familiar with Alpha Four, you may feel comfortable simply typing the expression instead of using the function keys and pop-up windows. Keep in mind, however, that the pop-up windows are wonderful memory aids and can help prevent entry errors, such as typos and use of invalid field names.

9. Next, press Enter twice. The cursor moves down to the **A**llow option. This option is the one you use to tell an index to permit only unique values. Place the highlight on **U**nique and press Enter.

10. Press F10 to create the index and return to the Main Menu.

Removing Duplicates in Existing Databases

Electronic database-management programs are more powerful than ever, but most have yet to conquer the ogre of eliminating duplicate entries from a database after it has been created and records entered. Alpha Four offers a method for finding: it marks every record that has a duplicate index key. The index key is the portion of the record that is also part of the index.

Assume that you have indexed a list on the last name, first name, and middle initial of several customers in the following manner:

    1   Dexter, Elizabeth
    2   Dexter, Liz
    3   Smith, John
    4   Smith, John H.
    5   Smith, John H.

Alpha Four would mark only the fifth name as a duplicate, because only Smith, John H. is an exact duplicate of another entry in the index.

To mark duplicate entries for deletion, you begin by opening a database in which you want only unique entries. Next, choose a primary index that can appropriately identify duplicate records. For instance, if you want unique names, the primary index should be on LASTNAME+ FIRSTNAME+MIDDLE; if you want unique part numbers, the primary index should be on the PART_NO field.

From the Main Menu, select **G**lobal Update/delete to display the **G**lobal Update/Delete menu. Then choose the delete Du**p**licate records option. Verify that the primary index is the one you want, and then press F10. (At the end of this chapter, there is more discussion about the range settings on this screen.)

After Alpha Four identifies records as having duplicate keys in the index, it marks them for deletion. Alpha Four does not delete these records; it simply prepares them to be deleted. (For a discussion of deleting records, see the section on packing a database in Chapter 3.)

Understanding How Index Files Work

Understanding index operation is not critical to your management or enjoyment of Alpha Four. But for those who want to know the way things work, however, this section delves into the internal workings of indexes.

When you create an index, Alpha Four actually creates a separate database with two fields for each record. Every record in the index file (the new database created by Alpha Four) corresponds to a record in the original file. For example, the personnel database of the boatyard looks like the following:

Record No.	Last Name	First Name	Years Employed
1	Tong	Sam	7
2	Tong	Lee	5
3	Makal	Tammi	6
4	Alexander	Zeb	9
5	Gomez	Sally	10
6	Makal	Doug	9
7	Alexander	Michael	11
8	Makal	Francis	8

Record numbers are assigned sequentially as records are entered into the database. When you index on the YEAR field, Alpha Four selects years and record numbers, sorts the years, and then drops the data from both fields into an index file as the following:

Years	Record No.
5	2
6	3
7	1
8	8
9	4
9	5
10	6
11	7

Note that the years are in the order you want, from the newest employee to oldest.

When printing a report or displaying records in Browse mode, Alpha Four first looks at the personnel index file, where it finds the newest worker. Then it gets the record number that corresponds to the newest employee in the original PERSONEL database. The technique of using record numbers to coordinate the order or sequence by which information is retrieved often is called *pointing*. The index file points to records in the PERSONEL file. When Alpha Four needs the record for the next newest worker, it advances to the next record in the index, picks up the record number, and uses that number to retrieve the next newest employee from the PERSONEL file.

Detaching Indexes

If you have worked with Alpha Four for a while, you probably have realized how important indexes are to the effective use of this software. More technical information about indexes, then, is in order when you find it necessary to use indexes in ways other than simply obtaining an ordered listing of a field.

When an index is created, it automatically becomes the current index for the database to which it belongs. In Version 2, you can use 15 indexes, in addition to the Record Number and Search List indexes, for a single database. For a simple mailing list, it is unlikely that you need more than two or three indexes. Some applications, however, demand the capability to browse through and view a group of files in other ways. For such applications, it is necessary to detach one index to make way for another. Detaching an index is a way of temporarily turning that index off.

The link between an index file and its parent file is dynamic. Each time a record is added to the database, a new record is placed in the index. A detached index, however, loses its dynamic link with the parent database. It is not updated automatically when records are added, deleted, or edited in the parent database. When the detached index is needed, it must be reattached and updated to resume the link with the actual database records.

The process of entering and editing data can be slow when a database that you are constantly updating has several complicated indexes. Detaching one or all of the indexes solves this problem, because Alpha Four does not have to keep updating the index or indexes whenever a record is changed. Naturally, you must update each index once you reattach it to the database.

In Version 1, you can attach an index that does not belong to a particular database file. You can do this when an index key field in the first database is the same as one in the second. If an index is attached to FILE A, Version 2 will not allow it to be attached to FILE B. Version 1 will allow this.

In Version 1, if an index belonging to FILE A is attached to and updated in FILE B, FILE A probably will not be able to read or use it again after it has been updated for FILE B. When this happens, Alpha Four tries to "resynch" the files. While the resynch message is on the screen, you may have to wait to perform other operations. (Until the resynch process ends, Alpha Four is too busy managing the files to do anything else.) Alpha Four probably will return to record number order after resynching unless you indicate otherwise.

Lack of understanding about when to update indexes is the root of many Alpha Four problems. That's why it is a good idea to update all indexes after resynching errors occur in high-use databases.

Updating, Attaching, and Detaching Indexes

To update an index, from the Main Menu, select the Indexes/Ranges option. Then select the Update Indexes option. From the next menu, you may choose to update some or all of your indexes.

To attach an existing index, select Index and Attach, and then choose from the displayed list of current indexes. You cannot choose an index from another subdirectory. When a file is attached to the current database, an arrow mark appears next to the index file name in the directory listing and the database to which it is attached appears as well. In Version 2, an index not currently in use is indicated with the word Unattached.

The Index Expression screen appears once the index is attached. Here you can give the index a brief description and change or confirm current index parameters as the following:

Allow:	All, Unique, and unique with Exceptions
Case Sensitive:	Yes No, and
Update Index:	(Yes/No)

If there have been any changes since the index was detached, you should choose Yes to update the index. You cannot change the index expression or filter definition at this point.

When an index is created or is reattached to a database, the name of the index is stored in the configuration file that Alpha Four maintains for each database. The file has the name of your database plus the extension .DR4 in Version 1, or .IDN in Version 2. You can use the DOS command TYPE to examine the contents of these files in Version 1. In Version 2, the information is stored in machine language and is visible but not readily understandable.

To detach an index, select **I**ndexes/ranges from the Main Menu. Then select the **D**etach an index option from the menu. You see a list of the indexes currently attached to your database. Move the highlight to the index name on this list, or type the letter indicating the index you want to detach. Notice that, as you move your cursor onto each letter, the file name of the index appears in the lower-left corner.

After an index has been detached, it must be attached before it can be used again.

Understanding Searches

The records in your database are always in some kind of order. You may wonder how this can be when they appear to be as jumbled as the bottom drawer in your basement workbench. Even if you do nothing at all about creating an index, Alpha Four still keeps the records in record number order, which is the order in which the records were added to the database.

What good is record number order to you? Record number order enables you to discover which were the last 10 records, for example, added to the database. This is significant, for example, when you are entering stacks of records and you lose your place. In this case, you can ask to view the highest record number to discover which was the last record entered.

But, whether your database contains 25 records or 250,000, the time will come when you want to work with a smaller group than the whole database. You may, for example, need to search for certain characteristics within the data on each record that identifies that record as one you need to examine, calculate, or print. You may want to view in a specific order the records that match your criteria.

If, for example, you search for residents in a certain ZIP code, you probably want to see them in order by last name or the name of their company. This means that you need to have the LASTNAME or COMPANY index prepared before the search is performed. The search table is illustrated in figure 4.3.

To create a saved search perform the following steps:

1. Select **S**earch list from the Main Menu. Alpha Four displays the Search Options menu.

2. Choose **C**reate/edit a saved search.

3. Select an unused letter between A and Z.

4. Select **T**able mode and type a description of the search that reminds you of its purpose.

5. On the Search Table screen, use F2 (Fields) to choose the field you want to examine. In a name and address file, you can choose the ZIP_CODE field as shown in figure 4.3.

6. Type an = sign in the Op. column.

7. Under the title Search for What?, you can enter the ZIP code data you want to see. Enter a valid ZIP code that you know to be in the data.

8. Press F10 to continue. Be sure to select the right primary index to see the records in order. The program then selects the records that match this criterion.

Records found in a search are held in a search list that keeps the records in the same index order as it did when the search was performed.

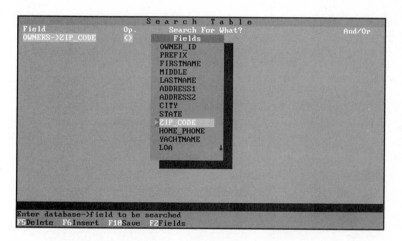

Define a saved
search by using
the Search Table.

Understanding the Difference between Range and Search

The distinction between a range of records and a search can be confusing. If you define a specific range of records, using the Range Setting capability, you probably want to view or browse your records using that range on what might be considered a temporary basis, but you can select that range any time you like. A search holds the found records in a separate, selectable list until a new search is run to find a new set of records. The active search list is one of the greatest advances Alpha Four has over ALPHA/*three*. Users of the earlier program cannot reselect a search list after changing to a new index.

In a range, if you use a date field to analyze your records, you can create a range that enables you to see records with dates greater than a certain date and dates not greater than a certain date. With a range such as this, you define two kinds of records: those between the two dates and all dates including those within the range. By making the range active or inactive, you can switch between the two as quickly as calling up the range setting screen.

Making a Filter Active

When the bottom line of your range setting screen is set to Active, as shown in figure 4.4, you know that when this particular range is selected, the Filter selects the records defined on the Filter expression line.

If you get a message that says No records found, resetting to Show: All, Filter: Inactive you may have a filter selected that is impossible for Alpha Four to handle. If, for example, a DATE > 01/01/93 is set in the filter and there are no records with dates greater than January 1, 1993, in the database, you see the error message.

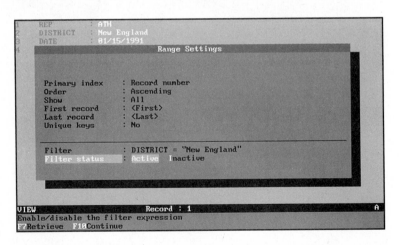

FIG. 4.4

The Range Settings screen with an active filter.

Making a Filter Inactive

There are two ways to solve the problem of the No records found message. The first is to add or modify records that match the criteria of the Filter. The second is to erase or deactivate the filter setting and save the filter in the Inactive position.

Defining Searches

Searches are designed to identify and select records that have specific characteristics. There are two kinds of searches: a saved search, or a one-time search. The program holds the found records in a search list, until you perform a new search, which overwrites the previous search in the computer's memory.

The search must be performed using a specific index, whether it is a record number or a complex combination of dates and dollars. The desired result is what determines which index to use for the search. Note that the search must be performed using the index that shows the records in the order you want to use them, because you cannot change the order in which the records are shown in the search list after the search is performed.

Using the record number rather than another index is noticeably faster, particularly for searches performed on less powerful computers. If time is a factor in your search, you may want to create an index in which you want to see the files, copy the database to a new database using that index, and do your search on the newly re-ordered record number database. (See the Copy command in Chapter 9.)

T I P

Using Expressions To Refine Data Retrieval

Searches, like indexes, can be created using the Table mode or the Expression mode. Table mode is used to let Alpha Four do the heavy work. If, for example, you want to find records for the month of February, but only for a certain region, and for sales greater than a certain number, you are asking the program to examine three different kinds of fields: date, character, and numeric.

When you use the Table mode, Alpha Four knows the difference between the kinds of fields and writes its own expression to perform the search. In fact, a requirement for creating all expressions is that the field types must be the same. You must convert both the date fields and the numeric field to a form in which the program can see it as a character field.

To make a date field look like a character field, you use the function CDATE(). To make the number field work like a character field, use the function STR(). Your search list will look something like that shown in figure 4.5.

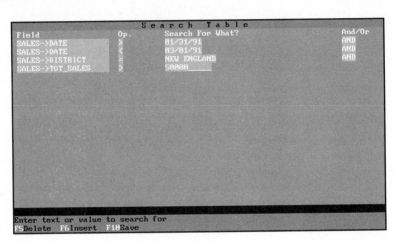

FIG. 4.5

Search Table filled with Date> 01/31/91 and date < 03/01/91 and district = New England and TOT_SALES > 50000.

Defining the Difference between .AND. and .OR.

Consider the difference between AND and OR in the search list. Using OR, you can search for records in which the date is 01/01/91 OR less than 01/31/92. If you search for records in that the date is greater than 01/01/91 AND 01/31/91, then only records that meet both criteria pass through the selection process. (See further discussion of .AND. and .OR. under sample searches following.)

Creating Indexes and Summary Databases

In this section, you need a small database with four fields and 20 records. You can follow along with the example, or use your own sales figures or create fields with names that are more meaningful to you.

In the sample database, there is a sales force of three representatives, five districts, and total sales figures for each salesperson for each month for each district. Each salesperson may work in more than one district.

Create a database with the name SALES. The fields should be as the following:

Number	Name	Type	Width	Decimal Places
1	REP	C	3	
2	DISTRICT	C	12	
3	DATE	D	8	
4	TOT_SALES	N	10	0

Enter the following records, remembering to use the Alt-F (repeat previous field) or Alt-R (repeat previous record) shortcuts wherever possible:

REP	DISTRICT	DATE	TOTAL SALES
ATH	Midwest	01-15-1991	23457
ATH	New England	01-15-1991	23467
FEG	South	01-15-1991	25460
FEG	New England	01-15-1991	31372
EMD	Midwest	01-15-1991	34323
FEG	Southwest	01-15-1991	54353
EMD	Midwest	01-15-1991	65434
EMD	Northwest	01-15-1991	65621
FEG	South	02-15-1991	23257

REP	DISTRICT	DATE	TOTAL SALES
FEG	Southwest	02-15-1991	23455
EMD	Northwest	02-15-1991	23467
EMD	Midwest	02-15-1991	54324
FEG	Midwest	02-15-1991	65466
ATH	New England	02-15-1991	65475
ATH	Midwest	02-15-1991	87645
FEG	South	03-15-1991	21278
EMD	Midwest	03-15-1991	44324
EMD	Northwest	03-15-1991	65422
ATH	New England	03-15-1991	65433
FEG	Southwest	03-15-1991	65467

You also must create the following indexes:

REP
DATE + TOT_SALES
DATE
DISTRICT + TOT_SALES

With this database and these indexes, you can perform a number of analyses in several different ways.

Creating a Summary Database

To summarize the example database to analyze the material by district, choose **Utilities, Summarize**, type the name **SUM1** at the bottom of the screen, and press Enter. Use F6 to select all the fields. Press F10 to Continue.

The type of summarization is shown with the default First. For field 2, DISTRICT, this should be changed to Count and on the fourth line, the summarization should be changed to Total. By moving your cursor onto the summarization options of each field, press the first letter of the option shown for that field. For example, press C to get count. Press F10 after making summary selections. Type in a description for your new database and press F10. The Summarization Selection screen should look like the following:

| | Summarization Selection | | |
Field	Name	Type	Summarization
1	REP	C	First
2	DISTRICT	C	Count
3	DATE	D	First
4	TOT_SALES	N	Total

On the range setting screen, choose the index that summarizes by the representative's initials and press F10.

This action creates a new database named SUM1 containing three records. When you choose the new database, you see that the record looks like the following in Browse mode:

REP	DISTRICT	DATE	TOT_SALES
ATH	5	01-15-1991	265477
EMD	7	01-15-1991	352915
FEG	8	01-15-1991	310108

You can perform this exercise with different indexes in the range setting screen and new names like SUM2 and SUM3. When you summarize on DISTRICT with COUNT on the REP field and TOTAL for TOT_SALES, the results should look like the following:

REP	DISTRICT	DATE	TOT_SALES
7	Midwest	01-15-1991	374973
4	New England	01-15-1991	185747
3	Northwest	01-15-1991	154510
3	South	01-15-1991	69995
3	Southwest	01-15-1991	143275

This analysis is impressive enough with just 20 records, but imagine how powerful this technique is with hundreds of records summarized in this manner. Naturally, all the usual operations for database management are available to the new databases: indexing, reporting, and exporting to other software (such as Lotus 1-2-3) for further analysis or exchanging with other users. (You can use this material again in Chapter 10 to illustrate special tips, tricks, and techniques.)

Performing Sample Searches

When you use AND with your search criteria, records must match two or more criteria to be found. When you use OR, records must match one or another of the defined criteria.

Using the sample SALES database, you can create a search that looks like the following:

DATE >= 01/01/91 AND
DATE < 02/01/91

The result of this search is only records that show dates during the month of January.

The criteria

DISTRICT = New England OR
REP = FEG

return records for New England and for representative FEG—a total of 12 records.

To illustrate the difference between AND and OR, notice that a search for

DISTRICT = New England AND
REP = FEG

returns only one record.

Mastering Global Update

The Global update menu contains five selections that represent a broad range of functions: Update field, Change case, Delete range of records, Undelete range of records, and delete Duplicate records.

Changing the Case
in a Range of Records

Case conversion is an uncomplicated function that is, in some ways, redundant in Alpha Four. It is odd that not only are there two other distinct methods to perform the same function, but this operation has survived with no noticeable change from ALPHA/*three*.

You can perform global change of case in six different varieties:

- To all uppercase
- To all lowercase
- To uppercase for the first character in a field only
- To uppercase for every word in a field
- To lowercase for all words and first letter uppercase
- To lowercase for all words and uppercase for each word in the field

The update process runs through a range settings screen that enables you to be selective in the conversion process. Generally, it may be easier to define a field with its case characteristics using field rules, as discussed in Chapter 5. Field rules force all data to attain the case characteristic as defined in the rule. If you need to change the case for a specific range of existing records but not for all records, then use the global update operation.

Another alternative to global case change is in the layout process for reports, forms, browse tables, and mailing labels. The choice of case conversion is available for all character fields in the layout process. This does not change the case of your fields permanently, however— only for the sake of display on the layout.

Updating a Field

Before globally updating a field, always back up your file. The changes are permanent and difficult, sometimes impossible, to reverse. The update discussed in this section is a simple one.

In Version 1.1 of Alpha Four, the capability to save up to 26 global update definitions was introduced. This means that while you are testing ways to perform complex updates, you do not need to retype the entire procedure. Again, a good practice is to create a dummy database on which you can test your updates before they do damage to your main files.

As many as five fields can be updated on the same pass in Version 1, while you can update as many as 20 fields using Version 2. Global update is used frequently in applications.

Performing Sample Global Updates

An example of using Global update/delete is changing prices on specific parts in an inventory database. Suppose that you get a letter from a distributor stating that certain products have been given a 7.5 percent price increase. Your inventory file contains one record for each product you carry. Because there is no way to identify the products with increased price other than with a manual review of your inventory file, you can put the database into Browse mode and scan the information, 20 records per screen. Mark each of the items that have a price increase for deletion by pressing Alt-D (Alt-U removes the delete mark).

CAUTION   Be sure to back up data before performing dramatic actions such as these.

When all records are marked, perform the following steps for the Global update:

1. Select Global update/delete from the Main Menu. Alpha Four shows the Global Update/Delete menu.

2. Select Update field, Create/edit update expressions.

3. Choose an unused letter between A and Z and type a description of the Global update that reminds you of its use. Press F10.

4. Select the PRICE field using F2 (Fields) to select from the pop-up window.

5. With your cursor in the Expression column, press F8 to open the Window, as shown in figure 4.6.

6. Use F2 to select the PRICE field again.

7. Type the following expression:

   PRICE * 1.075

   to increase the amount in the PRICE field by 7.5 percent.

8. Press F10 to save.

9. At the range setting screen, make sure that the choice in the third row, Show, is for only the Deleted records.

10. When you press F10, the update takes place on the records which have been marked. Remember to undelete the records marked deleted after the update has taken place.

11. Select **G**lobal update/delete from the Main Menu. Then select **Un**-delete range of records. On the third line of the range setting screen, change All to **D**eleted to reduce the number of records that will be examined.

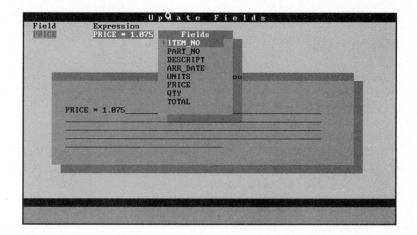

FIG. 4.6

Global update expression shows PRICE field increase.

As another example, in the sample SALES database, a new salesperson, with the initials PLF, takes over a group of accounts from someone who is leaving the company, whose initials are EMD. You can use a search list or filter for a global update to replace PLF with EMD.

The expression to use might read as the following:

REP if(REP = "EMD","PLF",REP)

In English, this expression says "If the representative's initials are EMD, replace them with PLF; otherwise, use the existing entry."

Summary

In this chapter, you examined the various methods Alpha Four offers for putting records in order and then retrieving the records. Defining an index creates an ordered list; defining a range selects a portion of that list. Because searches depend on indexes and ranges for their future output, you examined the ways that indexes, ranges, and searches work together. You learned to design searches and ranges to find the records you need to extract.

There are many uses for found records. The records contained in the search list are shown in the order of the primary index at the time that the search was performed. This makes a search list important for printing reports. The search list often is needed to select the records to be manipulated using global update. Working with a combination of these functions gives you a broad range of functions with which to control specific selections of your records.

In Chapter 5, you explore the power of field rules. With field rules, you can develop a variety of refinements to the standard data entry process. Field rules also enable you to establish rules for data entry to reduce errors and promote efficiency.

Creating Field Rules To Control Data Entry

If a little knowledge is dangerous,
where is the man who has so much
as to be out of danger?
Thomas Henry Huxley, Technical Education

Much of the great capability of your Alpha Four database comes from using field rules. Found under Database/set design, field rules help define the way the fields are displayed. This chapter gives a complete explanation of field rules and how they can be valuable in your work. Using field rules, you can accomplish the following tasks:

- Change all data to uppercase
- Multiply two fields
- Prevent the entry of too large or too small a number
- Offer a default for the input of an area code
- Automatically enter the correct ZIP code for any town
- Calculate 30, 60, or 90 days from DATEDUE
- Require double entry for a critical field

- Skip certain fields depending on the data in another field
- Prevent data entry errors

After you have used field rules to define the way Alpha Four handles entered data, you must consider how the material looks on an input form or a browse table. Combined with field rules, well-designed input forms and browse tables can enhance the productivity of most databases.

Writing Field Rules

To create field rules, perform the following steps:

1. Select the Field Rules menu from the main Alpha Four menu.

2. Select **D**atabase/set design. Alpha Four shows the Database/Set Options menu.

3. Choose **F**ield rules, **C**reate/edit field rules.

4. Select the field for which you want to write a rule and press Enter. The cursor moves into the lower window.

5. Use the arrow keys to move the cursor up and down on the first page of field rules. Press PgDn to access the second and third pages of field rules' options.

Selecting User-Entered and Calculated Data Fields

When you first start field rules, you see a screen with two windows (see fig. 5.1). The top window shows the first six fields in the database, the field type (character, numeric, date, logical, or memo), and the length of each field. In the lower window, you can see the name of the high-lighted field in the top-left corner. If you have entered no instructions, you see a message in this window that says, No rules defined for this field.

When you highlight any character field and press Enter, the cursor moves to the lower window, which displays the choices available on three pages. The first decision you must make is whether the field should be user-entered or calculated. Numeric fields can accept a range check of minimum and maximum value, as shown in figure 5.2.

```
                         F i e l d   R u l e s
    Field                Type    Value           Lookup
    OWNER_ID             C: 4    User-entered
    PREFIX               C: 8
    FIRSTNAME            C: 15
    MIDDLE               C: 8
    LASTNAME             C: 15
    ADDRESS1             C: 20

    PREFIX

    No rules defined for this field




    F10Continue   F9Define Rule
```

FIG. 5.1

The Field Rules screen has two windows; field names are shown in the top, and field rules are shown in the bottom.

NOTE   Two pages of field rules exist for numeric, date, and logical fields and one exists for a prompt message for memo fields.

```
                         F i e l d   R u l e s
    Field                Type    Value           Lookup
    CITY                 C: 15   User-entered    Database/Choice
    STATE                C: 2
    ZIP_CODE             C: 10
    HOME_PHONE           C: 13
    YACHTNAME            C: 20
    LOA                  N: 4

    LOA                                          Page 1 of 3

    Value           : User-entered
    Range Check     : Yes
    Minimum value   : 0
    Maximum value   : 0

    Default Mode    : None

    Increment       : None



    Enter the smallest value allowed
    F9Switch Window  PgDnNext Page
```

FIG. 5.2

Numeric, date, and logical fields have a different set of rules.

If you choose **C**alculated, all other options disappear. There can be no data entered from the keyboard. The calculation or expression that you enter on the next line completely governs the data entry in this field. You can, however, define a field as calculated and then change to user-entered. You could make this change, for example, as in Appendix D, where you step through the problem of separating one long data field containing NAME data into separate fields, such as PREFIX, FIRST, LAST, and SUFFIX. In this case, the field rule changing from a calculated field to a user-entered field has no effect upon the existing data.

Calculated fields are explored individually at the end of this chapter. Because calculated fields usually employ functions and expressions, more information about calculations is found in Chapter 13, which discusses expressions.

Understanding User-Entered Field Rules

When you choose user-entered field rules, new choices appear lower down in the window. Three pages of options exist for user-entered field rules (see fig. 5.3). These options include automatic case conversion, default entries, templates, masks, verification, and double entry of data. The options available for each field depend on the type of field. For example, Case Convert appears only for character fields; Range Check, Minimum Value, and Maximum Value appear for numeric fields.

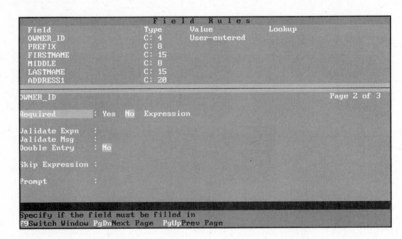

FIG. 5.3

The second page of the field rules for a Character field.

In the following sections, you learn about the available rules and how they are used.

CASE CONVERT

Case Convert is used only for character fields. Table 5.1 lists the available options.

Table 5.1 Case Convert Options

Option	Function
None	No changes to user-entered data.
Caps	Changes entered text to all uppercase.
First	Changes the first word in the field to uppercase.
Word	Changes the first letter of each word in the field to uppercase.
Lower	Changes entered text to all lowercase.
X	Changes all the text entered into the field to lowercase except the first letter in the field.
Z	Changes the text entered into the field to lowercase and makes the first letter of each word in the field uppercase.

Case conversion also is discussed in Chapter 4 in the section concerning **G**lobal update.

CAUTION If the data in this field is formatted for (F)irst or (W)ord, then a field containing the following data gives unexpected results:

None	(F)irst	(W)ord
O'Neil & deWolfe	O'neil & dewolfe	O'Neil & Dewolfe
State of New York	State of new york	State Of New York
Washington, D.C.	Washington, d.c.	Washington, D.C.

TEMPLATE

A *template* enforces a pattern into which data must be entered. Three examples occur frequently: telephone numbers, Social Security numbers, and ZIP codes. A template enables the user to define the *fixed* characters that belong in a field, such as the following examples:

(___)___-____   for telephone numbers
___-__-____   for Social Security numbers
_____-____   for 9-digit ZIP codes

Use some care with this rule, because you may run into difficulty. For example, if your data contains any telephone numbers from European countries, the area codes and exchanges may be replaced with city and country codes, which bear little resemblance to the familiar U.S. telephone numbers.

Also, if you append records from another database that does not contain this template, the parentheses may overwrite your numerals when a record is changed.

MASK

When you create a template to force the format of data entry by positions, the next step is to create a *mask* to define the kind of characters that can be accepted into the field. For letters, you have the options of A for capitalized alpha characters, a for any alpha character, 9 for numbers, and a space for anything. For example, if you want to write your telephone numbers in the old manner, you could make your template look like the following:

(999)999-9999

ALLOW EXCEPTIONS

Because there are many exceptions to this rule for telephone numbers, the next line asks whether the mask should be made a requirement or whether exceptions are allowed. Social Security numbers, for example, are all in the same format. You may want to require, therefore, that any entry conform to the definitions of mask as a method of error-checking.

DEFAULT MODE

Default Mode is available for every kind of field except the Memo field. Three choices exist for the default: None, Value, or Expression. None indicates that there is no automatic (default) entry.

Value enables you to create a default using the most common entry, the one that many of the entries contain. For example, in a name and address file of your customers, default value might be that most of them live in the same state. The *default* in the STATE field would have the U.S. Post Office's two-letter abbreviation for that state. When you set the default, you do not limit the possibilities for entry. Default entry is just a suggestion to the data entry person, not a requirement.

An expression in the default mode can make full use of the rich range of commands among the functions of Alpha Four. An expression can use fields from the current database, variables that have been set in scripts, and they can use any appropriate function. Remember that this is only a default entry. A default entry appears only during the initial creation of a record. When a calculation is in an expression in field rules, and the number in the total field for this default calculation is saved, the expression does not change when the numbers in the fields that make up the calculation change.

If you choose the calculated field rule instead of user-entered, the result of the calculation is dynamic; it changes as the numbers or data in the calculation change. When you save a calculation in the default expression, the result only changes with a new record entered by the user. Also, note that the F6 (Window On) and F7 (Evaluate) commands are available.

Examples of default values that are commonly found are expressions that define a default rate, such as the following:

> if(TAXABLE=.Y.,TOTAL*.05,TOTAL)

or the most frequently entered state field:

> "NY"

INCREMENT

For Increment, you can select None, Record, or Update. Record asks the program to enter the next available number after examining the previous number. When you enter your first record, you assign a beginning number. This is particularly helpful when numbering invoices or customer records when you plan to link this file with another in a set.

The Update option assigns the next number in sequential order each time a record is changed or updated. When you create the first record, you assign a beginning number. After that, each time the record is updated, the record defaults to the next higher increment. You can overwrite Update and Increment Record when you are working on the actual record in Enter or Change mode.

When you reach the bottom of these choices, press PgDn to go to the second page.

REQUIRED

If you answer Yes at this point, the program prevents the user from passing by this field without making a valid entry. You can carry the command further by defining the field rule with an expression that must evaluate to True in order to force the Required status. For example, if the purchase is charged to a credit card, fields CARD_NO and EXPIRE_DT must be filled with a valid entry but cannot be left empty.

You also can validate an entry by using Validate Expn. The user enters an expression that must evaluate to True, or the entry is rejected and a warning message is displayed, which is written by the user in the Validate Msg line. Such validation might indicate the following:

> SHIP_DATE>=ORD_DATE for order and ship dates
> DOB>=SYSTEM_DATE-(365 * 16) for police records to highlight
> the age of a minor offender
> ORD_AMT>=15.00 for credit card orders, which must exceed a
> minimum order amount

For further validation of an entry, you can force the user to enter the data twice by using Double Entry and the Double Entry Expression, which evaluates to True if the field must be entered twice.

SKIP ENTRY

Skip Entry enables you to define the circumstance in which the cursor skips a field entirely. Consider the following expression:

> (SHIP_NAME = "SAME")

If the user enters "SAME" to indicate that the same addressee is receiving the item as is purchasing it, then the address is the same and need not be re-entered.

In the case of a field that is filled with data lookup by a choice made in another field, you can force the cursor to jump over this field by writing the following as the Skip expression:

> .T.

PROMPT

Prompt enables you to write a help message that appears at the bottom of the screen whenever this field is entered or changed. This feature is particularly useful when the field name does not appear on the input form.

Creating Lookups by Using Tables or Databases

The differences between using a table or a database are significant and should be considered carefully. A *lookup table* is designed as part of field rules, and the data contained in the table is stored in memory with the other field rules when the database is in use. A *lookup database* is a separate file connected to the current file through the lookup definition. The lookup definition screen for either table or database lookups is shown in figure 5.4.

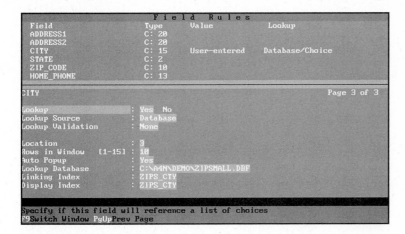

FIG. 5.4

The lookup source can be a table created in the current database or an external database.

A lookup table is used when you want to have quick access to a small amount of data that does not change frequently or substantially. A lookup table is limited to 255 rows and 6 columns of values. One column is used as the basis for the lookup and the other 5 columns fill associated fields.

Creating a Lookup Table

A good example of a lookup table is the record of entries in the database of the Dispatcher's Log for a police department. Several entries are required to indicate the last name, badge, and title of the officer involved in the incident. The entries are typed into the proper place when the user answers Yes to the following question:

```
Define lookup mapping now?  Yes  No
```

The database has a lookup table that looks like the following:

BADGE	TITLE	LASTNAME
1	Sgt.	Healey
2	Sgt.	Cuigini
3	Lt.	Allen
4	Dt.	Anderson
5	Ptl.	Shawn
6	Ptl.	Barber
7	Ptl.	Edwards

Creating a Lookup Database

The situation is different when you choose to define a lookup database. Three new lines appear on the menu. The program asks for the name of the Lookup database, the Linking index, and the Display index. The last two items are optional because the default is record number, but the right index is a time-saver if the lookup database has many records. The *Linking index* is designed to make the process of matching records faster. Lacking a Linking index, Alpha Four must start at the first record and work through the database to find the matching information. The Linking index must, of course, be defined before you get into the process of creating a Lookup link to another database. You can see the choices in figure 5.4.

On the last line of this screen, Alpha Four also asks you to select the order in which the data is to appear in the lookup window. As with Linking indexes, you can type the index name on the proper line or you can press F2 to display the list of indexes attached to this database.

At the end of this process, Alpha Four asks whether you want to perform lookup mapping. As shown in figure 5.5, lookup mapping is the act of choosing the fields from the lookup database that should flow into the current database. The user chooses which fields may appear in the pop-up window during data entry or during Change mode.

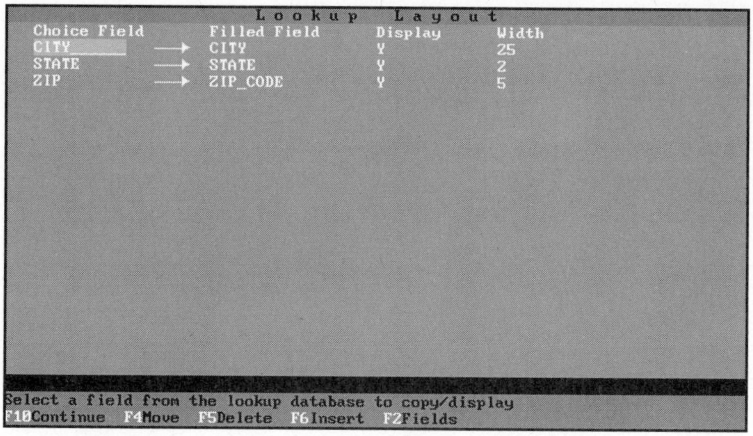

FIG. 5.5

Mapping a lookup database selects the fields to be viewed or filled in on your entry screen.

For Auto Pop-up, you can select Yes or No. If you choose Yes, the pop-up window appears with no request from the user. If you choose No, the user must press F3 (Choices) during data entry to display the pop-up window. The automatic pop-up feature works on only new records, not on records being edited. When existing records are being edited, the lookup is available, but only when you press F3 (Choices).

The location of the pop-up window is what is indicated in the next choice on the menu.

The Hidden 1 2 3 4 5 6 7 8 9 is analogous to the numbers on a touch-tone telephone. Hidden indicates that the pop-up window does not show on the screen at all. The numbers 1 through 9 describe the 3 x 3 square of the phone keys as parallel with similarly located places on the computer screen. The default is 3, which places the pop-up window in the top-right corner of the telephone pad, as shown in figure 5.6.

The Hidden choice is useful when you have defined the Lookup validation as Doesn't exist. This forces the user to enter a value that has no match on the lookup table. Displaying the list would have no value to the user.

You may want to keep records of various kinds of equipment, serial numbers, vehicles, weapons, and other items assigned to an officer. In this case, an officer's personnel file would be better served by a separate database designed to fill in fields describing the equipment assigned to the officer rather than a lookup table with more limited fields. The WEAPONS database would include fields, such as make, model, serial number, date of purchase, last date of maintenance, replacement cost, and much more information than is necessary in the officers' profile database. The OFFICERS database is linked to the WEAPONS database by an index in the WEAPONS database. In this example, you create an index called WEAPN_SN. The OFFICERS database must have fields that are ready to receive information about a piece of equipment, its make, model, serial number, purchase date, and maintenance date.

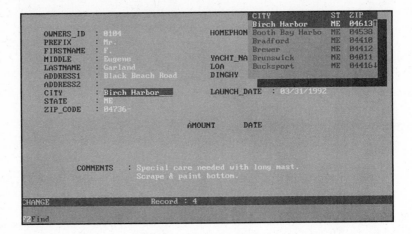

FIG. 5.6

Pop-up window position 3.

When the user enters the serial number of a weapon on an officer's record, the program can validate the number by checking with the lookup database to find out whether the number does or does not currently exist in the WEAPONS file. In Lookup validation, the choice of None performs no validation of the data. Exists rejects the entry if there is no match. Doesn't exist indicates that the entry is rejected if a match does already exist. This last choice effectively prevents duplication of data and should be used carefully. (See Chapter 4 concerning indexes.)

How do these lookup tables and lookup databases differ in practical use? The most important difference is seen in the effect of changes to existing records through changes in the lookup source. For example, using a parts list can automatically give you prices for billing. Any change in pricing in a table is reflected in new records only; whereas price changes held in an external database can reevaluate all records and take effect immediately in the entire database. A history of price changes may be maintained in the table method. The pricing of figures is always current if a Lookup database is used.

Exploring Lookups

Creating a calculated field in field rules is designing calculations in a *real* field. This process is different from a user-entered field. The sum that appears in this field is derived from other fields, functions or values; when the values in a related field or fields change, the result in the calculated field changes. This field cannot be changed by the user on the entry form. In fact, the cursor skips this field completely. The emphasis is on *real* fields. Although the user cannot enter data directly, the field responds to changes in other fields or conditions in the system, such as date changes.

To illustrate how this field rule operates, you can use an example in the database you created in Chapter 1, INVENTRY, which has nine fields. Only the following three fields need to be considered here:

Number	Field Name	Type	Length	Decimal Places
5	PRICE	Numeric	10	2
6	QTY	Numeric	5	2
9	TOTAL	Numeric	10	2

Select the INVENTRY file. At the Main Menu, select Database/set design. From the Database/Set Options menu, select Field rules, Create/edit field rules. Move the cursor to the TOTAL field and press Enter to move the cursor to the lower window to create a calculation in this field.

On the first line of the lower window, change the default of User-entered to Calculated. Press F2 (Fields), press Enter to select the INVENTRY database, highlight the field name PRICE, and press Enter. This places the word PRICE on the expression line. Next, press F3 (Functions) to view the range of possible operators. Select the asterisk (multiply) and press Enter. Finally, press F2 again to select the QTY field from the INVENTRY database. Of course, if you are sure of the field names and the function, you can type them directly without using the function keys. When your screen looks like the one in figure 5.7, press F9 to switch to the upper window. Then press F10 to save the field rule and return to the Main Menu.

You have now written your first expression. *Expression* is the term used by Alpha Four to signify a formula-like statement that is an interpretation of data, rather than the data itself. Not all field rules include expressions, but they all affect the way the data you enter looks and acts. For example, a formula that multiplies QUANTITY by UNIT_PRICE looks exactly the same in its field as the product of the two fields that contain the data.

The following is an example of the preceding idea:

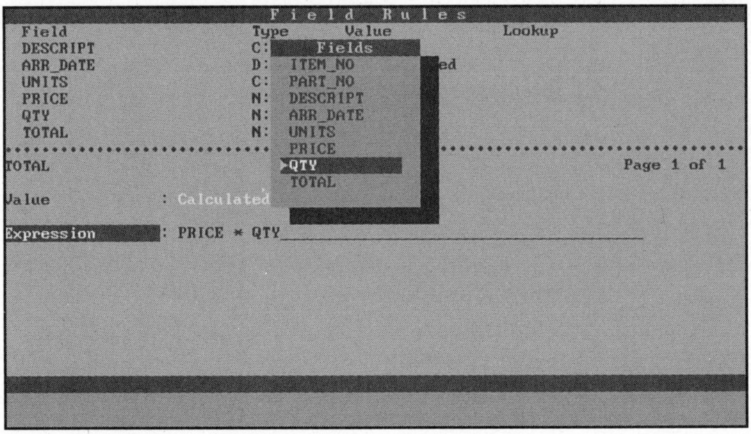

FIG. 5.7

Use the F2 (Fields) key to find the pop-up window containing field names.

if the value 3 = QUANTITY, and
the value 9.95 = UNIT_PRICE, then
expression QUANTITY * UNIT_PRICE = 29.85

The number 29.85 appears in the field where TOTAL has been calculated, but it is the result of a formula; therefore, it changes when the numbers in the other fields change.

Alpha Four enables you to use the point-and-shoot method to define the fields used in expressions from a pop-up window. When you press F2 (Fields) while the cursor is on the expression line, Alpha Four displays a pop-up window showing the field names from your database. You can select them by highlighting the one you need and pressing Enter.

Alpha Four's built-in functions also are available in the same manner by using F3 (Functions). Pressing F3 displays another pop-up menu. Six pages of options (accessed with the PgDn key) are associated with this menu. Each function is described on these screens with its own syntax, as shown in figure 5.8.

Functions are not necessarily easy to use the first time you try. Still, no one should put off learning and using expressions and functions. They are valuable and relatively easy to learn once you see their pattern.

The following are examples of times when you may want to use expressions:

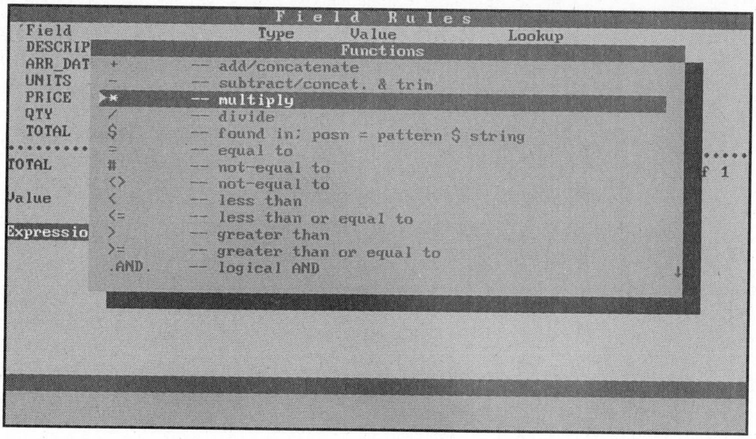

```
                        F i e l d   R u l e s
 Field                Type      Value            Lookup
 DESCRIP                    Functions
 ARR_DAT   +      -- add/concatenate
 UNITS     -      -- subtract/concat. & trim
 PRICE     **     -- multiply
 QTY       /      -- divide
 TOTAL     $      -- found in; posn = pattern $ string
 .........  =      -- equal to                              .....
 TOTAL     #      -- not-equal to                          f 1
           <>     -- not-equal to
 Value     <      -- less than
           <=     -- less than or equal to
 Expressio >      -- greater than
           >=     -- greater than or equal to
           .AND.  -- logical AND
```

FIG. 5.8

Six pages of functions are available to help you write expressions.

- To design a calculated field, such as QUANTITY * UNIT_PRICE

- To create a search that finds all dates greater than 01/01/90

- To perform a global update to make the TAXRATE change from .05 to .065

- To report the total value of all salaries for each department in your database

These examples are not complicated or difficult to execute. They do require an understanding of the mechanism used in their creation. You can learn more about expressions and functions used in these rules in Chapter 13.

Summary

Using field rules rewards you with reduced data entry, reduced errors, and greatly increased productivity. Complicated calculations requiring exacting accuracy need be set up just once, and then the computer can execute them again and again. Colorful, eye-catching effects can be achieved on forms and browse tables by using field rules.

Data verification and lookup capabilities are most effective as your applications become more complicated, but even simple applications, such as mailing lists with a city or ZIP code lookup, are greatly enhanced with field rules.

Learning to create field rules is a helpful introduction to concepts you can explore in Part III, where you work on designing and building your own applications.

Creating Reports

No one means all he says,
and yet very few say all they mean,
for words are slippery
and thought is viscous.
Henry Brooks Adams, The Education of Henry Adams

Five kinds of output are available from Alpha Four: reports (columnar), mailing labels, forms (for data entry and for printing), browse tables (for on-screen snapshots of your data and for quick editing of many files), and letters. Each of these five can be displayed on-screen for previewing, sent to the printer for hard copy, and saved to a file for further editing in a word processor.

This chapter explores the special characteristics of these five kinds of output to help you decide which one is appropriate for your particular need. The end of this chapter discusses the traditional columnar report format; the other four kinds of output are discussed in other chapters.

As you see them described, you may say to yourself, "Clearly, I need a report for this purpose and an input form for that." Don't be too quick to make that decision just because you are familiar with one kind of output or another. For example, perhaps you need a prompted user input field for an entry that is not contained in your database to create a letter that states the following:

Dear Sir:

Your account shows an overdue balance of (BALANCE). Please...etc.

Of course, this looks like a form letter, with the emphasis on *form*. The best way to deal with this issue, however, is within the letter format, the only one that permits a prompted message to the user saying: What's the overdue balance on this account?

In another case, if you require a three-column format for columns of records, it sounds like a columnar report, but mail labels are the only format that prints data in multiple columns from different records on the same line.

NOTE   Quick Start 1 has a list of the special characteristics of each output format.

This chapter introduces you to Quick Report techniques creating custom reports, developing calculated fields, calculating existing fields, summarizing data, and subgrouping reports for effective results.

Using the Report Writer

Report writing holds terrors for some people—victims, perhaps, of software with a less usable interface. With Alpha Four's report writer, you can generate a fine-looking report by completing the following steps:

1. Log into the database containing the data you want in the report. If you are working with the examples given in earlier chapters, use the OWNERS file.

2. From the Main Menu, select **Layouts**. Alpha Four displays the Layouts menu. Choose **R**eports and **C**reate/edit a report. Select an unused letter, A through Z. Choose **Q**uick Setup. Enter a descriptive title on the Report description line. Press F10 to continue.

3. Using F2, select several fields that you want to see as columns on your report. Watch the Column Used counter at the bottom center of the screen and stop before you go beyond 80 characters. Press F10 to go to the Report Layouts Screen.

4. To see the results of the selections you have made, press F10, select **P**review, and press F10 again. You should see the date, the page number, the column titles, and the first line of your report. Press the space bar to see the next line of the report, or press the Enter key to start and stop continuous printing.

5. When the report has run through the selected records, you can press PgUp and PgDn or the up- and down-arrow keys to review the report. Press F10 to return to the report layout to make revisions to the quick report. Press F10 to save the layout.

The preceding steps are just the basics. You could, if you wanted, alphabetize this report by NAME, CITY, PRODUCT, or even DATE. To do this, you simply choose a different index when you print. If there are number fields on your report, they are totaled automatically in the summary section when you use Quick Setup.

Defining Your Goal

A report is any presentation of your data in a readable, manageable, and printable form. Reports can list items in columns and show totals, counts, or averages at the bottom of each column.

Reports can be created in a single-record format—an input form. Using this type of report, the data can drop into a preprinted form, such as an IRS Form 1040 or a contract for services. Or a report can be a several-paged document that enters NAME, RANK, and SERIAL NUMBER into several pages of a government- or insurance-required form. Mailing labels and letters also are considered reports.

The following sections examine samples of each type of report.

Using Input Forms

Suppose, for example, that a criminal has been arrested. In New England, a seven-page form is required and may be even longer if the perpetrator is intoxicated. The arrest report forms require that the same data be used over and over again, such as name, address, date of birth, and so forth. A multi-screen input form can use data entered once and print it in several places throughout the arrest report, saving the police officer from repeatedly typing the data in each space on the form.

Although the Alpha Four Reference Manual for Version 2 states that 10 screens are available on an input form as in Version 1, 25 screens actually are available. These screens appear in View mode only when the form has been edited to show fields or text on the screens after the first screen. A screen represents about one-half of a typewritten page. Therefore, if you are designing a form to fill out a preprinted document, two screens (pages) would be needed for one 8.5-by-11-inch page. Legal documents, such as contracts, often are printed on 8.5-by-14-inch paper, which requires three screens of an input form.

Some early shipments of Version 2 contain a problem with printing input forms that are more than three screens long. If you run into this problem, Alpha Software will supply a patch to repair the difficulty. Call the company for instructions on how to receive replacement disks or to download the file from their bulletin board. Information about the bulletin board and support services are in Appendix A.

Using Browse Tables

A report also can be a spreadsheet-like browse table, designed to take existing data and manipulate the columns and rows to show relationships between one kind of data and another or a sequence of events. An example of this kind of report is seen in figure 6.1. In this browse table, the fields have been rearranged to make them more useful to the viewer. This report is very useful for quickly producing information on which you can act.

Browse tables, like input forms and other reports, can use fields from any file in the current set, including the SYSTEM database. (For more information, see the discussion of SYSTEM fields, later in this chapter.)

NOTE Input forms and browse tables can be edited on-the-fly. From View or **B**rowse mode, press **O**ptions **E**dit to edit the current screen. If you are developing your work for others to use, you can apply a password to the editing function during the edit phase. Also note that you can restrict the user's right to change record contents, to mark and unmark records for deletion, to enter new records, to change or define ranges, to select a new table or form, and to search and replace data.

Using Mailing Labels and Letters

A report can take the form of mailing labels—with personalized letters to match. Designing mailing labels and letters is explored in Chapter 7.

Using Columnar Reports

A traditional, columnar report presents data so that it gives summarized answers to questions you have about your data. Reports generally depend on various indexes or searches to give meaning to the columnar order. Columnar reports answer the following questions: *Who is where? How many? How much? Which month was best? Why?*

Sometimes you know the kind of report you need before you know what data you need to study. It may be necessary to work backwards from the reports you need to the data you have to make the reports.

LASTNAME	CONT_DATE	TOPIC	DISCUSSION
	12/08/1992	Offer to sell neighboring property	Bert stopped in to tell me that he is retiring next summer and would like me to consider buying his docks and storage sheds.
Jones	10/10/1992	Lost dinghy	Possible theft of property.
Jones	10/26/1992	Dinghy found	PD called with request for ID. Dinghy found wrecked in Bar Harbor. Called David.
Cooper	11/09/1992	Insurance	Dan Cooper of WorldWide Ins. Co. notified Dave that the insurance would be adequate to replace his oars but the dinghy was not covered.
Garland	12/06/1992	New instructions	Requested special care to varnish on hatch covers.
Smith	09/06/1992	Hurricane damage	Considering selling the remains.
Smith	10/18/1992	Potential buyer	Heard from salvage firm in Portland that value is approx. $12,500. He will not be happy.
Smith	10/20/1992	Salvage	Bad news from salvage. No buyers just now for wrecks.
Fredett	12/10/1992	New engine due in January	Eric wants to have this installed as soon as possible for early testing.
Faxon	11/15/1992	Haul/Launch instructions	

FIG. 6.1

A sample browse table.

You can save up to 26 reports, one for each letter of the alphabet. On files that have several users, duplications often exist that people believe they need. Several versions of one report may exist because each person has his or her own or because earlier versions were never erased. If you have reached the limit for reports in your database, review and compare the ones you have with the ones you really need. Sometimes the same report can be used to address completely different questions by changing the index and/or search. (See Chapter 4 concerning indexes and searches.)

T I P A notebook containing a list of the reports that you require and samples of the printed reports is a valuable tool. You should include in your notebook how to print critical reports, which index to use, and how to get the right range of records with searches or filters. Stored next to the computer, such a notebook can save hours of time and worry, particularly when the person who is experienced in the production of certain reports calls in sick or leaves town.

T I P Another 26 reports (and forms, mailing labels, and browse tables) can be created on the same database when it becomes part of a set. If you run out of letters to save necessary reports, make the database the parent in a set, although the relational function may not actually be needed. This will give you the option of 26 more reports on the same data.

Using Quick Setup versus Custom Report

When creating reports, you can choose from two options: **Q**uick Setup and **C**ustom Report. If you are a beginner, if you plan to stick to a column format, or if you are an expert in a hurry, you probably will prefer to use the Quick Setup.

In the Quick Setup, you can place the column heading, which is the field name, the line below the column heading, and the field itself with one keystroke. It takes a separate step for each of these selections in the Custom Report Writer.

To use Quick Setup, complete the following steps:

1. From the Alpha Four Main Menu choose **L**ayouts.

2. Select **R**eports

3. Choose **C**reate/edit a report, and then choose any unused letter in the alphabet. If there have been no reports created, A is presented as the default.

4. Next, select **Q**uick Setup.

   Alpha Four displays the Quick Report Parameters screen, which requests a longer description for your report. This description appears again later when you are deciding which report you want to edit or print, so give your report a name you will recognize. Your report title can be up to 40 characters long. You might, for example, type **Owners' names—by launch date**.

   The next three lines on the Quick Report Parameters are shown in figure 6.2.

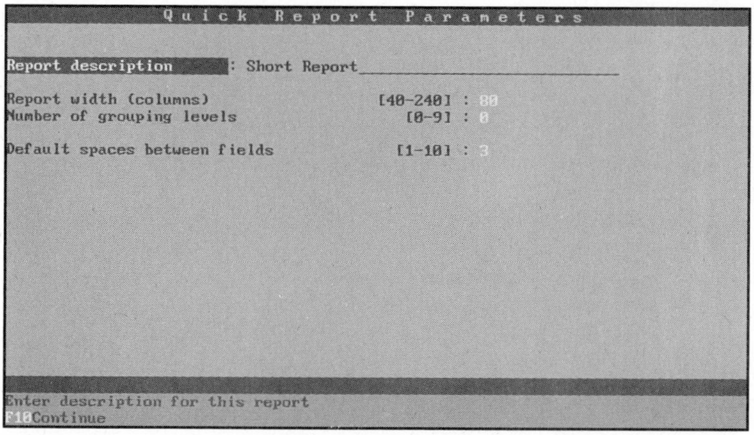

```
                Q u i c k   R e p o r t   P a r a m e t e r s

 Report description        : Short Report_____

 Report width (columns)              [40-240] : 80
 Number of grouping levels            [0-9] : 0

 Default spaces between fields        [1-10] : 3




 Enter description for this report
 F10 Continue
```

FIG. 6.2

The Quick Report Parameters screen.

5. First you provide information on how wide you expect your report to be (up to 240 characters).

6. Next, you select the number of grouping levels. *Grouping* refers to printing together records that are related to each other. In a name and address file, you could print records grouped by town or by ZIP code. Or, in a list of your friends, you could group the list by birthdays and break the report down by 12 months. (See Chapter 7 for more on grouping and subgrouping.)

7. The third line on the Quick Report Parameters screen asks for the number of spaces to be placed between each field. The default number of spaces between fields refers to the distance that the program automatically places between the columns on your report. This feature is useful if you want extra space or if you have few short fields for the report and you want them spaced out across the 80-column page.

If you want to take more control of the report-writing process, you can create a Custom Report. To create a Custom Report, complete the following steps:

1. From the Alpha Four Main Menu choose **Layouts**.

2. Select **R**eports.

3. Choose **C**reate/edit a report, and then choose any unused letter in the alphabet. If there have been no reports created, A is presented as the default.

4. Next, select **C**ustom Report.

   Alpha Four displays the Custom Report Parameters screen, which contains selections for printing the report, title lines, headers, margin and page break information, and more, as shown in figure 6.3.

A title, such as *Owners' names—by launch date*, tells the user that the file will print correctly only if the records chosen all have a launching date, and the Primary index for the printing is set for the date field, which tells when the boat is to be launched. Of course, this assumes that the index has been created before this point.

When creating a report, you need to plan ahead. Even a small sketch of your report will save you time in the long run. You should plan the fields, calculations, subgroupings, titles, and other details. Your drawing might include the column headings and page titles.

Such a drawing would ultimately look like figure 6.4. The design of the report shows the fields in the proper places in figure 6.5.

FIG. 6.4

Sketch your report.

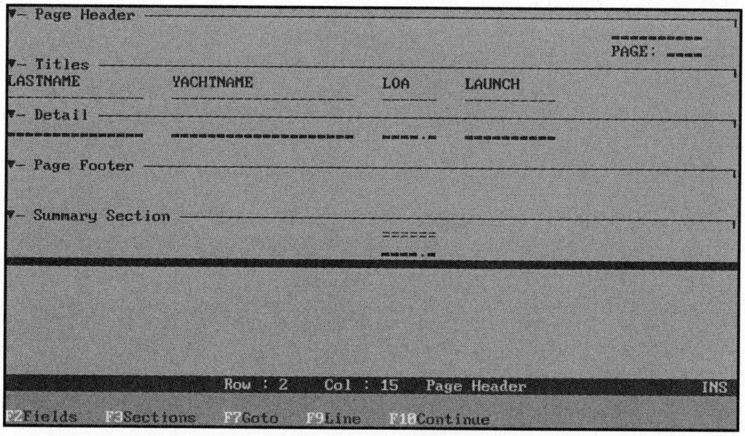

FIG. 6.5

The report to identify the dates for launching appears on the report editing screen.

Alpha Four assumes that because the LENGTH field is numeric, a TOTAL field must be created in the summary section. In the case of the length of the boats, the total is irrelevant and, therefore, should be removed. The report will look like figure 6.6.

			07-25-1991
			PAGE: 1
LASTNAME	YACHTNAME	LOA	LAUNCH
Smith	Sweet Sister	55.00	03-30-1992
Fenton	Wind Song	48.00	04-01-1992
Jones	Momma's Mink	64.00	04-01-1992
Garland	When Free	64.00	05-10-1992
Stanton	Blue Chip	28.00	06-01-1992
Smith	Sea Maid	20.00	06-15-1992

FIG. 6.6

Owners names by launch date.

Exploring Sections

Using Quick Report, the first screen asks for the names of the fields that represent the columns in your report—in this example, the column names are LASTNAME, YACHTNAME, LOA, and LAUNCH. When you are asked to enter the fields on the field selection menu, press F2 (Fields) to display the select Fields option. Press Enter to select the name of the current database and move the highlight to the field you want to select.

Creating a Database from a Report

In earlier chapters, you learned that databases can be designed based on the reports that they will produce. To use the following example, create a sample database called CHECKS containing the fields CHECK_NO, CHECK_DATE, PAYEE, ACCOUNT, AMOUNT, and RETURNED and containing the following information:

Number	Field	Type	Width	Decimal Place
1	CHECK_NO	C	4	
2	CHECK_DATE	D	8	
3	PAYEE	C	30	
4	ACCOUNT	C	25	
5	ITEM_NO	C	4	
6	AMOUNT	N	7	2
8	RETURNED	L	1	

With the CHECKS database as your current file, you can create a report that resembles a general journal of the transactions you record.

The output of this database will resemble a general journal of the transactions you record in the CHECKS file or a check register.

Alpha Four has several important fields that can be used in this report but that you did not create in your own database. As you create a report for the check register, notice that when you press the F2 (Fields) key and highlight the selected Field, there is also a choice called SYSTEM. This choice refers to a group of fields common to all databases no matter what fields are defined by the user. The fields in the SYSTEM database are created by the program, not by the user. In the SYSTEM database are system and report data, such as Page #, system date, index name, and more.

For your purposes, you should choose the name of the current database, CHECKS. This retrieves another pop-up menu showing the fields in the database. Using the up- and down-arrow keys, scroll through the list of fields and choose the fields that you want in your report by pressing Enter.

Choose, for example, the fields CHECK_NO, CHECK_DATE, PAYEE, ACCOUNT, AMOUNT, and RETURNED. As you select these fields, notice that the third line from the bottom of the screen says Columns Used:. As you choose fields to line up across the page of your report, Alpha Four keeps track of the number of characters required to show you the data in the fields. If the report is designed for 80 characters across the screen, the 81st and subsequent characters will be truncated when printed on 8.5-by-11-inch paper with normal margins.

In Version 1.1 and later, Alpha Four enables you to view a wide report by scrolling to the right when you print to the screen instead of to the printer. Of course, if your report must exceed the 80 character limit of the standard video display and the standard 8.5-by-11-inch page, then you must inform the program of this decision elsewhere (see the later section, " Using Formatting Options.")

NOTE Alpha Four also has an option for a report header that prints on the top of only the first page. This option must be selected by pressing F3 for sections and Insert section. If you insert enough lines to force a new page, the report header can serve as a title page to your report.

Choose the fields you want to see across the top of the report, and then press F10 (Continue). Alpha Four displays a visual representation of the report you have designed. The report layout screen shows the several sections that make up most reports. Notice that, as you move your cursor across the bright, dashed lines that represent the fields, the names of the database and field appear in the lower-left corner of the screen. In figure 6.7, because the highlight is on the field PAYEE in the database called CHECKS, it is represented by CHECKS->PAYEE.

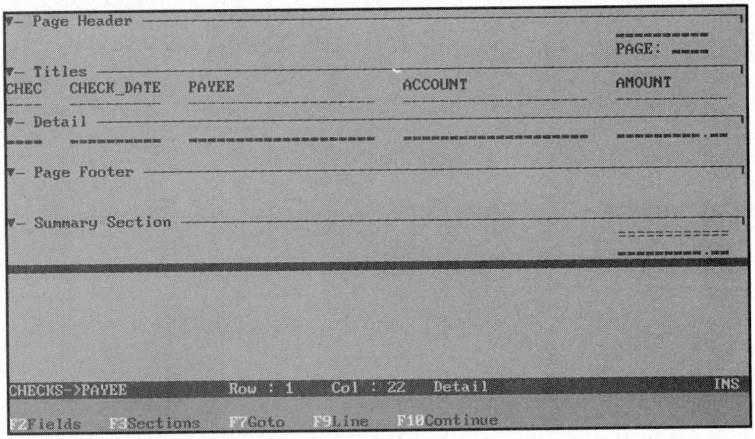

FIG. 6.7

A Quick Report showing fields from the CHECKS database.

Using a Page Header

The topmost section is called the Page Header. The header is printed at the top of every page. You can leave this section blank, but the fields automatically placed here by the Quick Setup procedure—SYSTEM ->DATE and SYSTEM->PAGENUMBER—are useful. A Report header, as compared with a Page header, does not appear automatically. Report headers appear only at the top of page 1.

For the header, use a description that identifies the report's significance in the Page header—dates, clients alphabetically by last name, or whatever signifies this report. This is the place for information about the report that you want to see on every page.

Using Titles

In the title section, there usually are only two items: the name of the column, and an underline character to emphasize this title. You can place an unsuppressible blank line in this section to improve the look of your report. To create an unsuppressible blank line, place the cursor anywhere on the line indicated and press Ctrl-Backspace. This creates a small, non-printing triangle △.

The line containing the △ does not close up at print time, although there is no other data to hold it. In Quick Reports, the names of the fields you selected in the initial field-selection screen are the default column titles. Thus, the example report form for CHECKS looks like figure 6.8.

- - - -Page Header - ■■■■■■■
                                                         PAGE: ■■■■
- - - -Titles -

CHECK   CHECK_DATE   PAYEE   ACCOUNT   AMOUNT   RETURNED
- - - - - - - - - - - - - - - - - - - - - - - - - - - - - - - - - - - - - - - - - - - - - -
△
- - - -Detail -
■■■■   ■■■■■■   ■■■■   ■■■■■   ■■■■■   ■■
- - - -Page Footer -
- - - -Summary Section -

                                                         =========
                                                         ■■■■■

Check register report with default settings.

Using the up-, down-, left-, and right-arrow keys, you can move your cursor around the screen to any location, add new fields, rewrite the title section, change the underline character, and adjust the report to your liking. You can personalize it, as shown in figure 6.9.

```
....Page Header.........................................
                            My Checkbook Report - ■■■■■■■
                            PAGE: ■■■■
....Titles..............................................

CHECK #   CHECK DATE   PAYEE   ACCOUNT   AMOUNT   RETURNED
-------   ----------   -----   -------   ------   --------

⌂
....Detail..............................................
■■■■    ■■■■■■    ■■■■    ■■■■    ■■■■    ■■
....Page Footer........................................
....Summary Section....................................
                                       =========
Check Totals                           ■■■■■■
```

FIG. 6.9

Enhanced check register report.

When the report is saved and you print it either to the screen or on your printer, it will produce the printout shown in figure 6.10.

```
                    My Checkbook Report  -  04-16-92
                                                      PAGE: 1
CHECK #   CHECK DATE   PAYEE   ACCOUNT     AMOUNT   RETURNED

2         04-03-1992   2       Payroll      16.50   Y
7         04-04-1992   2       Household    35.00   Y
8         04-14-1992   3       Household   150.00   Y
4         04-03-1992   1       Insurance   142.00   N
6         04-10-1992   2       Payroll      16.50   Y
9         04-15-1992   4       Supplies     79.00   N
                                          ======
                       Check totals        439.00
```

FIG. 6.10

Printed version of the check register report.

Using Details

The fields, shown as the dashed lines in figures 6.8 and 6.9, are in the Detail section. When the report is printed, the fields from each record appear in column form, one after another, as shown in figure 6.10. The Detail section may be expanded in depth by inserting more lines using F9 (Line) key. The most common reasons to do this are to place two or more fields together in the same area before the next record begins, and the need to print multiple lines from a Memo (or long character) field.

NOTE Alpha Four assumes that blank lines should be suppressed. To force a blank line to remain blank, place the cursor on the line that should be blank and press Ctrl-Backspace. This places the small house symbol on the screen to hold that line.

Using Page Footers

The Page Footer section is where you can define any calculation that helps the reader of the report interpret the data shown in the report— on a page by page basis. Page footers generally are useful for error checking. If the report total at the end is wrong, then you can check the figures, one page at a time, rather than line by line, until the error is detected. Using the Report Parameters screen, you can choose to have the footer printed on just the first page or on every page.

Using a Summary Section

Quick Report automatically creates a summary field for any numeric field you select using F2 and places these fields in the summary section. These fields are given the default setting of TOTAL and appear in the Define summary fields section. The summary section also is where you can place your own calculated fields as needed in the report. You may, for example, type the **Checks totals** and place the fields to follow in the summary section.

For example, in the checkbook report, you might want to know how many checks were written in the period this report covers. Move the cursor to the place in the summary section where the information should appear, and then press F2 to choose the CHECK_NO field from the CHECKS database. Alpha Four displays another pop-up box showing the following choices:

Summary
Value
First

Last
Count
Biggest
Smallest
Advanced

If you choose Value, the result on the report is the value in the field shown as the last record. Value refers to the actual contents of the field. If the field is a character field, such as CITY, the name of the city in the last record is the value displayed. In this case, you should select Count. This forces the report to calculate a count of how many records are in the report. When First or Last is chosen, only the value in the first or last record is shown on the report. This is useful, for example, to give emphasis to the first or last item in a range or grouping of records. The Biggest and Smallest options report on the largest and smallest data in the defined range.

 CAUTION If you choose Last when placing a date field in a summary section, the date that shows is the date of the last record, not necessarily the last date in the series of records.

Note that these options are for character and date fields. If you chose a numeric field, the options would include Total and Average. For a logical (True/False) field, the options include only **Value, First,** and **Last,** plus the **A**dvanced version of the same. Memo fields have no special options at all. The Summary Fields screen is shown in figure 6.11.

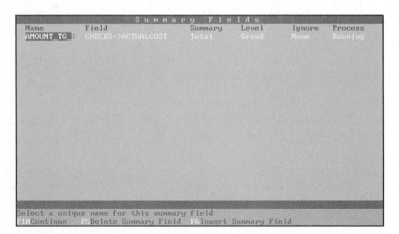

FIG. 6.11

Summary Fields appear in the SUMMARY database.

If you choose **A**dvanced, the program asks that you make choices that, otherwise, are installed as a default for the field. These are choices that relate to the field if it is in the summary section. Alpha Four permits you to use these choices in any section, but they rarely are used other than in a summary fashion. The Advanced definition is examined in greater depth in Chapter 7.

You may notice that once a field has been defined in the summary section, it does not disappear automatically when the field is removed from the report layout screen. If, during experimentation with your report, you create several summary fields and remove them from the screen with the Delete key, they are still in the summary section. When these fields are no longer useful on the report, you can delete them from the summary section using the F5 (Delete Summary Field) key.

When a memo field is selected, Alpha Four simply places the dashed lines on the report with no alternatives offered. Using the window, you can make the field scroll or word-wrap within a certain area of the report. Additional lines can be added and extra ones deleted, in the detail section or other sections, using the F9 (Line) key or Alt-I to insert or Alt-D to delete a row. The size of the window and length permitted for the memo field are defined in formatting Options (Alt-O).

Using Formatting Options

The process of placing fields can become confusing and the results not always what you expect. In Version 1.1 and higher, Alpha Four offers the chance to review the exact definition of the fields you have placed using the Formatting Options choice, found by pressing F2 and O for Options or Alt-O from the report layout screen. Formatting Options shows each field that has been defined as belonging on this report. It defines the source of the field, such as the current database, the SYSTEM database, or in the case of a set, one of the associated databases. Formatting Options also notes where the field is located on the report: the detail section, the page header, or the summary section.

Length versus Window

Changes may be made on this important screen to define certain characteristics of the fields, such as the length of the field or the window through which it is viewed, or the placement of data within the field (justification: left, right, and center). If the length of a field, such as CITY is defined as 20 characters, but you know that you need only 15 spaces for the longest city on your list, then you can save space across your report by changing the length of the field.

T I P	The + and - keys lengthen and shorten fields on which the cursor is resting.

Length, in this case, is different from, but related to, the defined length of the field. Take the example of a field, such as PROD_DESC (product description). This field probably needs 40 characters, but to fit this field into the desired layout design, you may only have room for 20 characters. By defining the window as 20 characters, a second line is added below the first record line into which the additional words in the Product description scroll.

Justification

The column headed Just defines the placement of text within the field: left, center, right, or none.

Data

On the formatting options screen, the column called Data permits the user to define an entry as Value or Unique. This refers to the case of a list that has duplicate entries. If Unique is chosen, the first occurrence of the data is printed, but subsequent occurrences of the data are not. This technique can improve the readability of many reports dramatically.

Format

In the Format column, the choices differ according to the kind of field being considered.

For character fields, the choices deal primarily with showing the data in upper- and lowercase. X adds wordwrap to long fields and memos.

In date fields, the choices consist of the several ways dates can be represented: MM_DD_YYY, DD_MM_YYYY, DD Month YYYY, or Month DD, YYYY.

The formats for numeric fields include the placement of dollar signs ($) and commas in appropriate places. You also can format a number to be printed in Extended format or English—you can print either *$25.00* or *Twenty-five dollars and no cents*, as on a check.

T I P

In the developmental stage of some complex reports, you often include the specific index needed for the report at the top of the sheet. Then, if the report prints in an unexpected way, the problem can be detected more quickly. The SYSTEM database field name for the index is INDEX_NAME.

The only mathematical calculation on the preceding report described for the CHECKS database is the total of the AMOUNT field in the Summary section. This calculation appears automatically when you choose the field during the Quick Report setup.

The Quick Report places a calculated TOTAL field in the Summary section for any numeric field you choose for your report: PARTS_NO, INV_NO, TAX_RATE, or any field defined as numeric, but not always appropriately selected. This is another reason why data, such as ZIP codes and parts numbers, should be stored in character fields, not numeric fields. Numeric fields do not hold leading 0s—the ZIP 02125 would give 2125 in a numeric field.

Several calculated fields can be used to enhance your Checks Paid report. Because you must review the data gathered into groups by the Payee, you must define more complex calculated fields. For example, rather than simply identifying the Payee by numbers, you might create a calculate field that you can call WHO. The process requires the following steps:

1. Press F2 to choose the Fields screen.

2. Choose Define Calculated Fields.

3. Enter the field name **WHO** and type the following expression:

```
if(trim(PAYEE)="Green Stationery","1",
if(trim(PAYEE)="Mike Smith","2",
if(trim(PAYEE)="Family Foods","3,"
if(trim(PAYEE)="CASH","4",
if(trim(PAYEE)="R & T Realty Trust","5"," ")))))
```

This expression, of course, can be placed all on one line, but for clarity you can add some spaces to make it easier to read.

After the Calculated field has been defined, it can be selected from the newly created Calculated database. This is a logical entity that cannot be managed in the same way as a database you create yourself because it is created by Alpha Four when you define calculated fields.

When you press F2 (Fields), you can see that the listing of databases now has four choices. As shown in figure 6.12, the calculated database has been added to the CHECKS, SYSTEM, and SUMMARY databases.

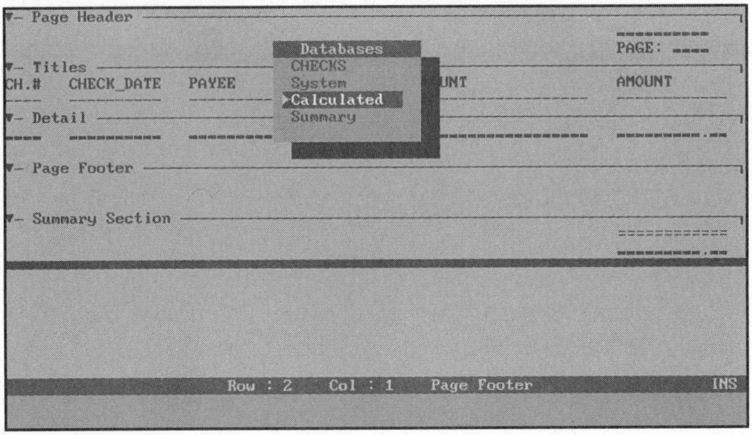

FIG. 6.12

The fields box now shows the Calculated database.

The real fields in your database appear in CHECKS. The DATE and INDEX_NAME and many more appear in the SYSTEM database. Your newly created WHO field appears in the Calculated database. Alpha Four has created another logical database called the Summary database in which you can find the TOTAL fields for the PAYEE subgroup and the grand total for the entire report. These last fields are given new names by Alpha Four as they are entered. The names reflect the kind of summary field they are, what grouping level they are on, and whether the field is preprocessed or calculated before the report is run (see fig. 6.11).

Preprocessing refers to the technique of telling the report to calculate certain fields so that other fields can be calculated using their data. If, for example, you were to ask the report to tell you what percentage of the total amount of all checks in this report was spent on each subgroup, you would need to ask the program to preprocess the grand total of all check amounts in order to divide that amount by the subtotal of each subgroup.

Applying Basic Formatting Options

Your first view of the report may give you a surprise. Fields that you thought were in the right position look different when only the data is showing. The data itself may need to be treated to make it look the way you want. Dates and numbers are particularly in need of formatting.

In Chapter 5, you learned that you could use the field rules to force capitalization to suit your needs. Similar functions apply in formatting options for reports, labels, forms, browse tables, and letters.

Making Lines Disappear

For character fields used on a report, there is one additional format that can be applied. The — (dash) can be used to make a line disappear if the field to which it is applied is blank. Suppose that you want a report of all checks you have written from your checkbook register that have been returned by the bank. You have a logical field for RETURNED, which contains Y or N. A second calculated field can test RETURNED to see whether the condition is True or False. The calculation will leave the field blank if the condition is false, but will enter CHR(127), the non-suppressible line character △, if the RETURNED field contains Y. The calculated test field is placed on your report with the — format. Thus, the data in the test field causes the entire line to be blank if the value in RETURNED is N.

The calculated field expression should look like the following:

```
IF(RETURNED,CHR(127),"")
```

Formatting Memo Fields

Memo fields are a special case on reports. The X format causes a multi-line memo field to break between words rather than breaking them apart in inappropriate places. If you want the memo field to print with its entire contents on the report, you must add the @ symbol, which tells the printer to accept the memo field and *expand* as required.

Occasionally you want to stack fields one above another in the detail section. This method works well unless there is a memo field involved. The following is a sample of the problem:

Name and address	Comments: (the memo field here)
Johnny Smith 132 Main Street Anytown, WI 30201	Johnny is a delight to have in our class. He is prompt and his homework is always well prepared.
Mary Mantoya 44 Broadway Anytown, WI 30201	Mary enjoys arithmetic more than most girls her age. She may wish to consider a future in teaching. She communicates well.

The memo field is interrupted by the second and third address fields below the name field. As this is plainly an unacceptable report, another format must be considered.

A possible solution to this kind of memo field difficulty is the following:

NAME	STREET	CITY/ST/ZIP
Johnny Smith	132 Main Street	Anytown, WI 30201
COMMENTS:	Johnny is a delight to have in our class. He is prompt and his homework is always well prepared.	
Mary Mantoya	44 Broadway	Anytown, WI 30201
COMMENTS:	Mary enjoys arithmetic more than most girls her age. She may want to consider a future in teaching. She communicates well.	

Formatting Numeric Fields

Number fields often refer to dollar amounts in reports. Alpha Four's formatting options offer nine different options for numbers, whether they are currency or simple numbers. The formatting symbols for number fields are listed in table 6.1.

Table 6.1 Formatting Symbols for Number Fields

Symbol	Effect
B	Blanks the number if the value is zero. Add to any numeric format.
*	Fills the leading blanks with asterisks, as on a check: *****$95,000.32. Add to any numeric format.
-	Used to suppress the whole line if this field is blank. Other fields on the same line will be deleted if this field is blank. B must also be used in this field because it is numeric and will usually display 0.00 instead of a blank.
C	Forces all caps for use with the extended formats: NINETY FIVE THOUSAND AND 32/100.
L	Forces words to print in lowercase in extended formats: ninety five thousand and 32/100.

Symbol	Effect
F	Forces the first letter of the field to uppercase when used with extended format: Ninety five thousand and 32/100.
W	Forces word-wrap when used with extended formats.
Y	Forces words to print in lowercase with the first letter of each word in capitals when used with extended formats: Ninety Five Thousand And 32/100.
Z	Forces words to print in lowercase with the first letter of the field in uppercase: Ninety five and 32/100.

NOTE The terms *expanded field* or *expanded number* refer to the elongation of the area in which the data is printed when the format is defined as extended.

Formatting Date Fields

Not only is date formatting available for nine different ways to write a date, but four of the extended date formats can be used with capitalization and word-wrapping functions as well. The codes to format dates are listed in table 6.2.

Table 6.2 Codes To Format Dates

Code	Format	Example
1	MM-DD-YYYY	01-07-1922
2	DD-MM-YYYY	02-12-1968
3	DD Month YYYY	2 February 1937
4	Month DD, YYYY	May 17, 1908
5	MM-YY	09-61
6	MM-DD-YY	09-19-61
7	DD-MM-YY	28-01-59
8	Month DDxx, YYYY	March 23rd, 1954
9	DD-MMM-YY	1-Feb-90

Saving and Previewing Your Report

As of Version 1.1, Alpha Four's report writer has included the **Preview** function to save you time while creating report layouts. Preview is included in both report layouts and mailing labels. This enables you to select F10 (Continue) to save the report but not leave the report writer, rather than select **P** for **Preview**. This choice brings up the range setting screen if the decision must be made to change the primary index, the range or records to be included in the report, or the filter.

If you are dealing with a small number of records or a sample database, you may see the report flash on and off the screen before you can get a look at the details. Press the PgUp key as often as needed to bring the top of the report back to view. From this position, you can press F7 (Window on/off) to split the screen. This enables you to see both ends of a long report at the same time. Use the right- and left-arrow keys to scroll through the columns and the Tab key to move between windows. The F8 (Size Window) key gives you control of the placement of the separation between the two windows.

Printing Your Report

After creating the layouts for your reports, forms, browse tables, mailing labels, and letters, the next step is printing your creation. This is where the rubber meets the road. Your great formatting skills and super tricks with indexing show here.

To print a report, a set of mailing labels, an input form, a browse table, or a letter, you select the **Print** option from the Main Menu. Alpha Four shows the five kinds of output listed on the Print Options menu. If you make a selection for which no layout has been created, Alpha Four displays a warning. If, for example, you select mailing labels but there is no layout for this output, you see the following warning:

```
You must first define a mailing label by using : Layout /
Mailing label
```

Press the Enter key or F10 to continue.

In the course of this chapter, you have created a report layout, so from the Print Options menu, select Report. A list of the reports you have created appear by their alphabetical designation and with the description you gave the report. Choose the report you want to print by moving the highlight to the name of that report and pressing Enter.

The range settings screen appears. On the range setting screen, all the functions described in Chapter 5 on Indexes and Ranges are available. When you have adjusted the selection of records using this screen, press F10 to continue. Next, Alpha Four offers three destinations for the printing: **S**creen, **P**rinter, and **F**ile.

If you select **P**rinter, one more screen appears, which asks you to identify the proper printer. The default printer can be used, or you can define one or more printer settings using the Printer Configuration menu. Press F10 to continue.

Defining a Printer Driver

Most of the decisions affecting the output have been made during the layout process. Some decisions, however, will be affected by the printer that you use to print your report.

To select a printer, you first must identify the printer driver available. From the Main Menu, select **O**ther. Alpha Four displays the **O**ther menu, which offers two choices: **I**nformation and **C**onfiguration.

Select **C**onfiguration, **P**rinter configuration, **C**reate/Edit Printer Configuration. If any printers already have been identified, they appear on the next screen. If none are chosen, select an unused letter between A and Z. A long list of printers with their model numbers appears. Use the up- and down-arrow keys to find the name of your printer. Press the Enter key to select that name.

Figure 6.13 shows the screen you see when you have selected a printer.

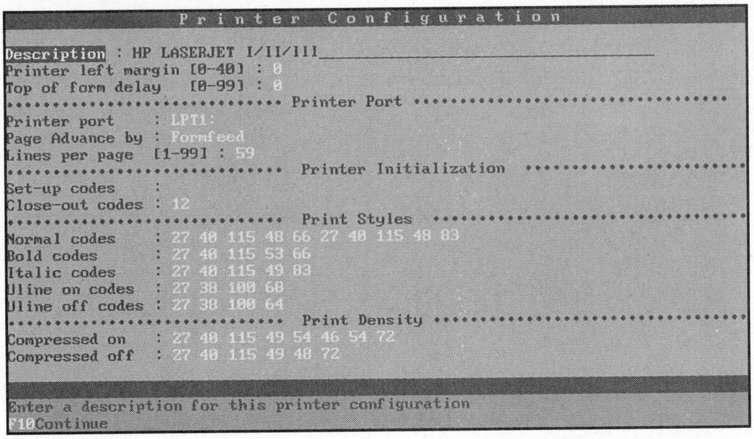

FIG. 6.13

The Printer
Configuration
screen with
settings for
Hewlett-Packard
laser printers.

This screen contains the numbers or settings that will be sent to your printer by the computer when you select this printer. If, for example, you select the HP LaserJet I/II/III printer, the default page length is shown as 59. If you select the HP LaserJet II Envelope 4-by-9.5-inch printer, the lines per page are shown as 24. You can change these numbers, but be careful in doing so. They have been designed and tested for the most common settings for each of these printers. If your needs are unusual, then you can make changes to adjust for them.

When you set a page length in a report layout, that setting overrides the default setting established by the printer driver. If you have problems making your report pages break in the right place, you may need to adjust the page length on the report itself and on the configuration screen for the printer you are using.

Summary

This chapter has outlined the basic information needed to create output using your database in the traditional columnar format of the report writer. The subject of sending your reports to the printer and how to set up your printer was explored. This chapter also touched briefly on the subjects of calculated fields, groups and subgroups, and summary fields.

Chapter 7 explores these topics further and examines other kinds of reports: mailing labels, browse tables, input forms, and letters. These reports are designed in the Layouts selection on the Alpha Four Main Menu. Each of these reports can be printed to the printer, to the screen, or to a file using the Main Menu Print option.

Developing Strategies for Special Reporting

Not believe in Santa Claus?
You might as well not believe in fairies.
Francis Pharcellus Church, *Is there a Santa Claus?*

In this chapter, you tackle interesting concepts of reporting. The details of selecting and formatting fields are discussed in Chapter 6, and you expand on that knowledge in this chapter. This chapter thoroughly examines the concept of subgrouping a report and explores mailing-label construction and form letter development.

In this chapter, your active participation in these projects is recommended. Unless you are experienced in other database projects or talented in visualization, performing the steps hands-on is the way you should follow this section.

Later in this chapter, two other databases are used with multiple sub-groupings and the indexes required to make reports work properly. The first database is INVOICE, which is created with 7 fields and 11 records. The second database, created in Chapter 4, is SALES. The SALES database contains 4 fields and 20 records. With these files, you will learn to manipulate the sections of a report and summarize data.

Letters are included in this chapter, because they are considered reports in the context of a database-management system. Merging data with letters is a frequent function in office and home business operations. Using Alpha Four, you can print your letters by using the existing functions or print the letters to an ASCII format to be retrieved and enhanced in a word processor or desktop publishing system.

Using Advanced Reporting Techniques

When you print a columnar report, Alpha Four usually shows the records one after another in the order in which they were entered. If you use the Index command, you will see the topmost selection listed by **A.**Record Number. This entry is followed by other indexes you have created, such as **B.**Last Name, or **C.**Zip Code. When an index is selected from the Main Menu to be the Primary Index, records appear in that order in View and Browse mode. Unless a report has been designed to use a specific index or range of records, it prints using the current primary index, unless the index is changed at print time (see Chapter 4 concerning indexes).

Often, however, you need to see records in groups. You may want to see all the records for a particular vendor or patient or donor grouped together with a total at the bottom. Whatever the business of your database, that business indicates the kinds of groups you need.

Consider a file of customer information. Each customer has one record containing name and address information. This information is a group: customer. Within that group, each customer can have several or many invoices. Invoices can be grouped by customer to show a total for all invoices for any or all customers. In this case, invoices is a subgroup; customers is the group. To put a still finer point on this matter, each invoice has one, several, or many line items. Line items are grouped together to make an invoice. Therefore, line items (level 3) are grouped by invoice (level 2), by customer (level 1).

A summary of the details is shown in figure 7.1.

```
Customer Allen
     Invoice 1              Qty      Price      Total
          Line item 1        2       2.00        4.00
          Line item 2        4       3.00       12.00
          Line item 3        1       1.50        1.50
     Invoice 1 Total                             17.50

     Invoice 3              Qty      Price      Total
          Line item 1        3       4.50       13.50
          Line item 2        2       3.00        6.00
     Invoice 3 Total                             19.50

     Invoice 5              Qty      Price      Total
          Line item 1        3       5.50       16.50
     Invoice 5 Total                 16.50

Total for Customer Allen                         53.50

Customer Jones
     Invoice 2              Qty      Price      Total
          Line item 1        2       4.50        9.00
          Line item 2        1       1.25        1.25
          Line item 3        2       3.00        6.00
     Invoice 2 Total                             16.25

     Invoice 4              Qty      Price      Total
          Line item 1        3       1.25        3.75
          Line item 2        2       1.25        2.50
     Invoice 4 Total                 6.25

Total for Customer Jones                         22.50

                                               =====

Grand total for all customers                    76.00
```

FIG. 7.1

Three grouping
levels.

If you count the list above, you find 2 customers, 5 invoices, and 11
entries listed as line items on the invoice. The line items are particular
items billed, goods, or services. The same item, or at least something
described with the same identifier, can be *sold* again and again. On an
invoice, a particular item may be identified generically by a part number or described rhetorically as the following:

Description	Quantity	Price	Total
Part No. XYZ	1 box	29.95	29.95
Customized Design Development	3 hours	75.00	225.00

Part No. XYZ is simply a designation of a particular item that has a price. A quantity figure applied to the item gives a total price. The extended prices added together give a total for an invoice.

To discover how many of parts No. XYZ have been sold, you do not need to know who has purchased them or on what invoice. You only need to examine a list of line items grouped by part number or description.

The next group up in the hierarchy is invoices, which represent the totals of the prices and which customer has or has not paid the total of the invoice. Therefore, invoices have little meaning without a relationship to the customer. The significance of the individual line items has been diminished. As you move up the scale of groupings to customer, you are interested in which invoices have or have not been paid. The individual line items have dropped out of significance entirely, and individual invoices have been reduced to the significance of merely one part of a whole: the total accounts receivable from one customer.

In fact, you can collapse the report into figure 7.2. This report shows only two groups: Customer and Invoice.

Customer Allen	Items	Total
Invoice 1 Total	7	17.50
Invoice 3 Total	5	19.00
Invoice 5 Total	3	16.50
Total for Customer Allen	15	53.50
Customer Jones		
Invoice 2 Total	5	16.25
Invoice 4 Total	5	6.25
Total for Customer Jones	10	22.50
Grand total for all customers		76.00

FIG. 7.2

Two grouping levels.

To reduce further the amount of detail that a report can give, the details of each invoice can be collapsed so that the report has only one group, Customer, which serves as the detail section of this report. Also, a *count* field on the number of invoices might be useful. In that case, the report looks like figure 7.3.

Customer	Invoices	Total Due
Customer Allen	3	$ 53.50
Customer Jones	2	$ 22.50
Total Accounts Receivable:		$ 76.00

FIG. 7.3

One grouping level; summary data only.

After you have created an index on the field or fields that provide the group, that index can become the basis of *subgrouping* a report. Because the columnar report format gives you areas in which to create headers and footers for groups, the group can be totaled, averaged, counted, or otherwise analyzed in comparison to other groups and in comparison with the total of the records in the report.

In figure 7.1, you have a detailed listing of invoices by customer name. In figure 7.2, you have an itemized account for each customer. In figure 7.3, you have an accounts receivable list.

Organizing Your Data

Now that you have read about the process, you can start organizing your data. First, you need the database with data that will perform properly. Using the techniques from Chapters 1 and 3, create a database called LINEITEM with the following fields:

Field	Field Name	Type	Width	Decimal
1	CUST_ID	Character	10	
2	INVOIC_NO	Character	4	
3	LINE_ITEM	Character	2	
4	DESCRIPT	Character	25	
5	PRICE	Numeric	10	2
6	QTY	Numeric	8	2
7	TOTAL	Numeric	10	2

You need 11 records showing 2 customers (Allen and Jones), 7 different products, and a total of 5 invoices. To save typing and verify your numbers, make TOTAL a calculated field with a field rule that multiplies PRICE * QTY as shown in Chapter 5.

Enter the following records into your LINEITEM database as shown in figure 7.4.

FIG. 7.4

Data entered without order.

ALLEN	1	1	Widgets	2.00	2.00	4.00
JONES	2	3	Gadgets	3.00	2.00	6.00
ALLEN	1	3	Hood Ornaments	1.50	1.00	1.50
ALLEN	1	2	Gadgets	3.00	4.00	12.00
JONES	2	2	Doo-dads	1.25	1.00	1.25
ALLEN	5	1	Jim jams	5.50	3.00	16.50
JONES	4	2	Crazy Weasels	1.25	2.00	2.50
ALLEN	3	1	Who Ha's	4.50	3.00	13.50
ALLEN	3	2	Gadgets	3.00	2.00	6.00
JONES	2	1	Who Ha's	4.50	2.00	9.00
JONES	4	1	Doo-dads	1.25	3.00	3.75

Notice how much easier it is to read and use the same list when it is organized and separated by a line as shown in figure 7.5.

FIG. 7.5

Data organized in a logical manner.

CUST	INVO	LI	DESCRIPT	PRICE	QTY	TOTAL
ALLEN	1	1	Widgets	2.00	2.00	4.00
ALLEN	1	2	Gadgets	3.00	4.00	12.00
ALLEN	1	3	Hood Ornaments	1.50	1.00	1.50
JONES	2	1	Who Ha's	4.50	2.00	9.00
JONES	2	2	Doo-dads	1.25	1.00	1.25
JONES	2	3	Gadgets	3.00	2.00	6.00
ALLEN	3	1	Who Ha's	4.50	3.00	13.50
ALLEN	3	2	Gadgets	3.00	2.00	6.00
JONES	4	1	Doo-dads	1.25	3.00	3.75
JONES	4	2	Crazy Weasels	1.25	2.00	2.50
ALLEN	5	1	Jim jams	5.50	3.00	16.50

Creating an Index

In figure 7.5, the list begins to assume greater visual significance when the first three records showing just Allen's Invoice No. 1 is separated by a line from Jones' Invoice No. 2. and the following records are arranged in a similar manner.

One index serves all three of these reports. To create this index, from the Main Menu, select Index/ranges, Create an index, and give the index a unique name. As shown in figure 7.6, you select CUST_ID, INVOIC_NO, and LINE_ITEM as the three levels of the index. You should select this as the primary index before starting to design these reports. In order to produce reports such as the ones in figures 7.1-7.3, you need to have this index to match the questions being asked.

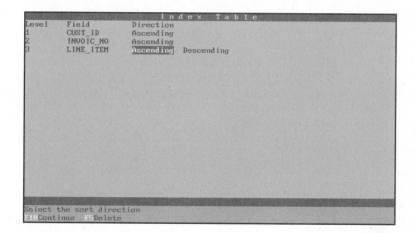

FIG. 7.6

Select three items to make a multi-level index.

Figure 7.1 has the most complex ordering system, because it is grouped on two different fields. In that table, the request is for the details of every invoice for every customer (in this case, only Allen and Jones). This index must be an index to identify the customer (CUST_ID), the invoice number (INVOIC_NO), and line items (ITEM_NO). The report returns the information on each line item on each invoice totaled and totaled again by customer.

In figure 7.2, you are asking the data for a summary of invoices for each customer. In this case, the response gives you the totals of five summarized invoices and the total for each customer.

In figure 7.3, the report summarizes the details to give just the totals owed by each customer and counts the invoices.

Complete the following steps to create the report shown in figure 7.1.

1. From the Main Menu, select **L**ayouts. Alpha Four responds with the Layouts menu. Select **R**eports, **C**reate/edit a report and choose an unused letter to identify the report. Choose **Q**uick Setup and give the report a significant name, such as Detailed Invoice Report.

2. On the Quick Report Parameters screen, make the number of grouping levels 2. Press F10. When you press F10, the Grouping Parameters screen appears. Select the two fields that represent the groups you want to see. To select the field for Group 1, press F2, select Fields, choose the primary database, and select the field representing CUST_ID as a Value. Press Enter. Press Enter again to drop to Group 2.

3. Repeat this process for the next group, selecting the INVOIC_ID. Press F10 to continue.

4. The next screen enables you to identify the fields that will be laid out in the detail section of your report. Use F2 to select LINE_ITEM, DESCRIPT, PRICE, QTY, and TOTAL.

5. When you are finished selecting these fields and press F10 to continue, the fields do not reach the right side of the screen. If you want the report to indent in a manner similar to that shown in figure 7.1, use the arrow keys, the Insert key, and the space bar to move titles and details to better positions. You can remove a field entirely by putting the cursor on the dashed line and pressing Delete.

6. Below Group 1 Header, type **Customer**. After this word, press F2 to select the CUST_ID field as a Value from the database. Move the cursor to the Group 1 Footer, below the TOTAL field in the detail section, and press F2 to select the current database. After pressing F2, choose Select Fields, and LINE_ITEM. Choose the field TOTAL with the designation of Total.

7. In the Group 2 Header section, type **Invoice No**. After this word, press F2 to select INVOIC_NO as a Value. In the Group 2 Footer section, move the cursor to a position just below the TOTAL field in the Group 1 footer. Press F2 to select the TOTAL field, again asking for the designation of Total, as shown in figure 7.7.

8. Press Alt-P to save and preview this report. Verify that the Range Settings screen shows the index for CUST_ID + INVOIC_NO + LINE_ITEM. Press F10 (Continue) to view the report.

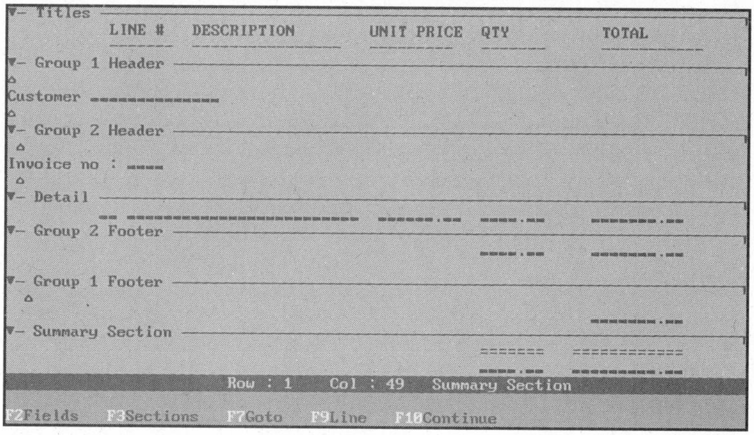

FIG. 7.7

The report layout
screen shows
Group 1 Header
and Footer fields
and Group 2
Header and
Footer fields as
well as a detail
section.

NOTE When the report looks the way you want, you can make the next revision by using save **A**s, instead of **S**ave, to create a new report.

You can revise the first report to create a new report that looks like figure 7.2. Select F3 (Sections) to delete the detail section and the Group 1 Header. Enter the invoice number as a value in the appropriate location within the Group 1 Footer section.

In figure 7.2, the question is asked: *What is the total for each invoice for each customer?* The answer appears in the Group 2 Footer.

Using Special Reporting Techniques

The **L**ayouts selection from the Main Menu brings you to the choice for **R**eports, **M**ail labels, **F**orms, **B**rowse tables, and **L**etters. Each choice except Letters gives you the option to **C**reate/edit, **B**orrow, or **E**rase. In the case of Letters, you cannot borrow because letters are independent, to a degree, of any single database. A letter created by using one database can be printed successfully from another, as long as the fields selected are the same in both files.

Borrowing a Format

Borrowing a format saves time and adds consistency. In Alpha Four, the term *borrow* refers to the time-saving capability of copying an existing report, form, label, or browse table from one file into another one. Despite the fact that all the fields may not match, borrowing the format saves hours of labor and can significantly improve consistency between reports of all kinds.

Using Save To Create a Support File

All five forms of output files use the A-Z designation to identify themselves. In the development phase, if you are working with a complex layout and want to test a new operation or restyle the layout or identify a new range of records to print, save yourself the time it takes to design a similar field. After a report, form, browse table, mail label, or letter has been designed and saved once, edit an existing document and, instead of using the F10 (Save) function, use save **As**. When save **As** is chosen, the program immediately asks you to select an available letter from a list of remaining letters. Remember, however, that Save and Preview will save under the original report name, so save **As** and Edit the new report letter before previewing changes.

T I P   Remember that another 26 letters are available by creating a set, using the *reporting* database as the primary database.

Refining Your Reports with Ranges and Filters

When you have finished the design of your report, you must be able to print the right records. Suppose that on a monthly basis your bookkeeper wants to see a summary of the invoices that remain unpaid. This effort will be frustrated by the lack of a summary other than the reports themselves. In Part II, you will create a *transaction* database called INVOICES that will become part of a SET in which each line item is a part. When you work in a set, the individual line items are linked to each invoice by the invoice number. A PAYMENTS database is necessary to receive payments from customers. Eventually, you post the payments to the TOTAL fields in INVOICE and add the amounts of payments to the CUSTOMER database. With this facility, you can search for specific invoices, by dates, by balances due, and other items.

You may want to filter the records to show only those with a balance greater than zero and an invoice date greater than 30 days after the billing date. However, this procedure must be based on another field that indicates payments made to cover each invoice. The following filter can be developed to display the date of the invoice and the condition of the total field:

> INV_DATE=>SYSTEM->DATE + 30 .and. TOTAL < 1

If you have a database in which a date field exists for this purpose, you can use the preceding filter. First, define and print the reports defined above. At the range setting screen during the print process, move the cursor to the Filter line. Type the filter on that line. Move the cursor to the Filter status line and make the filter Active.

In the current configuration, you cannot ask the software to show only the records where the invoice total is greater than X amount. To make this happen, you must transform the data into a set (see Chapter 8 concerning sets).

Creating Calculated and Summary Databases

When you create your database, the process of defining your fields and assigning them field names, types, and lengths produces physical fields that then mark the places where data is located in your computer. When you create a report using a calculated field and define a name and an expression that performs some computation or activity, this action creates a *logical* entity called the *calculated database*. When you place fields in summary areas of a report—or identify fields as operating in a summarizing manner—you are creating a logical entity called the *summary database*. Creating these fields establishes the new logical database, which then can be seen on the pop-up box when you select F2 (Fields), as shown in figure 7.8.

Fields that are created in the calculated and summary databases operate quite differently from *real* fields. To use the analogy of a spreadsheet, calculated fields work on rows of data, one record at a time across one or several fields. Summary fields work on columns of data, across one or several records. Figure 7.9 shows the rows of data regarding monthly expenses calculated. The totals at the bottom of the columns shows each month's data summarized.

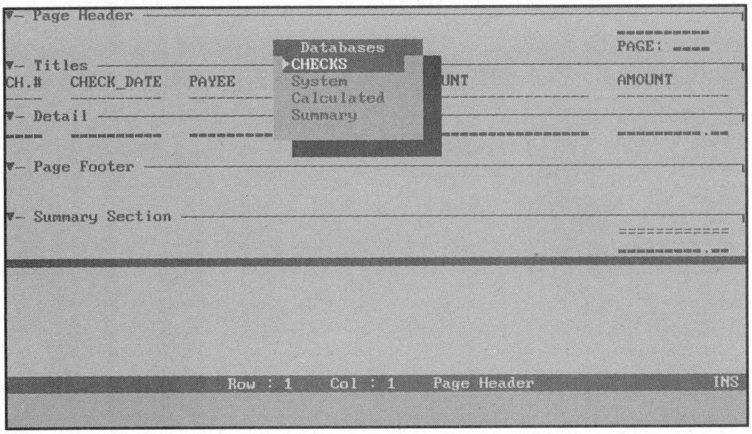

FIG. 7.8

Three logical databases exist on this report.

FIG. 7.9

A spreadsheet works with columns and rows.

Item	Jan	Feb	Mar	Total
Rent	900	900	900	2700
Food	234	214	432	880
Utilities	321	376	309	1006
Total	1455	1490	1641	4586

The fields in the column at the end of each row calculate the totals for each kind of expense. The fields in the row at the bottom of each column summarize the records of expenses for each month.

Using Calculated versus Summary Fields

When a field that has been created in the summary or the calculated database is placed on a report, the designation of that field is assigned a prefix to designate its origin. Alpha Four shows the name of the field preceded by its type. Consider the following example:

CALC->SALES_TAX or SUMMARY->BALANCEDUE

Calc means that the field SALES_TAX is from the calculated database, while BALANCEDUE is from the SUMMARY database.

When you create a Quick Report, Alpha Four automatically places any numeric field in the summary section (the bottom band of the report layout) and defines that field as a total. This feature works well when summarizing the field is appropriate. For example, in the LINEITEM database above, the field called SUMMARY->TOTAL is created (labeled Grand total for all customers) to summarize all the TOTAL fields. If you create a report in which a field, such as unit price, is automatically placed on a report during a Quick Report session, the result is probably not what you want. You can remove that field by placing the highlight on the field and pressing the delete key.

When a field is defined as a summary field, Alpha Four makes it part of a *logical database* known as the Summary Database. A field becomes a summary field when it is given the definitions known as **A**dvanced. The field can be viewed in the summary database by using Alt-U. From the summary database, you can change the way that field behaves. The summary database indicates the name of the field as it is used on the layout, the full name of the field and its database, the form of summary (First, Biggest, Smallest, Total, Count, etc.) when each field is defined, and the level of the responding record (Grand, Page, or groups 1 through 9).

If you want to use the summary functions automatically when you place a field on the layout screen, select **A**dvanced from the Summary box. Depending on the kind of field you are selecting, the program will give you the following choices:

Type of field	Choices
Character fields	Value, First, Last, Count, Biggest, Smallest
Numeric field	Value, Total, Count, Average, First, Biggest, Smallest
Date field	Value, First, Last, Count, Biggest, Smallest
Logical field	Value, First, Last
Memo field	No choices

Placing Fields in Custom Reports

When you place a field on a report by using the Advanced mode, you also can define the level of grouping to which the field belongs. If you are not using any subgroups on that report, there is no sense in defining a field as the total of subgroup X. However, if you are using subgroups and need to see the totals on the subgroups, the Advanced mode provides a vital function.

Figure 7.10 is an example of the Chamber of Commerce count of tourists visits each month. The detail section of the report has been removed. The subgroups are first on Town, second on Month. The Group 2 total is the number following the month. The Group 2 total is a calculated field that summarizes the details of group 2.

Town	Month	Total
Big Piney:	January	234
	February	321
	March	542
Jay Em:	January	234
	February	321
	March	542
Medicine Bow:	January	234
	February	321
	March	542

FIG. 7.10

A sample with two subgroups and one calculated field.

NOTE To calculate subtotals that appear above a detail section, remember to set the selection from Running to Pre-processing.

Averaging with Zeros

Occasionally, a numeric field placed in a summary database becomes part of a calculation that is affected by an empty record or a blank. One example is a listing that reports on the monthly totals of sales of several products, some of which may have no sales during a period. When the average price is needed, the problem is to tell the program whether a figure that is blank or contains a zero should be figured into the average.

By using Alpha Four, you can employ a method of defining a field called Ignore Mode. Found on the Summary Fields screen, Ignore mode gives you four choices for a numeric field: None, Empty, Zero, and Both empty and zero. For a character field, there are two choices: None and Empty.

To understand Empty versus Zero, consider a teacher and two students. The students have had five tests this semester. If a missed test can be made up, then the blank place on the list does not take the student's average down. If a missed test is gone forever, then the average includes the zero.

	Zeros count	Zeros don't count	
Dick	10	Jane	10
	20		20
	15		15
	0		
	25		25
Average:	(70/5=14)	(70/4=17.5)	

Defining Mailing Labels

You learn in Chapter 6 that creating great looking reports is easy when you correctly use the tools that are offered by Alpha Four. The same can be said for defining mailing labels, forms, and browse tables. Remember that all of these reports can be printed or saved to the screen and printed or saved to an ASCII text file on the disk as well as actually sent to hard copy output on a printer.

Making Mailing Labels

A mailing label must be designed in a database that contains the appropriate fields. You can think of numerous other uses for labels: file folders, file boxes, little boxes for tiny parts, jelly jars, and three-ring notebooks filled with class notes.

As with other Layout procedures, the first steps to creating a label are selecting a blank letter and filling in the Label Parameters screen, as shown in figure 7.11.

To create a mailing label, select a database with the appropriate name and address fields and complete the following steps:

1. From the Main Menu, select **L**ayouts. Alpha Four presents the Layouts menu. Select **M**ailing labels, **C**reate/edit a mail label. Select an unused letter between A and Z and type a description on the Label description line of the Label Parameters screen that will tell you what kind of label is defined.

2. For a standard printer, the most common label stock is two- or three-across (8 1/2"-by-11" paper, with or without tractor-feed edges). On the fourth line of the Label Parameters screen, place a 2 or 3. This can be changed to suit different paper sizes. Press F10 to Continue.

3. The next screen shows a sample of the proposed mail label with your cursor blinking in the top corner. Press F2 to select a field from your database. Select the FIRSTNAME, MIDDLE, and LASTNAME fields for the top line. Put the address fields below the names and the City, State, and ZIP code fields on the next line. If you have a business name to include on the label, the field should be the second from the top.

4. Text can be added to your label to enhance its usefulness. The F9 key lets you insert and delete lines, left, right and center justify lines, and fill to the end with a character. The F7 (Goto) key brings you back to the Label Parameters screen for refinement of your earlier size and spacing decisions. If the bottom line says: `Print labels on continuous-feed paper: Yes`, but you are working with a laser printer and single sheets of labels, change the message to `No`. This adds two new lines to the screen that enable you to define the output in terms of rows of labels per page and the placement of the top margin. Press F10 to Continue.

5. If you need to define a specific range of records or a certain printer, those decisions are made on the **R**ange and Print Settings screen, also found by pressing the F7 (Goto) key from the label layout screen.

6. When the label begins to look the way you want, press Alt-P to save and **P**review your work. A password can be on the Save screen. If a password is defined, the software requires that the password be given in order to edit the label. Press F10 to save the label definition.

Using Pre-defined Label Definitions

The F4 (Pre-defined Sizes) key is a great time-saver that takes a lot of the guess work out of the label-making operation. Press F4 to see a selection of label sizes with the label width and height ready to choose. In Alpha Four, Version 2, there are 26 choices including Cheshire and 11 other standard sizes from 3M and 11 more from Avery. You will want to consider the length of the data you wish to see on the labels, as well as your budget when buying labels.

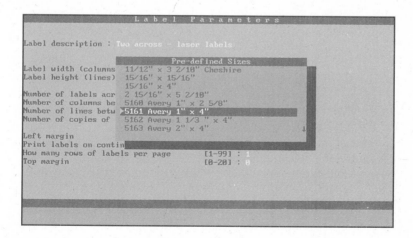

FIG. 7.11

The Label
Parameters
screen.

NOTE   There are only four pre-defined label sizes in Alpha Four,
Version 1.1 and below.

Two-across (two labels, side by side on the page) is generous and can
accommodate most names and addresses. However, if your purpose is
to make labels for small boxes for tiny parts to keep them safe on your
workbench, use a four- or five- or six-across label. One of the pre-
defined labels is the Avery 5267, 1/2"-by-1 3/4", a very small label, just
right to identify a data cartridge for tape backups or audio cassettes
(see fig. 7.12).

FIG. 7.12

You can select
standard size,
predefined labels
on this screen.

Individualizing Your Label for Your Needs

You can define your own label size. Suppose that you select the Avery 5161, which is 1"-by-4", a useful size for two-across labels. After you select the label, another box appears that requests advice on the size of type you want for the labels. The choices are the following:

	Label Size				
Characters per inch:		6	8	10	12	17
Lines per inch:	6	8			

The smaller the number of characters and lines per inch, the smaller the print and the closer together the lines. The normal or default choice is 10 characters per inch and six lines per inch.

Printing Multiple Copies of Labels

The number of copies of each label can be defined with a constant, such as 3, to indicate three copies to print every time. In Version 2, this field accepts a field name or an expression. This means that you can store the number of copies of a single label you want to print within each record. Further, you can define an expression to calculate how many copies should be printed, based on data in the record.

Suppose that you want to mail several documents to tenants with mailing addresses on Arlington Street but only one document to tenants of Berkeley Street. You can create an expression that checks the street address and calculates this matter for you.

Placing Fields on Your Label

The next step is to select the fields you want to see and place them where they should show. Use the shortcut Alt-F to select a field (Alt-T if you want to select the title with the field) or press F2 to choose other options. A name and address label will likely require that the fields are in the usual places, as required by the U.S. Postal Service.

Improving the Look of Your Label

To improve placement, you may need to insert or delete lines on the label. The F9 (Line) key produces these choices and several more that help you control the way the label prints. **L**eft, **R**ight and **C**enter justify controls placement of text, while **F**ill to end with a character enables you to decorate the label with any definable ASCII character you like. The Alpha Four Reference Manual Appendix contains a table of ASCII characters. With this as a guide, you can use a variety of symbols, such as the following:

♥   ☺   ♪♪   ✪   ↑   α

To create one of these characters, place the cursor where you want the character to appear, hold the Alt key down, as you would use the Shift key to make a capital letter, and enter the ASCII code number for that symbol using the numeric keys on the right side of the keyboard. For example, the heart symbol is 003.

If the results are not what you expect, check to make sure that the NumLock key is in the off position. When NumLock is on, the keys are used as numbers. When NumLock is off, those keys are directionals or, used with the Alt key, they produce the ASCII characters.

NOTE   ASCII stands for American Standard Code for Information Interchange. This is the common standard of symbolic communication between computers.

You must make a number of important decisions when you select the F7 (Goto) Key. If you choose label **P**arameters, you can redesign the size of the label and all other choices. **R**ange and Print Settings enable you to define both which records are to be printed and the index they will use, but also the output device which will be selected. This screen is important when labels must be printed with a specific printer or configuration (see sample 7.1).

Table 7.1 Range and Print Settings

Setting	Options
When to specify range settings	:Now at Print time
Range setting [A..Z, 0(Default), 1(Current)]	:1
When to specify output device	:Now at Print time
Output device	:Screen Printer File

continues

Table 7.1 Continued

Setting	Options
Specify Printer	:Now at Print time
Printer [A..Z, 0(Default), 1(Current)]	:1
Single Sheets	:Yes No
Compressed Print	:Yes No
Do Form-feed After Printing	:Yes No

The settings shown on table 7.1 are particularly useful when you are developing an application for other people to use. As the decisions you make on this screen reduce the decision-making at print time to a minimum. Those who are not familiar with manipulating the program will be grateful to you for using this feature.

As you save the layout of a mail label, the program offers the option of introducing a password of up to eight characters (Version 2 only.) If you define a password at this point, the label cannot be edited, borrowed, or erased without entering the right combination of characters. Once a password is defined, it can be removed by selecting **D**efine password and pressing **E**nter on the Enter the new password screen.

All reports, labels, forms, browse tables and letters are printed from the **P**rint choice on the Main Menu. If the index, range, and printer choices are left to be made at print time, the Range Settings screen appears when you select the report you wish to print.

Adding Special Emphasis to Mail Labels

Special emphasis can be placed on your labels by using boldface, italics, or underlining. This technique is the same in reports, forms, and letters. Print attribute flags, which are commands to your printer, are set into your label by placing special symbols at the place the emphasis is to begin and end.

The flags are shown below:

!b Turns **Boldface** on
!i Turns *Italics* on
!n Turns Normal on (turns boldface and italics off)
!u Turns <u>Underline</u> on
!o Turns Underline off

These flags are case-sensitive and the difference between upper-and lowercase is important. If you use lowercase, the printer recognizes the flag as a command and ignores the space it appears to take on the label. When the !b, for example, are deleted, the text moves to the proper location. If the flag is entered in uppercase, as !B, the printer replaces the flag with two spaces and begins the printing in the exact space where the field is placed.

Alt-I inserts a line and Alt-D deletes a line of text or fields in Label layout. Deleting a line brings lines below up on the label.

T I P

If an address field is blank, you usually expect that the software closes the gap between lines. For example, consider the label that has a field for COMPANY below the name of the addressee. If the COMPANY field is blank, the line provided for it should be suppressed. If there is a reason to prevent the suppression of the blank line, you can use Ctrl-Backspace to create the Δ symbol. This mark does not print on the label, but it maintains the line, although no date exists.

Suppose that you want to place all five parts of a NAME field on your mail label, and you know that the fields taken all together do not fit on the label you have chosen. The following expression, created as a calculated field (Alt-C), can solve the problem. Give the field an appropriate name, such as FULLNAME, then under Expression, type: **trim(PREFIX)+" "+trim(FIRST)+" "+trim(MIDDLE)+" "+trim(LAST)+" "+trim(SUFFIX)**. This expression concatenates the fields, which means that the words are strung together and trailing blanks are removed.

Punctuation can be included in an expression such as this. The following is another expression that you may find useful:

Name	Expression
CSZ	trim(CITY)+", "+trim(ST)+" "+ZIP

Notice that a comma is between the two double quotes after the CITY field.

The shortcut to **S**ave a mail label is Alt-S; the shortcut to save and **P**review is Alt-P.

T I P

Formatting Options on Labels

As with **R**eports, when you are designing a label, you can make detailed changes in the way the data looks on the printed piece. The F2 (Fields) key offers formatting **O**ptions, or you can use the shortcut, Alt-O to see a screen such as figure 7.13

Formatting options for mail labels give you control of the length of fields, the justification of their contents, and the case.

On the Formatting Options screen, you can see the fields that have been placed on the label. The second column shows the type of field, Character, Numeric, Date, or Logical. Memo fields cannot be used on mail labels. The second column tells the length of the field as it shows on the screen. There is no selection for Window as there is for reports, browse tables, and input forms, as multiline printing of a single field is not allowed on a label.

The third column offers Justification options, meaning that the selection of choices here moves within a field. Left justification means move text to left hand side of the field. Center justification calculates the length of the field and places the text in the middle. Right justification forces the text to fill to the right side of the field. Suppress means that the program removes all trailing blanks in the field and moves the following text to the left to fill the spaces.

Using Special Formatting for Labels

For special circumstances, you may need to fine-tune the formatting of your label design. Selecting **F**loat causes the data in the field to shift to the left if the preceding field contains the formatting option to suppress trailing blanks. The text in the following field does not shift. Trim forces the data in the field to print precisely where it is placed without regard to formatting in other fields. Text in following fields is shifted to the left. The Join option is like Float in that it causes the data in the field to shift to the left if the preceding field contains the formatting option to suppress trailing blanks. However, with Join, any text that follows is shifted to the left. (A detailed example of this is shown in the Alpha Four Reference Manual.)

Occasionally, you may want to add punctuation to your label. For example, CITY (comma) (space) STATE (space) ZIPCODE would be placed on the label in the following manner.

```
- - - - - - - - - - - - , - - - - - - - -‾- - - -
```

The dashed lines represent the fields, CITY, STATE, and ZIP code. If the CITY field is blank, the text, which is the comma, is deleted. This is called the After format. The same principle applies to Before. If a text character, such as a period, is placed on the label, such as after a PREFIX field showing Mr or Mrs, then the period is deleted and the next field fills in the empty space.

Using SYSTEM Fields on Labels

The SYSTEM database contains 22 fields that can be particularly useful on a mailing label. Table 7.2 contains a partial list to suggest what may be meant by some of the codes you see on mailing labels today.

Table 7.2 Fields Useful on Labels

Field Name	Function
CNTR_GRAND	Calculates the number of records printed and numbers each label as it prints.
DATE	Shows the current date, as your computer understands it. This is set at the DOS prompt and can be changed through SETUP or type DATE at the C: and enter correct data as indicated.
DB_NAME	Shows name of the file from which the label is printed.
DB_DESC	Shows the description of the file from which the label is printed.
DELETED	Prints the letter Y if record is deleted.
REC_NUMBER	Places the actual record number of each record on its label.

continues

Table 7.2 Continued

Field Name	Function
TIME	Shows the current time. See DATE.
INDEX_NAME	Prints the name of the index used to print the labels.
INDEX_DESC	Prints the description of the index used to print the labels.
INDEX_EQN	Prints the expression defining the index used to print the labels.
SET_NAME	Shows the name of the set used to print the labels.
SET_DESC	Shows the description of the set used to print the labels.

NOTE Formatting fields on labels follows the same pattern as is described for reports (see Chapter 7).

The combined use of indexes and subgrouping in Alpha Four's report writer enables the user to develop reports that print related records together, based on the value in a particular field. When the field that controls the *break* changes, the new group appears.

Using Subgroups

When the technique of using groups is called for, you may recognize a need to see your data in a new way: employees by town, alphabetically by last name; sales figures, highest to lowest, by the territory, by the salesperson, by the product, by the month. Any field can be used as a break field or manipulated into performing your needed calculations.

Calculated fields can be used to present the data to bring new meaning to your work. In several examples of sales figures for certain dates (figures 7.15-7.17), the data is indexed on the date field, then grouped on the date field.

Defining Ranges and Printers

A special feature of Alpha Four's report writer is the feature that gives the user total control over both the range of records to be printed and the printer with which they are to be produced. This capability is best illustrated by looking at a Range and Print Settings screen in Reports Layouts. When a report is being designed, you can press F7 (Goto) to find the screen shown in figure 7.14.

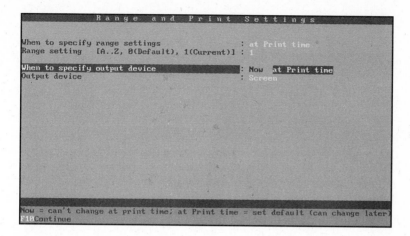

On this screen, you decide when the decisions are to be made about printing the current report. The important decisions that can be made here include the range setting and the specific printer. If a report is worthless unless printed with a specific index, the decision should be made here where the report itself is being designed.

You also should determine the width of the report as well. If a report is a standard 70 columns, then no decision needs to be made to change the default. If the report is designed to be more than 80 columns, perhaps 150 or 200 columns wide, then both the printer (landscape) and the font (compressed print) decisions should be made here.

Using Memo Fields in Reports

Memo fields present their own special problems in report writing. You use memo fields because they are undefined in length, except for the mechanical designation that memos are stored in blocks of 512K. A memo that uses up even one byte more than 512K takes a second block, whether or not the next block is filled with data. When a memo field is used on a report, you can define the number of lines it can fill, or you can make the definition self-expanding.

Indexing a Record

A small database with 4 fields and 20 records can help you work through the various ways that data can be summarized and indexed. You can use your own sales figures, but if you use the ones you find following, you can check your results. The sample database contains three Reps, five districts, and total sales figures for each Rep for each month by district. Each Rep can sell in more than one district.

This database was used in Chapter 4 to show Summarized databases and the Field Statistics function. The indexes listed here were created in Chapter 4. The first index has one level: REP; the second has two levels, DATE and TOT_SALES; the third index is only DATE; the fourth is the DISTRICT field and the field for TOT_SALES. These four indexes give you four different ways to analyze the data.

Start the report by using Quick format and a new letter. On the report parameters screen, make the number of grouping levels 1, select the REP field for Group 1, and give the program a default space between fields of seven. Then select fields: DISTRICT, DATE, AND TOT_SALES. On the layout screen, use the space bar to push the titles, underline characters and fields in the detail section over to column 20 and in the summary section to column 56.

Place your cursor on the top line of the Group 1 Header and press F9 and Enter (or use the shortcut Alt-I) to insert a line. Press Ctrl-Bksp to create the non-printing space holder: △. Below the △, type **REP**. Then select the REP field using Alt-F.In the Group 1 footer, follow the same procedure of adding a line with a △. Then use the hyphen to draw a single line to separate total sales figures from the detail section. Then place the TOT_SALES field defined as a Total below the line. Use Alt-P to save and preview the report (see fig. 7.15).

This report shows the data in three groups by Reps. The identical data broken down by the five districts rather than representatives shows quite different information. Try reversing the REP and DISTRICT fields and use the DISTRICT + TOT_SALES index (see fig. 7.16).

This report shows the same data indexed by DISTRICT, and TOT_SALES and Group 1 use the DISTRICT field to cause the group break.

The principles are the same for following report (see fig. 7.17). This report is indexed on the DATE field, and the group break field is DATE, as you might expect. However, the names of the months have been converted to English. Where the word January appears, a calculated field is looking at the DATE field through the expression: CMONTH(DATE).

	DISTRICT	DATE	TOTAL SALES
Rep.: ATH			
	New England	01-15-1991	23467
	New England	02-15-1991	65475
	New England	03-15-1991	65433
	Midwest	01-15-1991	23457
	Midwest	02-15-1991	87645
			============
			265477
Rep.: EMD			
	Midwest	01-15-1991	34323
	Midwest	01-15-1991	65434
	Midwest	02-15-1991	54324
	Midwest	03-15-1991	44324
	Northwest	01-15-1991	65621
	Northwest	02-15-1991	23467
	Northwest	03-15-1991	65422
			============
			352915
Rep.: FEG			
	Southwest	01-15-1991	54353
	Southwest	02-15-1991	23455
	Southwest	03-15-1991	65467
	South	01-15-1991	25460
	South	02-15-1991	23257
	South	03-15-1991	21278
	Midwest	02-15-1991	65466
	New England	01-15-1991	31372
			============
			310108
			============
			928500

FIG. 7.15

Sales figures by rep.

REP	DATE	TOTAL SALES

District: Midwest

ATH	01-15-1991	23457
EMD	01-15-1991	34323
EMD	03-15-1991	44324
EMD	02-15-1991	54324
EMD	01-15-1991	65434
FEG	02-15-1991	65466
ATH	02-15-1991	87645
		============
		374973

District: New England

ATH	01-15-1991	23467
FEG	01-15-1991	31372
ATH	03-15-1991	65433
ATH	02-15-1991	65475
		============
		185747

District: Northwest

EMD	02-15-1991	23467
EMD	03-15-1991	65422
EMD	01-15-1991	65621
		============
		154510

District: South

FEG	03-15-1991	21278
FEG	02-15-1991	23257
FEG	01-15-1991	25460
		============
		69995

District: Southwest

FEG	02-15-1991	23455
FEG	01-15-1991	54353
FEG	03-15-1991	65467
		============
		143275
		============
		928500

FIG. 7.16

Sales figures by district.

		DATE	TOTAL SALES

Month of January

ATH	Midwest	01-15-1991	23457
ATH	New England	01-15-1991	23467
FEG	South	01-15-1991	25460
FEG	New England	01-15-1991	31372
EMD	Midwest	01-15-1991	34323
FEG	Southwest	01-15-1991	54353
EMD	Midwest	01-15-1991	65434
EMD	Northwest	01-15-1991	65621

============
323487

Month of February

FEG	South	02-15-1991	23257
FEG	Southwest	02-15-1991	23455
EMD	Northwest	02-15-1991	23467
EMD	Midwest	02-15-1991	54324
FEG	Midwest	02-15-1991	65466
ATH	New England	02-15-1991	65475
ATH	Midwest	02-15-1991	87645

============
343089

Month of March

FEG	South	03-15-1991	21278
EMD	Midwest	03-15-1991	44324
EMD	Northwest	03-15-1991	65422
ATH	New England	03-15-1991	65433
FEG	Southwest	03-15-1991	65467

============
261924

============
928500

FIG. 7.17

Sales figures by month.

The preceding three reports, all printed using identical data, answer several questions you may want to ask: *Which representative sold the most in the month of January? In the New England area? Which District has the best sales over the three month period? Which month showed the largest total sales?*

Lettering Your Database

The purpose of the built-in editor in Alpha Four is to give you the capability of producing a form letter without leaving Alpha Four. You can create and save as many letters as your needs require by using the fields from the current database or set. Given the same names for the fields, you can use the same letter for databases or sets that were not current when the letter was created, because letters are not connected to a single file in the same way as reports, browse tables, forms, or mailing labels are linked to the database that is current when they are created.

Creating a Letter

To create a form letter, access the database containing the fields that will be needed in the letter and perform the following steps:

1. From the Main Menu, select **L**ayouts. Alpha Four shows the Layouts menu. Choose **L**etters, **C**reate/edit a form letter and type the name of your letter at the bottom of the screen. The three-letter extension .LTR is added by the program. Letter names must follow normal DOS rules, up to eight characters, no spaces.

2. The editor screen uses the paragraph sign, ¶, to show the end of a line or a carriage return. The club symbol, ♣, is used to indicate the end of the file. The editor with no text is shown in figure 7.18.

3. To begin a traditional letter with a date at the top of the page, select F2 (Fields) and choose the System database, not your current database. The System database contains a number of fields that are useful for letters. In this case, select the field named DATE. Formatting issues, such as justification and extended format, are defined on the next screen, shown in figure 7.19.

4. Place each field in the appropriate place on the letter using F2 to select the fields.

5. Type the text as you want it to appear on the letter. F4 (Block) is used to mark blocks to delete, copy, or insert in a new location. F3 (Commands) gives page formatting and printer commands: **I**nclude file, **P**age eject, **E**nable auto fill, **D**isable auto fill; **C**ontrol codes (for printer); **T**op margin; **B**ottom margin; **L**eft margin, and line **W**idth.

6. Save by using Alt-S or F10 to use save **As** or Save and **C**ontinue editing.

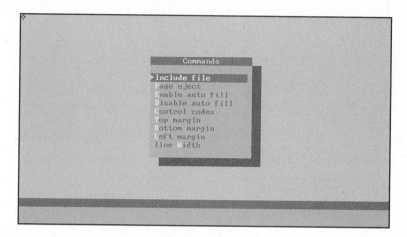

FIG. 7.18

The Commands menu is activated by F3.

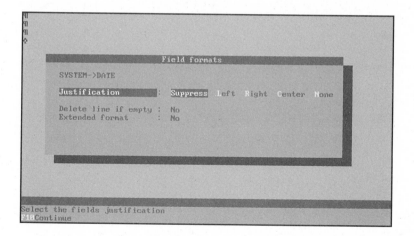

FIG. 7.19

Field formats are defined on this screen.

Figure 7.20 shows the layout of a letter. Two sample memos printed by using records from the OWNERS database and this letter would look like figures 7.21 and 7.22.

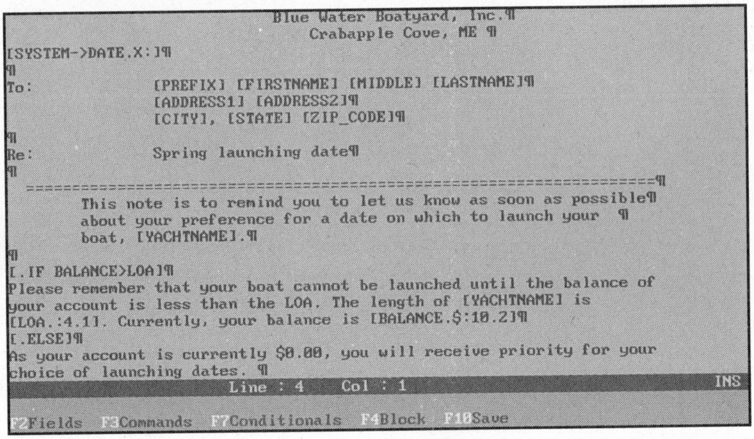

FIG. 7.20

A sample memo
on-screen.

FIG. 7.21

A sample printed
memo.

Controlling Page Layout

Include file tells the software to find a boilerplate paragraph (and where to find it) to be included at the specific location of the command.

The Page eject command forces the printer to start the next record on a new page. This command overrides the automatically calculated page break. This is particularly useful if your letter is short.

Blue Water Boatyard, Inc.
Crabapple Cove, ME

January 27th, 1992

To: Ms. Carole F. Sloan
        33 Bedford Road
        Acton, ME

Re: Spring launching date

==

   This note is to remind you to let us know as soon as possible about your preference for a date on which to launch your boat, Cheap Shots.

Please remember that your boat cannot be launched until the balance of your account is less than the LOA. The length of Cheap Shots is 34.0. Currently, your balance is $40.05

Thank you for sailing with us.

FIG. 7.22

A sample memo with different conditions.

Enable/Disable auto fill relates to ASCII text brought into Alpha Four from a word processor. This command forces the text to wordwrap based on the margins set in the letter. If this command is disabled, each line is treated as though it ended with a hard return which is interpreted as an end of paragraph symbol.

Control codes sends special formatting codes to the printer. These can be used to select a special font. Consult your printer manual for these codes.

Top/Bottom margins tells the printer where to start and end a letter on the page.

Left margin/line Width tells the software where to define the maximum line width from left to right sides.

Additional formatting is available in Letters using the attribute flags for boldface, italic, and underline. See the discussion of these flags in this chapter in the section "Adding Special Emphasis to Mail Labels."

Using Conditional Expressions

To use the conditional statement, select F7 (Conditionals) and choose IF. Alpha Four offers a box entitled [.IF] Expression into which you can type a statement that evaluates to true if you want the following paragraph to print. The example in the sample letter is: [.IF BALANCE > LOA]. At print time, Alpha Four examines each record to discover whether the number in the BALANCE field is greater than the number in the LOA field, which indicates the length over all of the boat. If the answer is TRUE, then the next paragraph is printed. If the answer is not true, then the paragraph that follows is printed.

You select the F7(Conditionals) key to select the [.ELSE] and [.ENDIF] commands. You also can include the [.ELSEIF] to make an additional condition. A nested ELSEIF statement can be up to five levels deep. Figure 7.23 shows the sample boatyard letter with conditional statements.

FIG. 7.23

```
                              Blue Water Boatyard, Inc.¶
                               Crabapple Cove, ME ¶
[SYSTEM->DATE.X:]¶
¶
To:            [PREFIX] [FIRSTNAME] [MIDDLE] [LASTNAME]¶
               [ADDRESS1] [ADDRESS2]¶
               [CITY], [STATE] [ZIP_CODE]¶
¶
Re:        -   Spring launching date¶
¶
================================================================¶
        This note is to remind you to let us know as soon as possible¶
        about your preference for a date on which to launch your   ¶
        boat, [YACHTNAME].¶
¶
[.IF BALANCE>LOA]¶
Please remember that your boat cannot be launched until the balance of
your account is less than the LOA. The length of [YACHTNAME] is
[LOA.:4.1]. Currently, your balance is [BALANCE.$:10.2]¶
[.ELSE]¶
As your account is currently $0.00, you will receive priority for your
choice of launching dates. ¶
                         Line : 4    Col : 1                      INS
   Fields  F3 Commands  F7 Conditionals  F4 Block  F10 Save
```

Your letter can contain conditional paragraphs to control the printing based on data in each record.

NOTE   These commands and expressions can be typed into the letter instead of being selected from the boxes.

Using a Word Processor

Most word processing software allows you to save your work to an unformatted ASCII file. You can write your letter in WordPerfect, WordStar, Microsoft Word, or any other product that permits a transfer to ASCII. (See your software manual for instructions.) It is easier to choose the field names and syntax commands when you are using Alpha Four rather than an external word processor. However, if you bring a file into Alpha Four from an ASCII file, you can place the fields in the appropriate places when it is in the Alpha Four editor.

Using Alternatives to Reports To Summarize the Data

There are at least three other ways to summarize the sample data shown in figures 7.15-7.17 using Alpha Four: remove details from a subgrouped report; enter expressions to summarize data using Field Statistics; and summarize the data to a separate database.

You can experiment with the first method by editing the detail sections of any of the three reports shown in the tables and removing all extraneous items from the report. For example, remove the detail from the DISTRICT report and save the report format under a new letter in order not to lose the original format. By leaving only the title section and the group header, you can print a report to look like figure 7.24.

Summarized report by District - For total sales

Page 1

District:	Total sales:
Midwest	374,973
New England	185,747
Northwest	154,510
South	69,995
Southwest	142,275

FIG. 7.24

A summarized report.

Using Other Kinds of Summarized Reports

Creating a report does not always have to be done from the Layout, Reports menu, at least if you accept the premise that a report is your data, arranged and summarized to be printed or viewed, in a format that you like. If you can use this definition, then there are two more kinds of summarized reports which you should consider.

Using Field Statistics

A second technique is to summarize the data using the Main Menu item Other, Information, Field statistics. Typing in the expressions shown in figure 7.25, produces a nonprinting report that looks like figure 7.26.

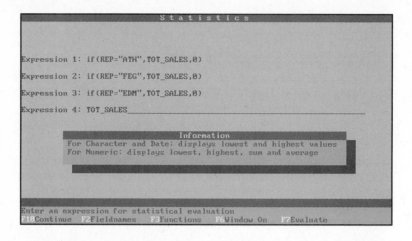

FIG. 7.25

Field statistics are requested by typing expressions into the four fields shown.

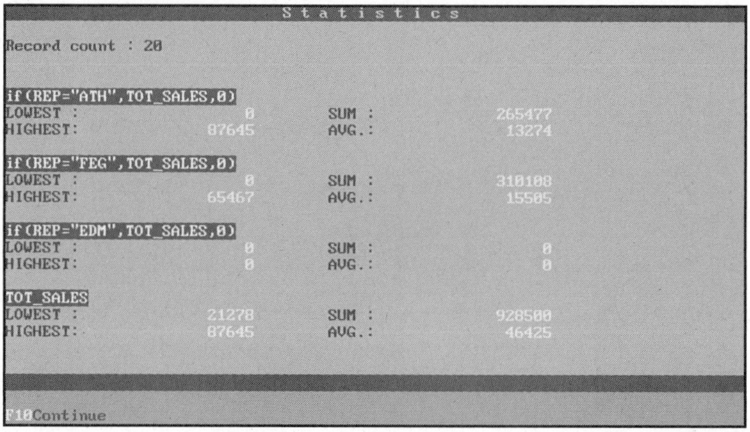

FIG. 7.26

Statistical output from the previous screens shows the highest, the total, and the average sales in each district.

These statistical reports require a fair amount of understanding of your data. There is no way to save the settings to perform this analysis except with a script. For these reasons, this technique is most successful when included as a macro in an application that automates the creation of this screen. While it is somewhat limited in having only four expression lines and lacking the capability to print the outcome directly, nevertheless, the information is valuable in this form for certain applications.

Any field, except memo fields, can be analyzed in one way or another in field statistics. Because field statistics show sums, averages, highs and lows, character fields cannot be analyzed in the same manner as a numeric field. An example of the statistical use of a character field can be understood by considering the SALES database again. To count the number of entries for a particular REP, the expression in field statistics is the following:

if(REP = "ATH" .and. DISTRICT = "New England", 1, 0)

The analysis examines every record for REP equal to ATH and for DIS-TRICT equal to New England and returns a 1 for each occurrence. The statistics total the number of 1s and show that as the sum. Highest, lowest and average are not relevant to the analysis, still the count is a quick way to retrieve data from your files. Adding to the sample above, if you change the DISTRICT field to TOT_SALES, you can see signifi-cance to two other fields, HIGHEST and AVERAGE, as well as SUM. The second field statistics expression is the following:

if(REP = "ATH" .and. DISTRICT = "New England", TOT_SALES, 0)

Advanced Version 2 users can employ the results of a Field Statistics analysis by creating a Dialog script that shows the current contents of the script variables called %SYS_STAT (1-4). A script variable exists for each of the four field statistics entries, showing the high, low, sum and average for each of the four. Whenever field statistics are run, the cal-culation is entered into the appropriate %SYS_STAT variable and can be displayed in a dialog box. (See Quick Start 3 on Applications.)

Using Summary Databases

The third way to achieve similar results is to choose **U**tilities, **S**umma-rize database. With this technique, you create a new database from the data in your file. The Summarize operation extracts records from the current database and summarizes them into a new file. To create a summarized file, perform the following steps:

1. If you are not already in the sales database, open it now. From the Alpha Four Main Menu, select Utilities. Alpha Four displays the Utilities menu. Choose **S**ummarize database and type a file name at the bottom of the next screen. The field selection screen, as shown in figure 7.27, lists the fields in your current database.

2. Press Enter to select or deselect a field. For this sample, select DISTRICT and TOT_SALES. (This field selection process operates in the same manner as that used to select fields to create a new browse table.) Press F10 to continue.

3. The next screen, illustrated in figure 7.28, shows that you can identify the type of summary activity required for each field. There are five districts in the SALES database. Therefore, the op-tion for each record in the summarized database should be the

first occurrence of that data. The TOT_SALES field is to be summarized with the total of each district's sales. Therefore, change the option to Total. Press F10 (Continue).

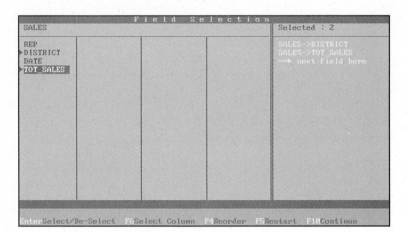

FIG. 7.27

Fields are chosen using the field selection screen to create a summarized database.

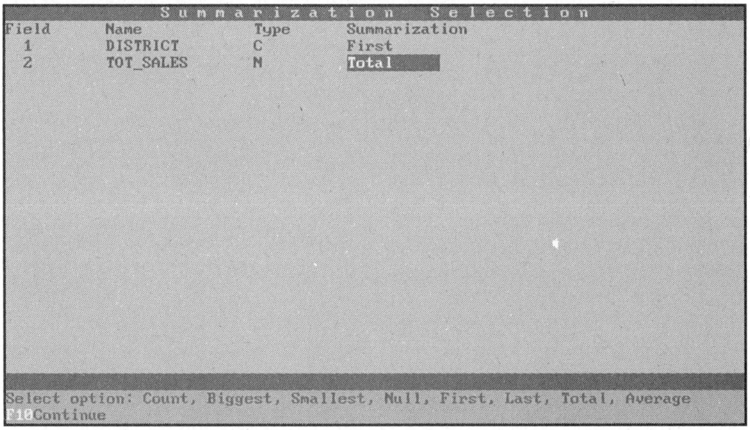

FIG. 7.28

The summarization selection is made on this screen.

4. The next screen enables you to give the summarized database a descriptive name for future identification. Typing in today's date in the description is frequently helpful. Generally, you should answer **No** to the question of Inherit support files as you may be creating quite different reports and forms for this database from those in the parent file. Press F10 to continue.

5. Success depends on selecting the right index on the next screen. The Range Setting screen must show as the primary index the

index that groups the primary field. In this example, the index is REP because the summary is to be made on the three sales reps. A filter can be used on the range setting screen to limit the record to be summarized.

Summary

This chapter highlighted techniques with which you can create especially useful reports. You may find that these skills allow you to create more informative reports with your own material. Special reporting is demonstrated with extensive use of sub-grouping techniques. Creating mailing labels and letters also add to the capabilities of using Alpha Four.

Field Statistics and Summarize database are used to demonstrate other analytical features of the software. Most of these activities will be examined again in upcoming chapters as they provide the basis for developing powerful scripts to implement the applications you design.

The next section of this book introduces the relational commands in Alpha Four. This section begins with Quick Start 2, a get-up-and-go session designed to take the mystery out of sets, post, join, subtract, and intersect.

PART

II

Intermediate Alpha Four

OUTLINE

QS2. Understanding the Relational
Skills of Alpha Four

8. Using Sets

9. Moving Your Data and Files

10. Using Alpha Four Tips,
Tricks, and Techniques

Understanding the Relational Skills of Alpha Four

Your system was liable to periodical convulsions,
overwhelming alike to the wise and unwise...
Edward Bellamy, Looking Backward

In this chapter, you use multiple files connected together to create a set. Although Alpha Four's relational capabilities are not the kind available on mainframe computers, they are more than adequate to handle most of the complex data-management problems of the average business.

Defining a Relational Database

A *relational database* manages two or more related files that supplement each other's purposes. Relational database management has twin goals: efficient data storage and rapid retrieval of records. The additional relational functions of Alpha Four, Post, Join, Subtract, and Intersect, give you additional capabilities that enhance these two objectives.

The concept of using a *set* in Alpha Four introduces a new range of activities. A set refers to the technique of linking multiple databases to make the data available between them. The link exists by a *common field* or *key* that exists in each database.

Strictly speaking, Alpha Four is not a true *relational database*. That term is more commonly used to indicate the large programs that reside in mainframe computers owned by big companies and governments, small and large. Alpha Four users also use the word *set* in a somewhat different way from dBASE programmers. This difference is significant because dBASE established the standard format for the *Xbase family*, and Alpha Software has made a determined effort to remain *compatible* with the dBASE and .dbf standard.

However, the word *set* in Alpha Four, refers to a group of files as one might refer to a set of golf clubs. The dBASE programmer uses the dBASE programming language to write an expression that establishes the link between files by using the following command:

> SET RELATION TO *<expression>*

Therefore, the term *set* needs to be interpreted for Alpha Four users. A set, in the terms of the Alpha Four software, is the definition applied to the result when two or more files are linked on a common field.

Preparing for Sets

If the purpose of a set is to store data more efficiently and to access data more rapidly, then entering and viewing data quickly and efficiently must also be a part of the plan. The first decision is which files must be linked. In Chapter 2, you defined a file called OWNERS, and in Chapter 4 you created another database called INVOICE. When two databases are linked or associated in a set, the purpose is to tie together records in the .dbf file by using a common field or a column of data that relates to both files.

Creating a Sample Set

To continue the theme of the boatyard, you have a database that keeps records about boat owner names and addresses, names of vessels, and other relevant data. As owner of the boatyard, you want to send bills for the materials or services provided to these owners. You can keep a database with INVOICE data, linked by a owner's ID number to the owner's records in the OWNERS.DBF file. You also have an INVENTRY.DBF containing inventory items, which was created in Quick Start 1. All three of these files can be linked together to create a set.

The linking of files helps you perform two tasks that are critical to database management: storing the data once and accessing the data efficiently in relation to appropriate records. When you link the OWNERS database with the INVOICE database, the result is a set. Still, one item is missing. The link between the owner file and the line item data is logically an invoice.

If you did not create the INVOICE database in Chapter 4, you can follow this chapter's examples if you create this file now as the origin of the invoice number to provide the link between line items and owners: INVOIC_ID in the INVOICE database links INVOIC_ID in INVOICES; the OWNER_ID in the INVOICE database links to the OWNER_ID in the OWNERS file. See Chapter 3 for details on creating a database.

To create the invoice database, you need the following fields:

Record Number	Name	Type	Width	Decimal Place
1	INVOIC_ID	C	4	
2	OWNER_ID	C	4	
3	INV_DATE	D	8	
4	LINE_NO	N	2	
5	ITEM_NO	C	4	
6	QTY	N	7	2
7	PRICE	N	7	2
8	POSTED	L	1	
9	TOTAL	N	8	2

Create a two-level index by using INVOIC_ID as the first line and LINE_NO as the second line. This index will provide the link to the other files. For help on indexing, see Chapter 4.

You must have a clear picture of which file will be the most active for current use because it will become the parent database. The first step in linking files is deciding which file will be the *parent* and which will be the *child*. Because the INVOICE file will form the link and will be the one in which additional records are created, the logical approach is to make this the parent file. When you select **D**atabase/set design, **S**et commands, you must have the two or more files ready to be linked.

The parent database uses the same data, whether it is in its original form or being used in a set. In this case, the INVOICE database is where the data will be located whether you view the data through a set or in the flat file. The same indexes that are defined for the flat file are available in the set. However, differences do exist. The flat file can have entirely different indexes active from the set. Forms and reports are not common to both files. In fact, to see the related records, you must edit the forms and browse tables to bring those fields onto the screen.

T I P   In extremely large applications, you may need to maintain more than the allowed number of reports, which is 26. To work around this limitation, you can make a duplicate of your set and start again with new reports and different indexes identified as primary.

 CAUTION   If you detach an index in a parent file that is currently the primary index in the original file, the parent file will revert to the Record Number index. With the availability of 15 indexes, this problem is substantially reduced in Version 2.

Before you create a set, answer the following questions:

1. Which files are included in the set?
3. Which fields link which file to which file?
4. Which index will be used to link each file to the other?
5. What is the common field between each linked database?
6. Is the link one-to-one (one customer number per invoice) or one-to-many (one invoice number to many line items)?

As you explore these questions, you should examine each of the intended child databases and verify that each is indexed appropriately. The OWNERS database is indexed on OWNER_ID; the INVOICE database is indexed on OWNER_ID; and the INVENTRY database is indexed on the PART_NO field.

After you answer these questions, you can create a set. For this book's example, make the intended parent database, INVOICE, the current file and perform the following steps:

1. From the Main Menu, select **D**atabase/set design. Alpha Four responds with the Database/**S**et Options menu.

2. Choose Set commands, **C**reate a set design and type the name **INVOICES**. (This name is plural, to distinguish it from the database called INVOICE.DBF.)

3. On the next screen, type in a description that will tell you what the set does, such as **Links OWNERS to INVOICE for invoices**, as shown in figure QS2.1

4. On the second line, verify that the primary database is INVOICE.DBF. If not, select F2 (Database Directory) to choose that file to be the parent (primary) database. Press F10 to continue.

```
                        S e t   D e f i n i t i o n


Set description   : Links owners to line items for invoices
Primary Database  : C:\BOATYARD\INVOICE.DBF
Show Mode         : All
Filter            :
Filter Mode       : Inactive









Enter name of primary database in set
F10 Continue   F2 Database Directory
```

FIG. QS2.1

The Set Definition screen is where the process of creating a set begins.

5. Press F2 on the next screen to select the linked file. The first link should be with the OWNERS database. On the second line (Linking Index) Alpha Four makes its best guess and offers the closest index name that it sees in the list. If you have more than one index, press F2 to select your choice of linking index. The connection between these files is, of course, their common field, which is OWNER_ID. The index in OWNERS that links to INVOICE is OWNER_ID. On the third line, Alpha Four tries again to give you the correct field. You may need to reselect the field by using F2. The field name in this case is OWNER_ID. Because only one client is associated with each invoice, the link will be one-to-one. On the fourth line, therefore, respond to the Link to? prompt with **First**, as illustrated in figure QS2.2.

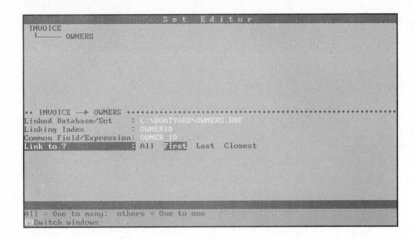

FIG. QS2.2

The Set Editor
screen is where
the links between
files are created.

6. The second link is with the INVENTRY database. Press F6 to add the second file. Because several line items may exist for each invoice, the relationship will be one-to-many, link to All. Press F9 to switch windows and F10 to save the set definition, as seen in figure QS2.3.

```
                            Set  Editor
INVOICE
   ├──── OWNERS
   └──── INVENTRY -- Inventory for Boatyard file




·· INVOICE ══▶ INVENTRY ·······················
Linked Database/Set       : C:\BOATYARD\INVENTRY.DBF
Linking Index             : INV_PART
Common Field/Expression: ITEM_NO
Link to ?                 : All




   Set: C:\BOATYARD\INVOICES
F5Detach Link  F6Add Link  F9Switch windows  F10Save
```

FIG. QS2.3

The second link
is one-to-many,
so the choice
is All.

When the linking process is complete, the program returns to the Alpha Four Main Menu in the new set. Check the top of the screen to note the name showing Current set: INVOICES.

Don't be surprised if the carefully crafted input form you have been using in the original of your parent file is missing. None of the previously defined supporting files come over to the newly created set except field rules. The form is still available in the flat file. If necessary, you can borrow the setting by using **L**ayout, **R**eports, **B**orrow. In the set, of course, you can develop even more stylish forms and browse tables by drawing in fields from any file linked in the set. You can view the data in those fields, but you cannot edit that data as it is derived from an existing *linked* database. The record that is seen in the form with fields from two or more linked files in a set is called a *composite record*, which means that two records are linked because they share the same value in the linked field.

Fine-Tuning with Link Parameters

You can further refine your sets by using the Link parameters function. The set with which you want to work must be the current set when you start this function. If you are currently logged to a single file, such as INVOICE.DBF, you will get a warning that says, There are no links defined. Cannot customize! This message indicates that you must make the set you want to customize the active file.

From the Main Menu, select **D**atabase/set design. Alpha Four responds with the Database/Set Options menu. Choose **S**et commands, **L**ink parameters.

The Link Parameters screen acts in a special way to include or exclude records based on several parameters. This screen is parallel in its purpose for the child file to the Set Definition screen shown in figure QS2.1. The difference is that the Set Definition screen is designed to operate on the parent file. The records in the parent file will be visible in the set according to the status of **A**ll, **N**ot deleted, or **D**eleted, any filter that may have been set, and the active or inactive status of that filter.

In the Linking parameters screen, three more tools are available. The Include parent if? choice enables you to include the composite record if there is a match, or if there is no match, in the child file. The default is to include the parent under any circumstance.

Show mode in Linking parameters works as it does on all range setting screens in Alpha Four: All, Not deleted, and Deleted. Filters also operate in the same manner in Linking parameters as on all range setting screens, as shown in figure QS2.4.

The last two choices on this screen are particularly useful if you are creating an application for others to use. To ensure that your user will see what you want them to see during a zoom operation in View or Browse, you can identify by letter any existing customized format. The default is the current form or browse table. Making this decision here can reduce confusion later, if the right forms or tables have been defined.

```
                        L i n k   P a r a m e t e r s
  INVOICE
    |----> OWNERS
    |----= INVENTRY -- Inventory for Boatyard file




.. INVOICE --> OWNERS ...........................................................
Include parent if ? : Always
Show Mode           : All    Not deleted   Deleted
Filter              :
Filter Mode         : Inactive
Zoom Form           : _
Zoom Browse         : _



  Set: C:\BOATYARD\INVOICES
Create composite records using all, deleted or non-deleted child records
F9 Switch windows
```

FIG. QS2.4

The Link Param-
eters screen
permits fine-
tuning of the
set's links.

Two functions discussed in this section are available in Version 2 and higher: Desktop and sWitch. Two other functions have changed significantly in the way they work: Post and Append.

Zooming around Your Files

When the indexes are working properly and you have the fields from all three databases on an input form, you can view some sample records to verify that the files are linked in the proper manner. The composite record combines the data from the linked files.

To create the input form or browse table to show fields from all linked files, edit an existing form or table or borrow from one of the source files and include desired fields.

After a link is created between files, you can travel between the files using the **Z**oom function. Zoom can be selected from the View or Browse screens to make a temporary change into a different database. The corresponding command, Unzoom returns to the original database. These are similar to the s**W**itch command (Version 2 only), which enables the user to switch between open files.

Zoom enables you to make entries to a child file. The child file is viewed as a source for the parent file. As such, the child file is used less frequently than the parent, at least for the current application. For example, when your INVOICES.SET is ready to go, you can quickly enter new line items for invoices by identifying the boat owner by his or her OWNER_ID and the product or service purchased by the ITEM_NO. Most of your boat owners' name and address records will already be in the computer in the OWNERS file. Those records are a source for the new INVOICE.SET and appear on the input form and in the browse tables. Only the OWNER_NO field, however, contains duplicate data. All other identifying information is stored just once in the original OWNERS database.

If an invoice for a new owner turns up while you are entering invoices for current owners, you can choose **Z**oom, select the OWNERS file, enter the new name and address data, and assign a unique OWNER_NO to that individual. After the record of the new owner has been saved, you can **U**nzoom again to the INVOICES.SET to complete the entry of an invoice for the new owner.

An alternative to using **Z**oom is to use the s**W**itch command. (See the discussion on Desktop files following.)

Managing Your Desktop

When two or more files are linked in a set, they are both considered by the computer to be *open* in the sense that you can zoom between the members of the set. In Version 2, Alpha Four retains a list of the open files and assigns numbers from 1 to 9 as a history of the order in which the files were opened. You can identify a group of files as a desktop. The desktop contains, in the order in which they are opened, the names of all files that you would like to access during a session. Perform the following steps to create a desktop:

1. From the Main Menu, select **C**hoose database/set. Alpha Four responds with the Desktop Options menu (see fig. QS2.5).

2. Choose **O**pen a database.

3. Select INVENTRY.DBF from the database directory.

4. Repeat steps 1-3 process and select OWNERS.DBF. Each time this is done, you access the new file. Each time a new file is added to the desktop, it appears on the Open Databases box like the following:

   ```
   1..C:\BOATYARD\INVOICES.SET
   2..C:\BOATYARD\INVENTRY.DBF
   3..C:\BOATYARD\OWNERS.DBF
   ```

5. When these files have been added to your desktop, press **C**hoose database/set and **S**ave current desktop. Give the desktop a name, such as INVOICE.

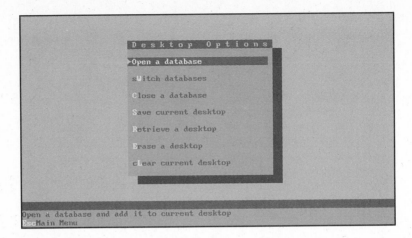

FIG. QS2.5

Desktop options
are listed on this
menu.

To create a desktop, you simply open all the files that are customarily
part of your daily database routine and save with a name relevant to
your work. You should give the desktop a descriptive name to tell you
what series of files are identified in this group.

When you create a desktop while you are working on a network, your
desktop files are stored in your private directory. The .dtn extension is
stored with whatever legitimate DOS name you choose to give your
desktop. When a desktop has been defined, you can sWitch between
files already open in the desktop.

After a desktop has been saved, you can add or remove file names from
the current group by opening the desktop, opening or closing that file,
and resaving the desktop with the same name. When the screen asks
whether or not to overwrite the existing file, answer **Yes**.

NOTE   A special desktop is defined using AUTOEXEC.DTN. If a
desktop of this name exists, Alpha Four automatically opens
all files named in the desktop when the program starts.

Understanding Zoom and Switch

The significance of Zoom is that if a matching record exists in the child
file, the computer finds that record when you call for the Zoom command. If no matching record exists, the program searches for the closest match. When Zoom finds a matching record, you can see that
record only during the Zoom unless you change the current index or do
a Find. The program displays Record 0 (see Chapter 8).

The program expects that when you are Zooming from View mode that you probably want to arrive in View in the child file. The same applies when you are Zooming between files using browse tables. When you return to the parent file, the command is **U**nzoom from view or browse. The original record, the one from which you originally did the Zoom, reappears.

The expectation is different when you use s**W**itch. First, you can only switch among any files that are open on your desktop. Regardless of which record you are viewing or browsing at the time, sWitch takes your view or browse for the first record in the new file, based on the current index in that file. If you are on the Main Menu when you decide to sWitch files, you are sWitched to the Main Menu on the new file.

Controlling Output from Sets

Creating reports with files linked in a set adds opportunities for enhancement that otherwise are unavailable. In this section, you will take the report created in Chapter 7, figure 7.1, and develop it further.

Enhancing Reports in Sets

You have used the input form and browse table to illustrate the options available with sets, but the fact that an input form can only show one child record at a time indicates that a different technique must be used if you want to produce an invoice for one of the boat owners in our INVOICES set. You need a report with two subgroups. The first subgroup is on the OWNER_ID from the OWNERS file; the second is on INVOIC_ID from the INVOICE file.

The Grouping Parameters screen contains the following lines:

```
Level    Field
Group 1  OWNERS->OWNER_ID
Group 2  INVOICE->INVOIC_ID
```

In Chapter 4, you examined the related issues of indexing and subgrouping. These topics are considered together because without careful indexing, subgrouping won't work and without the capability to create subgroups, indexing lacks effectiveness.

The printed report that results from the design shown in figure QS2.6 can be seen in figure QS2.7. Examine the items on this report and you will see all the basic elements needed to create an invoice.

Furthermore, by using fields from the OWNERS database, you can add clarity to the report still further by adding the name of the owner next to the total billing figure.

FIG. QS2.6

The Owner History Report screen includes the details of all invoices created for each owner.

Compare figure QS2.7 to figure 7.2 to see a few of the advantages of this report. One important item that has been added is the pre-processed total for Group 1. This calculation examines the totals associated with each invoice and accumulates them before printing the line on which the owners' names appear. In order for this calculation to happen, you must have defined the total fields in the summary section as the following:

Name	Field	Summary	Level	Ignore	Process
PRICE_T1	: INVOICE->PRICE	Total	group 1	None	Pre-Processing
QUANTIT_T2	: INVOICE->QUANTITY	Total	group 2	None	Pre-Processing
PRICE_T2	: INVOICE->PRICE	Total	group 2	None	Pre-Processing
QUANTIT_TG	: INVOICE->QUANTITY	Total	Grand	None	Pre-Processing
PRICE_TG	: INVOICE->PRICE	Total	Grand	None	Pre-Processing

When printed to the screen or the printer, the results will look like figure QS2.7.

11/28/1991
Page: 1

Client History Report by Invoice Number

Last Name	Invoice Date	Line	Item	Quantity	Total Price
Owner: 101 Fenton	Total: $23.00				
Invoice No. I002					
	09/09/1991	1	2001	12	6.00
	09/09/1991	2	2003	4	2.00
	09/09/1991	3	2000	1	15.00
	Total for invoice:		I002	17	23.00
Owner: 102 Jones	Total: $4,892.35				
Invoice No. I001					
	10/09/1991	1	2007	100	315.00
	Total for invoice:		I001	100	315.00
Invoice No. I003					
	10/10/1991	1	2003	2	1.00
	10/10/1991	2	2000	1	15.00
	10/10/1991	3	2009	3	38.85
	Total for invoice:		I003	6	54.85
Invoice No. I008					
	11/27/1991	1	2005	3	13.50
	11/27/1991	2	2006	2	9.00
	Total for invoice:		I008	5	22.50
Invoice No. I010					
	12/03/1991	1	2007	200	3000.00
	12/03/1991	2	2011	100	1500.00
	Total for invoice:		I010	300	4500.00
Owner: 103 Goullaud	Total: $372.05				
Invoice No. I004					
	11/27/1991	1	2004	300	225.00
	11/27/1991	2	2008	3	56.85
	11/27/1991	3	2009	5	64.75
	11/27/1991	4	2010	1	16.45
	11/27/1991	5	2005	2	9.00
	Total for invoice:		I004	311	372.05
	Total for this report:			739	$5,287.40

FIG. QS2.7

List of line items
and invoices
in a set.

By applying the techniques of subgrouping records and pre-processing calculations, you can quickly turn the report in figure QS2.7 into a summary of all of the information by removing the detail sections while leaving the totals for group 2 and the grand total, making a new report that looks like the following:

Invoice Number	Quantity Sold	Extended Price
I001	100	315.00
I002	17	23.00
I003	6	54.85
I004	311	372.05
I008	5	22.50
I010	300	4500.00
Total billing:		$5,287.40

A summary of the preceding detailed report.

Useful Samples of Linked Databases

Files can be considered linked in three ways in Alpha Four. The following section compares these operations:

The Set commands form a logical connection, not a physical link, between two or more databases that share common fields. The hands-on section of Chapter 9 gives you the basic steps of creating a set.

The Lookup database technique links two files on a specific field for the purpose of dropping information from one file into the other. In Chapter 6 concerning field rules, there is a hands-on tutorial for creating a lookup by using an external database.

A *visual* link is created when files are stored together in a Desktop. By using the sWitch command from browse or view and passing through the list of file names, the user can gain the impression that the files are part of a continuous series of data.

Posting Invoice Totals to Customer Files

Now you should have an OWNERS file and an INVENTRY file linked together in a set called INVOICES.SET that uses the INVOICE.DBF as its transaction file. Because each record in the INVOICE database represents one line item on an invoice, the total amount of each invoice is reported and printed in an invoice by using the set to combine the data properly. To keep a current balance for each customer, the POST command is available.

Post is a common term in accounting that refers to adding amounts in individual transactions to a summary record. For example, you would *post* your check to the gas company to a Utilities account and your paycheck to a Cash account. At the end of the month, the Utilities account and the Cash account show the total of several entries which were posted to each account.

Using the boatyard files as a posting sample, you would want to post the individual entries in the INVOICE.DBF to the OWNERS.DBF. To post, you must access the file that will receive the data from an external file. In this case, choose OWNERS.DBF as your active database and select OWNER_ID as the primary index. To post the INVOICE file to the OWNERS file, perform the following steps:

1. From the Main Menu, choose **Utilities**. Alpha Four responds with the Utilities menu.

2. Select **R**elational commands, **P**ost database.

3. On the next screen, highlight the INVOICE.DBF and press Enter. The Common fields screen appears (see fig. QS2.9). The common field in both of these databases is OWNER_ID. If you have given them different names, then you must change the first line on this screen to No.

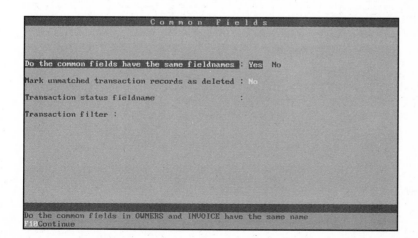

Common Fields

Do the common fields have the same fieldnames : Yes No

Mark unmatched transaction records as deleted : No

Transaction status fieldname   :

Transaction filter :

Do the common fields in OWNERS and INVOICE have the same name
F10 Continue

FIG. QS2.9

Common fields are identified for Post on this screen.

4. If your answer on the screen shown in figure QS2.9, line 1, is No, the next screen gives you the chance to give the name of the common field. In that case, the screen looks like figure QS2.10.

FIG. QS2.10

An expression that identifies the common field is created on this screen.

Within the figure:

Common Field Expression

Primary index description : Boat owners ID

Primary index expression : OWNER_ID

Common expression : OWNER_ID

Enter equivalent expression using transaction database fieldnames
F10 Continue F2 Fields F3 Functions F6 Window On F7 Evaluate

5. The next screen enables you to identify the fields to which the data is to be posted. Use the arrow key to place the highlight on the word None next to the field from the OWNERS file called CUR_BILAMT (see fig. QS2.11).

6. Change the None to Add by pressing the letter A. The highlight jumps to the column for the INVOICE database.

7. Press F2 to select the field TOTAL and press Enter. This means that the field CUR_BILAMT in the OWNERS file will have the TOTAL field in the INVOICE file added to the amount that currently exists in that field.

8. On the next line, select the letter R to cause the word Replace to appear and use F2 to select INV_DATE from the INVOICE file. This means that every time the data file is posted to the OWNER file, the date of the most recent invoice will be recorded.

9. On the field BALANCE, select A to add the field TOTAL to the owner's balance. Press F10 to continue.

Records in the INVOICE database are posted only to records in the OWNERS database when the OWNER_ID fields in both files contain the same data.

```
                    F i e l d   S e l e c t i o n
Num.    OWNERS          Operation       INVOICE
2       PREFIX          None
3       FIRSTNAME       None
4       MIDDLE          None
5       LASTNAME        None
6       ADDRESS1        None
7       ADDRESS2        None
8       CITY            None
9       STATE           None
10      ZIP_CODE        None
11      HOME_PHONE      None
12      YACHTNAME       None
13      LOA             None
14      DINGHY          None
15      LAUNCH          None
16      COMMENTS        None
17      CUR_BILAMT      Add             PRICE
18      CUR_BILDAT      Replace         INV_DATE
19      LASTPAYAMT      None
20      LASTPAYDAT      None
21      BALANCE         Add             PRICE____

Select field from INVOICE to post to OWNERS
F10 Continue   F2 Fieldnames
```

FIG. QS2.11

The Field Selection screen is where you identify the activity of each posted field.

NOTE Remember to make the index in the current database the same as the field that will be summarized in the posting function.

NOTE Alpha Four does not permit you to use the Post command from within a set.

Summary

Sets add great flexibility to the automation of our databases. The creation of sets is easy and can add a lot of power to an application. You may find yourself concerned that making more sets will use up lots of room on your computer. To illustrate to yourself that this is a minor problem, identify one of the sets you have been working with, one with plenty of field rules, search lists, reports and forms. Exit to DOS and do a directory of the file with the name of your set.

For example, if your INVOICE set is in a directory called C:\ALPHA4\ MYDATA, you should type: **dir invoices.***.

By using the DOS wildcard function, the asterisk, you are asking the computer to show you all the files that have the first part of their name INVOICE and any other appropriate three-letter extension. Generally, you will find files that end with extensions that suggest which program

(Alpha Four stand-alone or network version) and which kind of supporting file: I for Input forms, R for field Rules, U for global Update. These files will be very small compared to the .NDX and .DBF file if you have any significant number of records. The SET file itself is around 300 bytes and other will be from 1,500 to 5,000 bytes. A two-page letter in WordPerfect, with printer definitions included, is between 5,000 and 10,000.

This discussion is intended to encourage you to use sets to solve problems. Files that contain common data such as CUST_ID or PART_NO can be linked with either file serving as the parent or as the child. The perspective on the information changes and the purposes to which the data can be put changes, depending on which way the data is linked and upon the needs of the application. Don't be afraid to experiment.

Understanding indexing and the relationship between the files gives you the ability to utilize the relational commands and to build sets. In the next chapter you will look further into the new capabilities of reports and input forms in a set.

Using Sets

*Genius, in truth, means little more than the faculty
of perceiving in an unhabitual way.*
William James, Psychology

Using sets in Alpha Four requires a different approach to data management than using flat files. The process also is different from what dBASE programmers are accustomed to using. In fact, professional programmers actually have to learn to simplify their approach to multiple file use.

In this chapter, you create sets. Then you define forms, create reports, and examine the differences between creating these formats by using sets. In most cases, the skills you learned in Part I relate directly to the same functions used in sets. For example, defining input forms is very much the same process in sets as in flat files, except that you have all linked databases from which to choose your fields.

NOTE Two or more *single*—meaning flat—*files*—meaning databases—are linked together to create a set.

For this reason, Chapter 8 explains how the functions are different in sets. Refer to the appropriate chapter for corresponding information. Quick Start 2 gives you a brief overview of using the relational commands, making a set, and performing the Post command, but this chapter examines the set functions in detail.

Forging Links

The actual linking of the two or more data files in a set occurs on two levels. At the first level, you establish the common field and index with which the two files are logically connected. At the next level, Alpha Four gives you the capability of refining the connection to serve particular purposes.

Suppose that in the management of the sample boatyard, you have your OWNERS name and address file working well, but you want to track the phone contacts and results of meetings with your customers and other business contacts. You need a second database in addition to the OWNERS file, because there will be contacts and conversations with some customers over and over again, while others write a letter once a year and pay their bills at the same time. The OWNERS database and a CONTACT database can be linked to give access to each file for the data in the other. The CONTACT database should have the following seven fields:

Name	Type	Width
OWNER_ID	C	4
LASTNAME	C	15
CONT_DATE	D	8
TOPIC	C	30
DISCUSSION	C	254
ACTION	C	50
NEXT_CONT	D	8

The OWNER_ID will be the link to the set. LASTNAME provides easy data entry and retrieval in a lookup (see Chapter 5 concerning field rules) and provides an index for the quick Find command in View and Browse modes. CONT_DATE records the date of the event, conversation, or letter. TOPIC is for standardized entries or key words for sorting purposes, such as LAUNCH/HAUL INSTRUCTIONS, or INSURANCE INFO. The DISCUSSION contains a detailed version of the event. ACTION identifies the next event to take place in the relationship with this correspondent or customer. The NEXT_CONT field enables you to make a to do list based on the date you want to be prompted to take action.

Before you start to create the set, create two indexes in the CONTACT.DBF: a one-level index on LASTNAME and a two-level index using OWNER_ID and CONT_DATE. You also should verify that the owner's ID field in OWNERS is indexed.

To create the CONTAC.SET, perform the following steps:

1. Make the current database the CONTACT file. From the Main Menu, press **Database/set design**, **Set commands**, **Create a set design**. Type the name **CONTAC.SET**.

2. Type **Contacts, calls, and to-do reminders**. Be sure that the Primary Database is CONTACT.DBF. Press F10.

3. To identify the Linked Database/Set, press F2 and draw the highlight down to OWNERS.DBF. (If the linked database is in a different directory or drive, you can type the name on the bottom line or use the arrow keys to find the file in another directory.) Press Enter twice.

4. Press F2 (Index list) to select a name from the Linking Index. Select OWNERID. Press Enter twice.

5. When a field name appears on the Common Field/Expression line, this will be Alpha Four's best guess but may not be correct. The field that displays on the command field expression line is the field from the linking index.

   Press the space bar to erase that automatic entry. Press F2 (Fields) to select a field from the CONTACT database that will match the indexed field in OWNER. Select OWNER_ID.

6. On the last line, change the First to All to make a one to many relationship between CONTACT and OWNERS. Press F9 to switch to the top window.

7. To add another link, press F6 (Add Link) to identify another file. Repeat steps 3-6 using appropriate choices.

8. Press F10 (Save) from the top window to save this set.

Creating Forms and Browse Tables in Sets

To exploit the advantages of using a set, create a data entry form by using the fields from the linked files. When you go to View mode, you don't see any changes, except that you no longer have the forms that were created in the parent file (see fig. 8.1).

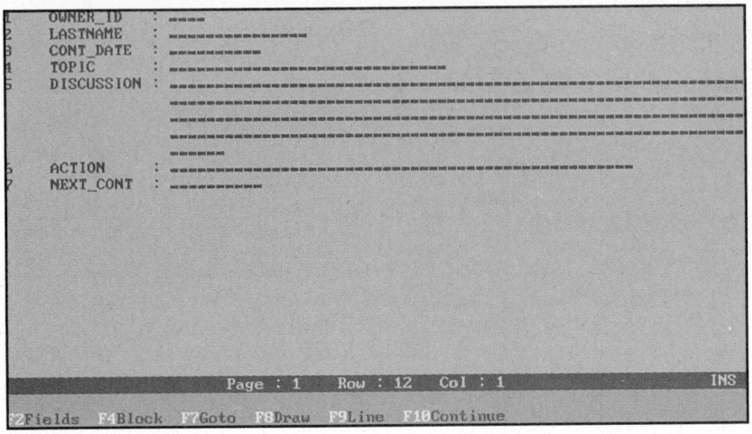

FIG. 8.1

The default form
in a set is the
same as the
default form in
the parent file.

Those forms can be borrowed for this database (see Chapter 4 concerning the borrow function), or a new form can be created by performing the following steps:

1. In View mode with the default input form on the screen, select **O**ptions, **E**dit the current form. The default form for the CONTAC.SET is shown in figure 8.1.

2. Using the skills you learned in Chapter 3, edit the form by moving fields, retyping text, and selecting files from the linked databases. Press F10 to save. A form in Edit mode is shown in figure 8.2.

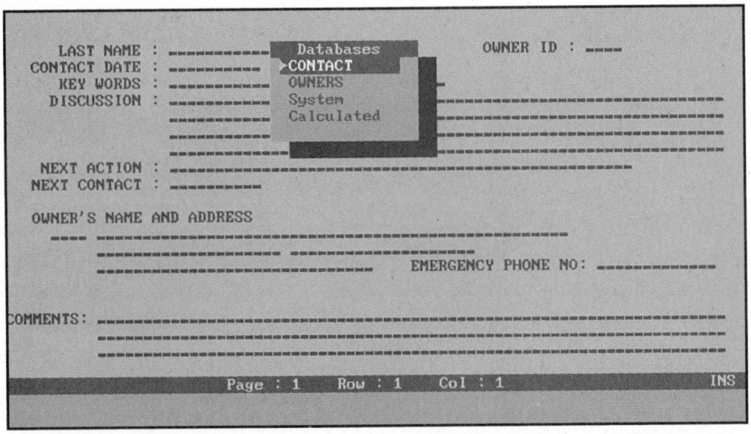

FIG. 8.2

Editing the form
by using sets
enables you to
use fields from
any linked file.

> When appropriate on a set, use a line or box to make a visual separa-
> tion of the fields taken from the parent (active) database from those
> in the linked (secondary) databases. This procedure can enhance
> the distinction between the files and clarify the purpose of the form.
>
> **T I P**

Entering Data in a Set

You can start the project by entering the customer data where it belongs, including an owner ID number that will be used as a line to the
CONTACT file (see fig. 8.3). To add new information to the CONTACT
file each time you are in touch with customers, the two files must be
linked with CONTACT as the primary database, or parent file, and
OWNER as the child file.

The OWNER data appears in the input form as soon as the correct
OWNER_ID number is connected by using a lookup defined in field
rules and linked by the OWNER_ID field in the CONTACT database to
the owner's number in the OWNER database. (See Chapter 10 for special tricks to aid data entry using entry forms and lookup databases.)

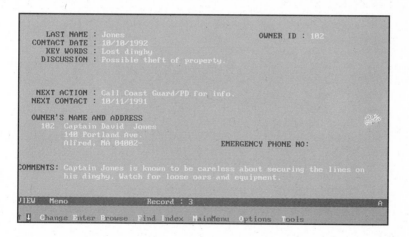

FIG. 8.3

The edited form
with data from
CONTACT.DBF
and
OWNER.DBF.

When you are entering data on your new input form, you cannot access
the fields that are derived from the secondary files. To make changes in
a record in the child file, access the related record and **Z**oom to the
OWNERS database. For example, if you are in contact with F. Eugene
Garland and he tells you that you have listed his address as being in

Birch Harbor but he is actually in Caribou, find one of the records showing Garland as the owner, press Z to Zoom, and choose the OWNERS database. If a related record exists, which does for this owner, the program zooms to that record in the linked file.

When you have completed the changes, remember to return to the set file by pressing U (or Options, uN-zoom) to Unzoom. This procedure returns you to the original record from which you zoomed. Notice that the field that was changed on the OWNERS record from Birch Harbor to Caribou appears to have changed when you un-Zoom to the CONTAC.SET record. The appearance, of course, is accurate because the record you see on the form is actually the data that is in the OWNERS.DBF.

Linking Parameters

When you are examining your records to add follow-up activities that have not been completed, you should define one set that shows records that have a relationship to owner's matters and another set that simply shows external activities not related to owners with existing records. Those other activities could include agreements with distributors, discussion of legal matters with Coast Guard or Conservation officials, or other local business problems. These are important records but can be excluded from the record to be viewed as part of the owner's concern. (See Quick Start 2 concerning link parameters.)

Because these matters do not refer to an owner's ID number, which is the linking field between OWNER and CONTACT, you can set the CONTAC set to include the parent file only if it contains reference to a record in the child (OWNERS) file. If no owner's record exists, the item in CONTACT is an entirely different kind of material. A second set can be designed to perform the opposite function. In the second case, the set includes the record in the parent file only if there is no child that matches the parents.

It will be convenient to be able to use two sets to see different kinds of data, knowing that we are really seeing and storing the same data in the same two databases. In this case, the sWitch command can do the job.

T   I   P   You can use this technique in many situations. Consider using it to view invoice records that have NO record of payment in the PAYMENTS database.

In this chapter, you create several sets to see how and why they work the way they do. Then, to make them as useful as possible, you examine the field rules, input forms, and reports, as they are related to issues in sets. Finally, you start putting scripts to work to make the sets easier to manage.

Creating a Set

The following steps are general guidelines to help you get better results when working with the design of your sets and databases:

1. Draw a picture of the relationships. Set them down on paper so you will remember them and follow a logical plan.

2. Prepare the primary and secondary files with indexes and field rules before you whip into action.

3. Design the sets, using the indexes to control relationships, based on knowledge of how the sets can work for you.

Choosing Sets versus Lookup Databases

A frequently asked question is, *When should I use a lookup database and when should I use a set?* Depending on the circumstances, you may need to use both simultaneously. A set enables you to see and use data in two or more files linked by the common field. The lookup database automatically enters the data from another database when used in the same set and serves to automate the linking process. With just a couple of keystrokes plus F3 you can enter the linking data and cause the screen to display the requested fields in the linked file.

Quick, accurate, and efficient data entry is the goal of most users. For that reason, you should focus on techniques, such as the lookup method mentioned above, which lend themselves to this goal. In the following section, you roll through the process of designing a functional data entry system for the CONTAC.SET discussed in Chapter 9. The parent file is CONTACT.DBF and the child file is OWNERS.DBF.

The purpose of this set is to enable you to view in sequence the records' instructions, requests, and problems with your clients. Each contact is recorded with the owner's ID number, as looked up in the OWNER database. When the link has been established and an input form created with fields from both databases, you can see each of the records in the CONTACT file click past as you press the up- and down-arrow keys while the linked record in the parent file remains the same on the screen.

Because the records are indexed on the OWNER_ID field and the CONT_DATE field, the conversations or meetings with each owner will be sequentially listed by date. If the index is made using OWNER_ID + invert(CONT_DATE), then the records appear in order from the most recent event to the earliest. This configuration is convenient as a means of keeping you up to date on the current status of the discussion.

Consider what would happen if the two files were linked with only the last record based on the date. Before the set is created, make preparation for the linking by building the indexes you will need. The linking index must be available and the linking field or expression identified. The contact file is linked to owners using ALL records in the set editor screen.

Creating Field Rules in a Set

Field rules accompany a database when it becomes the parent file in a set. When designing a database that has a number of lookups, calculated fields, case conversions, skip fields, and so on, remember to complete as many as possible of the field rules that will be needed in the new set. Of course, if you decide later that another field rule is needed, you can add it, but it will have to be done in field rules in the set as well as in the original file if you need it in both.

This principle is not true for other supporting files, such as input forms, browse tables, mail labels, global updates, and saved searches. These files will not travel with the original when it becomes the parent file. In some cases, there are files that are rarely used, except in a set. Don't waste time making reports and input forms for such a file. Save your time for making great things happen in the set; you should make those decisions and create the reports, forms, and browse tables after the set has been made. Then the fields from all the files can be included. If they are needed later in the flat file, the report, forms, and browse tables can be *borrowed* back and redesigned for the child file.

Determining Field Origin

Using the fields from two or more databases linked in a set is easy when you understand which functions allow you to choose from all the linked files. The following sections discuss basic operations and which files are available in each.

Creating an Index

When you create an index, the only fields available are those in the parent database. If you want to be able to *find* customers by last name, that field must be available in the active CONTAC.SET as the parent file. This configuration is a duplication of data that purists may say is unnecessary, but in most business applications, the practical advantage of being able to find items by a last name should override purity of technique any day.

Defining a Global Update

You can only update fields from the current, parent database. However, when you get to expressions, you will find that fields from CONTACT and OWNERS are available for creating an update expression. In other words, the field to be updated must be in the parent database. The expression that performs the update can be taken from a combination of the two or more databases in a set. In global update, the screen where expressions are created looks like figure 8.4.

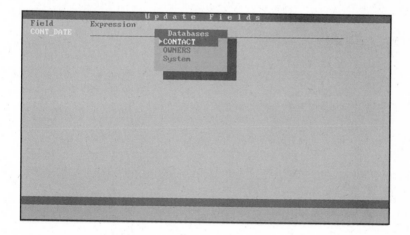

Creating Field Rules

Calculated fields can draw from fields in all linked databases. In Default mode, in the required expression, in data-validation expressions, in double-entry expressions, and frequently-used skip expressions, a field from any linked child database can be used in an expression. Unfortunately, when you set up a lookup table, the only fields available are from the parent or primary database.

Retrieving the Linked Data

To prompt the user to select an existing last name or owner's ID from the OWNERS database, you can define the same file that is linked in the set as the lookup database in field rules. When you select a last name or owner's ID as you create a record, the related information appears on the screen to complete the information about the owner. Therefore, you can create two lookup links: one on OWNER_ID and the second on LASTNAME.

You may observe that storing last names is redundant and therefore not strictly necessary to this database. You include the LASTNAME field here to demonstrate the benefit of linking on a unique identifier, such as the OWNER_ID, and on the far easier and more memorable last name of an owner.

As you create the entry form for the CONTACT + OWNERS set, select the LASTNAME field as the first one on the screen and the OWNER_ID as the second. The input form for your CONTAC.SET can look like that in figure 8.5.

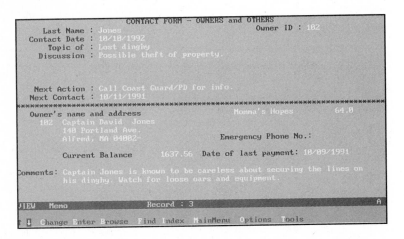

FIG. 8.5

Edit the input form for CONTAC.SET.

Notice that all the fields below the line of asterisks are from the OWN-ERS database. Because the primary activity of this form is to record the events relating to owners and boats, you rarely need to access the fields in the owners' file. When you need to change the data in an owner's record, you can press **Z** and press Enter to zoom to the OWN-ERS file, as described previously.

When you use Zoom to access a child file in a set, Alpha Four will zoom to the matching record if one exists. If no matching record exists in the

child file, Alpha Four zooms to a blank record that shows Record: 0 on the information line. You can automate the creation of a new owner's record by typing the information into this record. When the new owner's information is saved on the child file, uN-zoom by pressing U to return to the parent record (see fig. 8.6). By pressing Change and pressing F3 (Choices), you can see the newly recorded information pop into the waiting fields below the asterisk line.

NOTE The Zoom function is different in versions prior to Version 2.

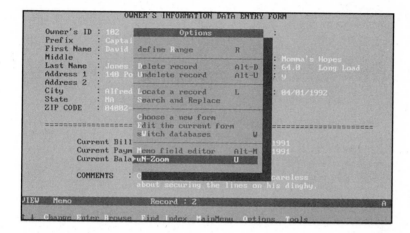

FIG. 8.6

The uN-zoom function in View mode.

Using Colorful Math

Alpha Four can perform calculations on any of the fields in all of the databases that are linked in a set. Suppose that you want to have the computer send you a signal when some event occurs. For example, if the balance of an owner's account is greater than $1,000.00 and the date of the bill is greater than today's date minus 30 days, make the data in the last name field blink.

The color expression is accessed while editing a form under the formatting options. Put your cursor on the field you want to put an equation in and press Alt-O then F6. The expression prompt appears. Type in your equation and press F10 and save the form.

Write the following expression:

    if(OWNERS->BALANCE > 1000 .and.
    (OWNERS->BILL_DATE < SYSTEM->DATE - 30), 135,7)

The English translation of this expression is the following:

If the total basic charge amount in the owner's record is greater than 1000 and the billing date is less than the system date (probably today) minus 30 days, then BLINK, otherwise, normal.

The Color Expression screen should look like figure 8.7.

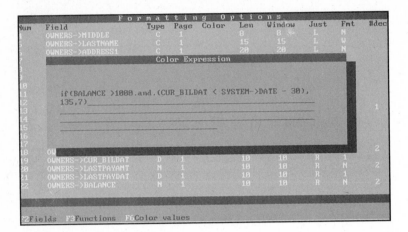

Color Expression compares overdue account with system date field to change the screen color.

Copying a Set

Although you can easily copy a database, copying a set is more difficult. Suppose that you are in a set and select Utilities, Copy. As you type a legitimate DOS name for the copy, Alpha Four creates the copy of the parent file of the current set and changes the name from .SET to .DBF.

CAUTION If you hope to copy the set in which you are currently working onto a floppy disk to take it home to work on it at night, be careful to examine the process carefully before you assume that you have successfully copied the set. Alpha Four copies the current database to a file using whatever name you type and carries the supporting files (forms, browse tables, reports, etc.) with it to the new file. *Alpha Four does not carry along the linked files, however.*

To copy a set, select each linked file that you want included in the copy process. Copy each one individually, remembering that the copy command never includes indexes. Say **Yes** to the question: Include supporting files? and copy the Set files using DOS.

To copy any set, perform the following steps:

1. Select *each* of the linked files in turn and use **U**tilities, **C**opy, and name the new file. For example, if you want to copy the file named OWNERS to a floppy disk in the A: drive, at the bottom of the screen, type the following name:

   A:\OWNERS

2. Press Enter. Use the range setting screen to select the appropriate index and the first and last records to be copied based on that index. Use the Filter to exclude unneeded records. For example, use **LOA > 0.00**. Repeat for each linked file.

3. From the Main Menu, press Alt-F9 to retrieve the function called DOS access. The Alpha Four software suspends itself temporarily. The next message you see on the screen is the following:

   ```
   Alpha Four DOS access.
   Type Exit to return to Alpha Four.
   ```

   When you access DOS, you can perform any of the normal DOS commands, including copy files. To find out how many files are associated with your set, use the DOS DIR command to view a list of these files. For example, if you are working on a set called CONTAC.SET, you can find all files by using the following DOS command:

   DIR contac*.*

   The asterisk (*), when used in DOS, is a wild card. This command shows you every file that begins with *contac*, with any two letters following (contacts), and any three-letter extension. The extensions include the files that contain the definitions of forms, reports, searches, global updates, browse tables, field rules, etc. While working at the DOS level, copy the appropriate files from the set to the new subdirectory or floppy disk.

4. When you want to use the copied files, several choices exist: use them on the floppy disk; copy them to the hard disk on a new computer in the same directory; or copy them to a different directory, possibly even a different disk drive, on a different computer. In any case, to use a copied file, any reference to a drive or subdirectory must match the current situation.

When you create a set, the file you create can recognize the drive and path where it finds itself and its linked databases. If the set is copied to a new drive or path, the statement that links the files automatically updates to the new location. Definitions of applications do not. If a formal, menu-driven application accompanies your work, adjustments need to be made.

T I P Remember that the Copy command does not include any index files. If you want to use an entire database and all of the supporting files, as well as the currently existing indexes, you can copy the files using the regular DOS copy commands. Copy the .NDX files as well as all others. In this manner, you can carry your entire set or single flat file application with you from one machine to another.

Carrying your entire database and all sets and index files around on a floppy disk should not diminish the vital significance of this data. In fact, if your files are small enough to fit on a floppy disk, this method of retaining a back up of your data is relatively easy and quick. If your files are too large for a floppy, the next choice is to split the file in half, copy record number 1 through X on one disk, and copy X to last record on the second disk. If space is becoming an issue, copy the support files only once and say **No** to the question for subsequent files. This process can be automated with a macro in an application or by using a script. (See discussions of scripts in Chapter 2 and applications in Chapter 11.)

CAUTION If you can back up your critical data on a floppy in a matter of several minutes, so can someone else. The .DBF format is easily transferable, printable, and usable in other software. If your data contains material that you do not wish others to have, consider an encryption software to *scramble* the .DBF file itself. Placing a password on the forms or restricting access to the enter, change, and delete functions only works at the Alpha Four level. Anyone familiar with DOS can find and copy a .DBF file for negative purposes. (Encryption, a different and more effective process than assigning passwords, is discussed in Chapter 14.)

Summary

In this chapter, you created a set and looked at the differences between using flat files and files linked in a set. Input forms and browse tables have distinct differences in both function and creation, but reports are more powerful but less different in sets.

More advanced Alpha Four activities require you to use DOS commands. The most important DOS commands are described here, but you may need a manual on the operating system for your computer.

Moving Your Data and Files

The greatest task before civilization at present is to make machines what they ought to be, the slaves, instead of the masters of men.
Havelock Ellis, Little Essays of Love and Virtue

So far in this book, you have learned how to create files (Chapter 2). You have learned how to enter data into records by using the keyboard or lookup rules or calculations, to view the data in the default view and browse formats, and to customize the view and browse formats to suit your needs (Chapters 3, 4, and 5). You have learned how to put your records in order by indexing on one or several fields (Chapter 4) and then how to report on and calculate the existing data to output to a printer, screen, or file (Chapters 6 and 7). You also have learned how to link two or more files to create a set, giving new perspective to your output and calculations (Quick Start 2 and Chapter 8).

The portion of this book that follows this chapter talks about swapping data in and out of temporary files; setting and carrying variables between files; and creating, overwriting, and erasing files and records as part of application development. Therefore, this chapter is designed to help you learn how to make these moves as single operations.

After your data has arrived safely in fields, records, and files in Alpha Four, this question may occur to you: *How can I move this data around to suit my different needs?* As a group, the commands to carry out this kind of activity are found under the menu heading Utilities. You also may need to move entire files around—perhaps copy all or part of a file to a floppy disk or to a backup file on the hard disk, erase a file, dupli-cate an existing file, summarize in one file the data from another file, and cross-tabulate a file to a new file. You can find these commands in both the Database/Set design and Utilities menus.

In Chapter 8, you considered the creation of sets, the basic *relational* function. Now in this chapter, you examine other commands that move data from one file to another: the Copy command, which creates an exact or partial copy of the current file; the Append command, which adds records to the current file; and the crosstab function (Version 2 only), which summarizes one file on different fields; the Import and Export commands, which pass data to and from external sources; and the relational commands Post database, Join database, Subtract data-base, and Intersect database. The summarize operation, which uses one file or a set of related files to create a summary of related records in a separate database, is discussed in Chapter 7.

Copying a File

The copying operation causes anxiety even for accomplished data man-agers if they are not acquainted with the procedures of working with DOS. (Chapter 3 also contains a brief discussion of the Copy com-mand.) You can copy a data file in one of the two following ways:

1. Let Alpha Four do most of the work.

2. Leave Alpha Four and do the job at the disk operating system level (DOS).

If you elect to make the copy by using DOS, you should know that there are many small files associated with each data file. These include the definitions of forms, reports, field rules, searches, global updates, the color palette definitions, the desktop files, the .UDN (user defined name), the script files, and many more. Using the DOS command, **COPY FILENAME.* A:** transfers most—but maybe not all—the files from wherever they are to the A:\ drive. You run the risk of missing related files that do not have the same name, such as script files. If you choose to copy a file by using the Alpha Four Copy command, then Alpha Four copies any pertinent files.

NOTE Index files are never copied when a database is copied.

To make a copy of the MYFRENDS.DBF data file, make MYFRENDS the active file and perform the following steps:

1. Choose the **U**tilities menu. Alpha Four responds with the Utilities menu. The first choice is **C**opy database. Press Enter to select this choice.

2. The next screen requests that you type the name of the new file that you are about to create. If you precede the name of the file with a drive or path setting, the new file will be in that location. For example, to make a copy of the file on a floppy disk in the A: drive, type **A:\NEWFILE** and press Enter. The next menu gives you the choice of taking all fields or making a selection. Choose **S**elected fields.

3. The next screen enables you to choose among the fields in the current file. Press the Enter key to select some or all of the fields, or press F6 to select the entire column of fields. F4 enables you to reorder the fields you have chosen. Press F10 (Continue) when the selection is complete.

4. The next screen is the Range Settings screen. Here, you can define which records will pass through to the new copy of MYFRENDS. If you use the Record number as the primary index, you have the same records in the same order as when the file was created. If you want to create a new file in a specific order, such as LASTNAME or CITY, without creating another index, select that index at this point. When you open the copied file, it will appear in that index's order.

5. On the range setting screen, you also have the usual range commands: Order, Show, First and Last record, Unique keys, and Filter. With these settings, you can select among the records you want to place in the new copy. Press F10 (Continue).

6. The next screen requests that you give the file a significant name that identifies the file. If the file is archival in nature, a good description might be **Copy of all records as of 10/01/92**. The last line asks whether you want to copy the support files. The support files include all forms, reports, search definitions, and so on. A current copy of the support files should be maintained, but you may need to save space on a single floppy by saying **N**o to this question. Press F10 to complete the process.

NOTE If you are copying a set, the field selection screen discussed in the preceding Step 3 enables you to choose among the fields from all related databases. The resulting file contains one record for each record identified in the primary database of the set.

Understanding the Relational Commands

The relational commands in Alpha Four are Post database, Join database, Subtract database, and Intersect database. Each of these commands performs a unique function in the world of database management.

Of the four, Post database is the most commonly understood and probably the most often used. With this command, you update the current database by posting from a second database. You deal with two existing files. The *master* file is the current database during a relational operation. The master file determines the index and common fields for the *transaction* file.

The other three commands use two files, the current or primary database and a secondary database, to create a third new, physical database called the *result* database.

The following list gives you brief definitions of all four commands:

- Post database applies data from the transaction file to the master file, a process that adds to, subtracts from, or replaces existing data.

- Join database combines two files containing fields from both "parents" based on the records in the primary file.

- Subtract database compares the records in two databases and copies into a third database the records that are unique to the first file.

- Intersect database is more discriminating, creating a third file by using only records that are common to both files.

The following commands are not considered relational, but because they "move data" they are discussed in this chapter:

- Copy replicates the current file, carrying some or all records in the current file to a new file, using a selectable index and range settings.

- Append adds records from the secondary file to the end of the list of records in the current file.

- Summarize accumulates data based on records in one file.

- Import converts data from external software data files to Alpha Four.

■ Export converts data to another format for use with an external software package.

■ Crosstab creates a new file based on grouping fields in the current file or set.

Table 9.1 shows how the relational functions within Alpha Four work. The table gives examples for the current file and secondary file names and the results of using the respective commands.

> Preparation for the relational functions means that you must be certain of the names of the two files that are needed for the planned operation. Verify as well that a common field is used in their indexes.

T I P

Table 9.1 Alpha Four's Relational Functions

Command	Current File	Secondary File	Result
Post	INVENTRY	PARTS	Updates prices in inventory
Join	INVOICE	OWNERS	Creates new file showing all records in INVOICE file and added fields with data from matching fields in OWNERS file
Subtract	INVENTRY	PARTS	Creates list of new parts not in current inventory
Intersect	INVENTRY	INVOICE	Creates new file showing only those records with a matching record in INVENTRY
Non-relational commands that move data			
Append	INVENTRY	PARTS	Adds new items (unique) to existing file
Copy			(See Chapter 3)

continues

Table 9.1 Continued

Non-relational commands that move data

Import	Receives data from other formats, ASCII, .WK1
Export	Sends sales figures to spreadsheet, word processor, or ASCII format
Summarize	(See Chapter 7)
Crosstab	Analyzes INVOICE database by customer purchases

A number of reasons exist for learning about and understanding the functions of the four relational commands, but you may find that you can simulate many of the operations offered by the relational utilities by using the set functions of Alpha Four. The customer file linked to the invoice file, for example, provides a simulation of what takes place when you use the Post database command. You can print a summary report from a set that gives the totals and year-to-date figures for customers or for particular invoices, but the totals are not stored in the customer data file unless they are posted from the transaction database. Commonly, a series of transactions is held during the period of verification (bids, quotes, orders, and so on) until they are completed. Then the files are posted to a summarizing record and cleared out of the transaction file.

In sets, no third file results from the Join database, Subtract database, and Intersect database commands. Instead, a logical database is created that always shows the changes made to the component files. Furthermore, changes that occur in the Post database command alter the data in the current file. If you compare this design with a one-to-one or one-to-many link between a parent and child file in a set, you can understand that you have no way to update a file without a certain amount of manipulation in a set, involving variables and scripts. (For more information, see Chapter 12.)

You need to understand at the outset that the new files created by Join database, Subtract database, and Intersect database are independent of their parent files. No dynamic link exists between these files. They are not updated by changes in their predecessors. On the other hand, if you create a script or menu choice in an application that exports specific data to a spreadsheet such as Lotus 1-2-3, you can create the same effect as a dynamic link, because updates can occur without user intervention.

NOTE Join database, Subtract database, and Intersect database operate with a range-setting screen, which means that you can define a specific range of records at the time of the operation or can retrieve a previously saved range. The Append and Post database commands do not utilize the range-setting screen.

NOTE A document in WordPerfect can contain a dynamic link to a spreadsheet. This feature is important if special formatting or a proportional font is required for your report.

Posting Data from One File to Another

To continue with the example used throughout this book, suppose that you have an INVENTRY database for the boatyard. This file contains records of the items that you carry in inventory for the convenience of your boat owners. Suppose that the distributors who wholesale these items to you are becoming modernized and have offered to send revised price lists on a disk in any format you prefer. Of course, as a user of Alpha Four, you reply that this effort would be a great convenience and ask to have the files sent in DBF format, the dBASE standard. (See Chapter 1 for more information on DBF file formats.)

After agreeing about the appropriate size floppy disk upon which you want the data to be sent, you settle down to work out the method for using the data when it arrives in the mail. (An alternative is to use a modem and log on to the distributor's bulletin board service and download just the records you want from the distributor's master file.) The issue is how to get the new data into your current INVENTRY file.

Understanding How Posting Works

The steps to posting correctly are sufficiently complex that you should try them on small sample files before you consider taking such dramatic action on "live" data. Almost certainly, you will want to design a small application or write a script file to manage this operation so that it comes out the same way every time. (See Chapter 12 for information on writing scripts and Chapter 11 to learn about creating application macros.)

To set up a practice example for the boatyard database, first you need to make sure that your INVENTRY file contains at least these seven fields:

Name	Type	Width	Decimal Places
ITEM_NO	C	4	
DESCRIPT	C	30	
ARR_DATE	D	8	
QTY	N	5	2
UNITS	C	25	
PRICE	N	7	2
TOTAL	N	10	2

You also must create a PARTS file to represent the distributor's list and then enter some records to be posted during the example. Some records should be the same as those listed in the INVENTRY file, others should be different, and the prices on the new list, of course, should be increased. (The price increase represents an economic law: "What goes up should never come down." This law is not, however, a rule of database management.) Your PARTS file should have these five fields:

Name	Type	Width	Decimal Places
ITEM_ID	C	4	
SKU_NUM	C	4	
DESCRIPT	C	50	
UNITS	C	25	
PRICE	N	7	2

Obviously, the two files do not match completely, and ITEM_NO and SKU_NUM do not appear to match. These inconsistencies do not matter to the projects you are going to undertake. When you use the Post database command, the data in the distributor's file changes the data in your INVENTRY file to show the current prices.

When you have the files fixed clearly in mind, proceed with the following series of steps:

1. Make the current file the one that you want to update from the external database. In the example, INVENTRY is the file to be updated from the external PARTS database from the distributor, so make INVENTRY the current file. Be sure that the ITEM_NO is the current index.

2. From the Main Menu, select **Utilities**.

3. From the Utilities menu, select **R**elational commands.

4. From the Relational Utilities menu, select **P**ost database (see fig. 9.1).

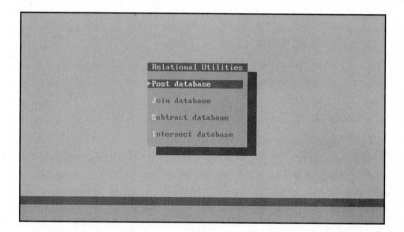

FIG. 9.1

The Relational Utilities menu.

5. Type the name of the transaction database, or use the up-arrow key to highlight the name. In the example, the name is PARTS.

6. Press N to indicate that the common fields do *not* have the same field names, and press F10 (Continue). Figure 9.2 shows how the screen looks at this point. If the field names in both files are exactly the same, you can press Y and the software makes the best match of field names. Leave the next three lines as they are for now. See the following section, "Marking Posted Records," regarding the purpose of these three selections.

7. Press the space bar to remove the default entry. Press F2 (Fields) to choose SKU_NUM from the PARTS database. This field matches the PART_NO in the INVENTRY database. Press F10 (Continue). See figure 9.3.

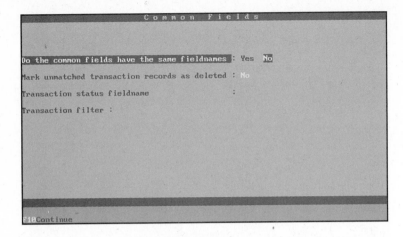

FIG. 9.2

Indicating that common fields do not have the same field names.

8. Press the down-arrow key to highlight line 6 the PRICE field, press R to change the *operation* to Replace. Press F2 (Fieldnames) to select PRICE from the PARTS database. Press F10 (Continue), as shown in figure 9.4. This process identifies the field or fields that will be altered during the Post command.

If the process has been successful, you see the program rapidly counting the number of posted records. Keep your eye on the screen. In a small file, this process happens very fast.

You can design a filter that excludes records not appropriate to your needs. Suppose, for example, that the distributor carries ski mobile equipment as well as the yacht supplies you purchase. The part numbers for ski mobile equipment begin with a 3000 series of numbers. This series must be filtered because you purchase other items in the 3000 range from another distributor.

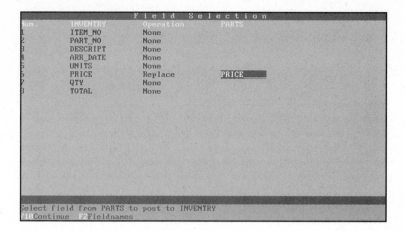

FIG. 9.4

This screen identifies the fields to be replaced when posting takes place.

To automate the Post procedure, you need to create a script file that repeats the process unfailingly—every time. Such a keystroke script reads as follows:

{ALT-F10}ipburpPARTS{ENTER}n{F10}item_id{F10}{DN:4}rprice{F10}

Marking Posted Records

Because of the nature of the Post database command, which changes data in your current file, you need to use a further measure of protection in addition to using a script. You need to mark the posted records with specific, identifying information. Then a field such as POSTED, defined as a logical field, has the responsibility of denoting whether a record can be processed with the Post database command. When a record is created, the default entry should be No. A Y in the field signifies that the record has been posted. At the time of posting, when you define the common field, the third and fourth lines are where you fill in the transaction status field name and the transaction field. If the field is called POSTED and the filter is .NOT. POSTED, the command proceeds just as you planned.

Distinguishing between Post and Append

The difference between **P**ost and **A**ppend is clear when you consider that append means add records, not replace part of matching records. The distributor's file could have a number of products that you do not intend to carry in your boatyard. If you use the Append command, the effect is quite different than if you post the new prices in matching records.

A major difference also exists between Versions 1 and 2 of Alpha Four with the Append command. In Version 1, the filter command alone can limit the record that will be posted. If you mistakenly post the same records more than once without using the marking technique to indicate that a record has been posted, you can continue to multiply similar or identical records in your primary file. In Version 2, you can establish that only *unique* records will be appended. New products in the distributor's PARTS file are recognized as not existing in your INVENTRY file, so they are added to the list. In addition, you can determine that a field such as QUANTITY, which does not exist in the PARTS file, remains untouched during the appending process. Therefore, your existing quantity information remains untouched.

CAUTION Like **G**lobal update, the Post and Append commands can do amazing amounts of work when they are set up properly. But they can do terrifying amounts of damage in a hurry if they are misused. Always back up your data before experimenting with these operations, and always practice first on small, test files before sacrificing real records to careless actions.

To use the Append command, follow these steps:

1. Make current the file that you want to update from the external transaction database. In the example, the INVENTRY database is the file to be updated from the PARTS transaction database from the distributor, so make INVENTRY the current file and use ITEM_NO as the current index.

2. From the Main Menu, select Utilities, Append, Unique to add only records that currently do not exist in the current file (INVENTRY in this case). See figure 9.5.

3. Type the name of the external database or use the up arrow to highlight the name. In this example, the name is PARTS.

4. Press N to indicate that the common fields do not have the same field names. (If you press Y to indicate that the field names are the same, the odds are high that you will get an error message. The only way around the error message is to press N and pass on to the next screen where you can examine the field names by using the F2 (fields) selection and verify the field you expect to use.) You can add a filter expression on the next line if appropriate. A common filter in Append is based on dates or dollars: DATE > {06/01/93} or PRICE < 500.

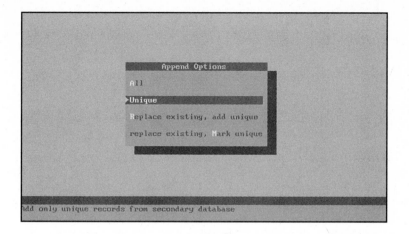

FIG. 9.5

The Append Options include the choice to exclude duplicates.

5. Press F2 (Fieldnames) to choose ITEM_ID from the PARTS database. Press F10 to continue. This action identifies the field that forms the link, based on the primary index in the current database.

6. Match the right fields from PARTS with INVENTRY's fields (see fig. 9.6). Then press F10 (Continue). The program shows the record count as the Append function proceeds.

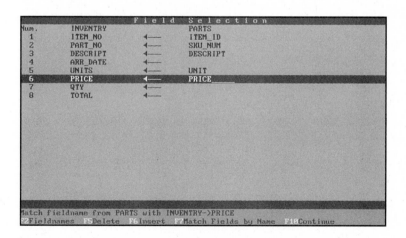

FIG. 9.6

The Primary Field Selection screen for the Append command.

Splicing and Dicing with Subtract, Join, and Intersect

These three commands compare two files and create a third file that contains records that do *not* match (Subtract); *do* match (Intersect) the secondary file, based on a comparison with records in the primary file; or, in the case of Join, the third file contains a *copy* of *each* record from both databases, regardless of the match.

Extracting Nonmatching Records with Subtract

To help you understand the use of the Subtract database command, take a look at an example. Suppose that you want to remove from database NEWSTUFF any records that are not represented in database MYPARTS. In Alpha Four, this decision involves using the Subtract database command. In effect, you create a new file to replace the primary file. The records are not actually removed. They just never get to the new file. Therefore, you can verify that the Subtract database command has given you the records you wanted by reviewing the result file for exciting new products that you want to add to your inventory without being distracted by listings of existing products. The result file contains any records that are not represented by the primary database, which in this case is your inventory file.

Suppose, for example, that the distributor sends you a list of new products, many but not all of which you believe are on your own list. Using the Subtract database command gives you a list of just the items that are not found on your current inventory, so you can give these items further consideration. Subtract database compares two files and creates a third file containing records that are unique to the primary database.

To use the Subtract database command, follow these steps:

1. Choose the PARTS database as your current file using SKU_NUM (representing the part number assigned to the part in both fields) as the primary index. This file contains records that match those that exist in your inventory and new products that are not in your file. From the Main Menu, select **U**tilities. Alpha Four shows the Utilities menu.

2. Select **R**elations commands, **S**ubtract database.

3. On the next screen, the program shows a listing of the database directory. Select as the secondary file your existing inventory listing: INVENTRY. Make sure that a valid index exists, such as SKU_NUM available.

4. You cannot get past the next screen unless the secondary file has been attached to a valid index. When you select an index, Alpha

Four moves on to the next screen, which asks whether the common fields have the same field name. You should reply No to this question, and access the Command Field Expression screen to verify that all indexes and expressions are properly selected. If the correct answer is Yes, this screen is bypassed.

5. The next screen enables you to create an expression or simply select a field using F2 (Fieldnames) in the secondary, which will serve as the link between the two files.

6. The next two screens show the fields from the primary and secondary files. On each screen, you select the fields that you want to see represented in the result database. Press Enter to select or deselect a single field, or press F3 to select the entire list. The triangle appears next to any selected fields. Press F10 to continue.

7. When both databases have been identified, the databases have been linked by their common fields, and the fields have been identified, the next screen asks you to type a name for the new database. For the example, type **newitems** as the intended name for the new file. Type a description that identifies the file for you, such as **new products to be reviewed for next year - 4/01/92.**

8. The next field shows a range-setting screen. The primary index refers to the one that was current when the primary file was placed into the Subtract process. At this point, you can enter further refinement by dates, seasons, and descriptive filters such as "list price > 25.00" and others. The secondary index governs which records are matched and by what field. Press F10 to continue.

The result of the Subtract operation is a third file in which one record is created for each record that is not found in common with records from the secondary file.

Creating a Third File from Two Files with Join Database

Have you ever discovered in your business that two departments are maintaining similar files with parallel information, with neither knowing that the other is partially duplicating its work? Have two groups ever taken the same or similar databases and gone off to do their own work, forgetting that another group was tracking the same customers/patients/students/donor/parts while they are keeping a log on the invoices/X-rays/grades/gifts/orders?

When this kind of inefficiency occurs, and you believe that the files could be more useful if the two groups compared their data, the Join database command can rescue the situation. This command works as long as both groups have common data, such as CUST_ID, with which to perform the operation. The field name does not have to be identical, but the information identifying a certain Customer Jones as GC104 in the primary file must be the same as that identifying the same Customer Jones in the secondary file: GC104.

Join database enables you to combine information from two sources, each of which shows common data in a specific field. The command produces similar results to those you see when you use a set with two files linked one-to-one. When two files are joined, the resulting file has some or all of the fields selected in the two databases. No change is made to the two original files. A new record is created for each selected record in the primary database. The range-setting screen is available with Join database.

This technique is different from that of the Append command. Rather than create a third file from the first two, Append adds records in the secondary file to the end of the existing records in the primary file. The Join database terminology is different from Post database as well. With the Post database command, the master file is updated by the transaction file. With Join database, Subtract database, and Intersect database, the primary or current database works with data in a secondary database to create a *result* database.

Suppose, for example, that the distributor who wholesales to you many of the items in your inventory file includes a new field in his next on-line data file, the one you use to update prices. The prices are all the same, but the new field contains information on manufacturers' warranties for certain products. You can add the new field to your existing records with the Join database command. What you need to do here is to create a new inventory file of the products you sell, with the additional field called WARRANTY. (To make the example work, you need to add the WARRANTY field to your sample PARTS database and add some data such as *Lifetime*, *1 year*, and *90 days* to files that already exist in the database.)

When you have the PARTS database prepared for the example, be sure that you have an index on PART_NO with which you can associate the PART_NO field in your INVENTRY database. Also be sure that you have enough room on your hard disk to accept the file, which will be larger, at least by one field, than the original INVENTRY database.

Then, to use the Join database command, follow these steps:

1. Make the INVENTRY database your current file. From the Main Menu, select **U**tilities. Alpha Four responds with the Utilities menu. Choose **R**elational commands, **J**oin database.

2. The next screen asks you to select the secondary database. Use the highlight to select the PARTS file, or type the name on the bottom line. The next screen shows the index descriptions that are available in the secondary file. Select the one that matches PART_NO.

3. If the two files have identical field names to refer to the part number, the next screen should have the answer **Yes**. If not, type **No** and choose the right field name on the common expression line, using F2 (Fieldnames). Press F10 to continue.

4. The next screen shows the fields in the primary database, in this case INVENTRY. Press F3 to select all the fields because this database is your file of selected data. Press F10 to continue. The screen should look like figure 9.7.

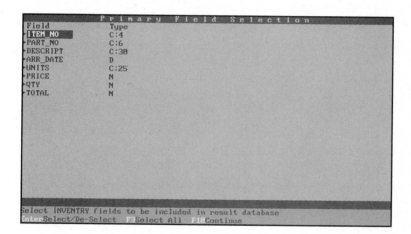

FIG. 9.7

Selecting fields from the primary file for the Join data function.

5. The next screen shows the fields in the secondary database, which is PARTS in the example. Highlight only the WARRANTY field and press Enter to select the one field. The right triangle mark, ▶, shows next to this field. The WARRANTY field will be added to the new database that you are about to create. Press F10 to continue.

6. On the next screen, type the name of the new inventory file that contains the warranty information. Use a name such as **new_invt**. Type a description, such as **Inventory List with Warranty Data, 01/01/93**. Press F10 to continue.

7. On the range-setting screen that appears next, be sure to select the index that indicates the PART_NO. Press F10 to complete the JOIN function.

The result of this exercise is a new file with the warranty information in a new field matched to the appropriate part number.

Intersecting Data Files

The third relational function is Intersect. With this command, you can create a third database that compares two files and contains only the records based on the primary file, which also exist in the secondary file.

As an example of how this command works, consider your inventory stock again. Perhaps a glance in the back room is enough to tell you exactly which products sell and which ones you want to eliminate and never order again. If the problem is bigger than this seat-of-the-pants method of inventory control, you can call up your INVOICE database, in which a record exists of each part number sold on an invoice. With this file and the Intersect database command, you can create a list of items currently listed in your inventory that have appeared in an invoice, indicating that these items should be kept in stock.

To use this command, you must have entered some sample data into your INVOICE database. Take the following steps to Intersect your INVENTRY field with your INVOICE database:

1. Make INVENTRY your current database, and select the PART_NO field to create an index upon which the comparison will be based.

2. From the Main Menu, select Utilities. Alpha Four responds with the Utilities menu. Select **R**elational commands, **I**ntersect database.

3. On the next screen, use the arrow keys to identify the secondary file that is to be compared to the current file. (In this example, select INVOICE to be compared to the INVENTRY information.)

4. The next screen requests that you identify the secondary index to use in this action. The index should reflect the link between the two files: PART_NO.

5. Next, you are asked whether the two files have identical field names. Select No to view the screen containing the Common Field Expression selections. Use F2 to choose the linking field. Press F10 to continue.

6. On the next screen, select the fields that form the primary database to be included in the result file. Press Enter to select or deselect the fields, or press F3 to select all fields. Press F10 to continue.

7. The selection of the secondary file's fields is done on the next screen as in Step 6. Press F10 to continue.

8. On the next screen, type a name for the new file, or overwrite a preexisting file if this procedure is part of a regular office process.

9. On the range setting screen, you can impose a variety of selections, including filters. Press F10 to continue.

10. One record is created in the file for each record that exists in the INVOICE database.

The result is that you have a new file containing one record for each item that appears on an invoice.

Performing Crosstab Functions

Cross-tabulation, which is available in Version 2 only, is another great weapon in your arsenal of ways to summarize data in a flat file or a set. The primary index chosen indicates which records are to be summarized and how. The primary file in the set defines the source of the primary index. The analysis is passed through a range-setting screen, so you can restrict the records based on the primary index, select for deleted or not deleted, and calculate based on filters.

Cross-tabulation enables you to define existing fields or calculated fields to be analyzed. The result is a new database that in Browse mode is analogous to a spreadsheet. The data in your original file is summarized on the existing fields or calculated fields you define, shown as the columns. The labels (field names) of the columns are the fields you define. The rows or records represent the summary of the grouping you define by the selection of the index.

Using the SALES database defined in Chapter 4 as a sample of how this process works, several reports are shown in this section. You can create these reports by defining three saved crosstab definitions. The definitions are similar in that the primary activity is summarizing the sales figures. The indexes and the column title fields change to create different effects.

The data in the SALES file includes the following:

REP	DISTRICT	DATE	TOTAL SALES
ATH	Midwest	01-15-1991	23457
ATH	New England	01-15-1991	23467
FEG	South	01-15-1991	25460
FEG	New England	01-15-1991	31372
EMD	Midwest	01-15-1991	34323
FEG	Southwest	01-15-1991	54353
EMD	Midwest	01-15-1991	65434
EMD	Northwest	01-15-1991	65621
FEG	South	02-15-1991	23257
FEG	Southwest	02-15-1991	23455
EMD	Northwest	02-15-1991	23467
EMD	Midwest	02-15-1991	54324
FEG	Midwest	02-15-1991	65466
ATH	New England	02-15-1991	65475
ATH	Midwest	02-15-1991	87645
FEG	South	03-15-1991	21278
EMD	Midwest	03-15-1991	44324
EMD	Northwest	03-15-1991	65422
ATH	New England	03-15-1991	65433
FEG	Southwest	03-15-1991	65467

The following indexes are also on hand:

1. REP
2. DATE + TOT_SALES
3. DATE
4. DISTRICT + TOT_SALES

The report in figure 9.8 was generated by the crosstab function in the SALES database, using calculated fields to accumulate the sales for each district based on the sales of each rep.

			02/10/1992 PAGE: 1
DISTRICT	TOTAL ATH	TOTAL FEG	TOTAL EMD
Midwest	111102	65466	198405
New England	154375	31372	0
Northwest	0	0	54510
South	0	69995	0
Southwest	0	143275	0
	265477	310108	352915

FIG. 9.8

Crosstab report on district sales.

The report in figure 9.9 accumulates the sales of each represenative based on the totals for each district.

					02/10/1992 PAGE: 1
REP	TOT. SW	TOT. NEW ENG	TOT. NW	TOT. SOUTH	TOT. MW
ATH	0	154375	0	0	111102
EMD	0	0	154510	0	198405
FEG	143275	31372	0	69995	65466
	143275	185747	154510	69995	374973

FIG. 9.9

Crosstab report by sales rep.

In the case of figure 9.10, the cross-tabulation is based on calculated fields, using the DATE field. If the DATE field places the sale in the month of January, that data becomes one summarized column; if the date is in February, that data is summarized in another column. This calculation is performed with the rep's initials as the index. Therefore, the sales figures show the January and February totals for each represenative.

REP	JAN	FEB
ATH	37452	76560
EMD	55025	38896
FEG	39586	37393
	132063	152849

FIG. 9.10

Crosstab report by month.

When you do a cross-tabulation, a new database is created with a name of your choice. Based on the way you define the crosstab, the results appear on-screen immediately after the calculation, or you can open the newly created database and examine the report later.

To use the crosstab function, follow these steps:

1. Select the database on which you want to perform a cross-tabulation, such as the SALES file. Create an index on the DISTRICT field.

2. From the Main Menu, choose **U**tilities. Alpha Four responds with the Utilities menu.

3. From the Utilities menu, choose the last item on the menu: cross **T**abulation.

4. Select **C**reate/edit a saved crosstab from the Crosstab options menu.

5. Select an unused letter between A and Z and give the crosstab definition a name that can help you recollect its meaning. For the example, name the file XT_SALES (for crosstab SALES). Then press Enter. The next screen shows the Crosstab description screen, as shown in figure 9.11.

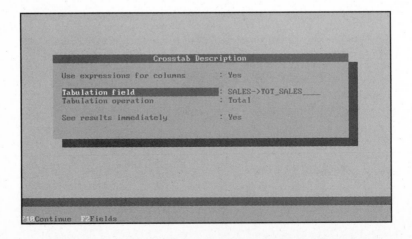

Crosstab Description

Use expressions for columns	: Yes
Tabulation field	: SALES->TOT_SALES_____
Tabulation operation	: Total
See results immediately	: Yes

F10 Continue   F2 Fields

FIG. 9.11

The Crosstab Description screen.

6. Choose **Yes** to indicate the use of expressions for columns, and press F7 to go to the Calculated Fields screen (see fig. 9.12). For this example, the fields are defined in the following manner:

Name	Expression
TOTALATH	REP = "ATH"
TOTALFEG	REP = "FEG"
TOTALEMD	REP = "EMD"

To end the field definitions, press F10 (Continue).

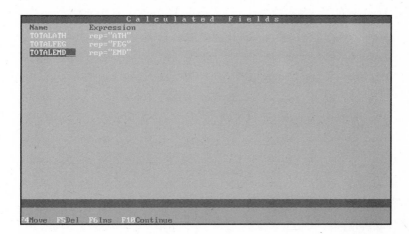

FIG. 9.12

Calculated fields in cross-tabulation.

7. With the cursor in the Tabulation Field field, press F2 and select the TOT_SALES field from the SALES database. In the Tabulation Operation field, select **T**otal. On the bottom line, select **Yes** to see the results immediately. Press F10 to continue.

8. On the next screen, the Range Settings screen, press F2 to select a primary index for DISTRICT. Press F10.

9. The next screen shows the records being calculated and another range-setting screen. Press F10 to continue. The result of the sample exercise should look like figure 9.8.

The final screen shown is a report created automatically by the cross-tab function. Without your needing to do more than give the file a name, the program has created a database, defined the fields, written a report, and printed the report to the screen. This report, of course, can be indexed and printed in the same way as any other database.

NOTE On the Crosstab Description screen, the first choice enables you to create your own field names and put them in order for the tabulation report. If you are satisfied to use the existing field, as shown in figure 9.13, press F2 to select the name from the currently active database. In this case, another line appears to inquire `Create names database: Yes No`.

If you answer **Y**es to the `Create names database` question, Alpha Four creates another database, based on the fields chosen. This file contains two fields, one for the name assigned to the field in the cross-tabulation, the second for the real name of the field in the original file. With these two fields, one record exists for each column in the new database. Alpha Four creates the new database by taking the name of your primary database and adding the underline character, as in MYFILE_. The purpose of this file is to give you a reference against which to match the names of the fields in the cross-tabulated database and the actual field values.

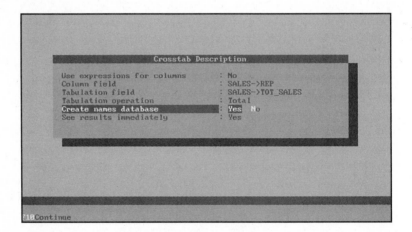

FIG. 9.13

Defining the column field from the current database.

Summarizing the Effects of Relational Commands

The Intersect database and Subtract database commands are parallel in structure. Both create a third file from the results of the activity. Intersect database makes a result file containing only the records for the primary database that have a matching record in the secondary file. Suppose that you decide to send an electronic listing of your overdue accounts to your collection agency. Intersect database enables you to create a third file by comparing your CUSTOMER file with the INV_PAID file. This database can be transmitted to your collection agent, who will give you faster service and perhaps a smaller charge. In this manner, no extraneous information other than the balance due and name and address data are sent.

With Subtract database, you get an opposite effect. The goal of the Subtract database command is to create a third database containing only records that are *not* found in the primary file. If you have a copy of last year's holiday greetings list and a copy of this year's list, for example, you can use Subtract database to examine the records in last year's file that don't turn up in this year's records. This analysis may cause you to wonder why these former friends or customers disappeared. Perhaps with improved customer contact thanks to the help of Alpha Four, you can win these customers back.

Almost universally, database software such as Alpha Four is used to manage mailing lists, a seemingly simple matter—unless you have tried it with more than 25 names. Just the matter of keeping the names and telephone numbers up to date can be overwhelming. Judicious use of these relational commands can make life with a mailing list much easier to bear.

Alpha Four's generation of form letters is simple and effective. A well-tended mailing list can keep those folks in last year's GOOD_CUS file from wandering off to the competition. (For more on the philosophy of mailing lists, please see Appendix D at the back of this book.)

The basic operation for the Subtract, Intersect, and Join commands includes these four steps:

1. Identify and log on to the primary file and select the index that is to form the connection with the secondary file.

2. Identify the fields that are to migrate to the result file.

3. Type a name that identifies the function and the primary database.

4. Make the appropriate changes to the range-setting screen.

Be sure to select the primary index that matches both files. The range-setting screen enables you to identify in the usual manner the specific records you want in the resulting database. A filter operates in this situation as in any other range-setting format.

Putting Yourself into the Import/Export Business

Suppose that someone has offered to share data, enter data, or update your list of data. Sometimes this kind of help seems to make more work than it's worth. When a single database becomes spread around, you begin to risk losing control of the information. You know how messing up your own work makes you feel. Just think how you would feel if you got a friend to help you do it. Lacking the control of well-informed supervision, your data is at risk.

If after all these warnings, however, you know that you can count on bringing files from one computer to another, from one office or business to another, from one software package to another, Alpha Four gives you the tools to do a great job.

Understanding ASCII

You undoubtedly are aware that many software packages can "talk" to each other through the common language called ASCII. The American Standard Code for Information Interchange establishes a format for DOS-readable, otherwise unformatted text. These files are generally the alternative rather than the primary output from most programs. If you want to see a sample of an ASCII file on your computer, type the following line at the DOS prompt in the root directory of the C: drive:

        TYPE C:\AUTOEXEC.BAT

The screen should scroll the English-like commands with which you start up your computer. These words are written in standard ASCII format, importable and readable by most software. Therefore, just about anybody can create an ASCII file that you can read with your Alpha Four software.

One step beyond this into the formatting of files is the DBF format used by all the Xbase software called compatible with dBASE, FoxPro, Clipper, and others. If your friend, business associate, spouse, or other significant person offers to create or share a list of data with you, you should probably accept. Be wary, however, that the addition does not create more work.

If the files you are planning to manipulate are in the ASCII format, you must take one step before you can add them directly to your current data. You must *import* them into a compatible format, using the Data

Import function of Alpha Four. This step is also necessary for data in a
1-2-3 Lotus or Symphony spreadsheet (WKS or WK1) or MultiPlan's
SYLK format, the early dBASE II format, VisiCalc's DIF format, or the PFS
and WordPerfect secondary document. The conversion of data from these
foreign formats is common custom for many database users.

Importing and Exporting

The import and export capabilities of Alpha Four are broad, powerful,
and relatively easy to learn. Alpha Four inherited these capabilities
from its predecessors, Database Manager II, which was subtitled, *The
Integrator*, and ALPHA/*three*. Here are the lists of exchanges that you
can make:

Data Import Menu	Data Export Menu
ALPHA database	ALPHA database
Manager II Ver. 2	Manager II Ver. 2
Lotus 1-2-3/Symphony worksheet	Lotus 1-2-3/Symphony worksheet
SYLK (MultiPlan file)	SYLK (MultiPlan file)
dBASE II DBF file	dBASE II DBF file
VisiCalc DIF file	VisiCalc DIF file
Character-separated ASCII file	Character-separated ASCII file
Table ASCII file	Table ASCII file
PFS file	PFS file
WordPerfect merge document	WordPerfect merge document
	Multimate secondary document

NOTE Importing and exporting are operations that are intended to
convert data files from one file format to another. If your
data is in the dBASE III- or dBASE IV-compatible DBF format,
you can view the data directly in Alpha Four with no need to
go through any other steps or conversion. If the data is in
dBASE II format, Alpha Four recognizes the file and performs
the proper conversions to bring the data into your file.

Dealing with Spreadsheets

If you are handed a disk with a 1-2-3 or Symphony spreadsheet to import, you may need to perform some preliminary steps to make the file readable. Spreadsheet users have the habit of placing descriptive titles at the upper-left corner of the work space and running the rows of data across and below this area. This material is extraneous to the designing of a database. Therefore you need to clean up the spreadsheet before handing it over to Alpha Four. In fact, a good way to make the data ready for your import to Alpha Four is to extract the rows and columns, using the Values command, and save the file under a new name if you do not want to alter the spreadsheet.

In general, the Import command can be relied upon to make good guesses about the data you are asking to bring into a file. In the case of an ASCII file, however, you must make two choices before you can get to the heart of the matter. First, is the file to import stored in character-separated ASCII or table ASCII? Answering this question in turn answers the second question: which format should you choose from the Data Import menu?

Talking to WordPerfect

When Alpha Four exports data to a WordPerfect format from a file with names and addresses, the program creates a header that contains the field names separated by the ~ (tilde) character. Each field ends with the WordPerfect 5.1 symbol, {END FIELD}, and each record ends with the {END RECORD} mark. The header of the WordPerfect file contains a listing of the field names as defined in Alpha Four. These are shown on page 1 of the WordPerfect document. If a blank record is included, the list shows {END FIELD} for each empty field and {END RECORD} at the end of the record.

When you exchange data with Multimate and WordPerfect, Alpha Four prepares its own file, examines the word processor's data for defaults, or asks you to make adjustments. If you prefer to use your word processor to print your form letters, you will find the import and export commands a useful technique. Alpha Four automatically looks for or adds the .DOC extension to Multimate documents and .MRG to WordPerfect files.

Summary

In this chapter, you have examined a number of ways to move your data from one file to another and from disk to disk. One last reminder is needed: Back up your files before you get involved with any of these operations.

It could be argued that the Summarize command belongs in this discussion. Because Summarize generally is used for the purpose of creating a file that can be used to reduce the complexity of advanced reporting projects, however, the discussion of that command is included in Chapter 7.

In the last part of *Using Alpha Four*, you explore the development of applications that automate the complex commands to which you have been introduced in this chapter. Using both the application generator and the scripting functions, you can anticipate nearly everything that you could want the database to do and put these items on menus. By reducing the amount of decision-making, you can reduce the potential errors and raise the productivity of your work sessions and your data-management system.

Using Alpha Four Tips, Tricks, and Techniques

*Private information is practically the source
of every large modern fortune.*
Oscar Wilde, An Ideal Husband

Many users ask the following question: *What are the shortcuts to using
Alpha Four—the ones you can't find easily in the manual?* Version 2 provides many new functions that aren't really shortcuts. Rather, they are
techniques for using a database, and these appear throughout this
book. This chapter discusses shortcuts that are not obvious Alpha Four
features. This chapter includes shortcuts for Alpha Four and other areas of computer operations.

These shortcuts apply to anyone who has enough familiarity with the
computer to expect and understand certain conventions, such as function keys, the Esc key, and standard DOS file management conventions.
These shortcuts apply even more to the nonprogrammer, the person
who categorizes himself or herself as *computer-illiterate*.

Get the Right Hardware

If your applications are small, you require few calculations or indexes, you have only two or three files to be swapped around and less than a few thousand records, then an older PC or XT model will do. If you are planning more extensive operations, save your time and your money. Buy a faster, more powerful machine, with extra memory.

Get the Right Software

Unless your applications are small, as described in the preceding section, get a copy of the latest version of Alpha Four. Alpha Software constantly makes the program better and faster. Version 1 was good, but Version 2 creates indexes faster, searches faster, and enables you to create applications faster.

Don't forget to add hardware or software mechanisms for backing up your data. As much as it is shown to save time—sometimes even jobs or lives—backing up data is a consistently ignored safety procedure. Tape backup systems are a paltry sum compared to the money necessary if your general ledger disappears, the subscribers to your magazine disappear in a puff of electronic carelessness, the diagnoses of your patients crash with your hard disk, or all the company's receivables are suddenly zeros.

Whether you consider yourself a novice or an expert, remember to protect your investment in your time and your data. Back up your files as often as is reasonable. The definition of reasonable is *How much can you afford to lose?* Big banks run redundant systems to protect themselves against data loss of any kind. A poet changes one word in his haiku that changes the meaning significantly, and he copies his file to another floppy disk. *Back up when losing your changes would cause a major inconvenience to recreate the work.*

Don't think it won't happen to you. Eventually you will lose data. Just imagine the feeling of relief and smug self-satisfaction when you produce the most recent back up, just hours old. You don't want to know the other feeling.

This chapter can make computing a little easier for you, but only if you use these hints with care. Even *experts* work too late, get everything just right, and hit **Erase, Yes** at the end. *Experts* also back up corrupted data over their previous good data. No one can protect you from these perils.

Write Down Your Procedures

Tedious and time-consuming as it seems, writing down the steps required to perform certain functions is valuable. This rule is a shortcut because it saves time in the long run. Write down the steps, correct the order of the menus, draw boxes and arrows to show how the data flows, type it up, and keep a notebook on each project, so you will be willing and able to review the material quickly the next time you come back to it.

These guidelines are particularly important when you are developing systems that are intended to last for a long time or to work for other people. If you are a developer, then documenting your work is absolutely critical.

If you are purchasing a system or guiding the work of someone who is developing a system for you, you should insist on seeing documentation to be used by others who may follow. You also must allow time and money for this documentation to be created. If this step is overlooked, you will be left with a system that no one except the designer can operate. Probably even that person, six months later when revisions are required, will have to waste time reviewing and becoming familiar with the material again.

Learn This Program Well

There are approximately 35 Alt-key shortcuts. There are nine ways to move data between files. There are at least three entirely different ways to summarize data for presentation. There is a difference between **F**ind and replace and **G**lobal Update. If you understand the subtleties of these differences, you will save yourself a lot of time. Matters such as these have been shown in various places throughout the book. This chapter deals with examples of ways people have used the program itself to accomplish great things.

Learn Applications and Scripts

Learn to create applications in Versions 1 and above, and learn the scripting capabilities in Version 2. Just the simplest matters, if they need to be performed repeatedly, can be hastened if they are on a menu that is well-tested and works unfailingly.

Using Shortcuts

Using shortcuts does not mean cutting short the time to do things right. In computing, it is rarely possible to cut short the time that it takes to perform tasks; using a shortcut means figuring out ways to do jobs with greater efficiency or insight, so that fewer steps must be taken, less computing time is needed, and more results are evident.

Changing Data in Records by Using a Calculated Field

Global update is a powerful tool for many purposes. One important feature is that the process operates with a range setting screen. There is another choice that can be effective, but only in specialized situations. That situation is generally in a development cycle or after a database has been in use for some time and you are working on field rules to fine-tune your data entry. You can reconfigure to add a new field; go to Field Rules and make it **C**alculated instead of **U**ser-entered; type in the expression or calculation; then reevaluate the database.

For example, in a name and address database, you might be asked to have a FULLNAME field for easy identification on pages 2 and 3 of an input form or to avoid the necessity of creating this kind of field in several different places in the database. If records already exist in the database and you are working in Field Rules anyway, create a calculation in your new FULLNAME field that reads like the following:

trim(FIRSTNAME)+" "+trim(MIDDLE)+" "+trim(LASTNAME)

When you reevaluate the file, the existing records will show the full name, and during data entry, the first, middle, and last names will pop into the FULLNAME field from that time forward.

Creating an Automatic Lookup on More Than One Category

Field	Choices are
COLOR	Black or Colors
STYLE	Wood or Plastic
MATERIAL	Regular or Fancy
CONDITION	New or Used

The preceding categories are mutually exclusive. An item is black or has colors. It is fabricated of plastic or wood. The price depends upon the combination of the eight choices, a possible of 16 combinations, and 16 possible prices. An item could be a BlackPlasticRegularNew or a ColorWoodFancyUsed or any of 14 more combinations. If there is a book value on the item, each choice can add another few dollars to the selling price.

The selection should be made in four one-character fields. A COLOR field will accept B or C, MATERIAL can accept P or W. Field rules will make this an all-caps field with the default of the initial of the word expected.

Create two character fields, each with a length of four. The first is a calculated field that will contain the following formula:

trim(COLOR)+trim(MATERIAL)+trim(STYLE)+trim(CONDITION)

The second field accepts the four initials as a default value. The reason is that a regular character field can accept a lookup, which a calculated field cannot. The second field can be over-typed to make a correction during editing but can be limited to accepting only the eight valid characters. The second field can be linked to a lookup in field rules. Depending on the circumstance, the lookup can be a table or an external database. The lookup can find the occurrence of the right combination, CWFN or BPRU, and put in the calculated price for that specific combination.

This example can be modified to suit a wide variety of multi-level definitions, not just pricing, but any kind of lookup that involves multiple conditions.

Changing the Colors of the Entire Screen

To change the colors on your screen, select Other, Configuration, Set screen colors. At this point, Versions 1 and 2 have very different interfaces. In most of the Alpha Four menus, the users of Versions 1 and 2 will see basically the same choices, but color configuration is one place in which the two diverge. For that reason, the two versions are discussed separately in this section.

Version 1

To fine-tune the color selection, place the highlight on the selection you want to change and select a color from the *palette* at the top of the screen. To make the screen easier to see on a black-and-white or monochrome screen, you can select the F2 (Black/White) setting (see fig. 10.1).

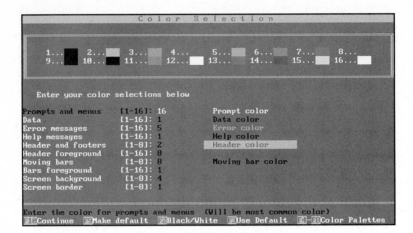

Color selection screen in Version 1.

Certain selections have [1-16] and others have [1-8] after the name. To be compatible with ALPHA/*three* for use on earlier, lower resolution color monitors, only eight colors were available in the original Alpha Four. Those are the [1-8]. Higher resolution added another 8 shades on six of the 10 choices. As you select each color by the number across the top, you will see the description on the right change color.

Beside the Black/White palette are five other pre-defined palettes that you can explore by pressing F4 through F8. Within each of these five, you can customize the screen by changing one or several of the parts. When you find a combination that pleases you, make it the default by pressing F9. If a favorite combination has been defined in this fashion, you can change the colors on a new file or one brought from a different computer by pressing F3 (Use Default).

After a personalized color selection has been made the default, any newly created files will contain these colors.

NOTE The *second* computer at home is frequently monochrome or black and white. If you have transferred your Alpha Four files from a VGA color screen to your laptop with an LCD (liquid crystal display) monitor and find that there seem to be some parts missing, such as the moving bar, the problem may be in the color settings.

Version 2

Users of Version 2 have the revised color setting screen shown in figure 10.2. The number of items over which you have control has doubled, and the color selection has broadened to the range of a VGA screen. The palette settings screen enables you to identify each of the existing colors and increase or decrease the percentage of red, green, and blue in the shade.

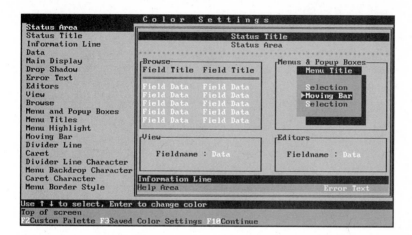

FIG. 10.2

Color selection in Version 2.

By placing the single line box over the color you want to change and pressing F9 (Switch Window), you can use the left- and right-arrow keys to reduce and increase the three component colors (see fig. 10.3).

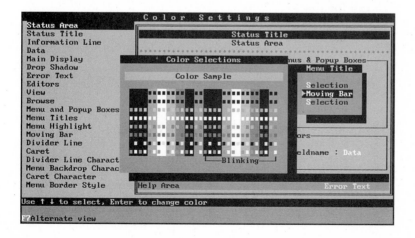

FIG. 10.3

Palette settings are flexible.

Series of color settings have been identified and given names appropriate to their shades. ARIZONA, CAPE COD, LAS VEGAS, LONDON, and NEWPORT are several of the names chosen to represent color schemes. You can select one of the pre-defined settings or modify an existing scheme and give it a name of significance to you or the database.

Using Colors for Help

When you are designing an application for others to use, remember that they may not know Alpha Four as well as you do. This means that they will be telephoning or writing you to ask for assistance on certain matters. This suggestion is designed to assist you when the inevitable calls arrive.

If you are using a pair of sets that show the same files but in different relationships, make the background of one set a light color setting and make the other a darker set of colors. Then when the calls come, you can start quickly to identify the problem by asking which color is shown on the background of the screen.

This tip applies even for an application that you are using. If you will be swapping back and forth frequently, make an obvious color change to tell you immediately which file you are checking at the top of the Main Menu.

During development of screens and reports, placing certain system fields right on the input screen is also helpful. For example, to give notice immediately about the current index, the system database contains three fields that track this matter: INDEX_NAME, INDEX_DESC, and INDEX_EQN. These fields, when placed in an inconspicuous place on your screen, such as the last line on the bottom, will give you quick access to information that you would otherwise need to return to the Main Menu to find. The current system date and time, of course, can usually find a spot on an input screen if work is time-sensitive.

NOTE When the TIME field from the system database is placed on the screen, it will show the current system time. That information will change only as the status of the record is changed by being opened, changed, saved, or reindexed.

Using Alt-F5 and Alt-F6 To Cut and Paste

If you haven't discovered the cut and paste functions of Alt-F5 and Alt-F6, you are in for a treat. Alt-F5 places the contents of a field into a memory location. Alt-F6 pastes the material back into a field. The paste can be performed repeatedly. This is extremely useful if you are developing a series of entries, for example, in calculated fields, in which a group of fields are needed to calculate on another series of fields, such as the following:

Field	Expression
FIELD1	if(trim(upper(NAME1="X","Y")))
FIELD2	if(trim(upper(NAME2="X","Y")))
FIELD3	if(trim(upper(NAME3="X","Y")))

You can write the expression once, put the cursor at the beginning of the Expression field and press Alt-F5. Then move the cursor to the next row, give the field a name, move to the expression line, and press Alt-F6. This will reenter the first line. To create FIELD1, FIELD2, FIELD3, etc., quickly, just enter a 0 in the expression to satisfy the program's need for a valid entry. Then, go back to the top and perform a paste routine with Alt-F6. Use the End key and the arrow keys to make changes to the "X" and "Y" parameters.

Organizing Records

When you need to index on a letter that is never seen on-screen, such as the following expression, you can describe almost any condition in your record. For example, to group names and address records by regions, use a ZIP code analyzer, such as the following:

    if(ZIP < 01700, "A", if(ZIP < 02100, "B", if(ZIP < 02500,"C","X")))

If you need to prioritize records according to some scheme of categorization that does not lend itself to a normal index, create a special character field, width 1, 2, or whatever you need, and use that field to designate a condition.

Suppose that you have a list of classmates, some of whom have given gifts to the school, some have come back to reunion, and some have sent their children to your alma mater. You can use this small character field to signify any or all of these conditions. Furthermore, if George finally turns up for the reunion on the 25th or springs for a new science lab, the status field can change with the flick of a digit.

The special PRIORITY field becomes a calculated field (in field rules) containing something such as the following:

```
(if.not.isblank(REUN_YR),"Y","N") +
(if(SON_DAUGHT = "S","S",if(SON_DAUGHT = "D","D","X") +
(if(GIFT < 50,"X",if(GIFT < 500, "L",if(GIFT < 2500, "M","H"))))))
```

The REUN_YR, SON_DAUGHT, and GIFT fields are prompted or required to have an appropriate entry as indicated. The PRIORITY field calculates on the three fields and shows a code such as the following:

YSL for a reunion buff with a son in the school and a gift of between $50 and $500 for the year

NXX for a non-reunion type with no children in the student body and no history of gifts to the school

Using Pseudo Fields To Prevent Unauthorized Data Changes

People who develop systems for others to use run the risk that their users can and will change data in records that should not be changed. Version 2 has two ways to prevent changes at the record level:

- You can restrict access on the Restrict Access Screen shown in figure 10.4. This selection prevents access to, or places password protection on, a broad variety of activities.

- On the **O**ther, **C**onfiguration, **D**efault settings screen, you can set Prevent change/enter to **Y**es. This restricts all changes and foils all attempts to enter new records.

Version 1 users must be more creative. Lacking the two features described above, users of Version 1.1 and below can use the following trick for sensitive data files.

On the input forms, rather than placing the *real* fields in the view and browse modes, the designer created matching fields for each of those with sensitive data. Using the **C**alculated field definition in **F**ield rules, the designer made a *mirror image* of the data. The calculated field's expression is simply the name of the field that is to be mirrored. Thus, the mirror field, not the real field, is placed on the input form or browse table to be accessible to users. Anyone with knowledge of Alpha Four would be able to track down the reason that the fields are not editable.

If the person is accessing the data through an application, that access can be limited to just those items. Unless you have a mechanism for simply appending data from another file, you must also have at least one screen for doing data entry.

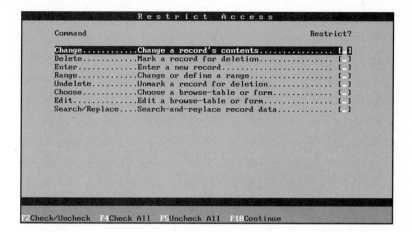

FIG. 10.4

The restrict access screen limits changes by users.

You can use a similar trick without the use of duplicate fields and field rules and create the same effect with calculated fields in view and browse mode. On an input form, create a calculated field for each field in question, and place the reflection, not the original, on the form. The disadvantage of this is the necessity to recreate the calculated fields for all forms or browse tables where they are needed.

Personalizing Your Work

Customize your input screen with lines top and bottom that are really fields filled with ----- or ■■■■■■. This field can be used to indicate a condition or state of the record: Favored Customer, Balance greater than $XXX.XX for INV_DATE > SYSTEM->DATE - 30, and more.

This simple, but effective, indicator shows the viewer who is in on the game how to read the message. An example is the input screen on the computer system that assists the host in a fine restaurant in Florida. This restaurant caters to tourists and the wealthy locals who patronize race tracks and other places offering entertainment with their meals. The host is expected to know how to treat the guests who have reservations. The reservations are called in to his station, and he calls up the screen that has the patron's personal preferences entered.

The host's entry screen has a bright line across the top and the bottom of the form. These lines are colored according to a special code: bright blue for best customers; bright red for favored clients; white background with a yellow line for regular customers; and a faint but flashing white line on gray background if there is a warning on a customer for difficult behavior.

To the uninitiated, the screen shows no clue about the assessment that has been assigned to the customer's patronage. The host only has to react for the few bright blue and the few flashing white line customers. The warnings exist for the protection of the staff. They do not want to make any problem for the friends of the owners, nor do they want to offer extra encouragement to customers who make difficult request for the restaurant.

Creating Scripts for Shortcuts

By using keystroke scripts, dozens of time-saving shortcut techniques can be developed if you see the need for them. It is not necessary to learn the scripting language to get great results from Alpha Four; however, if you have the time to automate certain functions, the experience may lead you into discoveries that will be helpful. For example, you may decide to keep a library of *tools* for your primary file.

The following are sample menu choices describing scripts that will be used frequently:

> sWitch to XXX.files
> Change Script Path
> Print report {list}

Creating Field Rules

Field rules accompany a database when it becomes the parent file in a set. When designing a database that will have a number of lookups, calculated fields, case conversions, skip fields, and so on, make as many as possible before the file becomes part of a set. (Quick Start 2 and Chapter 8 discuss sets; Chapter 5 discusses field rules.)

Verify that as much of the development of field rules as possible has been done before you create the link for a set. After the set has been created, any form, table, or report can be borrowed to suit the new configuration.

Use the example of the CONTAC.SET (found in Chapter 8) entry form with lookups on last name and owner ID. The owner ID lookup is linked to the owner's name index for display. Therefore, you can enter the first letters of the last name and the pop-up window shows that name.

Making Records Easy To Find

When you are using records, changing the data, adding new line items, or creating reports, the last thing you want to do is worry about a client's ID number, an insurance policy number, or for that matter, even some equipment's part number. Because you are dealing with an almost relational database and a scripting language that comes as close as necessary to blending English with logic, a compromise must be made. The compromise has to be with the purity of database design.

Looking up the information needed for the *next* record may have to be done based on a redundant field. Part numbers may need to be found initially by the first couple of letters of their description; customer's records are more easily maneuvered if they are indexed on the name rather than the CUST_ID field.

Using Subgrouping

A company with a mailing list of several thousand names in the Boston area needed to get a count of the list by ZIP code. The count had to be defined by the first three digits and the first four digits.

The solution to this issue is found in subgrouping with a proper index, as is the case with so many database problems. Alpha Four has the capacity for reporting on subgroups in a flexible manner. In this case, the reports had to be based on a three- or four-digit grouping. The actual index for the report is the ZIPCODE field. The expression for the calculated field for the first group looks like the following:

    substr(ZIPCODE,3,1)

The second expression looks like the following:

    substr(ZIPCODE,4,1)

As the number in the expression gets higher, the discrimination of the sort gets finer. The group of records that contained the same four digits was smaller than the group that contained the same three digits.

The next step in the process, after this refinement is understood, is to find a way to report the data discovered by these indexes. Depending on the circumstance, the best way to report the data will vary. A good way is to create an index by using ZIP code alone, then use the preceding expressions as the definitions of calculated fields in designing two reports. The expression for the reports is defined in the **G**rouping parameters as you are creating a report.

The next step is to create a report that looks like figure 10.5. The report to be printed must use an index defined with the same expression. The subgroup total counts ZIP code entries. The results for this report look like figure 10.6

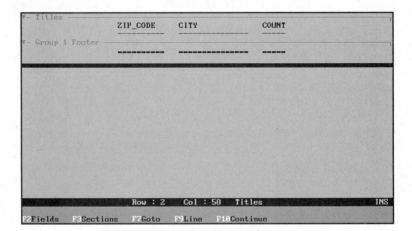

FIG. 10.5

This report has one sub-group, which counts ZIP code entries.

ZIP CODE	CITY	COUNT
01002	Amherst	5
01105	Springfield	1
01609	Worcester	34
01801	Woburn	277
01944	Manchester	127
02043	Hingham	168
02151	Boston	629
02401	Brockton	18
02540	Falmouth	49

FIG. 10.6

A ZIP code report counts values.

Summary

Half the fun of working with Alpha Four is devising faster, more elegant ways to solve the puzzles that develop in the course of creating business solutions.

This process has been explored here to illustrate some creative thinking that may assist your work. Many more shortcuts and special treatments are discussed in the last section of this book. Part III the how and why of writing applications, scripts, and expressions and documenting your work. With the background you have developed in Parts I and II of this book, these chapters should seem far more like the reward than the punishment for doing advanced application development in Alpha Four.

PART

III

OUTLINE

Advanced Alpha Four

QS3. Creating Applications and Scripts

11. Creating Applications

12. Creating Scripts

13. Using Expressions and Functions

14. Documenting Your Work

Creating Applications and Scripts

*You don't learn to hold your own in the world by standing guard,
but by attacking, and getting well hammered yourself.*
George Bernard Shaw, Getting Married

Quick Start 3 assumes that you have worked through Parts I and II of this book and are comfortable with the basic functions of Alpha Four and with the more advanced techniques of working with indexes, designing sets, moving data, and reporting. Now that you have discovered the range of functions that you have at your command, the time has come to put the pieces together as an application.

In this Quick Start, you get a hands-on session with the major issues of Part III. You design a small, menu-driven application, and you create dialog and keystroke scripts. You analyze the concepts of script variables and trigger scripts and create a desktop file.

Understanding an Application

There are two uses for the word *applications* in Alpha Four. The first usage refers to a series of commands brought together with a specialized menu to solve problems unique to a particular circumstance or business. Such an application might be designed to automate a retail sales department or a personnel tracking system. These applications are likely to have several layers of menus. Some may include separate menu systems designed to link together as subapplications.

The second kind of application can be viewed as a single module designed to be reused in recurring situations, specific to a certain file, or generalized to operate in many files. This small application accomplishes a certain task or series of tasks. Such an application might be a series of commands to address envelopes and mark which customers were sent which letter. Another would be a system you might develop for entering, editing, and viewing specific records based on a series of search lists or filters. These functions are needed in many database situations, so you can create a library of applications to be reused when the occasion arises.

In either case, an application is generally used from a menu. The menu establishes the order in which events take place and can show prompt lines for each item to encourage understanding of each selection. With the arrival of Alpha Four Version 2, the process of creating small, quick, menu-driven applications became easier than ever.

In a sense, macros and scripts have the same effect. Generally, as used with Alpha Four, the term *macro* refers to the recorded keystrokes in a menu-driven application. A macro can be made to {PLAY} a script. A *keystroke script* in Version 2 also is a series of recorded keystrokes, but there is no need to play the script solely from an application menu. A *dialog script* shows itself in the form of a pop-up box that can contain three types of entries: *Prompt controls*, *Button controls*, and *Display controls*.

In Quick Start 3, you design a menu-driven application with several entries. Then you create two kinds of scripts, a dialog script and a keystroke script. You also write a series of scripts that define and display a variable. Then you learn about trigger scripts. These examples lay the groundwork for Chapters 11 and 12 in which you develop an application by using macros and scripts tied together in a full application.

 In addition to applications and scripts, the other important concepts introduced in this Quick Start are script variables and desktops. These are both available in Version 2.

Creating Applications

An application is designed around a single file, such as CUSTOMER.DBF; a set that links two or more files, such as INVOICES.SET; or a group of files that are related but not linked, such as an inventory file and a payments file. The first step in designing an application is deciding which database will be the current file when the application begins. To make the Quick Start 3 examples operate properly, you need the files that you created in earlier chapters and some new ones.

You must have the following databases with which to manage your invoicing and receivables system: the INVOICE.DBF and INVENTRY.DBF working together in the INVOICES.SET. The next step is to create files that will receive the payments to the invoices and store the invoices and payments as a history of these activities. You need to create a PAYMENTS.DBF, a BILLS.DBF, and a LEDGER.DBF (see Chapter 2).

The PAYMENT data file contains the following data:

Name	Type	Width	Decimal Place
PAYMENT_ID	C	4	
OWNER_ID	C	4	
LASTNAME	C	15	
INVOICE_NO	C	4	
INV_AMT	N	10	2
AMOUNT	N	10	2
BALANCE	N	10	2
DATE	D	8	
POSTED	L	1	

The PAYMENT.DBF requires an index be created on the OWNER_ID field. The PAYMENT.DBF will become the parent file in the PAYMENTS.SET with OWNER.DBF linked on a one-to-one basis by using the OWNER_ID as the linking field.

The BILLS.DBF also is identified as a lookup in the PAYMENTS.SET in Field Rules. An additional function for BILLS.DBF is to serve as a history of invoices. Ultimately, you will not want to retain the details of each invoice, only the totals.

By putting the payments into a separate file, you can view them in sequence in the same manner as you did with the invoices in Quick Start 2. Create indexes for PAYIDNO and OWNER_ID. The PAYIDNO enables you to use the find command for a specific payment. The OWNER_ID enables you to post payments to the BILLS file and enter (Append) each payment as a transaction to a LEDGER database.

The BILLS data file contains the following data:

Name	Type	Width	Decimal Place
INVOIC_ID	C	4	
OWNER_ID	C	4	
INV_DATE	D	8	
AMOUNT	N	10	2
LASTNAME	C	15	
POSTED	L	1	

Index the BILLS file on INVOIC_ID, OWNER_ID, and LASTNAME. This file will be linked to the PAYMENT.SET to ensure that payments are identified with the proper invoice and owner. This database will be the lookup to invoices for the LASTNAME field in the PAYMENTS.SET.

The LEDGER data file contains the following data:

Name	Type	Width	Decimal Place
LEDGER_ID	C	4	
LEDGER_DAT	D	8	
ACTIVITY	C	10	
DESCRIPT	C	30	
OWNER_ID	C	4	
LASTNAME	C	15	
AMOUNT	N	10	2
DATE	D	8	

The LEDGER database serves in the same capacity as a listing of bills and payments in any business, household, or professional office. Each invoice billed to a customer (in this case known as an owner) becomes a receivable, and every payment made is logged into the ledger and posted to the owner's (or buyer's) file to reduce the balance due.

Enter several records of sample data to give yourself a sense of reality with these files.

Creating a Sample Application

To create the sample application, make the OWNERS file created in Quick Start 1 the current database on your computer, and complete the following steps:

1. From the Main Menu, choose **A**pplications. Alpha Four responds with the Applications menu. Select **C**reate/edit an application. Type the name **BOATYARD** on the line at the bottom of the screen, or choose your own appropriate DOS-correct file name. Type a description of the application on the description line on the next screen, which is the Application Parameters screen: **Boatyard Office Management System**.

2. On the second line of the Application Parameters screen, the program asks you to fill in the name of the startup database. Press F2 to select the INVOICES.SET.

3. The next two lines are designed for placement of default-setting data. In the case of a name and address file, the startup macro could be designed to select the index based on a LASTNAME field or a complex index, such as LASTNAME + FIRSTNAME + CITY. To teach the macro to the application, press the F3 (Learn Macro) key. The screen jumps back to the Alpha Four Main Menu and the Learn Macro box pops up, as shown in figure QS3.1.

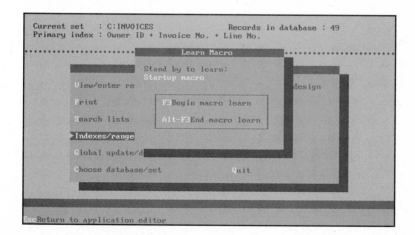

FIG. QS3.1

The Learn Macro box pops up at the start of creating a macro in an application.

4. Press F3 again to Begin macro learn. This step leaves you on the Main Menu, but the learn process is working. Notice the remark End:Alt-F3 at the lower-right corner of the screen. When you see this, you know that your keystrokes, mistakes, backspaces, Escs and all, are being recorded.

5. Press Index, **P**rimary index selection, and select the letter of the index you want, such as LASTNAME, and press Enter. You should define the macro by using the letter rather than the arrow keys to make selections, because the selections can change order in certain cases. Press Alt-F3 to complete the macro.

6. At this point, the startup macro line reads ipb, which translates to the keys you pressed in step 5. If you know the letter of the index you wish to select, these letters can be simply typed in from the keyboard.

7. On the next line, the Script path, you can define where the application is going to look for its scripts. Alpha Software has designed a special word for this circumstance: <DATAPATH>. This entry establishes that the current subdirectory is to be the place that the application will look for its scripts. For now, ignore the last two lines of this menu and Press F10 (Continue).

> **NOTE** Using <DATAPATH> means that you can change from one subdirectory to another and the application continues to find scripts, not in the original subdirectory, but rather in the subdirectory where the current file is located. If you need to hold the script path to a specific location, enter the full drive and path name in the script path setting line (Alt-F3,S).

8. There are two windows on the next screen. You can move between the windows with the F9 (Switch Window) key. In place of the default name, MAIN MENU, type the following:

BLUE WATER BOATYARD, INC.

BLUE WATER BOATYARD, INC. becomes the Main Menu heading for your application. Press F9 to switch to the top window.

> **NOTE** This title is longer than the space that appears to be available for the title. After the first menu item has been created, you can press F8 (Simulate) to observe the placement of the title as it will appear when the application actually runs.

9. Press F2 (Menu items). The screen should look like figure QS3.2. Select Insert a new menu item, or use the shortcut Alt-I.

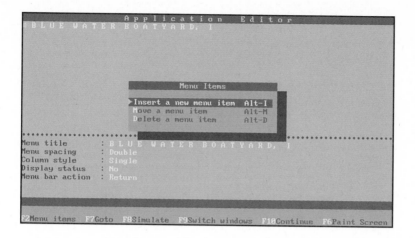

FIG. QS3.2

The Menu Items
screen appears
on the Applica-
tion Editor when
you press F2.

After Step 9, you continue to design your menuing system in the manner appropriate to your business. The Main Menu can contain commands that activate macros or the selection can take the user onto
submenus or to separate applications that are not included in the main
application (see fig. QS3.3). Use the Call-app or Goto-app menu action
to redirect the activities of the user.

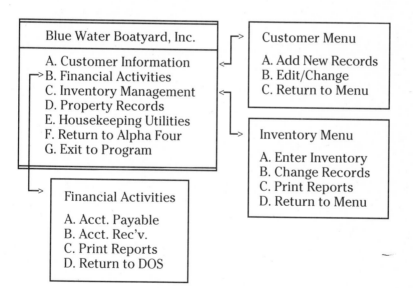

FIG. QS3.3

A sample menu
system for the
boatyard
application.

Creating a Macro in the Application Editor

Now that the initial setting up of the application has been completed, the next step is to create menu choices and attach macros to the menus.

To create the macro, you must complete the information on the Application Parameters screen. The steps for creating menu choices are similar to the ones required for the Startup macro. The first macro begins after you insert an undefined menu choice in the Application Editor. Your screen should look like figure QS3.4.

FIG. QS3.4

Define a new menu item with this menu.

To create the macro, perform the following steps:

1. After selecting the Insert a new menu item command, press Enter to switch to the lower window. Type **Enter new record**. Press the down-arrow key three times to put the highlight on the fourth line, Macro keys. Now you are ready to *teach* the program another macro in the same manner as you did with the Startup macro.

2. Press F3 (Learn Macro) to begin. Press F3 a second time when the Main Menu appears. Now press **E** to enter a record. You should see your cursor on the first field of your input form with an empty record waiting to be filled. Do not enter data here. Press Alt-F3 to end the macro. Alpha Four confirms that the macro has been learned. Press Enter to return to the Application Editor. For all that work, you should just see the letter e in the macro keys line. In cases such as this, it would be easier simply to type one or several letters on the macro keys line. Macros get more complicated soon.

3. With the highlight still on the macro keys line, press Enter to edit the macro. This action opens the Macro Editor screen, as shown in figure QS3.5

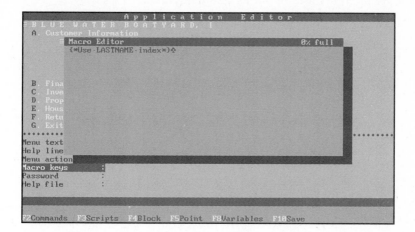

FIG. QS3.5

The Macro Editor screen has many options for more extensive operations.

4. In Chapter 11, the broad range of possibilities for macros is explained. For this sample, put in a reminder statement as a sample of the documentation you need for various lines in your macro. To create a reminder that has no program function, enclose your remark within curly brackets with an asterisk, as shown in figure QS3.5. The following is an example of a typical reminder: {*Use LASTNAME index*}. When the macro has been completed, press F10 to save it and return to the Application Editor.

Understanding Scripts versus Applications

Those who are proficient in developing applications by using the Application Editor in Version 1 and above will find scripts a delight for their speed and for their accessibility. To use a script from View or Browse mode can be a matter of two keystrokes. To run a menu choice from an application, you must be running the application and be on the correct menu of the application. Several more steps are required in applications than are required in scripting.

Before you give up all the applications that have been designed for earlier versions of Alpha Four, remember the major reason for using an application rather than scripts is to control or direct the user's activities. With a script, you have a sense of working more closely with the software. Using an application menu deliberately removes your user from the sense of proximity to the material and puts the focus on getting the job done. If your assignment is to take the user by the hand and guide the operations of his or her work, then an application is required. During the development of an application, you will discover that scripts are a necessity you never knew you needed.

The scripting power of Alpha Four lies in its concept of enabling you to design mini-menus or pop-up windows that perform tasks. In fact, when you are in View or Browse mode, if the right script exists, you are only one step away from a do-anything menu by using a new function, **Tools**. In practice, users create pop-up boxes with several menu choices shown on them. Some users call the pop-up box, *The Tools Box*.

Creating Scripts

The two kinds of scripts, *dialog* and *keystroke*, serve different functions but work together to produce applications. The name *keystroke script* suggests that these scripts are primarily designed to record and play back keystrokes, which the user teaches them in the process of their development.

Creating a Dialog Script

The name *dialog script* suggests the purpose of this kind of file: a means of communication between the user and the software. The dialog script creates a box in which the user can place three kinds of Controls: *Prompt control*, *Button control*, and *Display control*.

- The **Prompt** control asks for the user to enter data.

- The **Button** control executes a script containing instructions to the software (select index A; print mail labels, etc.).

- The **Display** control puts information on the screen for the user to see.

To get the hang of this procedure and to see how easy it is, you can make a dialog script with a Button control. Select the OWNERS file you created in Chapter 2 or a database of your own containing names and addresses. Verify that there is at least one report defined and one index created for the database you plan to use for this example.

To create a dialog script, perform the following steps:

1. Press Alt-F3.

2. The menu for Scripts appears, as shown in figure QS3.6. Choose the menu selection create **D**ialog script. Type **TOOLS** in the name field. Leave all of the other fields as they are and press F10 (Continue).

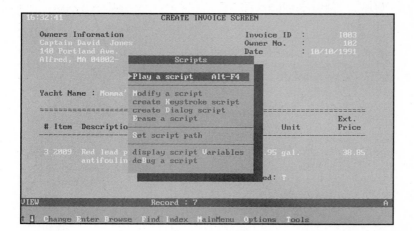

FIG. QS3.6

Alt-F3 produces the Scripts menu at the Main Menu or from View or Browse mode and many other places in Alpha Four.

3. The next screen is a box that will become the site for viewing a menu item. When complete, this dialog script pops up by simply pressing the letter **T** from View or Browse modes. On this dialog box, you can place a menu choice that enables you to do many of the things that an application can do but much quicker. Use the arrow keys to move your cursor to about one inch from the top and one inch from the left margin so that you can put the first item on the menu.

4. Press F2 (Controls) to see the Controls Menu. The screen looks like figure QS3.7. Three choices are on this menu, each one enables you to create a selection on your **TOOLS** menu. Choose Button control.

5. On the top line, Type **print Report** with a capital R. Next, type **PRT_REPT** on the Script line. Type **Print customer address report** on the Help line. Press F10 to continue.

6. Save the Dialog box with F10. To see your work, in View mode, press **T**ools. The new dialog box pops up. The Print report button cannot do anything yet, because the keystroke script has not yet been written.

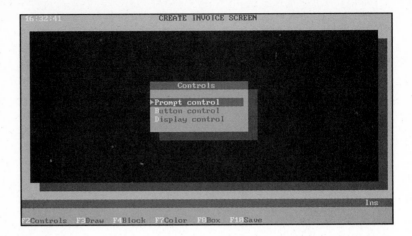

This menu shows the Controls available for these scripts.

The menu item that has appeared on your box shows the capitalized letter R highlighted. This is the same technique Alpha Four uses to indicate the Command key on its menus. Notice also that a prompt line appears on line 24 to instruct the user as to its purpose, in this case, Plays: PRT_REPT.

Creating a Keystroke Script

A *keystroke script* is a series of instructions to the software. To create a keystroke script, complete the following steps:

1. Be sure that there is a report defined with the letter A in your database; you can automate the printing of this report using the Print report command. The command on your TOOLS dialog box cannot print until you design the PRT_REPT script, as shown in figure QS3.8. The PRT_REPT script can be used to print your report. Press Alt-F3, create a **K**eystroke script; give it the name PRT_REPT. Type a description which states: **Print report A**. On the third line, press Enter to access the script editor and type the following:

    {ALTF10}pra

2. Press F10 to save your PRT_REPT script. From the Main Menu, choose View, Tools. You should see your menu box with one entry: PRT_REPT. Because only one item is on the menu, you can press Enter or **R** to select this choice. This should take you to the Range Setting screen for printing your Report A.

```
16:32:41              CREATE INVOICE SCREEN
 Owners Information                    Invoice ID  :      I003
 Captain David  Jones                  Owner No.   :       102
 140 Portland Ave.                     Date        : 10/10/1991
 Alfred, MA 04002-
 ─────────────────────── Keystroke Script ──────────────────
          Name           : prt_rept
 Yacht    Description     : Prints customer names report
          Keys/Commands   : {ALTF10}pra
 =====    Screen test     : No                              ===
 # It     Screen compare is off                             ce
 ─────
 3.20                                                        .85

                              Posted: T

 VIEW                  Record : 7                               A
  ⌐Learn keystrokes  F⌐Append learn  F10Save  EnterEdit
```

Now you should try the same method to create other choices for the
TOOLS pop-up menu. For example, the next step would be to provide
an alternative to the `Print report` file—perhaps a `Print another`
`report` file or `Select the primary index and print mailing labels.`

Remember that Alpha Four highlights the first capitalized letter on a
menu item to serve as a *hot key*. Rather than moving the highlight or
cursor to your selection, simply press the bold capitalized letter.
When there are several menu items shown on the dialog box, you
can select an item by pressing the Alt key in combination with the
capitalized initial of the command. As a designer of scripts and
macros, you must use care with the syntax to assure that an appropriate unique character is available for this purpose.

T I P

Using New Tools

Alpha Four has chosen the term *Tools* to represent a script that plays
automatically when you press one key. Tools is a script file that may be
considered *multi-purpose* because of its status as a user-definable item
on the View and Browse menus.

Tools is a generic script that appears in whatever file is current, when
you press **T**ools in View or Browse. Whatever script is given the name
Tools appears when the user selects this option from the menu.

A script that has been given the same name as the current file supercedes the Tools script. If a script called CLIENT.SCP exists, it will run in the place of a script named TOOLS.SCP when you press **T** on the View or Browse screens. A Tools-like file can be created for each user on a network.

Specializing File Names

You can recognize the type of file that you are working with by the three-letter extension that follows the name. In Alpha Four, the supporting files that are the definitions of all layouts, saved global updates, saved searches, and the data file itself shares the same first name. Their three-letter extension tells what the file represents in terms of the software. The OWNERS file holds the actual data in a file called OWNERS.DBF. All reports are assigned the name OWNERS.RNx with the *x* representing a letter A-Z. These names are assigned when you create the definition of a report in Layouts. The letter reflects the letter you choose for the report.

Types of files	Extensions	Function
Keystroke scripts	.SCP	Operational macros
Dialog scripts	.SCP	Displays or prompts for values & choices
Desktops	.DTN	Stores definition of files to be opened for an application
Color Definitions	.PAL	Saves custom palettes
User defined file	.UDN	Contains most recent form & browse table, color selection and other defaults specified by user
Search List Name	.SLN	Stores definition of the current search list
User count file	A4.NET	Defines the number of users allowed on the network

Types of files	Extensions	Function
Variables	.VAR	Script variables stored using the {VSAVE} command
Crosstab definitions	.XNx	Saved crosstab definition
Special Files		
Generic Hot Key	TOOLS.SCP	Script active on View and Browse modes
File-specific hot key	MYFILE.SCP	Takes precedence over TOOLS.SCP
Auto-executing script	AUTOEXEC.SCP	Used for establishing preliminary default settings
Auto-loading desktop	AUTOEXEC.DTN	If it finds this file, Alpha Four always loads this desktop first when the program begins
Start-up file	MYFILE!.SC	Executes when the MYFILE.DBF is opened
Special command	<datapath>	Sets script path to current directory

Managing a Desktop

The concept of a *desktop* is borrowed from Macintosh technology. On the Mac, files are opened and kept on a desktop to make moving from one document to another easy. The concept is the same with Alpha Four's Version 2 concept of a desktop. To sWitch between files on your desktop is vastly quicker, particularly with less powerful computers, than going through the process of opening a database.

You can open a series of files that you use on a regular basis and save the list under a specific name. Alpha Four applies the three-letter extension .DTN to identify its function as a desktop file. The desktop files are stored in the directory where the Alpha Four program is found.

As many as 10 files can be named in a desktop. They are listed in the order in which they were opened, 1 through 9 plus A. If you ask the program to open another file after the first 10 are defined, you get an error message that says the following:

> The current Desktop is full. If you continue, a database/set will be opened but won't be added to the current Desktop. You must close a database/set if you wish to add to the current Desktop.

This does not affect the desktop. As many files as you wish can be opened. None of their names appear in the sWitch command, but the desktop operates normally.

Opening a desktop is a matter that should be studied with care in the development of an application. Scripts are often written that carry the user from one file to another by using sWitch. The syntax reads: W3, which translates to *switch to file number 3 on the desktop*. Obviously, file number 3 has to keep its position as number 3 on the list. Otherwise, scripts will be playing with the wrong file. One way to ensure that your files will remain in the proper order is to define a script that re-creates the desktop if you need it.

Desktop files can get lost or misused, so creating a DESKTOP.SCP with documentation can be vitally important. You can save different desktops for different purposes. If your applications are large, you may want to define more than one desktop for a given application.

The reason you may need to work with this idea is that opening a desktop does slow down the process of starting an application. The actual opening of a desktop should be done when your application requires it, preferably at the start of a session. Desktop scripts can be documented like any keystroke script, so that you or your successor can easily understand the function of each file. The following is a sample desktop script:

```
{*Clear the current desktop*}
cl{*Choose OWNERS file*}
co OWNERS {ENTER}{*Choose INVOICES file*}
co INVOICES {ENTER}{*Choose CHECKS file*}
co CHECKS {ENTER}{*Choose PAYMENTS file*}
co PAYMENTS {ENTER}
```

Processing a Desktop

To save the preceding desktop, complete the following steps:

1. Verify that the currently open files are the correct files and that they are in the proper order for your application. From the Main Menu, choose **C**hoose database/set. Alpha Four responds with the Desktop Options menu.

2. Choose **S**ave current Desktop and type in a legal DOS name that signifies this file's importance to you. The program returns to the Main Menu.

To retrieve an existing desktop, complete the following steps:

1. From the Main Menu, select **C**hoose database/set. Alpha Four responds with the Desktop Options menu.

2. Choose **R**etrieve a Desktop and type the name or move the highlight to an existing desktop file and press Enter.

To erase an existing desktop, perform the following steps:

1. From the Main Menu, select **C**hoose database/set. Alpha Four responds with the Desktop Options menu.

2. Choose **E**rase a Desktop and type the name or move the highlight to an existing desktop file and press Enter.

To clear the current Desktop, perform the following steps:

1. From the Main Menu, select **C**hoose database/set. Alpha Four responds with the Desktop Options menu.

2. Choose c**L**ear current Desktop. The program returns you to the Main Menu.

Understanding Variables

Variables are pieces of data that serve many purposes. Data is entered into every field as a variable. The total of all line items for an invoice is a variable. The month for which you want to print a report is a variable. Today's date and the time are variables.

A distinction exists between two important classes of variables. The first class, *user-defined variables*, includes those pieces of data that are linked to a specific condition, such as the LASTNAME in record number 423. The second class is considered a *system variable*, such as those that are listed in the SYSTEM DATABASE. These variables include the name of the current database, the current date or time, the current index, or the record number. The difference is that the last name in record number 423 stays the same indefinitely. The current name of your database, the time of day, and the last name in the most recently viewed record are all subject to change every minute that you are using your computer.

Variables that Alpha Four users employ frequently are any items that are entered into the Table mode of a Search List, the components of a complex index, or the elements in a Global Update. Suppose that you want to print a report on records that show only the dates between February 1 and February 29, 1992. If you are working with a search list, the definition of the search looks like the following:

Field	Op.	Search for What?	And/Or
INPUTDATE	>=	02/01/92	And
INPUTDATE	<	03/01/92	

The variables are 02/01/92 and 03/01/92. If you are developing an application and setting up a query to establish the dates for which you want to run the report, the {PROMPT} should ask you to ENTER BEGINNING DATE and ENTER ENDING DATE. These two date entries become variables that the software holds for use in the search table.

Defining and Using Variables

A major difference between Alpha Four's Version 2 and earlier versions is that the user can take an active role in defining and using the variables needed to make the application effective. In this example, you can make two scripts that accomplish four operations, all with the goal of creating a usable element to display on the screen. Ultimately, of course, if you can see the variable, you can place it into a search, use it in a range setting screen, pass it to another file, or any number of other operations.

To create a usable variable to run from a menu, perform the following steps:

1. Make a dialog box that creates a location in which a variable can be shown.

2. Define a Display Control on the dialog box that identifies the variable and displays the contents of the variable after the variable has been set and retrieved to view.

3. Run a keystroke script that actually *sets* the variable, which means that this event gives the variable something to work on, a system field name, a database field name, or some other calculation or string of data to show as the variable.

4. Play the keystroke script that makes the variable current and retrieves the dialog box containing the Display control showing the variable.

> A script variable always is considered character type, no matter what kind of data is shown. It may be necessary to convert the variable to character type before it can be used in an expression.
>
> T I P

> **NOTE** After a script variable has been defined, it is valid until you quit the current session of Alpha Four. When you leave the program, the value of any variable must be reset when you return to the program. (See Chapter 12 concerning VSAVE() and VRESTORE() to retain the most recent values from one session to another.)

Creating a Variable

From the Main Menu, or from almost any other place in Alpha Four, you can define scripts. Work from the Main Menu to try creating a variable. Select the OWNERS database. To create a pop-up box showing the date and time, perform the following steps:

1. Press Alt-F3 to display the Scripts menu. Press **K** to create keystroke script. Give the script the name TIMEDATE. Press the down-arrow key to reach the field called Keys/Commands. Press Enter.

2. Type the following expression:

       {SET %time, TIME()}
       {SET %today, DATE()}
       {PLAY "SHOWTIME"}

   Press F10 to return to the Keystroke script screen and F10 again to save this script.

3. Press Alt-F3 to display the Scripts menu. Press D to create a dialog script. Type **SHOWTIME** on the Name line of the Dialog Script box. This is where you create the script that is called in step 2. On the Description line, type: **Script shows time and date**.

4. Make the following adjustments to the script: Row, 5; Column, 25; Height, 5; and Width, 25. Press F10 to continue. The box, approximately 1"-by-2", appears on your screen. Move the cursor one row down and four spaces to the right. Press F2 (Controls) and select **D**isplay control. Make the Width, 15 and type **TIME** on the variable line. Press F10 (Continue). Move the cursor down two rows and press F2 again to select **D**isplay control. Make the Width, 15 and type **TODAY** on the variable line. Press F10 (Continue).

5. Press Alt-F3 again and select **P**lay and highlight TIMEDATE. If you have been careful, the box that appears on the screen will show the current time on the top line and the system date showing on the screen. The time changes each time the macro is run.

Viewing the Variables

Another great tool for the designer is found on the Scripts menu with the display script **V**ariables selection (Alt-F3, V). Sixty system variables are already defined when you start your session of Alpha Four. Many of them are not active because they have not been set to contain data. Figure QS3.9 shows the Variables screen with system variables.

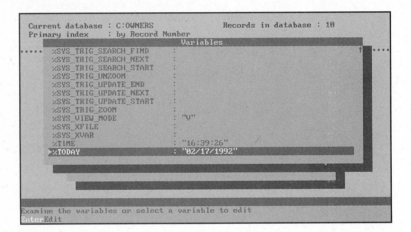

FIG. QS3.9

System variables and user defined variables.

The variables you create with keystroke scripts and dialog controls are active for the session only and must be reset when you want to use them in a new session. You can edit variables directly on the Variable Edit screen by highlighting the variable and pressing the Enter key as shown in figure QS3.10.

Using Triggers

Trigger scripts are special scripts that use the activity of the software to cause other actions to take place. *Trigger events* are such activities as enter, change, save, delete, or undelete a record, print a letter, perform a search, update a field, or zoom to a child file. There are 20 triggers events in Alpha Four. When a trigger is set, a value is stored in the system variable named for that trigger.

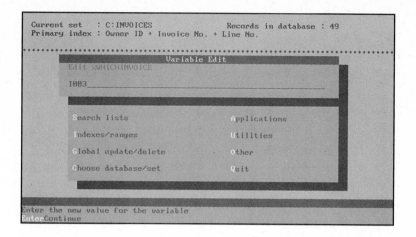

FIG. QS3.10

Variables can be
edited on the
Variable Edit
screen.

For example, when a trigger is set for the event of a Zoom to child file, what is *set* is the activity that the user wants to take place when the software gets the message to perform the Zoom function. The information that appears in the system variable for Zoom, SYS_TRIG_ZOOM, is the command that should run when the trigger event, Zoom, occurs. That information can be a script, another variable, or data.

The trigger variables are discussed in greater detail in Chapter 12.

Passing Data between Files with Triggers

A common request by Alpha Four users is a method of carrying data from one record to another, or to another database. The following trigger script carries the two items of data, the invoice number and the client ID to a child file.

Two scripts are needed. The first is a keystroke called TRIGZOOM. This script sets the system trigger zoom to another script called COPYFELD. The first script is the following :

Name:	TRIGZOOM
Description:	Triggers script at zoom to child file
Keys/Commands:	{SET %SYS_TRIG_ZOOM, "COPYFELD"}

The second script is called COPYFELD. This script copies the field INVOIC_ID from the set into a system variable that you create here called %INVOIC_NO. After the Zoom takes place, this script sets the child database to Enter mode, places the data saved in the variable %INVOIC_NO into the first field on the entry screen in the child database and then moves to the next field. In the second field, the script places the data saved in the variable %CUSTID from the parent file. The following is the second script:

Name:	COPYFELD
Description:	Copies invoice number into child file
Key/Commands:	{SET %INVOIC_ID, INVOIC_ID}
	{SET %CUSTID, OWNER_NO}
	{TRIGKEYS {e{%INVOIC_NO}
	{ENTER}{%CUSTID}{ENTER}
	{ALTD}{F10:2}U}}}

This script assumes that the child file contains the fields, INVOIC_ID, OWNER_NO, and INV_DATE. The script carries the two variables into the first two fields, executes the shortcut Alt-D command to enter the system date in the third field, then saves the record and executes the Unzoom function to return the user to the primary database. You could add any number of flourishes to this script. For example, if the child file had a lookup field into the customer database, you can add the {F3} command to access the lookup and enter the last name, first name, city, or whatever is required.

NOTE Unlike other scripts, trigger scripts are highly sensitive to finding spaces where they do not expect them.

Summary

Version 2 of Alpha Four contains 36 commands that operate as part of the scripts function. Based on the menu-driven aspects of the process, Alpha Software's marketing people consider their product to be the *relational database for non-programmers*. When you get involved with the scripting of this software, you may decide to give up your nice office and opt for the blue jeans and late nights of the stereotypical programmer—it's that much fun.

Alpha Four has outdone itself in its commitment to remain the *every-person's database*. While the FoxPro fanatics, Clipperheads, and dBASE diehards work at their coding, the Alpha Four beginner-turned-developer can take those late nights or leave them. Some people use computers as more than just a tool for doing repetitive functions, storing word processing documents, or calculating with spreadsheets.

Alpha Four users may willingly take teasing from programming colleagues to avoid becoming programmers themselves. However, when a program offers IF statements and the LOOPing capability, the line between full-blown programming and mere script-writing becomes blurred.

Certainly, the basic uses of Alpha Four, covered in earlier sections of this book, are effective without the use of scripts. *Alphanatics* who became involved with the software before the introduction of Version 2 know this. What scripting does at the simplest level is provide quick ways to record and replay repetitive operations. At a more advanced level, scripting gives you the power to automate your applications to the highest degree.

This Quick Start is intended to give the user who is familiar with Version 1 of Alpha Four a boost for using new features. The concepts of applications, scripts, desktops, variables and triggers are new to many users, but these functions should not be ignored in favor of comfortable habits. These functions add a new dimension to this program. Don't be afraid to try them.

Creating Applications

The best menu you could possibly design would read like this:
Monday, Tuesday, Wednesday, Thursday, Friday.
Adam Green, from a talk given to The Boston Computer
Society, Alpha Four Users Group, November 1990

Quick Start 3 introduces you to the concepts of menu-driven applications and scripts. This chapter takes you through the complete process of developing a simple application with the files developed in earlier chapters as the basis for the operations. The great value of an application is that, to a degree, it forces logical, sequential steps upon the user and provides an interface for those who do not understand how the application or the Alpha Four program itself works.

As with designing your database in the first place, describing your application on paper first saves time in the long run. The notes you write down should be translated to the application editor and become the structure from which your macros are suspended. The logic that carries the user from one menu to the next should be apparent in the drawings you create.

In this chapter, you examine the process of outlining your application. Using Alpha Four's Application Editor is similar in many ways to using outlining programs with word processing software. You can define major headings and subheadings. Then you can move the headings around and change them to suit your needs. The headings are the equivalent of menu items on your application. You can do this planning in a preliminary fashion on paper or with a word processor to get it a bit closer to right the first time.

Another feature of this chapter is the matter of presentation of your database. If the application is just for your own use, you can get away with certain do-it-yourself measures that are "just too much trouble" to put on a menu. If your work is to be presented to another person or group to use, however, all the preliminary thinking must be done before the application is turned over to the users. Nothing discourages a new user like menu items that do not work, reports that answer the wrong questions, or searches that leave out critical data. Down to the questions about removing obsolete records to upgrading to a new printer, everything must be included, or at least provided for, on a menu. In Alpha Four, a single menu can have as many as 24 operations, select other menus, or choose a different application. Figure 11.1 shows a typical hierarchical menu system with three levels.

Learning the Art of Menu Building

The term *application*, in the larger sense of the word for Alpha Four, means a menuing system that provides the user with a series of steps for solving a particular business, personal, academic, financial, or technical database problem. In many cases, the major headings for your menus look much like the primary office-type activities of your business. How nice it would be if your database operations could be summarized with the succinct clarity of Adam Green's quote at the beginning of this chapter. Indeed, the ideal is to make an application that, with no further intervention from the user, can accept a single keystroke for all the necessary functions of one day.

In the real world, no developer, with the possible exception of Adam Green, could create a menu system that would realize this ambition. In fact, the menus that commonly are used are function-based (Administration, Finance, Personnel, Marketing) with submenus offering time-linked weekly, monthly, quarterly, or yearly operations or other function-based choices, such as the following:

A. Post invoices to general ledger;
B. Delete records with zero balance, with start date greater than today minus 365;
C. Print labels for Monthly Meeting Notices.

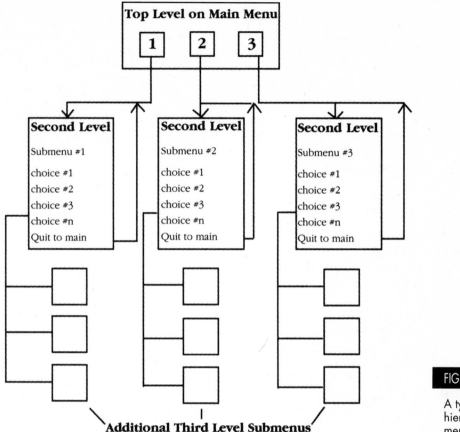

FIG. 11.1

A typical
hierarchical
menu flow.

Look at it this way: some occasions call for one coffee and a toasted English muffin, and others demand a more complicated meal of pheasant under glass. After your complicated procedure appears on a menu, backed up by a functional macro, you (or your users) should expect to have little or no further involvement beyond the response to prompts and normal editing functions. Like its culinary counterpart, your application's menu should have the capability to do your bidding without you, the designer, ever having to go through the developmental thought processes again.

How many steps, for example, are involved in printing a report based on a search list? The procedure might include the following:

1. Create and verify the right index for the XYZ report.

2. Design and debug search list.

3. Design and debug report.

4. Run search list.

   a. Which search list?

   b. Which index?

   c. When does it run?

5. Run report.

   a. Which report?

   b. Was this report done on wide paper? Compressed?

   c. Is this the right index?

   d. Which printer settings?

Steps 1, 2, and 3 on this list should be the activities in which you invest your time and thought. Steps 4 and 5 should not involve more decision making beyond selecting a clearly labeled item from a menu. Steps 4 and 5 should be combined on a menu as one simple choice: Run the XYZ Report.

This is a good time to remind yourself that during the development of applications, test files tend to proliferate. Saved searches as well as reports tend to multiply when you are in the throes of designing a system. While you are designing a menu system, you have a great chance to throw out the trash. Clean up the mess after you decide that you have a good version. It's all too easy to leave a trail of incomplete work behind as you fly through an application in Alpha Four.

Suppose that you have the following three test reports:

    F. Test report, version 4, 02/12/93
    H. Test report, version 2, 02/13/93
    T. Test report, version 3, 01/07/93

Were any of these any good? Which is the final version? Why? Pick the ones you need, give them names you can recognize six months after you created them, and put them on a menu.

You will be surprised to discover how easily you can create a menu-driven application in Alpha Four. The hardest part is surely the effort required to decide what functions belong on which menu.

T I P Remember to give menu titles names that can be identified with a capital letter. The first capital letter in a menu choice is the trigger for that command.

Planning Your Menu System

The special power of Alpha Four for the nonprogrammer lies in the ease of use of the Application Editor. The success or failure of the application depends on the care with which you plan and execute your menu system.

You need to observe a few rules about menu making:

■ Menus always should move from a Main Menu to a submenu and back again, never from one level 2 menu to another level 2 menu.

■ Plan the sequence so that activities flow logically from prior activities. Perform the search, for example, before printing the report.

■ Make the Main Menu choices as general as possible. The Main Menu should reflect any major divisions in the application.

■ Include a housekeeping menu to provide access to the utility functions, such as selecting a printer, packing records marked for deletion, and updating the indexes.

■ Always offer an exit (Esc) route from which the user may return to the Main Menu, quit the program entirely, or return to the Alpha Four menu.

Although in theory you are not limited to the number of activities that you can attach to an application, a practical limit certainly exists to the number of menu items that a user can master. You can develop applications that link to the main application, but the maximum number of entries that fit on one menu screen is 24. Each of these entries can in itself be the header for another menu that can bring up another submenu screen, which can contain 24 entries, and so on.

Your users may get worried and confused if they have to remember three levels of menus, even if each level has a clearly defined place and purpose. Two levels are better. Of course, this limit challenges you, the designer, to present activities in the clearest, most logical manner.

Defining the Structure

The definition of the application structure takes place in the first screen of the application editor. The decisions made on this screen determine the primary direction that the application is to take, and they should be at the head of your list of the menu items that will eventually make up your application. These decisions include the name of the start-up database or set; the defaults setting (defined in a start-up macro); the script path; the application banner; and the global escape and password restrictions for the entire application.

The definition of the application structure takes place in the first screen of the application editor, as shown in figure 11.2.

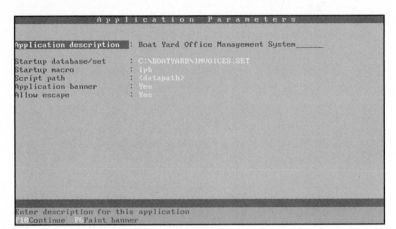

Application Parameters

Application description : Boat Yard Office Management System_____

Startup database/set   : C:\BOATYARD\INVOICES.SET
Startup macro   : ipb
Script path   : <datapath>
Application banner   : Yes
Allow escape   : Yes

Enter description for this application
F10 Continue F6 Paint banner

FIG. 11.2

The Application Parameters screen is where many defaults are established for running the application.

When the application gets underway, you can make the menus perform the following actions:

- Display an opening application banner
- Check password access to the application
- Show menu choices
- Ask the user for data (as in Which Invoice No.?)
- Perform searches
- Define default values
- Move data with Post, Join, Subtract, Intersect, Import, Export, Append, Copy, Erase, Pack, and Zap
- Summarize data with field statistics, summarize database, and cross-tabulate
- Change data with global update
- Create, edit, and delete records
- Create, update, attach, and detach indexes
- Print reports, mailing labels, form letters, and browse tables

- Select a range of records
- Mark records for further action
- Dial the telephone

Designing the Application

True to the message stated in earlier chapters, now is the time to take the functional outline you created before and translate that information into a menu. Remember to sketch your application on paper before you do it in the software. This section gives you a sample outline of an application. This application can represent the basic functions needed to operate a boatyard. Some of the reports, forms, indexes, and other items listed in this section have been developed in earlier chapters of this book. Others you may choose to work on yourself with the files created in your exercises.

Figure 11.3 shows the simplest kind of menu, used to introduce submenus, which is where most of the activity takes place. On this Main Menu, only the F and G options have keystroke macros attached. Selections A through F are headers that access submenus.

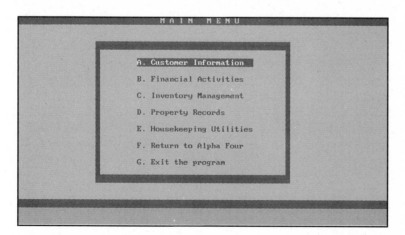

MAIN MENU

```
A. Customer Information
B. Financial Activities
C. Inventory Management
D. Property Records
E. Housekeeping Utilities
F. Return to Alpha Four
G. Exit the program
```

FIG. 11.3

A simple Main Menu for a business application.

The notes on a menu system for the management of a small business such as a boatyard might look like the following outline. Each major category becomes a heading on the menu. Each main activity is listed with notes about relationships and functions. As much as possible, items on the wish list become actions on a submenu.

Menu Headings	Wish List
A. Customer Information	Enter new owners' names; edit existing owners' records; print report of addresses and phone numbers; print report of instructions from boat owners; review current balances; send letters
Files:	CONTAC.SET
Indexes:	OWNER_ID, trim(upper(LASTNAME)), NEXT_CONT (date), LASTNAME only
Views:	Default, Entry form
Browse:	Default
Reports:	A. Name, Yacht name, LOA, launch date B. Name, address, emergency phones, comments
Description:	Links OWNER.DBF with CONTACT.DBF
B. Financial Activities	Enter invoices; enter payments to invoices; write checks; post bills and payments to ledger; print statements of overdue bills; print monthly/quarterly/yearly summary for bookkeeper
Files:	INVOICES.SET (links INVOICE.DBF with OWNERS and INVENTRY)
Indexes:	OWNER_ID, trim(upper(LASTNAME))
Views:	Default, Entry form
Browses:	Default
Reports:	A.
	B.
Description:	Links
C. Inventory Management	Enter new items; update list from distributors' files; analyze items not worth stocking; print report valuing stock; export data to spreadsheet for graphing
File:	INVENTRY.DBF
Indexes:	PART_NO, DESCRIPT
Views:	Default, Entry form
Browse:	Default

Menu Headings	Wish List
Reports:	A. Parts list with prices
	B. Inventory summary
Description:	Tracks items in the store
D. Property Records	Record data on tenants; record rent payments; send statements; enter records on rental properties; edit records of property
Files:	TENANTS.DBF, RENTAL.DBF, RENTPAID.DBF
Indexes:	
Views:	Default, Entry form
Browse:	Default
Reports:	A. Quick report: Who's where?
	B. Name, address, emergency phones, comments
Description:	Links three files for tracking rents and maintenance on apartments
E. Housekeeping Utilities	Select printers; pack databases; update indexes
F. Return to Alpha Four (assign password)	
G. Exit the program	

Creating a Sample Application

In Quick Start 3, you created the small application called MAILING.APP. In this chapter, you make a full application containing some of the primary elements of managing small business activities on the computer. Your activities may be quite different. As shown in the outline in the preceding section, the elements considered here consist of customers, billing, accounting, inventory, property management, and computer housekeeping. In the next section, you create the menu to tie them together as a unit, based on the work done in earlier chapters.

Creating the Menu

To begin an application, select the set or file that is to be the primary resource for the application you are making. In this case, you need a set that links INVOICE.DBF with OWNERS.DBF and INVENTRY.DBF. This set is called INVOICES.SET. Be sure that the indexes, reports, and desktop files exist before you start this process. Follow these steps:

1. From the Main Menu, choose **Application**. Alpha Four responds with the Applications menu.

2. From the Applications menu, choose **Create/edit application**.

3. On the line at the bottom of the page, type **boatyard**.

4. On the next screen, type a description of the application that reminds you of its significance: **Boatyard Office Management System**, for example.

5. On the next line, use F2 (Databases) to select the name of the primary set, INVOICES.SET in this example, to make sure that this set is listed as the start-up database/set.

6. The next line calls for the start-up macro. The decision here can make the difference between a fussy project, one that is slow to calculate, and one that is slower still to meet your needs for speed and efficiency. At this point you select the global defaults that will be needed for most or all of the application's activities. You should, however, guard against making the start-up macro so involved that the program takes minutes rather than seconds to come to life. For this example, press Enter and type:

   clcrBOATYARDipd

   This sample macro translates into English as follows: **C**hoose database/set, **cL**ear current desktop, **C**hoose database/set, **R**etrieve a desktop named BOATYARD, **I**ndex/ranges, **P**rimary index selection, **D**. Last Name.

7. Press F10 (Save) to save the macro.

8. The next line on-screen asks you to identify the script path. This path can be specific, as in C:\ALPHA4V2\DATA, or can reflect the need to move between several subdirectories by using the word <DATAPATH>. In this case, type **<DATAPATH>**.

9. The application banner is the next challenge. When you select **Yes** on this line, a new choice appears at the bottom of the screen. F6 (Paint Banner) enables you to make a distinctive opening screen that can identify the user or the application. The opening banner

in figure 11.4, for example, shows the name of the company and instructions for taking the next step. For the example, type **<Press Enter to Continue>**.

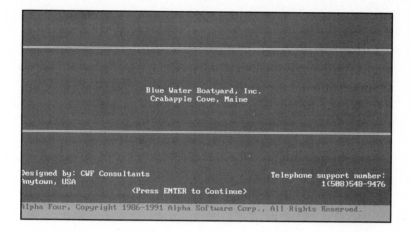

Blue Water Boatyard, Inc.
Crabapple Cove, Maine

Designed by: CWF Consultants
Anytown, USA
Telephone support number:
1(508)548-9476
<Press ENTER to Continue>
Alpha Four, Copyright 1986-1991 Alpha Software Corp., All Rights Reserved.

FIG. 11.4

A sample banner screen to introduce your application.

In the next section, you learn how you can enhance your banner to suit your purposes. The banner can be created at any time.

Dressing Up Your Banner

The banner for your application can serve several purposes. It can be decorative, informative, or promotional. If you are creating an application for your own amusement, menu banners are fun to make. You can waste a great deal of time beautifying and coloring the banner. On the other hand, if your application is for distribution to others, you may need to include information about the use of the program on the banner. Two important pieces of information to be shown on the banner are the telephone number where you can be contacted for technical support for your application, and the version of your application, if more than one has been created.

You can create two kinds of banners. The opening banner appears before the selections for the menu are available. The second kind of banner shows all menu items, as many as 24 on a single screen, and may carry out any color or design theme established in the opening banner. Both the opening banner and the next level of banner are designed with the same menu tools.

To initiate an opening banner, press F6 from the Application Parameters menu. The software responds with a blank screen including six menu items at the bottom. Two of the six show the color selections palette. If you press F3 (Draw), you see the palette, which gives you the color selections for drawing a line. In the next section, you learn more about drawing a line on your banner.

Drawing a Line

The palette offers both background and foreground color selections. As you move the cursor from one selection to the other, the Color Sample bar at the top of the palette indicates what the line you draw will look like on your screen. If you press F7 (Alternate View), the color names are identified. You make the selection of a color sample by moving the cursor to your choice and pressing Enter. The menu that then appears at the bottom of the screen offers three choices:

EnterDone   **1**Single line   **2**Double line

By selecting either 1 or 2 at this point, you can draw a single or double line with the color selection made on the previous screen. If you prefer, you can draw a box rather than just a line on your banner. In the next section, you learn how.

Drawing a Box

The procedure for drawing boxes is similar to that of drawing lines. You select the shape of the line character first. Press F8 (Box) from the menu at the bottom of the screen, and the eight choices of borders appear, labeled A through H. (The last selection, I, enables you to delete the box.) After you make a character choice, you select the color for the background and foreground of the box. The color selection palette appears, and you make the selection by moving the cursor to your choice and pressing Enter. At this point, you can draw the box by moving the cursor with the arrow keys.

Creating Template Screens

Template is a term that refers to something you can design once and use over and over again. In Alpha Four, it means a screen that you like and save for reuse in more than just the original menu location. You can make a different screen for any menu. If you save a specific screen as a template, the next time you go to the Screen Painter, you can press F9 (Options) and choose from the Options menu. The options for the Screen Painter are:

Use template screen
Save screen as template
Clear the screen
Toggle text/color link

After you have created a banner, you can save it by pressing F10 (Save). You can save the banner again as a template by pressing F9 (Options) and selecting Save screen as a template from the Options menu, thus creating a reproducible screen that you can use in other areas. When you go to a different menu and want to bring the banner onto the new screen, press F9 (Options) and select Use template screen.

Only one template can be current at any time, but you can save several templates in an application. The most recently saved template is the one that will be reused when you select the Use template screen choice from the Options menu.

You can use color in a template as an effective tool for imparting information. Lines such as the following can have the **$100** in a "blinking" color to get attention. You select one of the choices on the right side of the palette. As you place your cursor on one of these selections, notice that the color sample bar begins blinking to demonstrate what the effect will be if you select this choice.

```
A commission of $100 will be paid for leads of other
agencies that may want to purchase this program.
```

Changing Your Banner

If you make an error, lines or boxes become entangled, or colors go awry, you can clear the banner screen. Simply press F9 (Options) and choose the Clear the screen option. The program asks for verification:

```
Are you sure! Screen will be erased: Yes  No.
```

If the solution to your design problem is to start from the beginning with your banner, select Yes to clear the screen. (You can achieve the same effect by pressing Esc before saving the banner screen.)

Although the Alpha Four Reference Manual declares that you must enable the F6 key by choosing Yes at the Application Banner prompt, this statement is not accurate. You can create a banner at the opening screen or at any location where the cursor highlights the application editor and the menu definitions appear in the lower window. When the F6 (Paint Screen) menu choice appears, you can create a banner for that selection.

T I P

Adding the Details to Your Menus

Menus have a variety of styles in Alpha Four. Although the placement of the choices is linear, one following another, you can vary the look of each menu with more than just the banner. In this section, you learn how to choose your menu format and add menu items.

The final choice on the Application Parameters screen is Allow escape. If you can permit the user to leave the application and operate from the Alpha Four Main Menu, leave the choice at the default, Yes. Otherwise, the choices are to deny the escape choice or to place a password on the activity. If you select password, still one more line appears and asks you to enter the password for the escape function.

Spacing and Styling Your Menus

When you create a menu item and the highlight is on the line with the = mark, the lower window offers the following choices. Press F9 to switch windows.

Menu title	: (User entered)
Menu spacing	: Single Double Triple Quadruple
Column status	: Single Double Left Right
Display status	: Yes No
Menu bar action	: Return Stay Advance

You can type the menu title on the first line. You can achieve different effects by using all caps or by double-spacing the letters, as in the following:

B O A T Y A R D   A P P L I C A T I O N

The second choice, Menu spacing, enables you to choose whether one, two, three, or four lines fall between each menu choice. For this example, accept the default, but you can also experiment on your own.

The Column status option refers to the choice of placing the menu selections in a single column down the center of the screen or in two (double) columns in the fashion of the Alpha Four opening menu. Also, you can choose to see the menu item column in the left or the right half of the screen.

With the Display status choice, you decide whether to display the two lines at the top of the Alpha Four opening menu. These lines show the name of the current database or set, the number of records in the database, the primary index, and the number of records in the search list if the search list is current. These two lines disappear from the application menu if you select **No** for the Display status option. This choice can be made on each menu separately.

The last choice on this menu, Menu bar action, makes a distinction between the Main Menu and a submenu. This selection asks you to direct the actions of the application. When a menu item has completed its operation, the application can *return* the user to the application's Main Menu; force the user to *stay* on the current menu; or keep the user on the same menu but *advance* the menu bar to the next choice on the current menu.

Adding Menu Items

You can add a menu item at any level of the menu. The first menu item is the only one that is done for you, because it provides the first selection on the first screen, without which you have nowhere to go. All others are added to the top menu or are suspended from submenus. In effect, you are creating what looks like the outline designed at the beginning of this chapter. Each menu title is a major heading, and each menu item is derived from the wish list.

At any place where you want to add a new menu item, press F2 (Menu Items) or Alt-I. The words `Undefined menu choice` appear on-screen, and the cursor drops to the lower window to the line that reads `Menu text`. On this line, you type the words to describe what the menu choice is for, as it appears on the first level of choice. You can, for example, type the following:

Enter new client records

When this item appears on the application menu, the first capital letter (E in this example) is highlighted and becomes a hot key. The user can select this activity by moving the menu bar to this choice and pressing Enter or by just pressing the capitalized initial.

NOTE If you expect to run out of letters or find it awkward to discover mnemonic menu items, you may find that using the letters of the alphabet is more convenient than employing combinations such as this

> **E**nter new records
> edit/**C**hange records

In this manner, the two-line menu above becomes

> **A.** Enter new records
> **B.** Edit/change records

Adding a Help Line

The next line following the Menu text line asks you to type a prompt line for the user to see when the menu bar highlights this choice. If a menu choice is Enter New Records, for example, the help line might read, Enter data from new inquiry cards here. This line appears on the next to the bottom line of the menu screen, known as line 23. If the color selection for this part of the screen is incorrect or the message is not clear, you can change the usefulness of this entry by changing the shade by using the color palette definition screen from the Other on the Main Menu.

Adding the Action

The next line enables you to define the type of entry you are writing. The default answer is Macro. Other choices include Sub-menu, Call-app, and Goto-app. If you choose Sub-menu, the next line, designed to accept a macro definition, disappears. (Alpha Four generally shows only valid choices and expands those choices with prompt lines and the F1 (Help) key when the cursor is on them.)

If you select Call-app or Goto-app, you must have a related application available to enter into the definition. In this case, the next line asks for the name of the application that is to be called by this menu choice. At the completion of a Call-app, the user is returned to the main application. When the Goto-app is defined, the user is not returned to the main application. Instead, the application ends when the user completes the work in the subapplication.

You can password-protect any menu item. The password is applied at the next line of the application editor, the line after you define the menu action in the preceding section. Simply enter the word or letters you want to be the password. The user then needs to enter the password to select this item from the menu.

Helping the File

At this point you can express your creativity. You can write a quick ASCII file to be placed in the current directory by using the letters capability of Alpha Four or another text editor that enables you to create simple ASCII files. The line length should be less than 80 characters in width to make the help features useful. The drive, path, and file name should be included on the last line.

F9 (Switch Window) is the shortcut you use to move between the two major sections of the application.

T I P

When you feel that the time has come to examine the looks of your application use F8 (Simulate) to preview the menu action.

Creating the Macro

After going through all the preliminary steps to building your menu system, perhaps making a macro will seem anticlimactic. After all, Alpha Four teaches itself—or nearly so. As you can see from the menu choice at the bottom of the screen, when the highlight reaches the fourth line, Macro keys, a new item appears on the menu at the bottom of the screen: F3 (Learn Macro).

The making of a macro is as individualized as choosing a new pair of gloves, but much easier. You press F3 (Learn Macro) twice, and Alpha Four puts you onto the main Alpha Four menu. The instruction End: Alt-F3 shows on the help line at the bottom of the screen to remind you that you are in the Learn Macro mode.

The process from here is simply to use the initials of each command to create a macro. To create a menu item that updates all indexes in the current file, for example, you type the hot-key letters of the commands **I**ndex/ranges, **U**pdate indexes, and **A**ll. That's it. When Alpha Four returns control of the program to you after updating the indexes, you press Alt-F3 to end the macro. At that point, the program confirms the name of the macro that you have created, you press Enter, and the program returns immediately to the application editor.

That's not really it, of course. You can do a number of things with a macro that do not involve this automatic learning process. Many of the tricks that you are going to teach your application come originally from scripts that you create outside the Application Editor. For this reason, the chapters on application creation and script writing are close together. The two are closely related.

An example is the script you created in Quick Start 3. The script is called PRT_REPT. If you use F2 (Menu Items) to add a new item to your menu selection called *C: Print customer address report*, the macro can pick up the script that was created in Quick Start 3 which looks like the entry shown in figure 11.5.

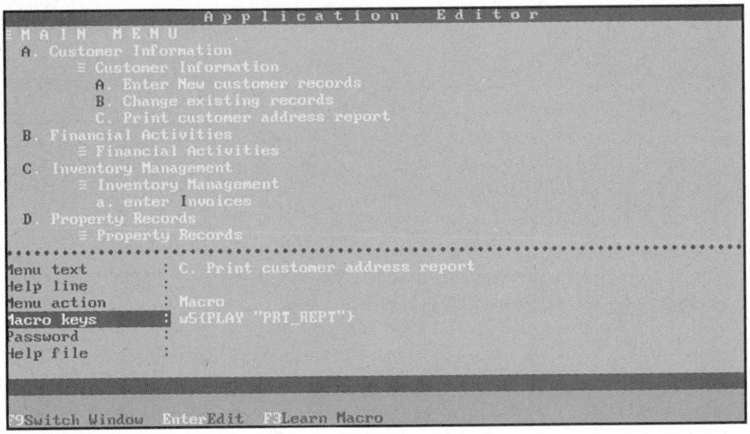

FIG. 11.5

The Application Editor showing the macro for printing a customer address report.

This macro is a mixture of a learned macro and a script. The macro reads

```
w5{PLAY "PRT_REPT"}
```

To create a macro, perform the following steps:

1. Press F2 (Menu Items) on the Application Editor screen to create an entry on the application screen. Press Enter to name the selection. Type **Print customer address report**.

2. Press the down-arrow key to get to the Macro keys line. Press F3 to display the Learn Macro box. Press F3 again to start the process.

3. Press **w5** to sWitch to the OWNER file, which is open on the desktop (defined in the start-up macro). Do not use arrow keys. Of course, if the fifth file on the desktop is not OWNERS, select the number that is.

4. Press Alt-F3 to end the macro, and press Enter to return to the application editor. The macro now reads w5.

5. Press Enter to edit the macro.

6. Press the End key to move the cursor to the end of the macro, marked with the ♠ symbol.

7. Press F2 (Commands).

8. As with many other pop-up boxes from which you select commands, fields, and so on, you can press the first one or two letters to find the word you are seeking. In this case, the word is {PLAY}. Therefore, type **pl** and note that the cursor jumps first to {PAUSE}, then to {PLAY...}. This technique works when choosing fields for equations and placement on layouts. Press Enter to choose this command.

9. What appears on-screen next is the first part of the command {PLAY} plus the rest of the expected syntax. With the cursor on the $, press F3 (Scripts) to view the list of existing scripts. For the example, type **prt** to get you in range of the choice you want: PRT_REPT. Highlight the proper script and press Enter. Assuming that your script path is set to the current data subdirectory, or to <datapath>, the selected script, PRT_REPT in this case, appears before the cursor and pushes the rest of the syntax to the right.

10. Press Del to remove the $script, but be sure to leave the right brace, }. You then have completed the macro.

11. Press F10 to save, and press F9 to switch windows.

You can fill in the entries on the application with a great variety of macros, many of which {PLAY} scripts designed from the Main Menu. Furthermore, you can create, edit, and erase scripts from within the Application Editor, as shown in figure 11.6.

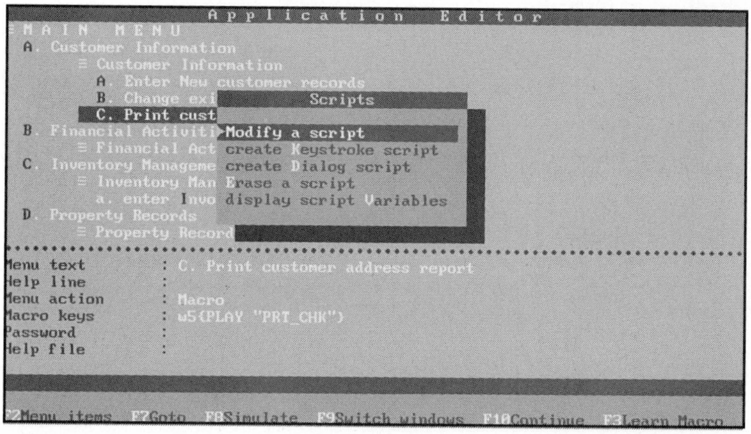

FIG. 11.6

Working with scripts from the Application Editor, by using Alt-F3.

Including Help Screens in Your Application

You can make your application especially professional by adding customized help screens to your menu selections. Place the name of the help file in the last line of the lower window. Press F2 (Help Files) for files that exist in the current subdirectory.

 **CAUTION**   You must add the three-letter extension HLP to the file name when you select it from the database directory. You also can enter the full drive and path name to assure that the proper help file is found by your application. Generally, Alpha Four accepts the name if you can "point" to it on-screen, but an exception exists in this case.

For short help screens, you can use the Alpha Four Layout Letters to write your message. Using the Letters function, however, results in a double-spaced message. You can experiment with your favorite line editor or word processing software to see which option works best for you. Remember that the help screen is only 60 characters wide and about 17 lines deep, depending on the software you select to create the file.

Calling and Going to Other Applications

As you learned in "Adding the Action," two kinds of subapplications are available to the application designer: the *call-app* and the *goto-app*.

Some data-management activities that are important to a business application appear to stand alone as activities that are not related directly to the Main Menu. If an application that uses Alpha Four information is designed to operate on your system, you can place a menu item on the menu to *call* another, separate application. To add to the flexibility of the application menu technique, you also can design a menu item to identify another application that causes the user to leave the current application and *go to* another application.

Calling and Going to a Subapplication

The first of these menu items is called a *call-app*. When you call up and then finish with functions on this separate application, the program returns you to the original application. If you design a *goto-app*, the intention is for the user not to return to the original application but rather to complete the work in the subapplication.

An example of a subapplication that should be designed as a goto-app is a section of work that deals only with managing data to be exported and imported to and from external files. This area of the program may be used by a specific individual for a specific period of time, both unrelated to the day-to-day activities of the application. In this case, the user of this subapplication accesses the import/export module from the basic application and exits from the program directly when the work is complete. In other words, the user does not need to work back and forth between this and other sections of the application.

The advantage of using the goto-app in this situation is that you can avoid any degradation of the speed of the computer system by removing this user from the other activities. Thus, the software is not trying to maintain indexes or other default values for the user in the Goto-app. The result should make the system operate with fewer delays.

Asking for an Application

One of the goals of the application designer is to remove, reduce, or restrict the user's access to the Main Menu. You can accomplish this purpose in a number of ways. The first of these is found in the procedure defined for the start-up from DOS. As the developer, you can create a batch file that starts an Alpha Four application in concert with a menuing system or shell such as the DOS Shell, Xtree Pro, Menu Maker, Automenu, or PC Tools. You can apply a number of *switches*, or options to the command line. These switches are discussed in Appendix XX. To start Alpha Four in version 2, using the OWNERS database in the D drive in the subdirectory \ALPHA4V2\BOATYARD and using an application named BOATYARD located in the C:\DATA subdirectory, for example, use this command:

A4 D:\ALPHA4V2\BOATYARD\OWNERS -A=C:\DATA\BOATYARD

The switch that tells Alpha Four to run the application named
BOATYARD is the -A=.

> **NOTE** Version 1 users have a different syntax. The same command
> line for Version 1 is the following:
>
> A4   D;\ALPHA4V2\BOATYARD\OWNERS /
> C:\DATA\BOATYARD
>
> The switch for this command is the forward slash, /, which
> comes before the application drive name, path name, and
> file name. (The / switch also is available in Version 2.)

Giving Yourself a Master Class

After many hundreds of hours of listening to users calling in on the
technical support lines, Alpha Software designers identified many of
the primary operations that their users attempt to conquer with this
software. Although it is neither their intention nor their business to
create applications for users, the software designers saw the value of
illustrating the most common situations with their demo programs.
The result for you can be a Master Class on Alpha Four.

Alpha Software has included in their demonstration files with Version 2
a well-designed sample of a simple invoicing system. The sample includes four sets and five database files, an application, and a
README.NOW file. Furthermore, more than 80 script files are attached to this demonstration.

Included with the demonstration files when you install Alpha Four is
an application called INVOICE.APP. You do not need to know much
accounting or even much computing to follow along with this demonstration. In simple terms, the program tracks invoices. This application
is probably the most frequently requested application at user group
meetings and on bulletin board sessions having to do with Alpha Four.
The directions for running this application can be found in the
README.NOW file, which is installed in the \ALPHA4V2\
DEMO\INVOICE subdirectory when the program itself is installed.

Generally, Alpha Software has avoided the use of README files, but the
volume of new information and changed functions that comes with
Version 2 forced the company to take this route to bring last-minute

information to the user. README files traditionally contain important information that software developers want to have their users possess. The information came too late to make it into the reference manuals, so it is packed into a nice, tight ASCII document and sent off with the software. You should print any files with persuasive names like README.DOC and README.NOW. The authors of the software are trying to tell you something. Better listen.

NOTE You can read or print a README.DOC or README.NOW file without leaving Alpha Four. Reading them often seems like too much trouble, but Alpha Four makes it easy. Although the results are usually not the quality of a high-grade word processing document, you can send these files to your printer by using the Letters function in Alpha Four.

This method is adequate for the purpose, and the effort is worthwhile for the tremendous amount of information and education that is included. To read or print a document not originally created by the Letters function, you must type the name of the document, including the complete drive and path name and extension. When Range menu appears, change the primary index to Record Number and the first and last record to 1.

Each menu choice in this demonstration application has two selections (view existing and enter new) for each of four components that many businesses require: Invoices, Customers, Inventory, and Purchases. A Reports menu offers reports on each of these components. In addition, two posting functions are included: Post sales to inventory and Post purchases to inventory. Nothing here is complex enough to discourage a beginner; however, the demonstration itself is worth study for even the most experienced Alpha Four user.

When you find the files relating to the invoicing application, for example, select Application from the Main Menu, select Create menu, and finally choose INVOICE.APP. You will discover that after the name of the application and the starting file are identified, the next line is a macro that calls a script. The command is {PLAY "startup"}.

If you examine the script called STARTUP, you find a number of activities that make an application run smoothly and give a professional air to the process, from setting defaults and retrieving desktops to establishing the right input form and resetting variables that might have been left from a previous session.

For starters, the {SCREENOFF} command keeps the various screens from flashing in front of the mystified user. The script documents its own activities by using the {WRITE} command to give the user a sense of the "behind the scenes" activities while various events are taking up his or her time. The following is the contents of the STARTUP script:

```
{SCREENOFF}
{WRITE 24,1,"Setting default settings.....    "}
ocd{up:2}y{F10}
{SCREENOFF}
{WRITE 24,1,"Retrieving Invoice Desktop.....    "}
crINVOICE{ENTER}
{SCREENOFF}
{WRITE 24,1,"Selecting input form....    "}
lfsb
{WRITE 24,1,"Setting initial values....    "}
{SET %new_recs, 0}
{SET %changes, 0}
```

You can learn by banging around this application. Try moving menu items and adding new ones, and observe the effect on the menu system. This approach is a good way to add to your understanding of menus and macros.

Summary

To suggest that any generic application you read about in a book can solve all your business/computer problems would be a monumental mistake. This book makes no pretensions to that goal, but this chapter has pointed the way to developing your own ideas about how an application can work for you.

In this chapter, you have explored the issues of creating a menu-driven application that can be used by you or by others. In order to take full advantage of this powerful capability in Alpha Four, you need to learn much more about how scripts and the application editor work together to give you close-to-programming capability.

Building on this chapter, you now can proceed to add polished scripts to your application.

Creating Scripts   2

*Work consists of whatever a body is obliged to do, and
Play consists of whatever a body is not obliged to do.*
Mark Twain, The Adventures of Tom Sawyer

NOTE Scripting is available for users of Alpha Four Version 2 and beyond only. Registered users of Version 1 have been offered the upgrade version for a very reasonable price. If you have not taken advantage of this offer, you can still contact Alpha Software and ask about the current policy.

In this chapter, you examine what a script is, how it is created, where it is located, when it is accessed, and how scripts can be tied together to make your application run smoothly.

A script contains a series of stored keystrokes, commands, or values that automate specific activities in Alpha Four. This definition is similar to the one for a macro. The difference is that macros are available only when you are working within an application. Macros are played from menu items in applications. Scripts can be played from almost anywhere in Alpha Four.

In Alpha Four Versions 2.0 and below, macros in applications are developed for extremely complex operations. The process of developing scripts has changed the way you can use macros. It is far easier, using Version 2, to design a series of modular scripts that can be tied together in a macro within an application. Then the scripts can be invoked by the macro on a menu line. Macros can play scripts, but a script cannot play a macro.

A script is a file that the user creates to customize the functions that he or she has to command. There are two kinds of script files: dialog boxes and keystroke scripts. Beyond this, there are several special scripts that have distinct purposes, prescribed names, and defined locations.

Setting Up for Scripts

There are three steps to consider regarding the use of scripts. First, you must select and prepare the site where the script operates. This refers to the .SCP file itself and the activity that is taking place when the script is to run. Second, the script must be created. Third, the script must be run, or *played*.

Scripts are played in several ways:

- By selecting a script from the Script menu.

- From a macro inside an application.

- By other scripts.

- By being selected from a dialog box as a menu item.

- By being triggered by an event that occurs within the program.

- By being named in such a way that it is automatically executed.

When a script has been played, the commands, keystrokes, or values that you put in the script are played back in the place where you designate.

Defining Special Purpose Scripts

Depending on how they are named and where they are located, certain scripts can behave in special ways:

- Start-up scripts are designed to play when Alpha Four is invoked and a database called. You can create a script to perform necessary startup procedures. This script plays automatically if it is named AUTOEXEC.SCP. If you do not want to give a script this name, then a startup script can be called in a command line using the -S=SCPNAME parameter.

- Open database scripts are named using the first seven (or less) letters of the name of the database; it runs automatically when the database is opened.

■ Quick scripts are played with Alt-F2. Alt-F1 is the quick record key. When you press Alt-F1, you automatically are in Learn Script mode. Notice that End:Alt-F3 appears in the bottom right of your screen. As long as this appears, you are recording a script with your keystrokes. Press Alt-F3 to end the recording session. Press Alt-F2 to play back a Quick script. Quick script is named UNTITLED.

If you become used to using the Alt-F2 to play a complex script, save a copy of that script under another name such as ALTF2, not UNTITLED.SCP. There is no warning if you are about to overwrite a Quick script.

T I P

HINT Creating a Quick script is a great way to test a keystroke script before naming and enhancing it. When a Quick script is created, the default name is UNTITLED.SCP. An UNTITLED.SCP can be edited using the Alt-F3 menu and saved with a different name. The next Quick script you create overwrites the previous one.

■ Hotkey scripts play from practically any location in the program. Hotkey scripts are named for the combination of the Ctrl key and a function key, 1 through 10. Thus, a script that you want to activate quickly from the Main Menu, for example, can be named CTRLF1 through CTRLF10, and the script plays when you press that combination.

■ Trigger scripts are activated when an event occurs within the software.

■ Tools scripts are played from a Tools menu. Scripts can be placed on a dialog box to provide the function and the appearance of a MENU.

Choosing Script Location

The place where the script is to be played is important. For example, consider the sample of the short keystroke script that was given in Quick Start 3. That script is designed to print a report. If from the Main Menu, you type **PRA**, Alpha Four expects to perform **P**rint **R**eport **A**. If the current screen shows anything other than the Main Menu, a script that plays the keystrokes **PRA** is likely to display an error message and stop.

NOTE The {ALTF10} command cancels the current activity and returns to the Main menu. Use this command at the beginning of a script to standardize the place where the activity starts.

Alpha Four provides the F3 (Learn keystrokes) capability so that for the initial creation of a script, the steps become obvious. In other words, if you start to create a script from View mode and the goal is to write a script that prints report A, then you are forced to leave View mode and go to the Main Menu in order to reach the Print menu.

This may all seem clear after you have gone through the process a few times, but at the beginning, the chain of events may be obscure. Using this Print Report A operation as an example, the steps are as follows:

1. Prepare to create a script.

   Select and prepare the OWNERS database that was created in Part I. Select the LASTNAME field as the first level of your index. Prepare a simple report with the LASTNAME field and several others to provide an example. Save the report using an appropriate letter, A through Z. (In the example, it is A.)

2. Create a script.

   From the View screen, press Alt-F3. Alpha Four shows the Scripts menu. Select create **K**eystroke script. On the top line of the next box, type **PRT_RPTA**, and type the description **Print Report A** on the next line. On the third line, press F3 to teach the keystrokes. Press Alt-F10 to access the Main Menu. Type **P R A F10** to complete the commands needed. Press Alt-F3 to end the learn mode. The script ends at the Print Destination screen, enabling the user to choose Screen, Printer, or File.

3. Execute (play) the script.

   Return to View mode and press Alt-F4. Select PRT_RPTA and press Enter. You should see the screens flash by as the script is being played.

Playing Scripts from a Tools Menu

There is an alternative to pressing Alt-F4 to play this script. The alternative is to play the script as a menu option from a dialog box. Dialog boxes pop up on your screen and can display data, request data from the operator, or play a script. Three terms define the options on a dialog box: prompt control, button control, and display control. The **P**rompt control requests input from the user, the **B**utton control plays a script, and the **Di**splay control shows data.

To create a dialog box, start from View mode and press Alt-F3. Alpha Four displays the Scripts menu. Select create **D**ialog script. Type the name of the current database. If you are using the OWNERS file created earlier, type **OWNERS**. This name identifies the script in a special manner, enabling you to access it with the **T**ools command. Give the script a description such as **Tools Box for Owners Database**.

You can use the F6 key to move the dialog box around the screen and the F7 key to change the size of the box. For now, set Row to 5, Column to 15, Height to 15, and Width to 30. Press F10 to continue. The dialog box appears. Move your cursor three rows down and two characters to the right. Press F2 (Controls) and select **B**utton control. Type **Print report A** on the top line of the next box. On the second line, press F2 and select the name of your Print Report script designed previously in step two. When you press Enter, the name of this script appears on the dialog box. Press F10 to continue. You see the dialog box showing the Button script description at the cursor location. In the lower-left corner, notice that the prompt line says `Plays: PRT_A`. This shows what script is to be played when that portion of the box is activated.

By giving the dialog script the same name as the current database, you have given it special properties. Any script so named becomes the Tools script for that database. If no script is named in this fashion, any script named Tools runs when you select **T** from the menu in View or Browse modes. You explore these techniques later in this chapter.

Using Script Variables

When you make a dialog box, three options are available: prompt controls, display controls, and button controls. The button control is associated with a script that must be created in a separate operation. The other two controls receive or display information that becomes a variable. When a dialog box pops up with a question that says `Which last name?`, this is a prompt control. The user is expected to type a name into the place provided. The information that is entered must be stored as a variable in the computer's memory.

The process of creating the prompt control establishes a location in the computer's memory in which the script variable is to be stored. The script variable can contain any appropriate entry that will fit in the space provided. This is one of several ways to create a script variable.

You can use the display control to show the contents of a script variable on a dialog box. You can examine the names and contents of script variables by pressing Alt-F3 and selecting display script Variable.

Understanding System Variables

Script variables are dependent on the user for their creation and management. A second kind of variable that is set by the actions of the program is called a *system script variable*. These variables are filled in as a result of events that occur within the program. A system variable, for example, may be %SYS_FIELD_NAME. This variable contains the name of the field in which the cursor most recently was located.

Defining System Variables by Programming

Some of these variables receive data without the user's intervention. Others, such as the %SYS_STAT variables, store data as a result of activities that are designed by the user. In any case, variables are seen on the Variables screen. Press Alt-F3 and V to view the System variables. These variables all have %SYS at the beginning of their names.

Setting Variables within a Script

Still another common method of defining a variable and identifying its contents is in the {SET} command. To employ this method, you create a keystroke script containing a line that establishes the relationship between a variable name and its contents. You can, for example, create a keystroke script that contains commands such as the following:

Command	Function
{SET %FILENAME, SYSTEM->DB_NAME}	Sets the variable %FILENAME to the name of the current database.
{SET %INVOICE_NO, INVOIC_ID}	Sets the variable %INVOICE_NO to the current contents of the field INVOIC_ID.

Command	Function
{SET %CURRENT_TOTAL, %SYS_STAT1_SUM}	Sets the variable %CURRENT_TOTAL to the amount identified in the system variable, %SYS_STAT1_SUM, which can be useful following a Field Statistics calculation.

The data stored in these variables is stored as character information.

Using Tools Scripts

To become familiar with the concepts of Tools scripts, select INVOICES.SET and go to View mode. Press Alt-F3 to display the scripts menu. Press K to create a Keystroke script. The steps to create this script are as follows:

1. Type the name **INVOICES** on the top line to establish that it will be the alternative to TOOLS as the default script. Type **Invoices TOOLS Script** on the description line, as shown in figure 12.1.

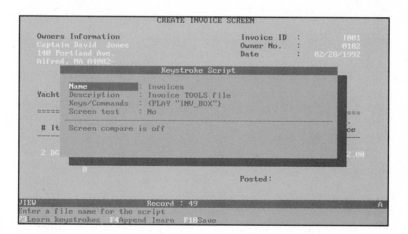

FIG. 12.1

The Keystroke Script starts with the definition screen.

2. With the cursor on the third line of the menu, press the Enter key to open the script editor box. Press F2 (Commands). The pop-up box that appears contains the commands available to the script. Press P and L. The cursor in the pop-up box jumps to {PLAY...}.

Press Enter to select this command. Notice that the command is placed on the script editor with the suggested syntax {PLAY $script}. Type **"INV_BOX"** and delete the syntax suggestion $script, leaving the curly bracket in place. The script should read {PLAY "INV_BOX"}. Press F10 to save the script. Press F10 to exit the Scripts mode.

You have declared that a script called INV_BOX exists, but you have not yet created that dialog script. Now you must make a script file called INV_BOX for the INVOICES script to play.

3. Press Alt-F3 to display the Scripts menu. Choose D to create a Dialog script. Type the name **INV_BOX** on the top line. On the second line, type **Main Menu for Invoice System**. In the next four rows, enter the following information:

Row	Type
Row	3
Col	18
Height	18
Width	46

Press F10 to continue. The dialog box that appears can serve as a menu for the Invoice System when you place various choices on it.

4. Place your cursor on the second line of the box and type **IN-VOICES TOOLS**. You can center this header by placing the cursor on the first letter and pressing F4 (Block). With the arrows, move the cursor to the end of the word TOOLS to mark the block. Press Enter to complete the marking process. Use the arrow keys to center the block of text. Press Enter to place the text in the new location. Alt-M is the shortcut to move a block. (You also can place the cursor on the first letter and use the space bar to push the text into place.)

5. Move the cursor on your screen three lines down and 1/2 inch from the left side of the box. Press F2 (Controls). Select Button. Type **1**. Enter **NEW invoice** on the top line. On the second line, type **NEWINV**. Press F10 (Continue). Press F10 again to complete this script.

6. Again, you have declared that a script exists that, in fact, does not yet exist. To create the script that is called for in step 5, from View mode, press Alt-F3 and press K to create a Keystroke script. Type

NEWINV on the top line. Type **Create a new invoice** on the second line and press Enter. Press Enter on the third line and type the following:

E{DN}{F3}{PAUSE}{ENTER:2}{DN}1{ENTER}{F3}

Press F10 twice to complete this script.

7. To see the results of your work, from View mode, select **Tools**. The dialog box appears. On a dialog box of this kind, you can place many display, button, or prompt controls, giving the appearance and function of a menu. To remove the dialog box from the screen without using a menu item, press the Esc key.

Carrying Data between Records

The capability to carry a piece of data from one record to another has been possible but not graceful in Alpha Four until the arrival of scripts and variables in Version 2. By setting the invoice number and the owner's identification number into variables at this point in your script, you have established the basis for entering additional lines to this invoice.

This technique can be used in a variety of applications. In this case, the variable reads the information about the two fields, INVOIC_ID and OWNER_ID, in the current record and retains the data. Then the script carries the data to the command to create a new record where the variables are entered in the first two fields, INVOIC_ID and OWNER_ID. (See Quick Start 3 for a Trigger script to carry data between files.) In the current example, the script to create a second line item on an existing invoice is the following:

    {SET %INV, INVOIC_ID}{SET %OWNER_ID, OWNER_ID}
    E{%INV}{ENTER}{%OWNER_ID}{ENTER:3}{F3}

Place this script on the Tols menu also. In the View mode, you can press **Tools** and view the alternate TOOLS script, the INV_BOX containing INVOICE TOOLS.

Summarizing the Operation

Here is a summary of how the process of creating a dialog box with a menu structure works. The dialog box starts the process.

Use the F6 (Position) and the F7 (Size) keys to make the box appear as you want. When you press F10 (Continue), the blank rectangle appears.

Place the cursor in the location where you want a menu item (button control) to appear. Press F2 (Controls) to define a menu item. Dialog boxes can contain three types of entries: *prompt controls*, which ask for a keyboard entry, *button controls*, which perform a command, and *display controls*, which display a message or variable. The process of selecting a script for a button control is shown in figure 12.2.

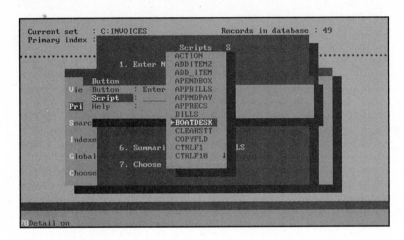

FIG. 12.2

Select script for
Button control.

Next you can create a prompt control to take information from the operator to set a variable. The Prompt definition box will be filled in like the following:

It says	*You type*
Prompt	**Which Invoice No.?**
Width	**4**
Window	**4**
Template	**I** (sets the default I for Invoice)
Mask	**A999** (forces a Capital letter and 3 numbers)
Variable	**%whichinvoice** (sets the invoice number as a variable)
Help	**Invoice numbers: Ex. I004**

Then, suppose that you want to switch among several files on your desktop. A useful item in a list of scripts is a SWITCHTO script that enters the letter W as a command. This requires a keystroke script that can be activated by a button control. To create the Button command, press F2 (Controls) and take the following steps:

It says	*You type*
Button	**Choose new file**
Script	**SWITCHTO**
Help	**Switch to new file**

This creates the possibility of activating this command, but until the script SWITCHTO has been created, nothing happens when you select this choice.

To create the Keystroke script for the SWITCHTO operation, press F10 (Continue) to leave the INVOICES script and start a new script. Press Alt-F3 and K to create a Keystroke script. Give this script the name SWITCHTO and type the description **Open Desktop to select new file**. At the third line, there are two ways to proceed. The first is the manual method, the second is the Learn method:

- Press Enter to access the script editor and press W.

- Press F3 (Learn keystrokes). Press W. At the View screen, note the message End:Alt-F3 in the bottom-right corner of the screen. You should press Alt-F3 to end the recording of the script.

At this point, you are ready to return to the dialog box already created and add to it the keystroke script you have written.

Understanding Trigger Scripts

Trigger scripts work differently from other scripts. Triggers are designed to respond to events that take place within the program. Hence, their use is event-driven.

Trigger scripts are played when a trigger event occurs. Each Trigger script is matched by a script variable that is set by a command executed with {TRIGKEYS}.

There are 20 trigger events in Alpha Four. Triggers happen to records and fields. They occur when letters are printed, when searches take place, when global updates are performed, and when the user chooses to Zoom and Unzoom.

Following is a list of the events that are triggers:

A new record is entered	Print a letter ends
An existing record is changed	A search begins
A record is saved	A search is processed

A record is deleted	A search match is found
A record is undeleted	A search ends
A field is entered	An update begins
A field is validated	An update is processed
A field is exited	An update is completed
Print a letter begins	Zoom takes place
Each record is printed in a letter	Unzoom takes place

Each trigger event has a matching script variable that corresponds to the named activity. Triggers operate only on real fields that exist in the database. Events related to fields cannot apply to calculated fields within reports, forms, browse tables, or letters.

The variables are found on the same screen as the other script variables. To see the list, press Alt-F3 and select display script **V**ariables. The following is a list of trigger variables:

SYS_TRIG_FIELD_ENTER	SYS_TRIG_REC_UNDEL
SYS_TRIG_FIELD_VALID	SYS_TRIG_SEARCH_START
SYS_TRIG_FIELD_EXIT	SYS_TRIG_SEARCH_NEXT
SYS_TRIG_LTR_START	SYS_TRIG_SEARCH_FIND
SYS_TRIG_LTR_NEXT	SYS_TRIG_SEARCH_EMD
SYS_TRIG_LTR_END	SYS_TRIG_UNZOOM
SYS_TRIG_REC_CHANGE	SYS_TRIG_ZOOM
SYS_TRIG_REC_DEL	SYS_TRIG_UPDATE_START
SYS_TRIG_REC_ENTER	SYS_TRIG_UPDATE_NEXT
SYS_TRIG_REC_SAVE	SYS_TRIG_UPDATE_END

Two scripts are required to run a trigger command. The first script sets the trigger variable. If, for example, you are writing a script that should play when a search begins, you create a script that sets the %SYS_TRIG_SEARCH_START variable that you want played at the trigger event, which is the beginning of the search. This script must be played when the work session begins in order to identify the action for this variable.

The second script plays when the Search function is activated. Whatever is defined in the second script is what happens at the beginning of the Search operation.

NOTE When writing Trigger scripts, be careful to keep spaces in the proper places. If the spaces are misplaced, the script will not run properly, or it will not run at all.

Planning Your Application

In theory, the development of a menu-driven application follows the creation of the databases, sets, indexes, search definitions, global update definitions, reports, input forms, browse tables, letters, mailing labels, import definitions, and cross tabulation definitions that you intend to use in the final system. In practice, there are generally bits and pieces that are added after the menuing system has started. The application development will proceed more quickly if most of the support files are already in place when you begin.

The first step in setting up your application should be to create or acquire a menuing system to introduce the application from the DOS level. This means using a software utility, DOSSHELL, AUTOMENU, or a series of batch files that you create yourself. Consult your DOS manual for creating a batch file. The command that you create for the menu should identify the method you use to log into specific files on your computer.

The assumption is that you will have more than one application on your computer or your network. If this is the case, the files for each application can be placed in their own data directories. On a network, the data files are kept in a shared directory where those with rights to the data can access them. In this case, each user also has a private directory—the location from which that user accesses Alpha Four. The normal process for accessing your files through Alpha Four is to call the files with a startup command. To start Alpha Four, you give the command:

    N:\ALPHA4V2\A4

This is the generic startup command for the Alpha Four, Version 2 program located in the N:\ drive, ALPHA4V2 subdirectory. Alpha Four remembers the place where the user is logged on when the program starts. This is the default location for certain files until Alpha Four learns about a different default location. It is important to understand this concept, because you can appear to lose scripts, default settings, and certain files by starting from a different directory.

Setting Defaults

If you have a subdirectory called \ALPHA4V2\BOATYARD and client tracking application named BOATYARD.APP in that subdirectory, you should make the startup command access the \ALPHA4V2\BOATYARD subdirectory first. From there you can issue the command N:\ALPHA4V2\A4, the N: referring to your own drive designator. In this manner, Alpha Four understands that you want the default information to be found in the \ALPHA4V2\BOATYARD subdirectory rather than in the \ALPHA4V2 subdirectory. It is worthwhile taking the time to understand this principle.

Identifying the Startup Directory

The next step is to identify the application and the program that you want to load first on this menu choice. In Quick Start 3, you designed an application called BOATYARD.APP. The startup file in the BOATYARD.APP is the INVOICES.SET. Therefore the startup command to access this set and this application from the BOATYARD subdirectory is as follows:

```
N:\ALPHA4V2\A4 N:\ALPHA4V2\BOATYARD\INVOICES - A=N:\ALPHA4V2
  \BOATYARD\BOATYARD
```

Of course, this is all on one line as a DOS command. You should substitute your directory, application, and file names for the ones shown.

Starting from a Different Directory

To carry this example one step further, assume that you also keep the records for your church to track donations on a weekly basis. The files for this application have no relationship to your business files. Therefore, you create a new subdirectory that contains the church files—the ALPHA4V2\CHURCH subdirectory. The startup file is named MEMBERS, and the application is called DONORS. The process to do this is as follows:

1. Create a batch file called CHURCH.BAT in your root directory. The batch file runs from your menu or by just typing the word **CHURCH**. The batch file contains the following lines:

```
D:                        (go to the D: drive)
cd\ALPHA4V2\CHURCH        (change to new directory)
D:\ALPHA4V2\A4 D:\ALPHA4V2\CHURCH\MEMBERS -A=D:\ALPHA4V2
  \CHURCH\DONORS
```

Alternative Starting Procedures

To add other options to the command line, the following switches are available:

- -A=Application name. This enables the user to identify the specific name of the startup application.

- -N=path. As in C:\ALPHA4V2\OUR_DATA. It generally is the place where the A4.NET file is located, this is the SHARED directory on a network. It is the location for files that are to be accessed by network users.

- -D=path. If the data path is not otherwise specified, this switch identifies the location of scripts.

- -S=STARTUP.SCP. If there is no AUTOEXEC.SCP, this switch identifies the script that is to run when Alpha Four begins.

Initializing the Application

Alpha Four has several ways to make files execute automatically:

- Two reserved file names—AUTOEXEC.DTN and AUTOEXEC.SCP—automatically are executed when the program finds them. The AUTOEXEC.DTN file contains the definition of a desktop; AUTOEXEC.SCP is a script file. Both files load automatically when the program starts in the subdirectory where they are located. These files are activated when Alpha Four begins, before a database file has been selected. This is similar to the AUTO123.WK1 worksheet that loads automatically when Lotus 1-2-3 is started.

- User-defined, automatically executed scripts—TOOLS.SCP, FILENAME.SCP, and FILENAM!.SCP—function only after you have selected a specific database. These scripts are identified as automatic by being named the same as the database itself. In other words, for a database file named INVOICE.DBF, a script file named INVOICE!.SCP runs the first time the INVOICE file is accessed. A second script called INVOICE.SCP runs when you select the TOOLS command in View or Browse modes. If a script name with the same name as the database does not exist, then the TOOLS.SCP will be activated when Tools is selected from View or Browse.

An example of this is the BOATYARD files. There are several files in the BOATYARD subdirectory. They work together to provide a method of tracking information for customer and invoice management. A Tools script can be defined that presents a menu of choices relating in an unrestricted manner to any file in the application. Tools is an easy-to-learn, easy-to-teach function. The function always appears on the View and Browse screens. Press T and the script executes. If the script is named TOOLS.SCP, it runs whenever you select Tools from View or Browse. If, however, you name a script INVOICE.SCP, that script takes precedence and plays instead of TOOLS.SCP when you are using the INVOICE database.

Automating Scripts with !s

The next important issue is to identify any other defaults that should be included in the process of initializing your application. These defaults can be set in three places:

■ In the startup script that is identified in the command line and plays when the Alpha Four program starts. The syntax for the startup script is the following:

-S=FILENAME.SCP

■ In the AUTOEXEC.SCP file that runs when the program is opened.

■ In a special script containing an exclamation point that runs automatically when a database is opened.

To create the third type of special script, you use an exclamation point as the last character of the file name before the three-letter extension. You use the first seven letters of the database file name followed by an exclamation point to name the script. In a database named INVOICE.DBF, for example, the automatically running script is named INVOICE!.SCP. If there are two files with the same first seven letters, only one of them is opened by this special script at one time. Either database will activate this script. INVOICES.SET and INVOICE.DBF both run INVOICE!.SCP when they are opened.

The defaults that can be set in the automatic scripts include the identification of certain variables needed for the operation of the application. You can, for example, create an application that takes data from INVOICE.DBF and posts the billing information to OWNERS.DBF. As part of the process, a variable can be set that stores the date that the post command was issued. This variable can be stored in a file created using the VSAVE{} command. The file created with VSAVE, for example, can contain a date that shows the last time a file was posted to the general ledger. The file can save a variable containing a date field that is set when the file is posted. Thus, a pop-up box can be designed that notifies the user that records should be posted or that they already have been posted for a period.

Saving Variables between Sessions

To save variables between sessions requires four separate scripts:

■ Script 1 creates the ASCII file containing the variables.

■ Script 2 restores the ASCII file data to the script variables.

■ Script 3 plays a dialog box showing the variable information, %POSTDATE.

■ Script 4 displays the variable %POSTDATE.

To save the existing variables at the end of a work session, you play the Keystroke script VARSAVE.SCP that creates the ASCII file VARSAVE. The expression for this script is:

{VSAVE "*", "VARSAVE"}

The VARSAVE file contains a line for each currently existing variable. This script should be played at the end of any work session to save the very latest information. The information in VARSAVE is restored by playing a companion script called RESTORE.SCP. This script must play at the beginning of every session. It contains the following expression:

{VRESTORE "VARSAVE"}

To play the VRESTORE script properly, it should be included in a startup procedure. In this manner, you can assure that the information stored from the previous session will be available for the next session.

To play the VSAVE script reliably, it must be included in the final sequence of an application, before the Quit command is executed to leave the system.

Locating the Defaults

The decision about where to place these default settings may teach you more than you want to know about why programmers sometimes are described as coming from a different planet. This kind of thinking requires looking deeply into the way things work in a computer. However, the most successful designers of systems for business uses are not necessarily programmers. They are people who know a particular business well and use Alpha Four to implement their ideas. Physicians, attorneys, salesmen, law enforcement managers, trades people, scientists, political activists, construction people, teachers—any professional thinker who tracks lists of items can make an application using scripts. Alpha Four provides the menu-driven functions and on-line support that are needed from your software. If you can master scripting, you can make your application safe, smart, and timesaving.

If this all seems a bit much, following is a check list for the items that may or must be considered:

- Where does the Alpha Four program start?
- Where are the application (data) files located?
- What should be the script path for this application?
- Which desktop file or files are needed?
- What TOOLS file is generic to this application?
- What variables have to be set for this application?

There are, indeed, a great many more decisions to make with Version 2 of this software. When a decision is made, it should stay made. This means inscribing your decisions in one or more scripts to play automatically.

For example, a decision that should not have to be made more than once is the preferred color scheme for your application. If your application for running the boatyard looks fine using BERMUDA, the name of one of the predefined color palettes that come with the program, but your baseball league scores look better in a red, white, and blue scheme you design yourself, then a color palette defined for each must exist in the drive path from which the program is started. Make a copy of the A4.PAL file that is found in the subdirectory where the Alpha Four files are installed. When the program opens from the \ALPHA4V2\BOATYARD subdirectory, BERMUDA is available. When you open your application from the \ALPHA4V2\REGGIE_J subdirectory, then RW&B is available.

Understanding .UDNs

The .UDN file contains the previously defined information that is stored by Alpha Four every time a file is accessed. Included in this information is the current selection of view and browse tables, color palette, printer definition and other selections specific to the database file or set.

An important rule regarding .UDN files is to be consistent about your startup procedures. Suppose, for example, that you have been in the habit of starting Alpha Four from the \ALPHA4V2 subdirectory and then moving to the \ALPHA4V2\BOATYARD subdirectory using the arrow keys. One day, you start the program from \ALPHA4V2\ BOATYARD and begin to access files that have not previously been started in the \ALPHA4V2\BOATYARD subdirectory. You must reset many defaults that you have been taking for granted. It appears that Alpha Four has forgotten all the current settings, such as the input form and browse table of choice.

This is because the first time that the application or file is viewed in the new directory, there is no .UDN field from which the program is able to choose the default settings. A .UDN file is created in the startup subdirectory whenever a file is retrieved in that subdirectory in the multiuser version of Alpha Four. In the single user version, the .UDN is saved with the database.

This means that, if you are putting files on a disk to send to another user, the .UDN files must accompany the application and the program must start from the subdirectory where the files are located.

Passing around the Scripts

The principle of application-specific information applies to the case of scripts, as well. Scripts, however, have their own special ways of being found by a program:

- ■ The script path command can be set by an instruction in the command line when you access the program.

- ■ The script path can be set by default to the subdirectory where the program was started.

- ■ The script path can be set to <DATAPATH>, which forces the file to examine only the current directory for the scripts.

There are two ways to execute a startup script:

- ■ The file AUTOEXEC.SCP, found in the default script directory, plays automatically when you start Alpha Four.

- ■ A script can be invoked by the -S=SCP_NAME parameter used in the startup command from DOS. This script takes precedence over a script named AUTOEXEC.SCP in the same subdirectory.

NOTE   Alpha Four stores certain configuration information specified by the user in the directory from which the program is accessed. This is particularly important in the case of use on a network system. User-specified information for network use is stored in the user's private directory. Network users should always start the program from the same private subdirectory so that the software can find the files it expects to locate.

Using Scripts for Accounts Receivable

Throughout this book, you have worked with different parts of the invoicing system for the boatyard. It is logical that you should add an accounts receivable section to the office activity. Accounts receivable enable you to keep track of the payments made against invoices in your system. The payment database can have a minimum of the fields listed in the following section. Additional fields that relate specifically to your needs can be added at any time. Additional indexes needed in your application can be created as you need them. Remember to keep notes as you make changes. Draw a picture of the relationships of your files and which file performs what function.

Adding Scripting Power to Sets Management

The discussion of the boatyard application began in Quick Start 1 with one file called INVENTRY.DBF. In Chapter 2, the file called OWNERS.DBF was discussed. To this, you added CONTACT.DBF to contain records of conversations, letters, phone calls, and meetings with owners and others involved with our business. To do this, you created a set called CONTAC.SET with CONTACT.DBF as the primary database and OWNER.DBF as the child file indexed on OWNER_ID. In Quick Start 3, you designed the beginning of an application for the boat yard. The application menu has the following entries:

> A. Customer Information
> B. Financial Activities
> C. Inventory Management
> D. Property Records
> E. Housekeeping Utilities
> F. Return to Alpha Four
> G. Exit the Program

The final steps in completing an application, for your own use or for someone else, is putting the scripts together and tying them into the menu system. In this section, you pull together the parts that have been set out in earlier work. To do this, you design scripts for the functions that lie behind the menu selection. Some of these functions are as follows:

- Print an invoice after completing the entry.

- Post today's invoices to a history file.

- Extract an ASCII file from an external program and add the data into the current files.

The nice part of this is that the way your business flows is the way your menu system should work. When you have created your menu choices and the scripts—and the forms, reports, indexes, and searches that go with them—then your application reflects the unique character of your operation in a way that no off-the-shelf software can do.

Using Field Statistics Variables

The field statistics command comes of age with Version 2 of Alpha Four. The software now gives you access to these variables in the same manner as any other variable. These variables can be seen in the list when you select the Alt-F3 (Scripts) menu. Select display script **Variables** to view the list. These variables are set when you run the field statistics operation.

The field statistics function is particularly useful for displaying a total for an invoice or a series of bills, or simply counting the occurrence of certain data. For example, to answer the question, "How many customer's addresses are in New York?," the query in field statistics is as follows:

    if(ST="NY",1,0)

This function creates a total in the SYS_STAT1_SUM variable that totals the variables that occur when the expression is true. Thus, the variable can be displayed in a dialog box that shows %SYS_STAT1_SUM.

There are four expressions in field statistics. Each returns a low, high, sum, and average figure for each expression, a total of 16 results. Also, there is one more variable called SYS_STAT_COUNT. Because field statistics operates with a range setting screen, the possibility exists that the analysis will be run on a search list or a filtered file. SYS_STAT_COUNT returns the number of records that were analyzed by the most recent field statistics operation.

NOTE Script variables are always considered to be character types, no matter what may be defined. So to perform mathematical operations on the data contained in a variable, you may have to convert the variable to the appropriate type. If, for example, SYS_STAT1_SUM returns the number of records with ST="NY", and SYS_STAT2_SUM returns the number of records with ST="CT", you can add the two with an expression that uses the VAL() function, such as:

VAL(%SYS_STAT1_SUM) + VAL(%SYS_STAT2_SUM)

Polishing Your Performance

Among the final items that you should attend to as a developer of applications containing scripts is the script library. The details of creating a LIBRARY.SCP are discussed in Chapter 14, but a brief description is needed here.

A *script library* is a file that is created when you have completed the debugging of all scripts you intend to use in a particular application. Alpha Four comes with an external program called A4LIB.EXE that you can find in the Alpha Four program directory. By running this program from DOS, you can collect a large number of scripts into one file. The syntax for running this program is as follows:

A4LIB LIB_NAME script1 script2 script3...

or

A4LIB LIB_NAME *.scp

In the first case, only the named scripts are added to the library script LIB_NAME.SCP. In the second case, the * DOS wild-card symbol causes A4_LIB to take all scripts in the current directory into the LIB_NAME.SCP.

You give the script any legal DOS name that is significant to you for this purpose. Alpha Four adds the three-letter extension so that LIB_NAME becomes LIB_NAME.SCP. When you create this script, you can either list the scripts one by one, as above, or you can use one of the DOS wild-card symbols, * or ?, to represent characters. Dialog scripts must remain in the directory because A4_LIB ignores them. All keystroke scripts except dialog scripts and LIB_NAME.SCP can be removed from the script path after the library has been created.

The developer should take note of this facility—untrained users will not stumble on keystroke scripts in their applications and become confused or worse, become creative, with the existing scripts.

Solving Real Problems with Scripts

Many users employ more than one software package on their computer. Frequently they see a need to pass information between Alpha Four and, for example, an accounting package or spreadsheet. The import and export functions discussed in Chapter 9 are a powerful feature of Alpha Four. Scripts can make them even more effective. The billing system called Timeslips is an example of a program on which people become dependent, despite Alpha Four's capability to perform many of the same functions. To include information recorded in Timeslips with other records created in Alpha Four, you must create two scripts in Alpha Four and a macro in Timeslips. Timeslips and many other programs have the facility of creating reports to export to a comma-delimited ASCII file. This file can be manipulated by Alpha Four.

The first step is to create a script that suspends Alpha Four temporarily to run Timeslips. This script assumes that Timeslips is on the D: drive, in the \TIMESLIP subdirectory:

```
{EXEC "D:\timeslip\tsreport",0,0}
```

This script suspends Alpha Four and runs a command to call up Timeslips. There is a matching script that retrieves the ASCII file created by Timeslips and appends the data to a history file. Timeslips contains a macro generator that can easily print relevant material to ASCII for importing to Alpha Four.

The second script logs to the ledger file and imports the ASCII data to a file called TS_DATA. The TS_DATA file is appended to the LEDGER file. This happens daily—the Timeslips file is overwritten to prevent the same data from being entered more than once. The macro in Timeslips calls for today's bills only. The posting is so quick that the process should be engaged every day. In this way, the record will always be complete and no one has to reenter any data.

Setting a Filter Using a Variable

This technique can be varied to set filter expressions to use a variable. You can design a dialog box with a prompt control that asks Which City?. When the user enters the name of a city, the name is entered as the data in the variable. Then when a report is run that uses a filter to select a specific city, the range setting screen looks like that shown in figure 12.3.

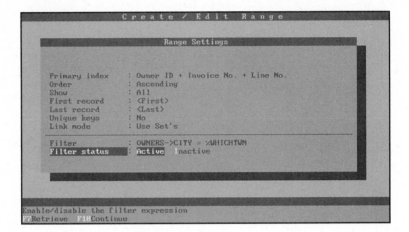

The Range Settings screen accepts a filter containing the variable set with a prompt control.

Unsettable Variables

Alpha Four stores several variables based on the condition of the current file. For example, %SYS_ID_FORM shows the letter representing the input form that is currently in operation. The variables are set by the software, not directly by the user. There is a system variable for each of the function keys, 1 through 10, when pressed with the Ctrl key. These are %SYS_CTRLF1 through %SYS_CTRLF10. Each of these can hold the name of a script file. Alpha Four plays the script when the corresponding key is pressed.

Script Commands Directory

The following is an alphabetical listing of the script commands in Alpha Four, including their category, syntax, and usage. Following is a listing of new script commands in in-line Version 2.00.04.

ABORT   Terminate script

Syntax: {ABORT}

Terminates a script that is being played. This command sends the user back to the Main Menu and removes the script from memory. This command also ends the playing of the script and returns to the application menu if an application is running, or it returns the user to the Alpha Four Main Menu if there is no application currently in effect. If the script is nested within another script, {ABORT} returns to the parent script. Compare the use of this command with {CANCEL}.

BEEP   Notification to user

Syntax: {BEEP}

Makes a sound with the computer's speaker. This is useful for notifying the user that an event has occurred. {BEEP} conveys the sense of an error as compared with the {TONE} command, which plays a selected note for a period of time. Compare the use of {BEEP} with {TONE}.

CANCEL   Terminate script

Syntax: {CANCEL}

Ends a script and returns to the active screen, not only to the Main Menu, as does the {ABORT} command. There is a difference in the two commands, based on the flow of activity. If your intention is to terminate an operation and return to the Main Menu, use {ABORT}, if the object is just to stop the script, use {CANCEL}. Compare the use of this command with {ABORT}.

CASE   Logical

Syntax: {CASE logical,command}

Provides a means of evaluating a series of expressions. The command accepts logical expressions and commands. If the first expression is True, the command that follows is performed. If the first expression is False, the next expression is evaluated. When the command finds a True expression, the command is executed and all further activity is ignored.

You can devise as many as 15 logical expressions for evaluation with a single {CASE} command. An example of how this might be useful is if you have an application for which you want to identify several legitimate passwords for performing data entry and editing functions. Create a dialog box with a Prompt control that asks the user to type in a password. This stores a variable, %PASSWORD. Next, create a keystroke script which looks like the following:

```
{CASE
    %PASSWORD="Professor".or.
    %PASSWORD="Music Man".or.
    %PASSWORD="Loveboat",{{PLAY "USER"}},
    %PASSWORD<>"Professor".or.
    %PASSWORD<>"Music Man".or.
    %PASSWORD<>"Loveboat".or.{{PLAY "NO_USER}}}
```

The USER script sets the **C**onfiguration **D**efault **P**revent change/enter to No. The NO_USER script sets the **C**onfiguration **D**efault **P**revent change/enter to Yes. See the {IF} command.

CLEAR   Defines or saves variables

Syntax: {CLEAR "variable"}

Clears specified script variables from memory. This command is useful, for example, if you run a series of Field Statistics or other calculations that result in data stored in variables, and you want to display the information in a dialog box.

The {CLEAR} command accepts a specific variable or a wildcard definition that identifies several or all script variables. For example, {CLEAR "%CURRENT_PO"} removes the data representing the current Purchase Order Number from memory. To clear all of the %SYS_STAT variables, use: {CLEAR "%SYS_STAT*"}.

NOTE   During script development sessions, variables may be created that are later to be discarded. If this occurs, there is no way to erase the variable directly. If there is nothing stored or restored for the variable, it will not appear the next time you access Alpha Four.

DEBUGOFF   Debug script

Syntax: {DEBUGOFF}

This command is the companion to {DEBUGON}. Together they present a means of debugging a troublesome script. {DEBUGOFF} turns off the action of {DEBUGON}. By causing the debug operation to appear at a location in a script where problems begin to occur, you can pinpoint the difficulty your script is encountering. When you use the standard debug function from the Scripts menu, the script must run from the beginning. With the {DEBUG} commands, the activity can be directed to a particular area of the script.

DEBUGON   Debug script

Syntax: {DEBUGON}

This command is the companion to {DEBUGOFF}. See {DEBUGOFF}.

ENDAPP   Application control

Syntax:{ENDAPP}

To force a script to return to the Main Menu, use {ENDAPP}. This does not simply end the script. It takes the process further to return the user to the application menu, if an application is running or to the Alpha Four menu if there is no application in effect at the time that {ENDAPP} is encountered. If the current script is part of an application that is invoked by another application, the {ENDAPP} returns control to the *parent* application.

EXECCLR   Runs external program

Syntax: {EXECCLR program_name, par1, par2}

Suspends your current work in Alpha Four and accesses an external program. In order to do this, Alpha Four must write a file to the disk that captures the current data that it needs when you return from the excursion into word processing, spreadsheet, or other activities. (See discussion of __A4xxxxx.$A4 files.)

This command has three parts. The parts are separated by commas. The first part is the command to execute the program. The second part tells Alpha Four whether you wish to create a parameter database during this operation (0 for no, 1 for yes). The third part identifies the amount of memory that you wish to allocate to the running of the external program. A zero in this location indicates that the program should give all available memory to the program.

If you tell the program to create a parameter database by placing a 1 in the second part of the expression, Alpha Four will define a unique name for that file. However, you can specify the name with a {SET} command by using the system variable %SYS_XFILE. The expression is the following:

    {SET %SYS_XFILE,"TEST.DBF"}

Where the program name is expected, you should use the complete drive and path name. For example, to execute WordPerfect from the \WP51 subdirectory, the command would read as the following:

    {EXECCLR "C:\wp51\wp",0,0}

Numerous, detailed examples are found in the Alpha Four Reference Manual. A companion command is {EXEC}.

EXEC   Runs external program

Syntax: {EXEC program_name, par1, par2}

Similar to {EXECCLR}, this command executes an external program. The difference is that {EXEC} does not clear the screen to

accommodate the external program. The majority of programs that you are likely to use do clear the screen before they are executed. {EXECCLR} is designed to perform the clear screen function, but {EXEC} is not.

GOTO   Redirect action of script

Syntax: {GOTO :label}

Enables the user to have more control over the execution of his or her script. A parameter is required for execution. The parameter is called a label. The label is a colon followed by a letter, A through Z. The command looks like the following: {GOTO :A}.

The label tells the script to pick up the next step of processing at the target location. The next location is identified by a matching entry such as {:A}. A companion command is {LOOP}. By combining these two, you can develop a sequence of instructions for creating multiple records based on user input.

IF   Logical

Syntax: {IF logical, command [,command]}

Enables you to design an expression that analyzes a statement and, based on its status (true or false), take a certain action (command). The expression is evaluated from left to right. In other words, the expression reads: IF (this statement is true), then (do command). If the statement is not true, the expression ends. More often the statement has another section. The translation, then is the following:

IF (this statement is true), then (do this command), else (do the other command)

Each command or series of keystrokes that represent the action to take if the logical expression is true must be able to stand on its own as an activity. If you have difficulty making the IF command work, separate the parts of the command and test each one separately.

You can place the commands in sequence to evaluate until it finds a true statement or it runs out of statements. For example, you can assign an index key to a record by writing a calculation for KEYFIELD such as the following:

IF(PRICE < 10,"A",IF(PRICE < 50, "B", IF(PRICE < 100, "C", "D")))

The record containing a price of 30 fails the first test and passes the second; therefore, the expression stops processing and assigns the letter B to that record. If a record fails each analysis, then KEYFIELD receives a D. The companion to the command is {CASE}.

LOOP   Redirect action of script

Syntax: {LOOP :label, variable}

Similar to the {GOTO} command, {LOOP} allows you to define the number of times that an action takes place. Where {GOTO} just directs the flow of a script to a label location, {LOOP} adds the variable in which is stored a number or expression that evaluates to a number, indicating the number of times that the command should be performed.

Each time the command is executed, the program reduces the number stored in the variable by one. When the number stored is equal to 0, the execution of the instruction stops. All variables are stored as characters. However, the operation of {LOOP} sees the variable as a number. The companion to the command is {GOTO}.

MAINMENU   Application control

Syntax: {MAINMENU}

Gives the user access to the Alpha Four Main Menu and its functions from within an application. The operation of this command ends when the user presses the Esc key. Escape returns the user to the application menu.

As a part of an application, you may want to consider that this command is for the more advanced user who is permitted use of the Main Menu commands. You can put a password on this choice on the application menu.

NOCLEAR   Screen control

Syntax: {NOCLEAR}

Provides an instruction to a script. The issue is the way the screen appears to the user. If you want a dialog box to remain on the screen, place {NOCLEAR} at the beginning of the command.

ONERROR   Error handling

Syntax: {ONERROR {command}}

Manages the processing of a script. When an error occurs, what happens? This command answers. It is here that the script says, *if a problem develops here, do something else.* Officially, this is called a custom error handling system. This command identifies the process that will occur if an error occurs. You can identify a direction to take if an error occurs. This command takes precedence over Alpha Four's Error messages. {ONERROR} inserts a message that offers Continue as the option, rather than the normal message.

ONESCAPE   Responds to key press

Syntax: {ONESCAPE {commands}}

After a certain amount of time using Alpha Four and other computer programs, the Escape key begins to be second nature for the little finger of the left hand. Whenever there seems to be no other solution, press {ESC}. This may be habit for the human, but it is just a command like any other for the computer. {ONESCAPE} provides an improved means of canceling whatever process may have been begun at the point that the user decides to use Escape. This is done by causing the program to return straight to the Main Menu without going through the usual process of stepping backward through a series of menus.

After the program has returned the user to the Alpha Four Main Menu, Alpha Four resets the behavior of the Escape key to normal.

ONKEY   Responds to key press

Syntax: {ONKEY key,{command}}

Enables the user to define a script that sets a block of commands that are activated when a specific key is pressed. You can assign as many as 64 keys to an ONKEY mapping at one time. You can define regular alpha and numeric keys such as A, 1, and &. You also can map what are called the *extended keys*, such as the function key F10, the combination of Alt and A (Alt-A), and Esc, (the Escape key). If your choice is an alphabetic ASCII key, Alpha Four understands the letter in upper- or lowercase. In other words, it is case-insensitive for {ONKEY}.

When a key that has been defined by the {ONKEY} command is pressed, Alpha Four activates the *script fragment* associated with the key. It does not pass the key through to the program. If you want the key that was pressed to be passed through, you must include a reference to that key in the script fragment.

To clear a key that has been identified by an {ONKEY} command, you must issue another {ONKEY} command with a blank script fragment, such as {} in the following:

        {ONKEY "{F10}",{}}

This command clears any previous ONKEY attachment to the F10 key. After this command is issued, the F10 key behaves normally.

ONMAIN   General script commands

Syntax: {ONMAIN {command}}

In the event that you want to keep the user from accessing the functions on the Alpha Four Main Menu, use {ONMAIN} to define the command that should occur instead. For example, the script fragment, {ONMAIN {b}} can be placed at the end of a search sequence. Thus when the search is complete and the screen would normally return to the Main Menu, the script goes to browse mode to show the records held in the new search list.

PAUSE   **Responds to key press**

Syntax: {PAUSE}

Causes a script to be suspended until the Enter key is pressed. Compare this with the {WAITKEY} command, which causes a script to be suspended until a user-defined key has been pressed.

When writing a {PAUSE} command, remember that the Enter key, which terminates the {PAUSE} command, is not recognized as the normal Enter key. If the script calls for an Enter at the point that the {PAUSE} is ended, then you must use a second {Enter} command to continue the script.

PLAY   **General script commands**

Syntax: {PLAY "script"}

Executes another script. Frequently, this means that a *current* script is suspended when a new script presents itself to be executed. As long as the script can be found on the current script path, it is available to {PLAY}.

A frequent use for this command is in combination with the {SET} command. For example, you may have defined a script that creates a relationship between a user-defined variable and the data in a particular field. Such a script as SET_INVOIC is the following:

　　　{SET %invoic_id, INVOIC_ID}

The preceding expression reads as *Store in the variable named INVOIC_ID the data found in the field INVOIC_ID.* To use this command, you need the following {PLAY} command:

　　　{PLAY "SET_INVOIC"}

Therefore, if the preceding expression is a script named SET_INVOIC, it can be used to look at the record currently shown on the screen and capture the data called for in a specified field (in this case, INVOIC_NO), and store that data in the variable %INVOIC_ID. This is important because once the data is stored in the variable, it can be used in any number of ways: searches, filters, reports, forms, other expressions, and to create records in related databases.

Commonly, this technique is used to capture data in a parent database where the expected child record does not yet exist, and drop it into a linked record in the child file.

An example of this is in a donor tracking system. The information comes in quickly to the data entry person. The files are set up to lookup an existing donor when a new record is being created. The user has a stack of donor cards or checks, the names on most of which have already been recorded in the DONOR file. The active (primary) database is the DONATION database. Every donation must be attributed to a specific donor. As an entry is created, if the donor has not been recorded in the DONOR file, the donation itself must still be recorded.

You can write a script that solves this problem. When a record is created for which no match is found in the linked file, the user is trained to zoom to the lookup file and enter the appropriate information into a new record. At this point, the DONOR_ID must be brought back to the original record and inserted into the appropriate field to establish the link between the donation and the donor. It is here that the *capture* takes place. The DONOR database probably is set to accept new donor information by assigning a unique identifier to each new record. It is this unique identifier that is stored in the variable DONOR_ID. When the data entry person has finished creating this record, a script causes the program to *unzoom* and enter that DONOR_ID into the record of the donation.

The {PLAY} command can accept as many as 10 levels of nested scripts. When a script calls for another script to {PLAY}, the first script's activity is suspended. At the end of the child script, the script that called the child script resumes. A companion to this command is {SHOW}.

PROMPT

Syntax: {PROMPT, variable, length}

Operates in much the same way as the PROMPT command in macros designed for applications. This command produces a prompt box that asks the user to enter the appropriate data. Generally this has been replaced in scripts with the PROMPT control, which appears on a Dialog box.

In defining the command, you must identify the variable in which the data is to be stored and the length of the field available for the user entered data. For example, the script entry might be the following:

```
{PROMPT "%INVOIC_ID", 4}
```

When the script containing this expression is played, a small prompt box will appear. The data entered in this box becomes the current contents of the variable, %INVOIC_ID.

This is useful for the occasion when it is inappropriate to have a Dialog box to accept the user input. Compare the use of the {PROMPT} command to {PAUSE} and {WAITKEY}.

READ

Syntax: {READ variable, row, col, length}

Reads a specific location of the screen and uses the data there as a variable. For example, a script can read the screen and gather the information in a calculated field, such as ACTUAL_AGE (a calculated field based on data of birth), and make it a variable although there is no stored field that keeps that data in an individual's record. Hence, like {SET}, the purpose of this command is to store current data in a variable.

The command reads the specific characters at the stated location on the screen, by row, column and length.

RPL   Runs external program

Syntax: {RPL code, par, result, error}

Gives access to Alpha Software's memory resident programming language RPL. You can use the {RPL} command to initiate RPL routines when RPL is active in your computer. RPL is sold as a separate product from Alpha Four.

SCREENFREEZE   Screen control

Syntax: {SCREENFREEZE}

Holds the current screen while script commands are being executed. This prevents the *slide show* effect as a script is playing. Compare this with {SCREENOFF}, which causes the screen to be blank while a script is playing. Different scripts call for different treatment, depending in part on the time it takes to perform the script's activities.

If the object is to give the user the impression that the computer is working quickly and properly, you may want to use {SCREENFREEZE} for a brief session while the script gathers results, performs a search, does a global update, and so on. If the activity is expected to take any length of time, you may want to use {SCREENOFF} instead of {SCREENFREEZE}, then include a {WRITE} command to send a Patience, please..... message to the user. Other companion commands include {SCREENON} and {SCREENOFF}.

SCREENOFF   Screen control

Syntax: {SCREENOFF}

Like {SCREENFREEZE}, {SCREENOFF} is used for aesthetic purposes. The operation of a script looks more professional if the activities that it performs are hidden from the viewer. Leave {SCREENOFF} and

{SCREENFREEZE} out of your scripts until you have completely finished the editing process. Other companion commands are {SCREENON} and {SCREENFREEZE}.

SCREENON   Screen control

Syntax: {SCREENON}

Turns the screen back on after the script processing is complete. Other companion commands are {SCREENFREEZE} and {SCREENOFF}.

SET   Defines or saves variables

Syntax: {SET %variable, characters}

Stores data in a script variable. The contents can be keystrokes or commands or a combination of the two. The contents are held as a character string. Data representing dates and numeric values are stored in character strings that can be reinterpreted in other circumstances in their original form.

The following are two examples. A dollar amount stored as a variable can be used in a comparison with other dollar figures, such as: IF %NEWPRICE > %OLDPRICE, %NEWPRICE, %OLDPRICE. Depending on the circumstance, Alpha Four understands the interpretation or the user must help with a function, such as VAL(DOLLARAMT). Using dates in an example, you can define two variables, such as %FIRSTDATE and %LASTDATE, and create a script that uses these two in a saved search to identify records that pertain to a specific, user-definable period of time.

The {SET} command rounds off numbers, in spite of decimal points that show on the screen, while {READ} takes the data literally. {SET} sees the number 19.95 and interprets the character string as 20. {READ} sees 19.95 and returns 19.95. The {SET} command can only be used to capture such data if the data exists in a field that is currently placed on the screen in View or Browse or if the field is used as part of an expression in a calculated field in the current layout. In the case where it is inappropriate to use the field on the current layout, if that field is used as part of a calculated field, neither the field itself nor the calculated field needs to be placed on the form for the {SET} command to function properly.

SHOW   General script commands

Syntax: {SHOW "script name"}

Enables you to place a dialog box on the screen for a comment or instruction to the user. Used to reassure the user that something is taking place on his or her behalf, the dialog box can be displayed after a {SCREENOFF} command has removed the script processing from view.

{SHOW} also can present dialog boxes to serve as mini help screens. {SHOW} does not permit other controls that might be on the dialog box to operate. Compare the function of this command with {WRITE}.

TONE   **Notification to user**

Syntax: {TONE frequency, duration}

Plays a tone with a numeric value and a duration in 1/100ths of a second on the computer's speaker. This can be useful to alert the user when a task is completed. Compare this command to {BEEP}, which has no frequency or duration.

TOOLEND   **General script commands**

Syntax: {TOOLEND}

Returns the user to the View or Browse mode and shows the screen from which the user invoked the TOOLS script. Compare the function of {TOOLEND} to the {ONMAIN} command.

TRIGKEYS   **General script commands**

Syntax: {TRIGKEYS {keystrokes}}

Plays back keystrokes within a script invoked by a trigger event. Trigger events are occurrences that take place within the program. A trigger events occur when certain activities take place regarding fields and records, global update and searches, the printing of letters, and zoom/unzoom operations. Triggers occur under the following circumstances:

> Fields are entered, validated or exited
> Global update is started, record is updated, command is completed
> Print letter command given, letter prints, letter is finished printing
> Records are created, edited, deleted, undeleted, or saved
> Searches are started, record is evaluated, match found, search ends
> Unzoom occurs
> Zoom occurs

In order for a trigger script to operate, the {TRIGKEYS} command must be issued. With {TRIGKEYS}, you identify the keystrokes you want to play. The program holds them for processing until the end of the trigger event.

VRESTORE   **Defines or saves variables**

Syntax: {VRESTORE "filename"}

Reloads script variables that have been saved in the named file, which is a file name such as RESTORE.VAR. Generally, this file is stored in the subdirectory where the data files are located. When the companion command {VSAVE} has been used to save current script variables to a disk at the end of a session, those variables can be restored rather than having to be re-created.

This command can also be used to maintain a set of variables that do not need to be kept current—just available. In other words, if information is held in variables that change throughout a work session but you want to return to the original data when a new session begins, then the {VSAVE} command would be used only to create the *permanent* variable file.

In a third instance, variables can be restored that normally do not change but which can be made to change with a new circumstance. Suppose that within a work group, certain individuals swap functions for different projects. In one instance, James is the project manager, Maureen is the engineer, and Denis is the director. These names must appear with the proper title on documents needing signatures. When a project ends, these individuals rearrange their jobs suitably for the next project. Their names can be stored using a prompt command and {VSAVE}. When a new project shuffles the roles again, the variables can be revised and made permanent, at least until the next shuffle.

VSAVE   Defines or saves variables

Syntax: {VSAVE "%pattern", "filename"}

Identifies the variables that are to be saved and to name a file that is to contain the information to be restored by the companion command {VRESTORE}. The information saved with {VSAVE} is stored in ASCII format with the extension .VAR.

For example, you can store such variables as %WHO, %WHEN, %WHERE, and %WHY. The command to save these variables can read as the following:

   {VSAVE "%WH*", "FACTS"}

If you want to save the data in every variable, the pattern should be "%*". To save the data in the 17 %SYS_STAT variables, use the pattern "%SYS_STAT*".

The information that is stored in the manner can be used as any comma-delimited ASCII can be used. For example, the data can be imported into another .dbf file by using the Utilities, Import data function. The data can be made available to other users on a network, and it can be viewed by using the letter function (Main Menu, Layouts, Letters, Create/edit a form letter. Viewed in ASCII, the variable name appears with an equals sign, followed by the stored contents, such as the following:

WHO=MaryAnn & Arlene
WHEN=04/01/92
WHERE=1 NORTH AVE
WHY=

WAITKEY   Responds to key press

Syntax: {WAITKEY}keystroke

Suspends the action of a script until a certain key is pressed. The key that is named is not passed through to the program. It simply reactivates the script. This command has numerous functions and extends the range of its companion command {PAUSE}, which only waits for the Enter key.

WAITSCRN   General script commands

Syntax: {WAITSCRN row, column, characters}

Suspends the activity of a script until a specified screen appears and shows the specified characters in the proper place. The parameters for this command are the row (1 - 25), the column (1 - 80), and a character string as long as 80 characters. The command is similar to the Screen test that can be defined at the start of a keystroke script, except this can occur during the process of execution of a script. Compare the function of the commands {WAITKEY} and {PAUSE}.

WRITE   Screen control

Syntax: {WRITE row, col, characters}

Sends a message to the user. The message generally is intended to allay user impatience when the software and the computer are working to produce results. A typical example is the period that it takes for the computer software and hardware to get together about which files are being loaded. If you have designed a DESKTOP script and included it in the startup procedures with your program, then the startup may take a bit longer than it would without the DESKTOP. However, the payoff in time is realized over and over again during the use of the files if you use more than one file. A peaceful message, such as Thanks for waiting or Loading the files, occupies the space during the time it takes to complete the procedure.

The {WRITE} command places that message on the screen. Generally, this is best shown on a screen that has been cleared with the {SCREENOFF} command.

New Script Commands

The following commands are new to Alpha Four in-line Version 2.00.04.

ALLOWKEYS

Syntax: {ALLOWKEYS $keys, {*doelse}}

Enables you to restrict the user's access to specific keys when playing scripts, where *$keys* is the string of allowed keys and **doelse* is a script command to play if the user enters a restricted key.

If *$keys* is blank, all keys are allowed. If a user presses Ctrl-Break or Alt-F10, restrictions are canceled.

WAITFOR

Syntax: {WAITFOR #*seconds*}

Pauses a script playback for a number of seconds specified by the variable.

WAITUNTIL

Syntax: {WAITUNTIl $*time*}

Waits until a specific time is reached, which can be specified to the second, in military or civilian format. Civilian format can use *pm* and *am* endings. Time intervals should be separated by a colon.

Summary

Computer consultants know that users love Alpha Four, but most barely scratch the surface of what the program can do. If you have followed the examples through sets and beginning scripts in this chapter, you have come a long way toward knowing what this software can do. You have started to design sets, build indexes, and work through some simple scripts.

Using Expressions and Functions

*Logical consequences are the scarecrows of fools
and the beacons of wise men.*
Thomas Henry Huxley, Animal Automatism

A *command* is an instruction that you give the software from the keyboard or through an *expression* that executes a command in place of your own key press. Commands in the View and Browse modes are on the menu and on submenus, such as Enter, Change, Delete, Undelete, Find, Index, Options, Main Menu, and Tools.

Functions are the language of the software, and their purpose is to manipulate data. A function has two parts, the name and the *argument*, as ISBLANK(LASTNAME). The function ISBLANK( ) takes the data in the field LASTNAME and returns an answer that tells whether the expression, which is the combination of the function and the argument, is true or false. If the current record shows no entry in the LASTNAME field, the response is .T. for true. An argument can be an expression that contains other functions.

In another example, the function MONTH( ), used with the argument (HIRE_DATE) looks like: MONTH(HIRE_DATE). When the function and the argument are combined into an expression, the result shows a number representing the month, 1 through 12, of the data in the field HIRE_DATE in the current record.

An *operator* is a mathematical, relational, string, or logical symbol.

Mathematical operators are used to perform simple math on numbers or numeric equivalents, such as the multiplication of the following two fields:

(PRICE * QUANTITY)

A relational operator is used to compare two fields, such as the following:

if(TOTAL_PAY < TOTALBILLS, "Watch it!", "No problem...")

A logical operator examines the *true* or *false* condition of an expression. For example, the expression here selects customer records showing the condition is *true* when the ID is 1234 or 2345. The .OR. is the relational operator in the following expression:

CUST_ID = "1234" .or. CUST_ID = "2345"

The expression, then is a combination of functions, operators, and values that calculate to a value. An expression also can contain field names and script variables.

Learning Syntax Rules

As with any written language, there are a number of rules you must follow to be understood. Each of the expressions and functions in Alpha Four has its own set of rules, called *syntax*, that govern the way you structure the command.

Where To Use Expressions

Alpha Four users need expressions in nearly every part of the program. Expressions are used to create calculations of all kinds: calculated fields in all layout activities, forms, reports, browse tables, mail labels, letters, field rules, creating indexes, searches, filters, global updates, cross tabulations, relational operations, and field statistics.

Syntax Rules for Functions

Four kinds of data exist for arguments: character, numeric, logical, and date. Functions can interpret numbers, character strings, logical values, and dates if they can be evaluated to the proper data type. This means that certain arguments may need to be converted to be interpreted properly. For example, if you want to include a character field in an expression with a number, the number must be converted to character format, such as the following:

CHAR_FLD + STR(NUM_FLD)

Using Expressions for Data Entry

Expressions can be used in nearly every aspect of using Alpha Four but seldom with more impressive results than when used to enhance or accelerate data entry. An example of this is the use of an expression to interpret data in another field and respond based on the data. For example, in Massachusetts, there is a sales tax on products but not on services. Therefore, if you have a STATE field and a PRODUCT field, you can write a default or a calculated field for TAX_AMT that reads: if(STATE="MA".and. upper(PRODUCT) ="SERVICE",.0 , .05).

Using the Clipboard

When you are designing an expression, there are occasions when you want to place a portion of your work into a clipboard to move or copy it to another area. Place your cursor on the beginning of the expression you want to place on the clipboard, press Alt-F5 to enter (or clip) the data into the clipboard, and move the cursor to a new location. Paste the contents of the clipboard into the new location using Alt-F6. You can paste repeatedly with the same clip, but the clipboard holds only one clip at a time.

Using Operators

Simple expressions can be combined with operators to make a more complex expression, but each type of data must be used (or converted to use) specific operators. For example, to use a date field with a character field, the date field must be converted to character format. An index expression that orders invoice numbers by the date of the invoice would be the following:

INVOIC_ID + CDATE(INV_DATE)

The arithmetic operators are the following:

+   Addition
-     Subtraction
*   Multiplication

/	Division
**	Exponentiation
()	Parentheses

The character operators are the following:

+	Concatenation (to combine two character strings)
-	Concatenation with trim
$	Substring inclusion

The relational operators are the following:

<	Less than
<=	Less than or equal to
>	Greater than
>=	Greater than or equal to
=	Equal to
<>	Not equal to

The date operators are the following:

+

-

When comparing date values, the higher the value the later the date. You can add a constant to a date: (LEND_BOOK + 30 = BOOK_DUE).

The logical operators are the following:

.NOT.	Negative
.AND.	Logical AND
.OR.	Logical OR
()	Parentheses

Using Pattern Matching

The *Pattern matching* technique used by Alpha Four for comparing character values depends on a setting that is established in the Default Settings screen. You can check the current setting from the Main Menu. Select **O**ther, **C**onfiguration, **D**efault setting screen. There are three choices: Exact, Case, and case-Insensitive. When you install Alpha Four initially, the default setting is case-Insensitive, which does not force a match on case or length. If you change the setting to **E**xact, then a comparison of two strings must match in every respect, character for character, and be the same length in order for the two to be considered equal.

Alpha Four Version 1 users are accustomed to using the TRIM() function to force the evaluation of an expression to ignore trailing blanks. The **E**xact match method is equivalent to this. If the default setting is set to one of the other two choices, length is ignored as a criterion for comparison.

Stepping through an Expression

You can create expressions in every part of the Alpha Four program. In some places, the program takes you by the hand and helps the process. Two of these places are the **S**earch lists and **I**ndexes/ranges. When you want to create a saved search or an index, you have two options: Table mode and Expression mode as shown in figure 13.1.

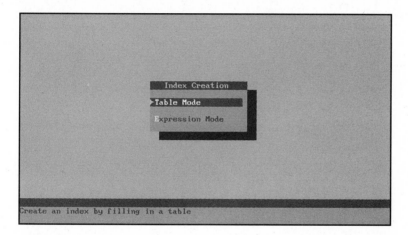

FIG. 13.1

The Table and Expression modes are offered for indexes and searches.

When you select Table mode, Alpha Four takes care of converting mismatched fields and writes the expression for you. For example, if you are working in the OWNER database and want to create a three-level index with OWNER_ID, INVOIC_ID, and LINE_NO, follow these steps to create a complex expression using the Table Mode, as shown in figure 13.2:

1. From the Main Menu, choose **I**ndex/ranges. Alpha Four shows the Indexes/Ranges menu. Select **C**reate an index. On the bottom line of the screen, type the name you want to identify the index, such as **OWN_INVDT** to indicate OWNER, INVOICE, and DATE. Press Enter to begin the process. Select Table mode from the Index Creation menu. Press F10 to Continue.

2. On the next screen, press F2 (Fieldnames) to select the OWNER_ID. Press the down-arrow key to go to the second line and select INVOIC_ID using F2. Press the down-arrow key again to go to the third line and select LINE_NO in the same manner. Press F10 to Continue.

3. Alpha Four's next screen shows the index expression with the first two fields concatenated or joined together with the plus sign; the third field, a number, is converted using the str() function, as you can see in figure 13.2. Press F10 to continue.

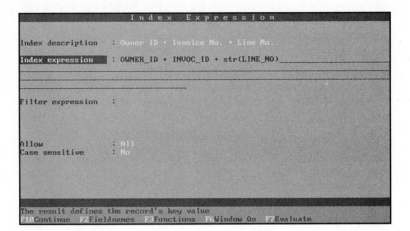

The Index Expression is created by the program in Table mode.

When you cannot achieve the desired effect using table mode in Indexes and Searches, the expression choice is available. Suppose that you want to assign a letter, A, B, or C to a group of records, based on a range of data, such as the following date field:

if(INV_DATE < {01/01/92},"A",IF(INV_DATE < {06/01/92},"B","C"))

An expression such as the preceding cannot be created in Table mode. Therefore, you must use Expression mode and type the expression using the F2 key to retrieve field names, F3 to get functions, and F7 to evaluate the expression.

In Field Rules, opportunities to write expressions are numerous. Expressions can be designed for calculated fields, default entries, required fields, validation expressions, to force double entry of data, and in skip expressions. Figure 13.3 shows the field rules screen that contains several rules that accept expressions.

Solving Problems Encountered with Expressions

The following are the most common problems that users encounter while trying to create effective expressions. These also apply to scripts in many cases.

■ Field names and drive/path names are misspelled or misrepresented. Always choose F2 to select fields in expressions or to select commands in designing scripts. Also select F3 to choose scripts and F8 to identify variables to insert into scripts.

■ Field types are mixed due to mismatching character, numeric, and date fields in the same expression without conversion. The solution is to make sure that they all return the same type of data. Also, verify that an expression that is performing a calculation returns the same type as the target field.

■ Parentheses, (), and curly braces {} are unbalanced. Count the number of left and right parentheses to verify that they match and that they are in the correct positions.

■ Logical statements don't give the right results. Separate parts of a compound expression and analyze each separately. If the parts are working properly, consider the logical part, such as the following:

If(CDOW(PAY_DAY)="Monday","Monday","")   (this works)

or

If(CDOW(PAY_DAY)="Tuesday","Tuesday","")   (this works)

Both of these expressions will work fine, standing alone. When you want to compare the two by combining them, the result may be somewhat different from what you expected. An expression that attempts to compare both operations will fail if the logical operator in the expression reads AND. PAY_DAY logically won't be Monday *and* Tuesday.

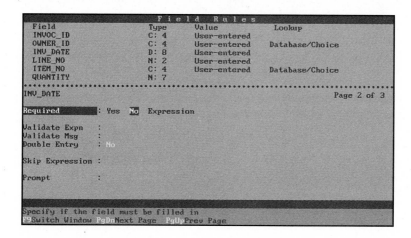

Field Rules			
Field	Type	Value	Lookup
INVOC_ID	C: 4	User-entered	
OWNER_ID	C: 4	User-entered	Database/Choice
INV_DATE	D: 8	User-entered	
LINE_NO	N: 2	User-entered	
ITEM_NO	C: 4	User-entered	Database/Choice
QUANTITY	N: 7		

INV_DATE   Page 2 of 3

Required   : Yes No   Expression

Validate Expn :
Validate Msg   :
Double Entry   : No

Skip Expression :

Prompt   :

Specify if the field must be filled in
^Switch Window PgDn Next Page PgUp Prev Page

FIG. 13.3

The Field Rules screen has several places to write expresssions.

Demystifying IF Statements

An IF statement is an expression that evaluates to a logical answer, true or false. IF statements are used when there is more than one condition to be decided logically.

An IF statement consists of the following three parts:

1. The question of fact: a statement that must be true or false, such as the following:

   (STATE="MA")
   (DOB - SYSTEM->DATE > 65)

2. The effect if the question evaluates to true.

3. The effect if the question evaluates to false.

If the answer to the question of fact is true, the first response is shown, otherwise the second response is shown.

IF statements are used in calculated fields, global updates, indexes, searches and filters, color expressions, and any place where you want Alpha Four to make a choice for you between two answers: Yes or No. For example, is the state Massachusetts? If so, the sales tax is .05; or else, 0:

   IF(STATE="MA",TAX_RATE = .05, 0)

The preceding is a simple IF statement. If the STATE is equal to Massachusetts, the tax rate field shows .05, otherwise, 0. However, if statements may be inadequate to answer the real question. For example, consider the following:

   If(BILLDATE < SYSTEM->DATE - 30,"Overdue","")

The translation of the preceding is: *if the billing date is less than today minus 30 days, print "Overdue", otherwise ""* (which represents blank.)

However, the fact that a billing date was more than 30 days ago doesn't mean that the bill is overdue. That description also depends upon whether the bill remains unpaid. Therefore, the following compound IF statement is needed:

   If(BILLDATE < SYSTEM->DATE - 30 .AND. AMT_DUE > 0,"Overdue","")

The translation of the preceding expression is: *if the date due is less than today's date minus 30 days, AND the amount due is greater than 0, print "Overdue", otherwise ""* (which represents blank).

The following are the three parts to a simple IF statement:

IF(question of fact, response to true, response to false).

When you are writing an IF statement, take the three parts separately and check each for the proper syntax. Remember that the true response and the false response must be expressed with the same data type. For example, the following expression does NOT work:

IF(BILLDATE<SYSTEM->DATE-30 .AND. AMT_DUE > 0,"Overdue",AMT_DUE)

The preceding expression will produce the dreaded `Operand type mis-match` error statement. To make the preceding expression expression work properly, one of the responses must be changed to match the other in data type. In this case, the field containing the numbers, AMT_DUE must become a character string by the application of the STR() conversion. Therefore, properly written, the statement is the following:

IF(BILLDATE<SYSTEM->DATE-30.AND.AMT_DUE> 0,"Overdue", str(AMT_DUE,6,2)

The *cascading* IF statement tests the following conditions:

```
if(GRADES < 50, "F",
     if(GRADES < 60, "E",
          if(GRADES < 70, "D",
               if(GRADES < 80, "C",
                    if(GRADES < 90, "B", "A")
```

The *nested* IF statement allows the result portions to contain additional tests of logic. An IF expression can be embedded within another IF statement. Alpha Four allows up to 10 levels of nested IF statements within one expression.

Using Dates

Date fields tend to give people trouble when they are used with other fields. They are often shown in expressions as character strings. The data represent a date, such as "12/24/92", by using CTOD("12/24/92"). This is the sort of conversion that is needed, for example, in a filter expression to limit the records shown as: PAY_DATE > CTOD ("12/24/92").

This expression also can be written PAY_DATE > {12/24/92} with exactly the same results.

Using Automatic Dating

In Field Rules, you can define a rule with a date expression that automatically fills as you create the record.

Using Dates in Field Rules

Default entry: Create a default entry using the SYSTEM->DATE to show today's date as the date a new record was created.

Calculated entry: Place a date field such as UPDATE in as a calculated field to show when a record was revised.

Using Global Update with Dates

To cause a date field to be empty, use CTOD(" ") or {}. To empty a date field if a character field evaluates to true, such as the following:

    IF(CHARACTER = "ABC", {}, DATE)

To update a date field if the field is blank, use the following expression:

    IF(DATE = {}, {04/01/92},DATE

    or

    IF(DATE = {}, CTOD("04/01/92"),DATE)

Using Indexes, Searches, and Filters with Dates

In the following example, you can combine a character string with a date field to create an index that puts people's names in order alphabetically and with a date field:

    LASTNAME + CDATE(DOB)

You can search or filter for records that show dates between two birth dates of 01/01/1925 and 01/01/1945 by using the following example:

    CDATE(DOB) >= "19250101" .and. CDATE(DOB) <= "19450101"

To make dates come out in the right order when used in an index expression, you must use the following correct functions:

CDATE(DATE_FLD) returns earliest to latest dates:

05/17/1908
01/07/1923
11/02/1964
02/02/1968
01/01/1991
01/31/1991
04/21/1992
05/25/1992
01/20/1993
05/09/1993

INVERT(CDATE(DATE_FLD) inverts the day, the month, and the year:

05/09/1993
01/20/1993
05/25/1992
04/21/1992
01/31/1991
01/01/1991
02/02/1968
11/02/1964
01/07/1923
05/17/1908

When you have trouble with an expression, try creating an index in Table mode using the fields you are using in the other location. Notice how Alpha Four combines the fields: Dates become CDATE(), Numeric fields use STR(). This may shed some badly needed light on a murky subject.

T I P

Alpha Four Functions List

The following is a listing of all functions that are available in Alpha Four with a brief description of each and the syntax and examples where appropriate.

ABS( )

Syntax: ABS(numeric expression)

Returns the absolute value of a numeric expression.

ACOS()

Syntax: ACOS(numeric expression)

Shows the angle size in radians for the numeric expression.

ADDMONTHS()

Syntax: ADDMONTHS(date expression, number, number)

Adds a stated number of months to a date expression and returns the resulting date. The expression examines the result for a valid date. If the result is an invalid date, such as 09/31/93, the next valid highest date is shown: 09/30/93. Therefore, ADDMONTH(DATE_FLD,1) = 09/30/1993 when you add 1 month to DATE_FLD, 08/31/93.

ADDYEARS()

Syntax: ADDYEARS(date expression, number, number)

Adds a stated number of years to a date expression and returns the resulting date. Like ADDMONTHS, ADDYEARS examines the result for a valid date. If the result is an invalid date, such as 02/29/93, the next valid date is shown: 03/01/93.

ASC()

Syntax: ASC(character string)

Returns an ASCII number that represents the first letter of the string of characters. Compare the inverse function provided by CHR(). Consider the following example:

    ASC(CITY) -> 83, if CITY is "Somerville"
    ASC("S") -> 83

ASIN()

Syntax: ASIN(numeric expression)

Shows the angle size in radians for the numeric expression, which is the sine value. The sine value must be from -1 to +1.

AT()

Syntax: AT(character expression 1, character expression 2)

Seeks the first location of a character string and shows the number that represents the location of that character.

ATAN()

Syntax: ATAN(numeric expression)

Shows the angle size in radians for the numeric expression. The expression must be between - /2 and + /2.

ATAN2()

Syntax: ATAN2(numeric expression 1, numeric expression 2)

Shows the angle size in radians for the sine (numeric expression 1), and the cosine (numeric expression 2) of the same angle.

BOF()

Syntax: BOF()

Refers to Beginning Of File. The expression tests whether the record pointer is showing the beginning of the file. BOF displays TRUE if the pointer shows the beginning of the file. Otherwise, the function returns the logical FALSE.

CCVALID()

Syntax: CCVALID(character string)

CCVALID automatically removes blank spaces and dashes to evaluate whether a given character string, representing the number on a credit card, is a valid number.

CDATE()

Syntax: CDATE(date expression)

Accepts a date expression and converts it to the format that is usable with other character expressions. Expressions must evaluate the same data types. Therefore, when a date is to be used in an expression, it must be converted to a character type. The result of this conversion is that the date assumes the YYYYMMDD format.

CDOW()

Syntax: CDOW(date expression)

CDOW returns the Day Of Week from a date expression. For example, New Year's Day is on Friday when the expression reads: CDOW (datefield) if the date field contains '01/01/1993'.

CEILING()

Syntax: CEILING(numeric expression)

Returns the smallest integer that is greater than or equal to the numeric expression. Compare to the function of ROUND().

CHKDIGIT()

Syntax: CHKDIGIT(character expression)

Calculates a checksum digit for a string of numbers.

CHR()

Syntax: CHR(numeric expression)

Accepts a numeric expression that represents an ASCII character and shows the corresponding ASCII value.

CMONTH()

Syntax: CMONTH(date expression)

Shows the name of the month for date expression. Similar to CDATE().

COS()

Syntax: COS(numeric expression)

Returns the cosine value of the numeric expression in radians.

CTOD()

Syntax: CTOD(character expression)

Accepts a character expression and converts it to a data type that is readable by other date fields so that the data can be used as a date.

DATE()

Syntax: DATE()

Depends on the actual date that is set within your computer, called the system date. Used as a default expression in Field Rules, it offers today's date to be entered into a field.

DAY()

Syntax: DAY(date expression)

Returns the day of the month, 1 through 28, 29, 30, or 31, depending on the month.

DBF()

Syntax: DBF()

Shows the name of the current database. Compare to the use of SYSTEM->DB_NAME.

DELETED()

Syntax: DELETED()

Shows the logical response TRUE or FALSE, in response to the condition of the record, deleted or not deleted.

DIFFERENCE()

Syntax: DIFFERENCE(character expression 1, character expression 2)

Compares two character expressions for the range of difference between them based on the soundex value of each. If the two are close, the value shown is 4. If there is no relationship, the value is 0. The range is only between 0 and 4. Compare the use of the function, SOUNDEX().

DMY()

Syntax: DMY(date expression)

Converts a date function into the form: DD Month YYYY. Thus, '01/01/92' returns 1 January 1992.

DOW()

Syntax: DOW(date expression)

Examines a date expression and returns the number of the day in the week, Sunday being 1, and Saturday being 7.

DTOC()

Syntax: DTOC(date expression)

Accepts a date and returns it in the form of a character string, MM/DD/YYYY.

DTOR()

Syntax: DTOR(numeric expression

Accepts the numeric expression representing angle degrees and converts them to radians.

DTOS()

Syntax: DTOS(date expression)

Added to Alpha Four Version 2 to remain compatible with dBASE IV. The function is the same as CDATE() as it converts a date expression into a character string in the form YYYYMMDD.

EOF()

Syntax: EOF()

Refers to End Of File. The expression tests whether the record pointer is showing the end of the file. EOF displays TRUE if the pointer shows the end of the file. Otherwise, the function returns the logical FALSE.

EXP()

Syntax: EXP(numeric expression)

Returns the exponent of a number or numeric expression.

FIELD()

Syntax: FIELD(numeric expression)

Returns the name of the field in the position named in the numeric expression in the current database. If the third field in the current database is LASTNAME, the value returned for the expression FIELD(1,3) is LASTNAME.

If this function is used in a SET, the expression assigns a number to the file in which the field is located. The primary file is number 1. The next file connected in the set is number 2, and so on. Therefore, if the second file in a set contains a field called LASTNAME as the third field, the expression (FIELD 2,3) returns LASTNAME, not the contents, just the field name.

FLOOR()

Syntax: FLOORING(numeric expression)

Returns the largest integer that is less than or equal to the numeric expression. Compare to the function of CEILING().

FV()

Syntax: FV(payment, rate, periods)

Calculates the future value of a series of equal payments yielding a fixed interest rate, over a time period. The rate is defined as the interest rate per period. Therefore, if the interest rate is given as a yearly figure, you must divide the rate by 12. Enter interest as a decimal number. Compare this with PV().

F_UPPER()

Syntax: F_UPPER(character expression)

Forces initial capitalization on a character expression. Compare this with W_UPPER().

IF()

Syntax: IF(logical expression, expression 1, expression 2)

IF expressions begin their calculation by evaluating the first logical expression to discover whether it is true or false. Based on that decision, the function continues to the first expression, or the second expression, to execute the command therein. If the logical expression is true, the first expression is executed. Otherwise, the second expression is executed. See also the IIF() function.

IIF()

Syntax: IF(logical expression, expression 1, expression 2)

Same as the IF function. Alpha Four provides IIF to assure compatibility with dBASE IV.

INT()

Syntax: INT(numeric expression)

Truncates the numeric expression to an integer, discarding all decimal places.

INVERT()

Syntax: INVERT(expression)

Reverses the order of an index. This works on numeric, character or date type material.

ISALPHA()

Syntax: ISALPHA(character string)

Returns TRUE if the first character of character string is a character.

ISBLANK()

Syntax: ISBLANK(expression)

Checks for any entry in a field. In Version 2, this function works on logical and date expressions, not simply on character fields.

ISLOWER()

Syntax: ISLOWER(character expression)

Checks whether the first letter of an expression is lowercase. If the condition is true, the function returns TRUE.

ISUPPER()

Syntax: ISUPPER(character expression)

Checks whether the first letter of an expression is uppercase. If the condition is true, the function returns TRUE.

LEFT()

Syntax: LEFT(character expression, numeric expression)

Returns the number of characters from the character expression specified in the numeric expression starting at the left end of the expression.

LEN()

Syntax: LEN(character expression)

Returns the number of characters in the specified character expression.

LIKE()

Syntax: LIKE(character expression 1, character expression 2)

Returns TRUE if the contents of character expression 1 are identical to the contents of character expression 2. However, the expression also accepts wild-card symbols, * and ?. This function is case-sensitive. Compare its use with that of the operator $.

LOG()

Syntax: LOG(numeric expression)

Returns the natural logarithm of the numeric expression.

LOWER()

Syntax: LOWER(character expression)

Converts the data in the character expression to lowercase. Compare this function to ISLOWER(), ISUPPER(), and UPPER().

LTRIM()

Syntax: LTRIM(character expression)

Removes leading blanks in the character expression. Compare with use of RIGHT(), LEFT() AND RTRIM().

MAX()

Syntax: MAX(numeric expression 1, numeric expression 2)

Returns the larger of the two expressions. Compare this with MIN().

MDY()

Syntax: MDY(date expression)

Accepts a date expression and shows a formatted character string in the Month DD,YYYY format. Compare the related function, DMY().

MIN()

Syntax: MIN(numeric expression 1, numeric expression 2)

Returns the smaller of the two expressions. Compare this with MAX().

MOD()

Syntax: MOD(numeric expression 1, numeric expression 2)

Returns the remainder of dividing numeric expression 1 by numeric expression 2. Compare the uses of FLOOR() and INT().

MONTH()

Syntax: MONTH(date expression)

Returns the number of the month in the date expression. January is 1; February is 2.

PAYMENT()

Syntax: PAYMENT(principal, rate, periods)

Shows the amount of the payment required for a loan given the principal, the rate, and the periods. The rate is the interest rate per period. If the interest rate is a yearly figure, divide the rate by 12. The periods is the number of payments for the life of the loan. For example, a mortgage for 25 years has 300 periods. Compare this function with FV() and PV().

PV()

Syntax: PV(payment, rate, periods)

Shows the present value of equal regular payments at a constant interest rate for the periods given. If the rate is compounded monthly, divide the interest rate by 12.

RAND()

Syntax: RAND()

Returns a random number each time the record containing the function is opened.

 Mathematicians have questioned the statistical value of micro computer-generated random numbers. Check with your statistician before relying on this method.

RECCOUNT()

Syntax: RECCOUNT()

Evaluates the number of number of records in the current database. For use with Version 1, this function must use a different syntax: RECCOUNT(RECNO()). Compare the functions DBF() and RECSIZE().

RECNO()

Syntax: RECNO()

Shows the system's number that is assigned to the current record.

RECSIZE()

Syntax: RECSIZE()

Shows the number characters held for each record in the current database. Compare this function with DBF(), and RECCOUNT().

REMSPECIAL()

Syntax: REMSPECIAL(character expression)

Removes all non-alphabetical and non-numeric characters and spaces from the character expression.

REPLICATE()

Syntax: REPLICATE(character expression, numeric expression)

Repeats the same character expression, the number of times given in the numeric expression).

RIGHT()

Syntax: RIGHT(character expression, numeric expression)

Shows the number of characters in the character expression that are specified by the numeric expression. Compare this function with AT(), LEFT(), LTRIM(), and RTRIM().

ROUND()

Syntax: ROUND(numeric expression 1, numeric expression 2)

Rounds numeric expression 1 to the decimal places specified in numeric expression 2. Compare the use of ROUND to CEILING(), FLOOR(), INT(), STR(), and VAL().

RTOD()

Syntax: RTOD(numeric expression)

Converts the numeric expression to degrees. Compare this function to the following: ASIN(), ACOS(), ATAN(), ATAN2() DTOR(), SIN(), COS(), and TAN().

RTRIM()

Syntax: RTRIM(character expression)

Removes the trailing blanks for the character expression indicated. Compare these functions: LTRIM(), TRIM(), LEFT(), and RIGHT().

SIGN()

Syntax: SIGN(numeric expression)

Shows a number to represent the sign (+ or -) of the numeric expression specified. If the numeric expression indicates a negative number, the function returns 0. If the expression shows a positive number, the value of the SIGN function is 1. Compare with the function ABS().

SIN()

Syntax: SIN(numeric expression)

Returns the sine of the numeric expression in radians. Compare the uses of the following: ASIN(), ACOS(), ATAN(), ATAN2(), COS(), DTOR(), RTOD(), and TAN(),

SOUNDEX()

Syntax: SOUNDEX(character expression)

Shows a four-character expression that represents the phonetic equivalent of the character expression. Compare with the function DIFFERENCE().

SPACE()

Syntax: SPACE(numeric expression)

Automates the placement of spaces within a character string that contains two or more strings. The number of spaces is defined by the number or numeric expression.

SQRT()

Syntax: SQRT(numeric expression)

Shows the square root of the numeric expression.

STR()

Syntax: STR(numeric expression [,length] [,decimals])

Converts a number to a character string with a specified length and number of decimal places. The definitions of length and decimal places are optional. The default length is 10, with the default value of decimal places is 0. Compare this function with VAL().

STUFF()

Syntax: STUFF(character string 1, number1, number2, character string 2)

Replaces part of the character string 1 with character string 2. The value shown in number1 is the starting place for the replacement. The value of number2 is the number of characters in character string 2 to replace in character string 1. Compare the functions LEFT(), RIGHT(), and SUBSTR().

SUBSTR()

Syntax: SUBSTR(character string 1, numeric expression 1, numeric expression 2)

Extracts a portion of character string 1, starting with the character defined by the position of numeric expression 1 and continues for the number of characters defined in numeric expression 2. Compare this function with AT(), STR(), and STUFF().

TAN()

Syntax: TAN(numeric expression)

Returns the tangent of the numeric expression, expressed in radians. Compare functions of ASIN(), ACCOS(), ATAN(), ATAN2(), COS(), DTOR(), RTOD(), and SIN().

TIME()

Syntax: TIME()

Shows the current time as known to the computer system, shown in the format HH:MM:SS.

TOSECONDS()

Syntax: TOSECONDS(time value)

Shows a time value in seconds. Compare this function to TOTIME().

TOTIME()

Syntax: TOTIME(seconds, format, decimal places)

Accepts a value for times in seconds and converts that value to a character string formatted for time, using the defined format. Compare this to TOSECONDS().

TRANSFORM()

Syntax: TRANSFORM(expression, character string)

Enables the user to design a customized format for an expression.

TRIM()

Syntax: TRIM(character expression)

Removes the trailing blanks from the specified character expression.

UPPER()

Syntax: UPPER(character expression)

Converts the data in the character expression to uppercase. Compare this function to ISLOWER(), ISUPPER(), and LOWER().

VAL()

Syntax: VAL(character expression)

Accepts character data that shows numerals and converts these characters to numbers. This function returns a 0 if it encounters a nonnumeric character ahead of the numeric characters. Compare this function with STR().

WORD()

Syntax: WORD(character expression, numeric expression)

Takes a character expression and extracts the word specified by the numeric expression. If the numeric expression is shown as a negative number, the calculation operates from right to left rather than from left to right. For example, in a field containing the name, John Quincy Adams, the results will be the following:

```
WORD(NAMEFIELD,1) = "John"
WORD(NAMEFIELD,-1) = "Adams"
```

Compare this function with W_COUNT().

W_COUNT()

Syntax: W_COUNT(character expression)

Examines the designated character expression and shows the number of words within the group. Compare the function of WORD().

W_UPPER()

Syntax: W_UPPER(character expression)

Forces initial capitalization on each word in the character expression. Compare this with F_UPPER().

YEAR()

Syntax: YEAR(date expression)

Accepts a date expression and returns only the year. For example, the date field containing 01/01/1997 will show only 1997. Compare the functions, YEAR() and DAY().

ZBLANK()

Syntax: ZBLANK(numeric expression)

Accepts a numeric expression and returns a right-justified character string. Compare the use of this function with STR() and TRANSFORM().

Summary

Many Alpha Four non-programmers view expressions with horror, but this reaction is probably more cultural than it is a reflection of the difficulty of writing an expression. The discussion here and the examples in the Alpha Four Reference Manual can get you going. Between the scripts commands and the functions offered in this program, you can create highly complex calculations with little more than sound logic and fill-in-the-blanks programming. Of course, producing complete and professional applications takes a little longer.

Documenting Your Work

He danced along the dingy days,
And this bequest of wings
Was but a book. What liberty
A loosened spirit brings.
                        Emily Dickinson, Life in a Library

In this chapter, you discover methods of making your work more accessible to your users and more manageable for you. Although a program is designed for a single purpose, rarely is one so clearly designed that little or no documentation is required.

Documentation begins with the original design: the flow charts, cocktail napkins, and backs of envelopes that inevitably serve as parts of the overall plan for an application. Alpha Four has provided a Runtime Module and four other utility programs that enable you to produce special files and reports that describe the field names, the set designs, field rules, scripts, and structure that you have created.

As the application designer, you can get a great deal of help from judicious use of the companion programs A4DOC.EXE, SCRIPTED.EXE, A4LIB.EXE, and A4STRPDT.EXE. The Runtime Module is a companion program in a slightly different class from the others.

Using the Runtime Version

The first of the companion programs that should be discussed is the Runtime Module that Alpha Software sells separately from the main Alpha Four program. The runtime generator gives the user the right and the capability of distributing applications to others without a *live* copy of Alpha Four.

When you call up the Runtime Module, the program sees your applications but cannot access any of the files directly. The user is limited to the menu created by the designer and must function with the reports, forms, mail labels, and browse tables that are provided.

Installing the Runtime Product

The Runtime module, offered by Alpha Software as a separate product, is designed to help a developer to create a stand-alone application that can be sold without including the Alpha Four program. A company might wish to use this process to distribute a specific application to several branches or offices. The Runtime Module leaves the end user without the capability of performing many of the design/create functions normally part of the Alpha Four program.

To develop an application with the Runtime program, the designer must have a full copy of Alpha Four with which to work. This reduces the cost of using the Alpha Four system in two ways. Only one copy of the program is purchased. And the time needed for training and technical support is reduced because users do not have access to the full program. If end users cannot create and change things in the program, presumably they will use it as it was designed to be used.

The end user of the Runtime program will not be able to create databases, sets, forms, labels, reports, field rules, indexes or new applications. From the Main Menu, the following commands are not available to the user:

Index/ranges	Create an index; edit an index; create/edit a range; erase a range
Database/Set Design	Set commands; Create a new database; Field rules; Reconfigure database
Application	Create/edit application, erase application

Layout	Form	Create/edit; Borrow; Erase
	Reports	Create/edit; Borrow; Erase
	Mail labels	Create/edit; Borrow; Erase

The Runtime program enables the end user to view and change data and add new records. The browse tables are available, but only as designed by the developer, and are not changeable by the end user. Reports, mail labels, and input forms are available only as the developer has designed them. Letters, however, are the exception to this rule. The end user can employ the normal procedures to create, edit, print, and erase form letters for their own use. Filters can be created by the user in the print menu and in the append and import/export functions. They cannot be created from the Indexes/ranges menu. All the Utility commands work normally, including the selection of printers and changing of screen colors.

After the Runtime module has been created, the developer can place it on a floppy disk and send it off to the user. The installation process is facilitated by a batch file that will create a subdirectory on the user's hard disk and copy the files from the floppy disk to the subdirectory.

There is an important difference in the creation of the application for this kind of distribution from the method normally used to create applications that are to remain on the user's own disk. The difference is in the method of dealing with the definition of the Startup database/set.

The usual designation of the C:, D:, or other drive is missing but the drive path and .DBF file name, \ALPHA4\INVTORY.DBF, are there. As long as the program is installed in the subdirectory that is designated, the application will operate correctly. If this path is incorrectly defined, the Application will not function.

Assuming that the user will be instructed to operate his application from the \RUNTIME subdirectory, a batch file can be included on the floppy disk. It will create a subdirectory on the designated drive, copy all the files onto that drive, erase the installation batch file from the hard disk, and start the program. To create the batch file, type the following:

```
A:\ COPY CON INSTALL.BAT
ECHO OFF
%1
MD\RUNTIME
CD\RUNTIME
COPY A:*.*
DEL %1\RUNTIME\INSTALL.BAT
A4RT /RUNTIME\MY_APPLC
```

The %1 represents the replaceable parameter used in DOS. The instruction to the user then says to log onto the A: drive and type the word **INSTALL** followed by the drive designator, such as the following:

```
A:\ INSTALL C:  (to install on the C: drive)
A:\ INSTALL D:  (to install on the D: drive)
```

The developer places the A4RT.EXE file on the distribution disk in place of the usual A4.EXE, which is the primary program file of Alpha Four. Lacking the A4.EXE file, the Runtime users cannot alter the program that they received. Distribution of the A4.EXE file is a violation of the *one user on one machine at one time* license to use Alpha Four.

The Runtime Module also includes an encryption procedure that guards the application from alteration, even with the full package of Alpha Four. If the encryption is not employed, users with the full program can alter the files received from the developer. If the files are encrypted, users cannot change the files. The encryption is an irreversible process. Therefore, the developer is advised to keep a separate copy of the application before encryption takes place.

Using A4DOC

Of the three *editor* programs included with Alpha Four, A4DOC is the most well-developed. It operates with a menu that enables the user to select the documentation of databases or sets, applications or scripts. The documentation of databases and sets helps you select whether you want to produce the information about the structure of a database or set, about applications only, or about scripts.

 NOTE If you plan to print the documentation data to a file for further enhancement in a word processor, use a printer defined as GENERIC. Remove all printer codes in the printer definition. Alpha Four includes codes for bold face in the printed files. The use of a GENERIC definition should remove most of the unwanted symbols.

Using A4DOC To Document a SET

Alpha Four understands that the documentation of a single database should be different from that reported for a set. Therefore, the report includes a representation of the tree structure of the set, if you choose to see it.

The following example is the result of using A4DOC to examine the INVOIC.SET. Notice that A4DOC.EXE documentation shows dialog boxes and keystroke scripts, whereas SCRIPTED.EXE only works with keystroke scripts.

```
Set Structure for C:\TEST\INVOIC

Set Tree Diagram

C:\TEST\INVOIC» -- Invoice

HEADER --
    ═══════DETAIL -- Invoice detail lines

  Link Parameters

HEADER ───────> DETAIL

    Linked Database/Set     : C:\TEST\DETAIL
    Linking Index           : DET_CLIN
    Common Field/Expression : OWNER_ID
    Link to ?               : Last
    Include parent if ?     : Always
    Show Mode               : All
    Filter Mode             : Inactive
    Zoom Form               :
    Browse Form             :

Parent Database

HEADER
        Field         Type   Width   Decimal Places
    1.  INVOIC_ID       C       4
    2.  OWNER_ID        C       4
    3.  LASTNAME        C      15
    4.  INV_DATE        D       8
    5.  TOTAL           N       8          2
    6.  PAID            C       1
    7.  PAYMENT         N       8          2
    8.  PAYDATE         D       8
    9.  BALANCE         N       8          2

  Child Databases

DETAIL
        Field         Type   Width   Decimal Places
    1.  INVOIC_ID       C       4
    2.  OWNER_NO        C       4
    3.  LINE_NO         C       2
    4.  ITEM_ID         C       4
    5.  DESCRIPT        C      25
    6.  QUANTITY        N       4          0
    7.  PRICE           N       8          2
    8.  LINE_TOTAL      N       8          2
```

Using A4DOC for Script Documentation

This is the first of two methods for documenting the activities of scripts. In this case, the Macro Call Tree is among the options. The tree represents the way that the scripts work together in sequence.

```
Script Documentation for CASEZOOM

Dialog Script Information
Name         : CASEZOOM
Description  : Select Zoom functions
Row          : 5
Col          : 15
Height       : 7
Width        : 27

Text         : Just Zoom
Control Type : Button
Script       : JUSTZOOM
Help Text    : Make no changes, just Zoom
Row          : 4
Column       : 5

Text         : Make new record
Control Type : Button
Script       : MAKENEW
Help Text    : Carry info from here to there
Row          : 5
Column       : 5

Text         : Report Field Stats
Control Type : Button
Script       : FIELDSTT
Help Text    : Make field stats on matching record
Row          : 6
Column       : 5

Script Documentation for CASEZOOM

Macro Call Tree

CASEZOOM
   |------------- JUSTZOOM
   |------------- MAKENEW
   |                 |------------- TRIGZOOM
   |                 |------------- COPYFLD
   |------------- FIELDSTT

Script Documentation for DESKTOP
Keystroke Script Information
```

```
Name        : DESKTOP
Description : Loads current desktop
Macro       : {ALTF10}crtest{ENTER}vt{ENTER}
Screen test : No
```

Script Documentation for MAINMENU
Dialog Script Information

```
Name        : MAINMENU
Description : Play instead of A4 menu
Row         : 3
Col         : 3
Height      : 11
Width       : 75

Text          : Exit to Alpha Four Main Menu
Control Type  : Button
Script        : ALTF10
Help Text     : None
Row           : 3
Column        : 6

Text          : Zoom Choices
Control Type  : Button
Script        : CASEZOOM
Help Text     : Select events for Zoom
Row           : 3
Column        : 45

Text          : Switch to other files
Control Type  : Button
Script        : SW
Help Text     : None
Row           : 5
Column        : 6

Text          : Show total of this invoice
Control Type  : Button
Script        : TOTL_INV
Help Text     : Sets this invoice & does Field Statis-
tics
Row           : 5
Column        : 45

Text          : Load Desktop
Control Type  : Button
Script        : DESKTOP
Help Text     : None
Row           : 7
Column        : 6
```

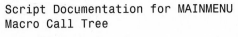

```
Script Documentation for MAINMENU
Macro Call Tree
```

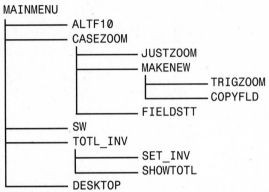

```
MAINMENU
    ├──────────── ALTF10
    ├──────────── CASEZOOM
    │                   ├──────────── JUSTZOOM
    │                   ├──────────── MAKENEW
    │                   │                   ├──────────── TRIGZOOM
    │                   │                   └──────────── COPYFLD
    │                   └──────────── FIELDSTT
    ├──────────── SW
    ├──────────── TOTL_INV
    │                   ├──────────── SET_INV
    │                   └──────────── SHOWTOTL
    └──────────── DESKTOP
```

The Macro Call Tree is a graphical illustration of the relationship between the Dialog Box CASEZOOM and the script that work from that level. CASEZOOM appears on the MAINMENU dialog box because it is played from that location. Hence, the relationship between that file and its Buttons, Displays and Prompts is shown.

Editing Scripts with SCRIPTED.EXE

This program translates the scripts you have written into ASCII format for further manipulation. You can edit, change, create new, delete, perform find and replace operations, and any other work required that your word processor can do. For example, if you have a series of scripts that refer to a file named CUSTOMER.DBF in one application and would be appropriate for use in another application with a PATIENT.DBF, many word processors allow you to define a *find* string, CUSTOMER.DFB and replace any occurrence with PATIENT.DBF.

The manipulation of SCRIPTED.EXE requires at least a minimal understanding of DOS operations on your computer. The assumed configuration for all Alpha Four system operations is that you are working with an IBM-compatible DOS system, Version 3.1 or higher. The assumption also is that you are able to manage basic DOS conventions and commands and understand the concepts of subdirectories. See your DOS manual for further questions on the Disk Operating System of your computer.

The syntax for SCRIPTED.EXE is the following:

SCRIPTED -[options] filename(s)

Type **SCRIPTED**, any necessary options, which are described below, and the file names that are to be edited or documented.

SCRIPTED.EXE is installed when the Alpha Four, Version 2, program is installed. Log to the subdirectory where the Alpha Four Version 2 files are located. From the DOS prompt, type **SCRIPTED**. This does nothing but show a screen describing the options and necessities and indicating how to run this program.

Following SCRIPTED, you can issue optional instructions about the specific scripts that are to be examined, such as the following:

SCRIPTED *.scp

> Takes all scripts in the current directory and converts them to a default output file called SCRIPTS.ASC

SCRIPTED -O=C:\A42\SMITHCO\INVOICE.DOC INV*.SCP

> Takes all scripts that begin with INV in the C:\A42\SMITHCO\ subdirectory and converts them to an output file called INVOICE.DOC

SCRIPTED -P=C:\A42\SMITHCO\SCRIPTS C:\WP51\DOCS\INVOICE.DOC

> Directs the program to extract the script files found in the C:\WP51\DOCS\ subdirectory in the INVOICE.DOC file and places them in the C:\A42\SMITHCO\ SCRIPTS subdirectory

SCRIPTED.EXE has the distinction of working two ways. Any file with an extension .SCP is assumed to be a script that you want converted to ASCII format. On the other hand, any file you designate to SCRIPTED that has any extension other than .SCP, is assumed to be an ASCII file that you want converted to scripts.

This means that after you have converted a group of scripts to ASCII, and brought them into a word processor, and completed work on them there, you can then convert them back out to .SCP files using the -P switch.

When you work with keystroke scripts in your word processor, be sure to stay within the limits of what a script can do. Keystroke scripts cannot contain more than 3,000 characters. Single script commands may not contain more than 1,000 characters. The totals do not include comments placed within commands. Any text placed in a command enclosed by {* *} is considered a comment for purposes of documenting your work. Use Tabs, not spaces, to format your scripts.

NOTE Some word processors insert spaces where you think a Tab is placed. This may cause problems when you play the script. The spaces are interpreted as keystrokes.

The following documentation of several sample scripts was created with SCRIPTED and edited in such a way that the descriptions of the scripts and the macros are easy to read and understand.

```
Script Documentation for A4DOCUM

Name        : A4DOCUM
Description : Execute A4DOC program
Macro       : {EXEC "c:\a4n\a4doc", 0, 0}
Screen test : No

Script Documentation for A4SCRIPT

Name        : A4SCRIPT
Description : Execute SCRIPTED program
Macro       : {EXEC "c:\a4n\scripted", 0, 0}
Screen test : No

Script Documentation for CHARGE

Name        : CHARGE
Description :
Macro       : {TONE 196,125}{TONE 261,125}{TONE 329,125}{TONE392,125}
              {TONE 0,1000}
              {TONE 329,105}{TONE 392,115}
              {CANCEL}
Screen test : No

Script Documentation for DOAPPEND

Name        : DOAPPEND
Description : Append payments to Rental
Macro       : muaatemp{ENTER}{F10:2}v
Screen test : Yes

Script Documentation for DOGLOBAL

Name        : DOGLOBAL
Description : Do Global update
Macro       : gura{F10}
Screen test : No

Script Documentation for TOTL_INV

Name        : TOTL_INV
Description : Show total of this invoice
Macro       : {SCREENFREEZE}
```

```
{PLAY "SET_INV"}
{ALTF10}oif
if(invoic_id=%INVOIC_ID,line_total,0){ENTER}
if(invoic_id=%INVOIC_ID,quantity,0)
{F10}{F2}b{F10}V{F10}{PLAY "SHOWTOTL"}V
```

Screen test : Yes
Screen text : Detail Section
Top   : 3,5   (This defines the row and column where the
                    screen text, "Detail Section" begins.
Bottom   : 3,18 (This defines the row and column where the
                    screen text, "Detail Section" ends.

Script Documentation for SET_INV

Name   : SET_INV
Description : Set invoice no. to current item
Macro   : {SET %invoic_id, INVOIC_ID}
Screen test : No

NOTE The Alpha Four Reference Manual notes that "when a script library is played, the scripts in that library are all loaded and can be called by other scripts. However, only the library name will appear in the list of scripts shown when you choose the Play a script command." In fact, the enscripted files do appear unless they are removed by the developer. Be sure not to eliminate dialog boxes when you remove or rename the scripts.

Stripping the Desktop

Stripping the desktop refers to a program that is available from Alpha Software for the purpose of removing the drive and path designations from a desktop file.

When you have defined and saved a desktop file that loads the filenames that you need, whether it is done on a regular basis for an application or simply for convenience, you may decide that you want to move the desktop file to a different drive or subdirectory. This is particularly important for developers who are creating files that will be used elsewhere on an unknown computer.

This program operates well when the A4STRPDT.EXE and the target desktop files are located in the same subdirectory. To execute the desktop file drive and path stripper, log on to the subdirectory where those files are located. At the DOS prompt, type **A4STRPDT**, the name of the desktop file **FILENAME.DTN**, and press Enter.

Creating a Library of Scripts with A4LIB.EXE

A script library, as compared with a Library of Scripts, is a file that holds a number of Alpha Four scripts designated by you and combined into one file. There are several reasons for using an A4LIB script:

- You can collect a group of individual scripts into one file that can be easily copied or moved with your application.

- The number of scripts showing in the Alt-F4 Scripts menu can be reduced to just the dialog scripts and the Library script itself, which cannot be modified.

- After a library is loaded, it stays active until you exit Alpha Four.

Running A4LIB.EXE

A4LIB.EXE is only accessible from DOS and is usually found in the directory where Alpha Four, Version 2 files are located. A4LIB.EXE operates in the following two ways:

- You can type the command **A4LIB** followed by the name of the library script to be created, followed again by the scripts you want included.

- You can use an input file created with your word processor, EDLIN, or DOS's copy con command.

To create a scripts library file, perform the following steps:

1. Log on to the database containing the scripts you want to incorporate into the library, making sure that your script path is set to the desired directory. From the Alpha Four Main Menu, press Alt-F9 to access DOS. You can verify that the scripts you need are available at this point by typing **DIR *.SCP**. This command produces a list of any files in the current directory that end with .SCP.

2. Note the names of the scripts you want to include in the library file. Then type **copy con LIBENAME**, and press Enter. This line is followed by a blank line on which you type the name of the first file for your library, such as DOAPPEND. Press Enter at the end of that line and type the next name **POSTPAYS**. Continue until all the required script names are entered, each on its own line. The screen looks like the following:

```
C:\ALPHA4V2\TESTFILS\copy con libename
DOAPPEND
POSTPAYS
PRT_REPT
```

(The script names should be the names of your scripts, not the book's.)

3. When you have completed the list, press F6, the DOS end of file command, and Ctrl-Z. This saves the file as LIBENAME. The computer should reply 1 file(s) copied.

   This procedure has produced an input file that can now be used to create the library script itself.

4. Assuming that your A4LIB.EXE file is in the C:\ALPHA4V2 sub-directory, you now type the command to execute the A4LIB.EXE and perform the job of creating the library script. Type the following, allowing for your own system configuration and file names:

C:\ALPHA4V2\TESTFILS\A4LIB LIBENAME @LIBELIST

The program should reply Creating LIBELIST. Then it shows a list of the names of your scripts, saying Adding: *filename* to LIBELIST for each of them. At the end, the program says The script library LIBELIST has been built.

In a future version of Alpha Four, this procedure may be added to the other add-on programs. This procedure takes a little practice but works.

When the LIBELIST script file has been finished, you can remove the scripts that have been incorporated with A4LIB. If you want to edit the scripts again in the future, rename them with a memorable extension, such as .SP. Then if necessary, you can rename them back to .SCP for further work and recreate the A4LIB with the changed version.

Prototyping with Alpha Four

The whole idea behind Alpha Four is that anybody with a need for a data-management program can use it without the need to go to school to learn programming, to provide a new tool for those who have done programming and who know that writing code takes a long time.

As a tool to create a prototype for demonstration purposes, Alpha Four has become a favorite of developers who use FoxPro, Paradox, and Clipper products. These software packages have programming languages that developers use to make the data perform in certain ways, to create screens (forms), and design reports for the end user. Many developers have found that nearly everything can be accomplished in Alpha Four that is needed to show as a demo for a potential client.

Some of these other programmable databases also have *front-end interfaces* for the nonprogrammer to use to get into the data. With Version 2, Alpha Four has begun to close the gap between Alpha Four, Version 1 and the programmable databases. Certainly, one of the most powerful, new features of Version 2 is the scripts, which are, in fact, a *scripting language.*

If it scares or bores you to think of yourself as a programmer, remember that Alpha Four has done most of the hard part. You are really developing rather than programming. The hard work that Alpha Four has done for you is the writing of this language with which you can *teach* the program what you want it to do. By pressing the F3 key during script writing, Alpha Four will record the keystrokes you type and save you the trouble of retyping each instruction when you want to accomplish some operation.

| T I P | Now that you have reached into the deepest regions of Alpha Four, you may want to provide a Help file for your own users like the help files you find when you press F1. Help files are described in detail in Chapter 11. |

Making Your Own Library

This discussion refers to a library of files, as compared to a library of scripts. As you begin to develop your skills with Alpha Four, you may find routines that you like for performing certain operations. When the routine is perfected, you may also discover that it can be made to apply to other files or applications. These routines (or scripts) become your library of stock answers to repeated situations. They may be as small as a finely-crafted script or expression, or they may be a complete, stand-alone application to perform routine tasks: mark files deleted with date greater than {x}, append records to HISTORY, and pack the database.

To qualify as part of your library, the stand-alone module should be complete with a sample database containing one TEST record with appropriate fields, index and range settings, and reports, forms, and browse tables definitions in place.

Using Pictures in Documentation

When creating documentation for others, you can enhance your work and make it easier to understand if you include screen shots to illustrate what the user will see on his or her screen. This book was created with a combination of HOTSHOT Graphics by Symsoft, of Incline Village, Nevada, and COLLAGE, by Inner Media, Inc., of Hollis, New Hampshire. Both are easy to learn and to use, and each has a special place in the business of documentation of software.

Summary

This chapter has taken aim at the finishing touches, the matters that are often left undone for want of time or understanding. Attention to these details will make your work more polished and more sellable— even if your only buyer is yourself.

These tips should make you feel that Alpha Four is a fine contribution to the database market of the 1990s, a facility that anyone who knows his or her own business can use to manage that business even more successfully in the challenging days of personal computing that are still to come.

Other Resources for Help

Many software companies pride themselves on their ability to present totally bug-free software. Alpha Software has put together a solid piece of work in Alpha Four, Version 2, a task which they undertook from the ground up, to incorporate entirely new technology including networking, vastly improved indexing, a new color palette, and many more features explored at length in this book.

Because of the range of new items, the continuing growth of the product, and their attempts to respond to the market pressure to get the new version onto customers machines, Alpha Software went to press with their Reference Manual before every new feature was ready for documentation. Therefore, they elected to include a number of items in README files, which are installed in the program directory when you install your software.

One is called README.DOC and is located the directory where you install the program. The second is called README.NOW and is in a subdirectory under the main program directory, called \DEMO\INVOICE. The readme files describe a number of items that have been covered in this book, and they indicate the publisher's attempt to keep you as up to date as possible.

NOTE Sample files with the examples from this book are available on 5 1/4" or 3 1/2" disks from Computers Without Fear, Inc., P.O. Box 1027, West Falmouth, Massachusetts, 02574; (508) 548-9476; CompuServe 71147,2071; or the CWF Bulletin Board (508) 540-8777.

Alpha Software has provided every possible assistance to the author and has tried to keep everyone aware of bugs and bug-fixes as they come on the scene. If you encounter problems with your copy, your first step is to check this book for any reference to the difficulty. If your problem does not appear in these pages, you can telephone Alpha Software in Burlington, Massachusetts, for information about your problem. The technical support telephone number is manned from 10 a.m. to 7 p.m., Mondays through Fridays at (617) 272-3680.

If you have a modem, you can call the Bulletin Board at Alpha Software and leave messages for the SYSOP (System Operator) who will leave a reply for you in a day or so. You also can leave comments or questions for other users on that board. Lively discussions can be found on many topics of interest to Alpha users. The bulletin board number is (617) 229-2915. The FAX machine at Alpha Software is a somewhat slower, but perhaps easier, method of getting questions answered. The FAX number is (617) 273-1507.

Other on-line services that support active conferences or forums on Alpha Four include CompuServe and Prodigy. Like the Alpha Software Bulletin Board, these are accessible by modem. Unlike the Alpha board, these two are by membership subscription only. Membership and on-line charges apply. The world of on-line services is extremely interesting. Altogether, the facility can be entertaining, educational, and expensive for the unwary. Be careful that you understand the charges when you sign up for one of these commercial services.

The tech support people at Alpha are bright, well-informed, and monumentally even-tempered. You will need to give them your registration number when you call. They are trained to help you with technical questions, *not* to help you design applications. They will do their best for you.

If there is a problem with a certain portion of the software, Alpha has offered to supply *patch* by mail, on disk, or by way of a downloaded file from their Bulletin Board. You should take advantage of this service if you encounter a problem.

Installation Procedures

The installation procedures for Alpha Four, Version 2, are completely menu-driven. The disks are labeled and each is installed in sequence. You should note that after the first release of Alpha Four, certain additions and corrections were made to the software. Packages shipped after May 1, 1992, should be the revised version, known as Release 2.00.04.

The number of the release is shown on the bottom-right corner of the status screen (F3 from the Main Menu) when you have completed your installation procedures. At the beginning of the installation, Version 2.00.04 asks the user to identify a preference for currency: U.S., Canada, U.K. and Other. You know that you are installing this version if you see a screen that looks like figure B.1

To install Alpha Four, complete the following steps:

1. Start your computer and access the root directory on the hard disk where Alpha Four is to be installed. From the DOS prompt, change to the root directory, so the screen looks something like the following:

    C:>

2. Put the Installation Disk in drive A: and close the door. Type **A:** to log on to the floppy drive. Type **SETUP**. The program begins to install itself on the hard disk by asking whether you can see three different colors in the boxes on the screen. If not, this indicates that you are working on a monochrome or black-and-white screen.

Alpha installs a different set of screen instructions, called drivers, for color monitors and black and white screens.

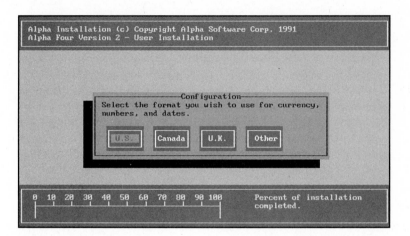

FIG. B.1

The currency
configuration
screen for
installation of
Version 2.

3. The installation program needs the name of the drive in which the installation disk is located (probably A:, possibly B:). The window shows A:\ as the default. If you wish to change the default, simply type the correct information in the Path field, highlight OK and press the Enter key.

4. The next question is whether you want the full installation with tutorial and sample files, or just the basic program alone. If this is the first time you are doing the installation, you probably want to see the full package. Later, when the tutorial files are not needed, erase the subdirectories that are created and replace them with subdirectories with logical descriptions pertaining specifically to your work.

5. The computer asks to which drive you would like the software installed. The reply should be the full name of the location where you would like to see the software. A sample answer is the following:

       C:\ALPHA4V2\

6. The installation program now begins to copy files onto your hard drive and shows you the percent of completion of the installation with a moving bar.

   Finally, if you did not choose the full installation, the program asks whether you want to install the tutorial and sample files. If you have ample space available on your hard disk, install these files.

As the installation procedure continues, the screen shows the percent of installation completed and an inquiry regarding the date format desired if you answer OTHER to the format screen (see fig. B.2).

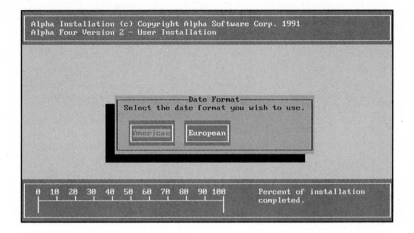

The percentage of installation completed and the chosen date format.

Using the Network

2

In 1992, Alpha Software released the second version of Alpha Four. This long-awaited version has numerous advances over the previous version, which in itself was a great addition to the world of personal and professional database management. The advent of Version 2, however, added the great advantage of networking capability. In this appendix, you will learn about the installation and use of the network version of Alpha Four, Version 2.

Installing Alpha Four on a Network

You can install the multi-user version of Alpha Four on a single-user system or on a computer that is connected to a network. To the user, the operation of the two versions is basically the same, from the point of view of the program itself. Of course, the multi-user version, when properly installed on a local area network, can give access to all users who have rights to the area to have simultaneous access to the applications on the shared directories of the network.

The multi-user version runs on all IBM PC compatible network systems that operate with DOS 3.1 or higher record and file locking protocols. Most Novell and other NetBios-compatible systems are acceptable. Other compatible network software includes: 3Com 3+, LanMaster by Microsoft, Banyan Vines, LANtastic by Artisoft, Main Lan, and the IBM PC Network.

Counting Users

When you purchase one copy of the multi-user version of Alpha Four, you enter a licensing agreement for one user on a network. For each user who is expected to function on the network and to have simultaneous access to the data in Alpha Four, one copy of the network version must be purchased.

The number of users who can access the software at the same time is defined by the user count, which is increased by the addition of other copies of the multi-user version or LAN packs. The first user who logs onto the Alpha Four software on a network is considered User 1 of 1. The information that other users can access the system is stored in the A4.NET file, traditionally stored in the subdirectory where the program files are located. If the A4.NET file is located in a different directory, then you must specify where the files are located in the command line when you start the program.

Network packs are also available for the purpose of adding users to the network. The packs are available in LAN 5-Pack and, for larger installations, the LAN 30-pack.

NOTE   Alpha Four displays the user count on the status screen in two ways. From the Main Menu, select **O**ther, **I**nformation, **S**tatus. The screen that appears shows a number of items about the configuration of the network, including the file sharing mode and the A4.NET drive and path. This screen also shows the number of users on the network and the maximum number of users who are authorized to use the network.

Using Password-Protection

If you are the designer of the application running on the network, you will decide which user has access to what commands and what files. Some users may be restricted from making changes at the View and Browse level, others may be given very broad powers to work with the application. Password-protection is available at almost every level of using Alpha Four.

Each or some items on an application menu can be protected. Individual files can be restricted within an application. Separate areas of the operation of the database can be allowed, protected, or given a password. Under the **A**pplications menu, the choice **P**revent/allow file alterations administers limits to reports, forms, browse tables, mail labels, ranges, and searches.

In individual databases, each file can be password-protected against a user trying to modify a file. Both reconfiguration and the Zap command can have a password applied. Carrying this still further, individual layouts can be protected for every level, from entering records to deleting records. (See Chapter 3 concerning editing forms and browse tables.)

Network Limitations

There are eight functions in using Alpha Four on a network that require that no other user be logged onto that file. These commands are Attach an index; Create an index; Detach an index; Erase an index; Reconfigure a database; Update an index; Pack; and Zap.

If more than one user is using the database, Alpha Four cannot give exclusive use to that file to any user. Therefore, if any of these selections are requested, an error message will occur.

Further restrictions exist when you preprocess summary fields and perform some special page formatting when printing reports. The database will be locked to prevent changes and to forestall the creation of new records during the printing process. The file will be accessible for viewing, however, during the printing session.

Default Settings on the Network

Network preferences are established on the Other, Configuration, Network settings screen from the Main Menu. If the network is set to Exclusive mode, you can change that choice for that session only, at the time that the file is opened. The original setting is reestablished when the next attempt is made to open a file.

If the network settings screen is set to Shared mode, you also can set the Update records command to change the number of seconds between screen refreshes when Alpha Four shows changes that other users have made to their files. The default is 60 seconds. If you have a speedy system, the auto-update feature should be set for a shorter period.

The Shared configuration directory can be specified when you issue the startup command by adding the -N=path command. This command tells the program where to find the A4.NET file.

Private Directories

Each user who needs to work with Alpha Four must have his or her own private directory to which full access rights have been assigned. User-specific information is stored in this subdirectory, in files with the .UDN extension. Each file has a .UDN extension that is updated every time the user accesses a file. Information about the default input forms and tables, color preferences, and printer data is stored in this file.

Further information about the defaults regarding indexes is stored in another associated file with the .IDN extension.

Search lists also are stored in the private directory with the extension .SLN. This means that more than one user can maintain a search list although the files are being accessed by a number of different people.

To start the program from any subdirectory other than the directory where the program is located, you must have a path command in the autoexec.bat file that designates the program directory. Be sure that users do not switch to files in a shared program directory to access the program.

Using Scripts on a Network

The private directory is the customary location for scripts for different applications. This directory can be set with a command-line switch in the startup file. The switch to tell Alpha Four that a path\filename is being changed is the -D=path command.

The designation <datapath> can be issued during a startup script named autoexec.scp that designates that the scripts are located in the current directory, no matter what. Another script can be identified to set the path when a file is opened. This is the file named with the !. This script automatically runs when a file is first accessed. See Chapter 11 concerning applications for further information on this subject.

Sharing with DOS

The file called SHARE.EXE is necessary for the proper management of a number of networks. This file comes with all versions of DOS 3.1 and higher. This command should be loaded through the autoexec.bat or during the network log-in routine. Although many networks do require this command, Novell NetWare does not need to receive the SHARE command.

The following files are located in the private directory:

- FILENAME.DTN, desktop definition files

- FILE_SET.SLN, the current search list

- FILENAME.$A4, an image of current Alpha Four stored when the program is swapped out to memory during the DOS access command or during a script playing the {EXEC} or {EXECCLR} command

- A4.DFL, the last used database or set and default settings, such as color, currency symbol, and default printer information

- FILENAME.HPL, a temporary file created when the program prints to the screen

- __A4xxxx.VM, a temporary file that remains after memory disruptions, which can be caused by the Disk Full error during reconfiguration or index creation

- A4.PAL, definition of custom color palettes

- A4.PNx, printer drivers.

The following files are found in the shared configuration directory:

- A4.ICx, saved import settings for character-separated ASCII files

- A4.IFx, saved import settings for VisiCalc or DIF files

- A4.IFx, saved import settings for Lotus 1-2-3 and Symphony worksheets

- A4.ISx, saved import settings for Multiplan/SYLK files

- A4.ITx, saved import setting for table ASCII files

- A4WPPx, saved import settings for WordPerfect files

- A4.NET, user count information

The capability of running on a local area network in Version 2 adds functionality to Alpha Four far beyond earlier versions of the software. Other than this issue, the network and the stand-alone versions are basically the same in Version 2.

Alpha Software's technical support department has had extensive experience with the installation of Alpha Four on a variety of networks. If you encounter difficulty, be sure to write down the messages that you receive on the screen and get in touch with the Alpha Four technicians. They are very capable of assisting you with this matter.

Problem-Solving Sample Expressions

Expressions for Personal Names and Prefixes

Problem: You have a database containing the names of 2,500 college alumni. There is a long field containing first name, sometimes middle initials, last name, and sometimes Juniors, III, M.D., or Esq. in a fourth position. There is no field for Mr., Mrs., or other prefixes. You must separate these fields so you can send letters to Mr. So-and-so with the salutation reading in a friendly manner, such as *Dear First Name*.

Solution: There are a number of problems in this situation, and the situation itself is not uncommon. The bad news is that where data is simply missing, such as the Mr. and Mrs., you will just have to add that data the hard way, one record at a time. This is a matter of judgment. Are Fran and Lou ladies or gents? Without some other clue, there is no way to know. The Frans and Lous among us are probably used to getting mail addressed to the wrong sex. When it is possible to do so, it is still considered more polite to send a letter with a gender-specific prefix.

Thank goodness that Ms. came along just in time to save us all from having to make yet another possibly alienating computer-generated goof. Unless you are certain of a woman's status and preference, for business (not social) purposes, you should select Ms. for a woman's prefix.

From this point, you must be the judge as to how accurate you want the database to be. Does this list represent most favored clients or members of the Board of Directors? If so, the mailing should be perfect. How annoying it is to get mail addressed to a misspelled name or wrong address stating the following:

> Dear *So-and-So*:

> Because of our personal knowledge of your status as a leader in the *(fill in the blank)* field, we want you to:

> [ ] Spend some money

> [ ] Attend our seminar

> [ ] Accept this credit card

> [ ] *(fill in the blank)*

If your decision is that the mailing list does not demand perfection, then you can select from the techniques discussed below, or try them all.

 CAUTION When trying any of these suggestions, test them on a small sample before you touch your data. Even when you think you've got all the right moves figured out, *back up your original data*. No excuses matter if you lose information.

Without doing anything to change the long NAME field, the first step to getting the names separated is to reconfigure your database to add five new fields: PREFIX, FIRST, MIDDLE, LAST, and SUFFIX. Using field rules, define each of these fields as CALCULATED, and put in the appropriate expression. To start, if Mr. and Mrs. appear in more than just a few fields, use the following expression, substituting the name of your long field where NAME is used:

```
PREFIX    (if("Mr." $ NAME, "Mr.",
              if("Mrs." $ NAME, "Mrs.",
              if("Dr."$ NAME, "Dr.",""))))
```

Send this calculation through and reevaluate the field rules before doing the next expression.

 NOTE A calculated field will not accept changes from the keyboard. After the field is filled, you may wish to change the field rule to a default value.

Next, you should find out whether there is anything in the PREFIX field. If there is an entry in PREFIX, then the calculation for first name should place the second word rather than the first word in FIRST, as in the following:

> FIRST   if(isblank(PREFIX,word(NAME,1),word(NAME,2))

From this point on, the problem changes. Now it is necessary to calculate backward from the end of the NAME field, that is, the SUFFIX field. You need to know whether there is data in the SUFFIX field. The first problem is to know how many words are in the name field. The following expression is used in a calculated field to count the number of words in the long NAME field:

> if(isblank(word(NAME,1)),0,if(isblank(word(NAME,2)),1,
> if(isblank(word(NAME,3)),2,if(isblank(word)NAME,4)),3
> if(isblank(word(NAME,5),4,5)))))

This will count up to five words in a name. If you know that there are more than a few six-word names, you can add another level to this cascading IF statement.

> **NOTE**   *Cascading* means that if the record being tested fails the first test, in this case, if the NAME field is not blank, the expression falls through to the next level of the test. If the record fails to be blank in the second word of the NAME field, the expression performs the next test, and so on.

If the record being examined contains five words, the strong likelihood is that the fifth word is a SUFFIX. In this case, you want the contents of word five to be placed in the SUFFIX field. This only applies if the PREFIX field contains appropriate data, i.e.: Mr. or Mrs., or the like. Therefore, if the PREFIX field is blank, it is more than likely to be a real suffix, such as Jr., IV, or Ph.D.

Taken all together, these actions provide you with an expression for Global Update that will solve the problem. The reason you switch at this point from creating Calculated fields in field rules to using Global Update is that with Global Update, you can define a range of records to use.

To update the MIDDLE field with the proper selection from the NAME field, create a global update on MIDDLE as the following:

> MIDDLE   if(isblank(PREFIX),word(NAME,2),word(NAME,3))

Save the expression, but pause at the range setting screen to create a filter that counts the words as in the following:

> Filter: count>=3

And make the filter status Active.

In this case, you should limit the range setting screen by defining a filter for the COUNT field equal to 5.

This section introduces a number of rather sophisticated activities, but you should see that each one taken separately is simple to understand. You will find that learning such techniques as outlined here will help you think through solutions to similar problems.

The same problem comes up in the case of a single, long field, which contains City, ST, and ZIP code information. In such a situation, the separation of data is easier to manage. None of the United States has more than two words, except the District of Columbia, and even there, the Post Office calls it DC. Few cities are identified with more than two words, the great exception being West Palm Beach. These rare exceptions can be dealt with on an individual basis.

Of course, all of this discussion regarding first and last names becomes academic in situations where you are dealing with Asian, Indian, and African names, some of which do not follow the standard order of the English-speaking world. As a human being, you may find these differences interesting. If you are trying to make simple calculations on a computer, the differences become challenging.

Tips and Traps for Mailing Lists

How to *get into trouble* with a mailing list:

1. Copy someone else's file CONTACT.DBF to your computer, where you also have a file called CONTACT.DBF. What was his is now yours—and yours is *gone.*

2. Copy an updated file from one machine in your office to the same file name on another machine in the office where two people have worked on both files. Which file is updated in which records?

3. Append the records from the floppy back-up disk you were keeping just in case, back onto the carefully sculpted list from which you had recently deleted all those folks you decided were never going to return your calls.

4. Keep your mailing list, patient list, invoice records, whatever, on a machine that is not adequate to the job. This is a lesson that more than a few people have had to learn the hard way. An absolute *must* is a computer with a reliable hard disk, a reliable floppy disk, and reliable power, both from the wall and from the machine itself. A good quality surge protector is a minimum, but a poor quality surge protector is sometimes worse than nothing, offering

nothing more than the illusion of safety. An uninterruptible power supply (UPS) also serves to protect your computer equipment against dips and surges in the current. The little motors in the hard drive will get sore if asked to run on less than the standard 60 cycles. The cost of a UPS is relatively high, compared to the rest of the computer system, but compare the cost to the replacement cost for your data. A UPS is an insurance policy that pays off every day.

If it takes a half-hour to index your mailing list of 5,000 names, give that computer to the nearest grade-schooler if you can find one who will take it off your hands. The machines that many schools have at the high school level are generally faster than this kind.

If you are paying someone to maintain your mailing list, or worse, doing it yourself, what is happening while your computer takes time off to think about things? You are losing money.

If your hard disk is too full and a crash occurs in the middle of an indexing or reconfiguration of the file, you stand a great chance of losing your data, your job, your employee, your friend, or whatever is involved. And you are losing money.

5. Put your favorite customer list in the hands of someone who used to (or intends to) work for your competition. A business magazine recently estimated that retailers lose more dollars through larceny of data out the employees entrance than from shoplifting out the customer entrance.

How to *get out of trouble* with your mailing list:

1. Generally speaking, a good strategy is to make one person responsible for maintaining a mailing list. Depending on the size of the list and its importance in your life or business, a raise in pay may be needed to indicate the level of concern that you have for the data. Naturally, make sure that your equipment is designed to do the work you are asking it to do.

2. Training on the techniques of data management is a good idea. This may consist largely of a self-paced tutorial such as that included with the Alpha Four manual. If you are clear about the purpose of the files you are keeping, they will stay in better condition. Formal training, of course, can shortcut the learning process dramatically and reduce the bad habits that can develop from the imperative need to get the job done and find out what's happening later.

3. Verify regularly that backups are being made on floppy disks, tape backups, or at least in a separate part of your computer. Unless you are on a well-managed network system with proven reliability

about restoring lost data, a bit of personal protection is in order. The generally accepted rule is to keep two copies (father and grandfather) of backup information. Use two sets of disks: set A and set B. Depending on the amount of change that takes place over a period of time, you should back up your data daily, weekly or monthly. For inactive files that you want to be able to access, but only infrequently, get a good dust-proof disk box, and store the records on a floppy, carefully labeled, in the box. Then label the box. These things tend to multiply.

4. Keep the activities simple. Using scripts and applications helps a great deal when complicated or lengthy procedures are required. A menu that pops up with a familiar outline is comforting when the phone rings and you lose track of where you are in your work: *Do I run this report from the SLS_Q192 file or from the PRFTQ192 file? Do I use the INV_DATE index or the ORD_DATE index?*

5. Make these decisions once and put it in a script file with documentation. Then write down the instructions in a notebook that is kept near the computer for the users of the database—and for yourself. Better still, write up a short but complete users' manual just to outline the steps needed to perform the basic functions of the database. (See Chapter 14 on writing documentation for applications.)

Menus for a Sample Application

A volunteer organization dedicated to environmental, economic, and historical issues on Cape Cod has developed an application designed to manage 6,000 records in a membership database with 35 fields. Those working on the records are all volunteers, mostly part-time, and largely retired persons with little or no computer experience. The volunteers do all the data entry and maintenance for the 6,000 records.

One of the members, considerably more than a little computer literate, designed an outstandingly effective application in Alpha Four. His goal was to structure the application in such a way that his helpers would be accurate, efficient, and comfortable in their own jobs.

The one-page instruction sheet for the volunteers is easy to understand and clear in the ideas presented. The top line is the following:

To Start   *Turn on red wall switch to right of computer and remove plastic dust cover.*

The last line of the instructions is the following:

To Finish   *Please cover the keyboard and computer with the plastic dust cover and turn off red wall switch.*

Instructions cannot get much easier than that. These instructions are not intended, nor understood to be, patronizing or demeaning. The people using the equipment are truly contributing to an important cause, and while hardly realizing that they are doing so, they are gaining new skills and confidence. This has proven to be a win/win situation for everyone.

The methods used by this volunteer are worth studying because it is not just retired volunteers who want their work to be simple. The new introduction of a computer into an office can be so traumatic as to cause people to leave their jobs and the company. Everyone loses in this situation. Therefore, the goal of an application developer must be to minimize the user's learning and simplify the activities. Provide the user with a means of performing the necessary operations in a way that matches as closely as possible the actions they were doing before the computer invaded their lives.

Even in a situation where an application is extremely complex, the menus can be designed to reflect logical groups of activities.

It would be grand if all the repetitive functions we must perform every day could be placed on a menu in this manner. Until we work out a way to train the computer to make our beds and brush our teeth, this will just be a silly fantasy. Still, the lesson is important: *Keep it simple.*

The following are the two menus used by the Cape Cod volunteers:

```
M A I N   M E N U

Browse Membership Records
Change Membership Records
Enter New Memberships
print Total Membership Roster
print Journal of Membership Receipts
print Mailing Labels
return to DOS Menu
```

When the user selects the sixth line or presses **M** for **M**ailing Labels, the following screen appears:

```
L A B E L   M E N U

1. Permanent Addresses ONLY
2. Seasonal and Permanent Addresses
3. Return to Main Menu
```

There are, of course, other elements to this application that carry the users further in functionality. Monthly and annual reporting, posting membership dues and donations, statistical analyses of receipts and so on, are done by those with more understanding of the software and the needs of the organization. The point of the application shown here is that it works so well.

The single data-entry form makes extensive use of the error-checking capabilities offered in Field Rules. Pop-up windows showing look-up tables and look-up databases assist the user in making certain choices. Default entries, such as MA in the STATE field, shorten the process and reduce keystrokes. The template rule, which defines the telephone number with parentheses and dashes, reduces data entry errors. The Prompt command places a brief instruction on the screen to remind the user of what kind of data should be entered into the field.

Favorite Expressions from Alpha Four Techs

Problem: Create a script that passes a variable, %b to a variable in a batch file for EXECCLR.

Solution: {SET %b, "01/05/69"} {set %d, "c:\test.bat" +%b} {EXECCLR %d 0, 512}

Problem: Force a character field to return the character name (January, February) of the date field plus one month.

Solution: CMONTH(CTOD(TRIM(LTRIM(STR(IF(MONTH(DATEFIELD) = 12,1,(MONTH(DATEFIELD)+1)))))+"/01/91"))

Problem: Calculate how many days are in a month depending on a date field.

Solution: if(DATEFIELD={},0,if(DAY(DATEFIELD + 31)=1,31,DAY (DATEFIELD + (32 − DAY(DATEFIELD)) − (DAY(DATEFIELD + (32 − DAY(DATEFIELD)))))))

Problem: Calculate age in years. The following is one of several used to perform this task.

Solution: YEAR(SYSTEM–>DATE) − YEAR(DOB) − if(left(dtoc(SYSTEM–>DATE),5)) < LEFT(DTOC(DOB),5),1,0)

Problem: Import Lotus 1-2-3, Version 3 files.

Solution: Go to 1-2-3 and save the 3-dimensional file as a traditional worksheet (.WK1) file. This converts the file in such a way that you can import the file into Alpha Four.

Problem: Convert files created in ALPHA/*three* to Alpha Four, Version 2.

Solution: There is an intermediate conversion program called A3TOA4.EXE that is supplied by Alpha Software for those who encounter this difficulty. If you have letters that need to be converted, ask for A3LETTER.EXE as well.

Problem: Display names stored as Last, First, Middle in the form, First Middle Last. *<FIELD LENGTH>* means you enter the digit corresponding to the field length of your name field.

Solution: if("," $ NAMEFIELD .and. at(",", NAMEFIELD) < at(" ",NAMEFIELD), rtrim(right(NAMEFIELD,*<FIELD LENGTH>* – (at(",", NAMEFIELD)+1))) +" "+ left(NAMEFIELD, at (",",NAMEFIELD)–1), NAMEFIELD)

Problem: Display names stored as First Last as Last, First.

Solution: rtrim(right(NAMEFIELD, *<FIELD LENGTH>* –(at(" ",NAMEFIELD))))+", " + left(NAMEFIELD,at(" ", NAMEFIELD)–1)

Error Codes in Alpha Four

Problem: DATA FILE LIMIT: RECORD OUT OF RANGE

Cause: Index file is out of order. This error occurs when you select an index that was created for another database or when that file was deselected; records were entered, deleted, changed; and the index was selected again.

Remedy: Update that index. If updating doesn't work, deselect that index and create a new one.

Problem: ILLEGAL ARGUMENT

Cause: Calculated or computed field equation that results in division by zero; an equation could result in a division by zero if nothing appears in the denominator field—even temporarily.

Remedy: Change default recalc. mode to manual (other on main menu), or include "if" in the equation: "if(*put denominator fieldname here*=0,0,equation)".

Problem: UNABLE TO WRITE PRINTER DRIVER FILE

Cause: Incompatible setup codes within the printer driver file.

Remedy: Delete setup codes.

Problem:	EVALUATION ERROR: *Xxxxxxxxxxx*
Cause:	Improper syntax, function, or a mixture of character, date, and/or numeric fields.
Remedy:	Recheck field type and syntax.

Problem:	ERROR RESYNCING
Cause:	Problems placing an entry within an index.
Remedy:	Update or rebuild index.

Problem:	ACCESS ERROR IN RANGE
Cause:	Bad linking index in a set or no valid records in a range.
Remedy:	Varying fields, lengths, or types may be in the linking index, or linking index may be bad. Also may be caused by using the same index for more than one database.

Problem:	OUT OF MEMORY
Cause:	Not enough RAM memory to open the database or set that you are choosing.
Remedy:	Check the Config.sys file in the root directory to verify that `files=40` and `buffers=32`. Also check whether any other programs are memory resident.

Problem:	ERROR UPDATING INDEX
Cause:	Indicates a corrupt index file.
Remedy:	Update or rebuild indexes.

Problem:	ERROR ADDING KEY TO INDEX
Cause:	Ran out of disk space while creating or updating index.
Remedy:	Delete necessary files and re-create or re-update index.

Problem:	ERROR READING DATABASE RECORD
Cause:	*In a set*, indicates that you are sharing indexes between the parent and child. *In a flat file*, may indicate a bad index or corrupt data.

Remedy: *In set*, verify that indexes are created in separate databases.

    In a flat file, attempt viewing in record number order. If
unsuccesful, try copying database out. If unsuccesful,
you have bad data. Perform a **chkdsk/f** command and
restore the backup.

Problem: CRITICAL ERROR: UNKNOWN COMMAND ERROR ON DRIVE C

Cause: Attempting to print with a bad index.

Remedy: Update or rebuild the index.

Problem: ZOOM STACK FULL ERROR

Cause: Attempting to zoom without unzooming.

Remedy: Unzoom, and try again.

Problem: EVALUATION ERROR: NO EXPRESSION

Cause: Field rules defaults may be set to expression mode with
no expression, or required rules have no expression.

Remedy: Check field rules and make necessary corrections.

Problem: WRITE ERROR

Cause: Occurs while indexing. May be running out of disk
space while trying to write an index.

Remedy: Can create a file called X_A4_X.DR4

Problem: ERROR OPENING X_A4.DR4

Cause: Running out of disk space when running a search or
indexing a file

Remedy: Clear adequate disk space.

Problem: EVALUATION ERROR: ILLEGAL OPERAND

Cause: If this error occurs when entering records into a database, then you have a division by 0 in field rules.

Remedy:	Replace equation with the following: F1=numerator F2= denominator:

> Version 1: **if(f1=0,0,f1/if(f2=0,1,f2))**
>
> Version 2: **if(f2=0,0,f1/f2)**

Problem: ERROR 1 PARSING KEY INDEX *XXX*

Cause: Bad index on a lookup table.

Remedy: Go to child, and create new index using same key values with a different name for the index. Then lookup rules, and change the linking index to the new one.

Problem: ERROR: NONEXISTENT FIELD

When evaluating an equation in reports or forms.

Cause: The equation contains a calculated field that is not a physical field in the database but one that was created in the form.

Remedy: Modify equation or field.

Problem: WARNING: UNEXPECTED END OF FILE

Cause: Usually caused by importing a database that has illegal characters in the field names (*!$^%%&).

Remedy: Change the field names to eliminate those characters.

Problem: ERROR OPENING DBNAME.DR4

Cause: Not enough files set in the CONFIG.SYS.

Remedy: Change the file to contain the statement FILES=60.

Symbols

! (exclamation point), 370-371
* (wildcard), 257
_ (field name divider), 63

A

A4DOC utility, 420-424
A4LIB.EXE utility, 428-429
{ABORT} command, 379
ABS( ) function, 403
access, restricting, 51, 351-352, 440-441
ACCESS ERROR IN RANGE error
   code, 456
accounts receivable (scripts for), 374
ACOS( ) function, 404
activating windows, 48
active filters, 132
ADDMONTHS( ) function, 404
ADDYEARS( ) function, 404
Allow escape command, 344
{ALLOWKEYS} command, 392
Alpha Four
   development, 38-40
   installing, 435-437
   starting, 13-14
Alpha Software
   Bulletin Board, 434
   contacting, 434
   Technical Support Team, 52
Alt-key shortcuts, 291
American Standard Code for Information
   Interchange (ASCII), 203, 284-285
analyzing fields, 220
AND statement, 134, 138
Append command, 105, 262, 269-271
Application Editor, 314-315
applications, 308, 331-332
   banners
      boxes, 342
      enhancing, 341-342
      lines, 342
      modifying, 343
      saving as templates, 343

calling, 350-352
command line switches, 369
compared with scripts, 315-316
converting, 12
creating, 309-313, 339-343
   with Runtime Module, 418
default
   locating, 371-372
   setting, 367-371
designing, 337-339
directories, 368
including .UDN files, 372-373
initializing, 369-371
planning, 367
structure, 335-337
switching, 350-352
arguments, 393-394
ASC( ) function, 404
ascending sort order, 114-115
ASCII (American Standard Code for
   Information Interchange), 203, 284-285
ASIN( ) function, 404
AT( ) function, 404
ATAN( ) function, 404
ATAN2( ) function, 405
Attach an index command, 441
Attach command, 129
attaching indexes, 129
attributes, 54
auto flush settings, 50
Auto Pop-up, 153
automatic dating, 402
automating
   data entry, 75-76
   scripts with exclamation points (!),
      370-371
averaging with zeroes, 198-199

B

backing up files, 290
backup copies, 103-104
banners, application
   boxes, 342
   enhancing, 341-342
   lines, 342

modifying, 343
saving as templates, 343
{BEEP} command, 379
Black/White palette, 294
blank lines
suppressed, 173
unsuppressible, 171
blinking fields, 94
BOF() function, 405
borrowing formats, 194
boxes
as highlights, 88
drawing, 342
break fields, 208
Browse command, 68
Browse mode, 74
data entry, 75
field editing, 90-92
browse tables, 26, 90-92
color, 92-94
creating sets, 97, 247-249
data entry, 96-97
default, 74-76
defining, 79-82
editing, 79-82
printing, 182
record viewing, 89
reports, 162
Browse tables command, 79
building menus, 332-334
button control, 359, 364-365

C

calculated
databases, 195
entry, 402
calculated fields, 29-30, 59,
82-86, 144-146, 196-197
creating, 85-86
editing, 292-293
formatting, 177
Calculated fields screen, 29
calculating
date fields, 453
field rules, 18-21
Call-app command, 346, 350-351
calling
applications, 350-352
subapplications, 351
{CANCEL} command, 379
cancelling deletion, 102
cascading, 447
IF statements, 401
{CASE} command, 379-380
Case Convert field rules, 146-147
case-Insensitive, 396
cases, 138-139
categorizing data, 58
CCVALID() function, 405
CDATE() function, 134, 403-405
CDOW() function, 405
CEILING() function, 405
Change mode, 71

character fields, 59, 64, 95
data entry, 72
formatting, 78, 176, 179
sort orders, 115
types, 54
character operators, 396
checking field rules, 22-23
child files, 229
CHKDIGIT() function, 405
Choose database/set command, 13
choosing output, 25-27
CHR() function, 406
classes, Master, 352-354
{CLEAR} command, 380
clipboards, 395
CMONTH() function, 406
codes
error, 455-458
formatting, 217
COLLAGE program, 431
color
browse tables, 92-94
expressions, 255-256
palettes, 293, 342
screen
Version 1, 293-294
Version 2, 295-296
Color Sample bar, 342
Column status command, 344
columnar reports, 162-164
columns, 171-172
command line, 369
commands, 393
accessing, 46
Allow escape, 344
Append, 105, 262, 269-271
Attach, 129
Attach an index, 441
Browse, 68
Browse tables, 79
Call-app, 346, 350-351
Choose database/set, 13
Column status, 344
Control codes, 217
Copy, 105, 262-263
Create an index, 441
create Dialog script, 359
create Keystroke script, 358
Create/edit a browse table, 79
Create/edit a form, 76
Crosstab, 263-264
Define password, 204
Detach, 130
Detach an index, 441
display script Variables, 366
DOS, 257
Enable/Disable auto fill, 217
Erase an index, 441
Export, 263-264
Find, 95, 98
Float, 206
Forms, 76
Global update, 292
Goto-app, 346, 350-351

Import, 262-264, 286
Increment, 19
Index, 186
Intersect, 262-265, 276-277, 282-283
Join, 207, 262-265, 273-276, 283
Layout, 41
Left margin/line Width, 217
Locate, 99
Menu bar action, 345
Pack, 102-106, 441
Page eject, 216
Post, 262-263, 269-270
Print, 41
Range, 98
Reconfigure a database, 111, 441
relational, 262-265, 282-283
save As, 194
{SCREENOFF}, 353
scripts, 379-391
Search, 99, 101
Search and replace, 99-101
Share, 443
startup, 367
Sub-menu, 346
Subtract, 262-265, 272-273, 282-283
Summarize, 136, 262-264
sWitch, 237, 250
Top/Bottom margins, 217
Trim, 207
Undelete record, 102
Update an index, 441
Update Indexes, 129
Window On, 48
Zap, 441
Zoom, 97, 234-237
common
    fields, 228
    keys, 228
compatibility, 12
    downward, 12
composite records, 233
compound indexes, 117
CompuServe on-line service, 434
conditional expressions, 217-218
contacts, 257
context-sensitive help screens, 48
Control codes command, 217
controlling page layout, 216-217
converting
    applications, 12
    files, 454
Copy command, 105, 262-263
copying
    deleted records, 105
    files, 260-261
    sets, 256-258
    text blocks, 74
COS( ) function, 406
count fields, 189
Create an index command, 441
create Dialog script command, 359
create Keystroke script command, 358
Create/edit a browse table command, 79
Create/edit a form command, 76

CRITICAL ERROR: UNKNOWN COMMAND
    ERROR ON DRIVE C error code, 457
Crosstab command, 263-264
Crosstab Description screen, 282
crosstab functions, 277-282
CTOD ( ) function, 406
currency
    name settings, 50
    symbol settings, 50
cursors, 46
custom reports
    creating, 166
    placing fields, 197-198
customizing
    data entry, 27-28
    input forms, 82-83
    input screen, 299-300
    screens, 27-28
cutting, 297

D

data
    arguments, 394
    backing up, 103-104
    calculated field, 292-293
    carrying between records, 363
    categorizing, 58
    editing, 75
    entering
        automatically, 75-76
        Browse mode, 75
        browse tables, 96-97
        character fields, 72
        date fields, 73
        in sets, 249-250
        logical fields, 73
        memo fields, 73-74
        numeric fields, 72-73
        records, 17-18
        View mode, 71-72
        with expressions, 395
    linked, 254-255
    mirror images, 298
    needs, 60-63
    organizing, 24-25, 189-190
    passing between files with trigger
        scripts, 327-328
    posting between files, 265-269
    protecting, 89
    pseudo field, 298-299
    reporting, 30-33
    retrieving, 133, 254-255
    strings, 95
    structure, 61
    summarizing, 277-282
        without reports, 219
    Unique, 176
    Value, 176
DATA FILE LIMIT: RECORD OUT OF
    RANGE error code, 455
databases
    basics, 37-38
    calculated, 195

creating, 14-16, 61
   extracting non-matching files, 272-273
   from reports, 168-175
   intersecting files, 276-277
   joining files, 273-276
designing with indexes, 118-119
development, 38
lettering, 214-218
logical, 197
lookup, 151, 251-252
   creating, 152-154
planning, 55-59
protecting, 51
reconfiguring, 120
relational, 227-228
reporting, 194
summary, 197, 221-223
   creating, 136-137, 195
   numeric fields, 198
SYSTEM, 207-208
terminology, 54
transaction, 194
date fields, 54, 59, 65, 210, 401
   calculating, 453
   emptying, 402
   entering data, 73
   formatting, 78, 181
   sort orders, 115
DATE() function, 406
dates
   Field Rules, 402
   format settings, 50
   operators, 396
   separator settings, 50
dating, automatic, 402
DAY() function, 406
dBASE
   compatibility settings, 50
   standard, 101
DBF() function, 406
dbQuick4T, 39
{DEBUGOFF} command, 380
{DEBUGON} command, 380
Default mode, 148-149
defaults
   applications
      locating, 371-372
      setting, 367-371
   browse table, 74-76
   entry, 402
   input form, 70
   settings
      networks, 441
      screen, 48-50
Define password command, 204
defining
   application structure, 335-337
   browse tables, 79-82
   data needs, 60-63
   fields, 196-197
   global updates, 253
   input forms, 76-79

mailing labels, 199
passwords, 204
print drivers, 183-184
printers, 208-209
ranges, 208-209
searches, 133-134
variables, 324-325
definitions, GENERIC, 420
Del keys, 46
delete marks, 22
deleted records, copying, 105
DELETED() function, 406
deleting
   cancelling, 102
   fields, 87
   records, 101
   text, 74, 87
descending sort order, 114-115
designing
   applications, 337-339
   databases, 118-119
   indexes, 113-114
   records, 301-302
desktops
   creating, 235-236
   managing, 321-322
   processing, 322-323
   stripping, 427
Detach an index command, 441
Detach command, 130
detaching indexes, 128-130
detail portions, 119
Details, 172
determining field origins, 252-253
dialog boxes, 363-365
dialog scripts, 308
   creating, 316-318
DIFFERENCE() function, 407
directories
   private, 442-443
   startup, 368
display control, 359, 364
Display index, 152
display script Variables command, 366
displaying personal names, 454
dividing field names, 63
DMY() function, 407
documenting
   sets with A4DOC, 420-424
   with pictures, 431
DOS commands, 257
DOW() function, 407
downward compatibility, 12
drawing
   boxes, 342
   lines, 342
drivers, print, 183-184
DTOC() function, 407
DTOR() function, 407
DTOS() function, 407
duplicated software errors, 113
duplicates
   eliminating, 124-125
   removing, 126

E

editing
  browse tables, 79-82
  data, 75
  input forms, 77-78
  scripts, 424-427
editor programs, 420
eliminating duplicates, 124-125
emphasizing mailing labels, 204-205
emptying date fields, 402
Enable/Disable auto fill command, 217
End key, 74
{ENDAPP} command, 381
enhanced data entry, 89
enhancing application banners, 341-342
Enter key, 46
entering
  data
    automatically, 75-76
    Browse mode, 75
    browse tables, 96-97
    character fields, 72
    date fields, 73
    in records, 17-18
    in sets, 249-250
    logical fields, 73
    memo fields, 73-74
    numeric fields, 72-73
    view mode, 71-72
    with expressions, 395
  records, 66-68
entities, 54
  logical, 195
entry
  calculated, 402
  default, 402
EOF( ) function, 407
Erase an index command, 441
ERROR 1 PARSING KEY INDEX error
  code, 458
ERROR ADDING KEY TO INDEX error code,
  456
error codes, 21
  causes and solutions, 455-458
ERROR OPENING DBNAME.DR4 error code,
  458
ERROR OPENING X_A4.DR4 error code,
  457
ERROR READING DATABASE RECORD error
  code, 456
ERROR RESYNCING error code, 456
ERROR UPDATING INDEX error code, 456
ERROR: NONEXISTENT FIELD error code,
  458
errors
  duplicated software, 113
Esc key, 41
EVALUATION ERROR: error code, 456
EVALUATION ERROR: ILLEGAL OPERAND
  error code, 457
EVALUATION ERROR: NO EXPRESSION
  error code, 457

exclamation points (!), 370-371
{EXEC} command, 381-382
{EXECCLR} command, 381
EXP( ) function, 408
expanding memo fields, 179
exploring lookups, 154-157
Export command, 263-264
exporting files, 285
  to WordPerfect, 286
expression boxes, 21
Expression mode, 133, 149
  creating expressions, 397
Expression windows, 21
expressions, 155-157, 297, 393-394
  color, 255-256
  conditional, 217-218
  creating, 397-398
  data entry, 395
  examples, 453-454
  personal name, 445-448
  prefixes, 445-448
  problem-solving, 398-399
  storing in clipboards, 395
  uses, 394
extended keys, 384
extensions, 257, 321

F

F_UPPER( ) function, 408
Fastback backup program, 104
field rules, 18, 143
  calculating, 18-21
  Case Convert, 146-147
  checking, 22-23
  creating, 18-19, 144, 300-301
    expressions, 398
    sets, 252
  dates, 402
  Increment, 149
  Prompt, 150
  Required, 150
  saving, 21
  Skip Entry, 150
FIELD( ) function, 408
fields, 54, 61
  analyzing, 220
  blinking, 94
  break, 208
  calculated, 29-30, 59, 82-85, 144-146,
    196-197
    changing data, 292-293
    creating, 85-86
    formatting, 177
  character, 59, 64, 95
    entering data, 72
    formatting, 78, 176-179
    sort orders, 115
  common, 228
  count, 189
  creating, 59
  date, 59, 65, 210, 401
    calculating, 453
    emptying, 402

entering data, 73
  formatting, 78, 181
  sort orders, 115
defining, 196-197
deleting, 87
editing in Browse mode, 90-92
length, 175-176
logical, 59, 65
  entering data, 73
memo, 59, 67, 95, 148
  accessing, 73
  entering data, 73-74
  expanding, 179
  formatting, 179-180
  saving, 74
moving, 87
names, 61
  dividing, 63
  rules, 63-65
numeric, 59, 64
  entering data, 72-73
  formatting, 78, 176, 180-181
  sort orders, 115
  summary databases, 198
origins, determining, 252-253
placing, 81
  custom reports, 197-198
  mailing labels, 202
psuedo, 298-299
real, 154, 195, 298
replotting, 100
selecting, 20
statistics, 219, 375-376
summary, 173-175, 196-197
text, long, 95-96
types, 54
updating globally, 139-141
user-entered, 85, 144-146
wordwrapped, 90
files
  automatically executing, scripts for,
    369-370
  backing up, 290
  child, 229
  converting, 454
  copying, 260-261
  creating, 65-66
  data
    passing, 327-328
    posting, 265-269
  desktops
    creating, 235-236
    managing, 321-322
    processing, 322-323
  exporting, 285
    to WordPerfect, 286
  extensions, 321
  flat, 53
    summarizing data, 277-282
  helping, 347
  importing, 285
  intersecting, 276-277
  joining, 273-276
  libraries, 430

linking, 246-250
  comparing types, 240
  master, 262
  parent, 105, 229
  private directory, 443
  README, 433
  resynching, 129
  scrambling, 258
  subgrouping, 121-130
  support, 194
  transaction, 262
  .UDN, 372-373
  zooming, 234-235
Filter line, 48
filters, 98, 112
  active, 132
  inactive, 133
  report, 194-195
  setting with variables, 378
Find command, 95, 98
finding
  records, 301-302
  strings, 424
flags, 83
  print attribute, 204
flat files, 53
  summarizing data, 277-282
Float command, 206
FLOOR() function, 408
footers, 173
form letters, creating, 214-215
formats
  borrowing, 194
  spreadsheet, 68
  table, 68
formatting
  calculated fields, 177
  character fields, 78, 176-179
  codes, 217
  date fields, 78, 181
  mailing labels, 206-207
  memo fields, 179-180
  numeric fields, 78, 176,
    180-181
Formatting Options, 175-178
  applying, 178-181
forms
  input, 26
    reports, 161
  sets, 247-249
Forms command, 76
found records, 25
front-end interfaces, 430
function keys, 42-43
functions, 393
  CDATE(), 134, 403
  complete listing, 403-415
  crosstab, 277-282
  ISBLANK(), 393
  MONTH(), 393
  STR(), 134, 403
  syntax rules, 394
  TRIM(), 396
FV() function, 408

G

GENERIC definitions, 420
Global update command, 292
Global update menu, 138
global
  case change, 138-139
  updates, 253
{GOTO} command, 382
Goto-app command, 346,
  350-351
grouping records, 186

H

headers
  Page, 170
  Report, 170
headings, menu, 337
help
  lines, 346
  screens, 350
helping files, 347
hiding lines, 179
highlights, 46
  boxes, 88
  lines, 88
Home key, 74
hotkeys, 319
  scripts, 357
HOTSHOT Graphics program, 431

I

{IF} command, 382
IF statements, 217, 400-401
  cascading, 401
  nested, 401
IF() function, 408
Ignore mode, 198
IIF() function, 409
ILLEGAL ARGUMENT error code, 455
Import command, 262-264, 286
importing
  files, 285
  Lotus 1-2-3, 454
  spreadsheets, 286
inactive filters, 133
Increment command, 19
Increment field rule, 149
Index command, 186
indexes, 24, 95, 115-117
  attaching, 129
  compound, 117
  creating, 25, 114, 117-120, 191-194
  database design, 118-119
  designing, 113-114
  detaching, 128-130
  Display, 152
  eliminating duplicates, 124-125
  filters, 112
  how they work, 126-128
  Linking, 152

purpose, 112
reconfiguring databases, 120
sort orders, 114-115
speed, 113
unique, 125
updating, 129
Indexes\ranges menu, 117
indexing records, 210-213
individualizing mailing labels, 202
initializing applications, 369-371
input forms, 26
  customizing, 82-83
  default, 70
  defining, 76-79
  editing, 77-78
  painted, 88
  printing, 182
  reports, 161
input screens, 299-300
Ins key, 46
Insert mode, 71
inserting text blocks, 74
installing
  Alpha Four, 435-437
  networks, 439-441
  Runtime Module utility,
    418-420
INT() function, 409
integrated software, 37
interfaces, front-end, 430
Intersect command, 262-265, 276-277,
  282-283
invoices, creating, 188
ISALPHA() function, 409
ISBLANK() function, 393, 409
ISLOWER() function, 409
ISUPPER() function, 409
items, menu
  adding, 345-346
  protecting, 346

J

Join command, 207, 262-265, 273-276, 283
justification, 176

K

key combinations, 42-46
keys
  Alt, 291
  common, 228
  Del, 46
  End, 74
  Enter, 46
  Esc, 41
  extended, 384
  Home, 74
  hot, 319
  Ins, 46
  PgDn, 74
keystroke scripts, 308, 425
  creating, 318-319

L

labels, mailing, 27
  creating, 199-200
  defining, 199
  emphasizing, 204-205
  fields, 202
  formatting, 206-207
  individualizing, 202
  modifying, 203-208
  pre-defined sized, 200-201
  printing, 182, 202
  reports, 162
  sizing, 203
languages
  R P L, 39
  scripting, 430
Layout command, 41
Layouts menu, 193
LCD (liquid crystal display) monitors, 294
Learn Macro mode, 347
Left margin/line Width command, 217
LEFT( ) function, 409
LEN( ) function, 409
length of fields, 175-176
lettering databases, 214-218
letters, form, 27
  creating, 214-215
  printing, 182
  reports, 162
libraries
  file, 430
  script, 376-377, 428
    creating, 428
Library of Scripts, 428
LIKE( ) function, 410
limitations of networks, 441
line items, 187
lines
  application banners, 342
  as highlights, 88
  blank
    suppressed, 173
    unsuppressible, 171
  Filter, 48
  help, 346
  hiding, 179
  prompt, 41
linked data, retrieving, 254-255
linking
  files, 246-250
    comparing types, 240
    parameters, 250-251
Linking index, 152
links
  parameters, 233
  visual, 240
liquid crystal display (LCD), 294
lists, mailing, 448-450
Locate command, 99

locating
  defaults, 371-372
  scripts, 357-358
LOG( ) function, 410
logical
  databases, 197
  entities, 195
  operators, 394
logical fields, 54, 59, 65
  entering data, 73
long text fields, 95-96
lookups
  databases, 151, 251-252
    creating, 152-154
  exploring, 154-157
  mapping, 152
  tables, 151-152
{LOOP} command, 382-383
Lotus 1-2-3, importing, 454
LOWER( ) function, 410
LTRIM( ) function, 410

M

Macro Call Tree, 422
macros, 308
  creating, 347-350
  creating in Application Editor, 314-315
mailing labels, 27
  creating, 199-200
  defining, 199
  emphasizing, 204-205
  fields, 202
  formatting, 206-207
  individualizing, 202
  modifying, 203-208
  pre-defined sizes, 200-201
  printing, 182, 202
  reports, 162
  sizing, 203
mailing lists, 448-450
Main Menu, 40-41
{MAINMENU} command, 383
mapping, lookups, 152
margins, 217
marking
  records, 22, 101-103
  text blocks, 74
masks, 148
Master Classes, 352-354
master files, 262
matching, Pattern, 396
mathematical operators, 394-395
MAX( ) function, 410
MDY( ) function, 410
Memo Editor, 67
memo fields, 54, 59, 67, 95, 148
  accessing, 73
  entering data, 73-74
  expanding, 179
  formatting, 179-180

reports, 209
saving, 74
memos, 67
Menu bar action command, 345
menus
    building, 332-334
    creating, 340-341
    Global update, 138
    headings, 337
    Indexes\ranges, 117
    items
        adding, 345-346
        protecting, 346
    Layouts, 193
    Main Menu, 40-41
    Options, 83
    planning, 335
    Scripts, 41
    spacing, 344-345
    styling, 344-345
    tying scripts into systems, 374-375
MIN() function, 410
mirror images, 298
MOD() function, 410
modes
    Browse, 74
        editing fields, 90-92
        entering data, 75
    Change, 71
    Default, 148-149
    Expression, 133, 397
    Ignore, 198
    Insert, 71
    Learn Macro, 347
    Overwrite, 71
    Table, 133
        creating expressions, 397
    View
        defining input forms, 76
        entering data, 71-72
modifying
    application banners, 343
    mailing labels, 203-208
monochrome settings, adjusting for, 50
MONTH() function, 393, 411
moving
    fields, 87
    text, 87
multiple record viewing, 89

N

names
    field, 61
        dividing, 63
        rules, 63-65
    personal
        displaying, 454
        expressions, 445-448
needs, data, 60-63
nested IF statements, 94, 401
networks

default settings, 441
    installing, 439-441
    limitations, 441
    passwords, 440-441
    scripts, 442
    user limits, 440
{NOCLEAR} command, 383
None default mode, 148
numeric fields, 54, 59, 64
    entering data, 72-73
    formatting, 78, 176, 180-181
    sort orders, 115
    summary databases, 198
numeric formats settings, 50

O

on-line services, 434
one-time searches, 133
{ONERROR} command, 383
{ONESCAPE} command, 383-384
{ONKEY} command, 384
{ONMAIN} command, 384
open database scripts, 356
operators, 393
    character, 396
    date, 396
    logical, 394
    mathematical, 394-395
    relational, 394-396
Options menu, 83
options, *see* commands
OR statement, 134, 138
organizing
    data, 24-25, 189-190
    records, 297-298
OUT OF MEMORY error code, 456
output, 159
    choosing, 25-27
Overwrite mode, 71

P

Pack command, 102-106, 441
packing records, 101, 104-106
Page eject command, 216
Page footers, 173
Page headers, 170
page layout, 216-217
painted input forms, 88
palettes
    Black/White, 294
    color, 293, 342
parameters
    link, 233
    linking, 250-251
parent files, 105, 229
passing variables, 453
passwords, 204
    network, 440-441
pasting, 297
patches, 434

paths, script, 373-374
Pattern matching, 396
    settings, 50
{PAUSE} command, 385
PAYMENT( ) function, 411
personal names
    displaying, 454
    expressions, 445-448
PgDn key, 74
pieces, set, 121-123
placing fields, 81
    custom reports, 197-198
    mailing labels, 202
planning
    applications, 367
    databases, 55-59
    menus, 335
{PLAY} command, 385-386
playing scripts from Tools menu,
    358-359
point-and-shoot method, 20, 156
pointing, 128
portions, detail, 119
Post command, 262-263, 269-270
posting
    data, 265-269
    transactions, 240-243
pre-defined label sizes, 200-201
prefixes, 445-448
preprocessing reports, 178
prevent change/enter settings, 50
previewing reports, 182
print attribute flags, 204
Print command, 41
print drivers, 183-184
printers
    defining, 208-209
    selecting, 183
printing
    mailing labels, 202
    reports, 182-183
private directories, 442
    files, 443
Prodigy on-line service, 434
programs
    COLLAGE, 431
    editor, 420
    HOTSHOT Graphics, 431
{PROMPT} command, 386
prompt control, 359, 364
Prompt field rule, 150
prompt lines, 41
protecting
    data, 89
    databases, 51
    menu items, 346
    pseudo fields, 298-299
prototypes, 430-431
pseudo fields, 298-299
PV( ) function, 411

Q

quick scripts, 357
Quick Setup reports, 165-166

R

R P L language, 39
RAND( ) function, 411
Range command, 98
Range Settings screen, 23
ranges, 97
    comparison searches, 131-132
    defining, 208-209
    refining, 194-195
{READ} command, 387
README files, 433
real fields, 154, 195, 298
RECCOUNT( ) function, 411
RECNO( ) function, 411
Reconfigure a database command, 111,
    441
reconfiguring databases, 120
records, 54, 60
    carrying data between, 363
    composite, 233
    creating, 17
    data entry, 17-18
    deleted, copying, 105
    deleting, 101
    designing, 301-302
    entering, 66-68
    extracting non-matching,
      272-273
    finding, 301-302
    found, 25
    grouping, 186
    indexing, 210-213
    marking, 22, 101-103
    multiple, 89
    organizing, 297-298
    packing, 101-106
    retrieving, 103
    summary, 240-243
    viewing, 23, 74
RECSIZE( ) function, 412
refining
    data retrieval, 133
    reports, 194-195
relational
    commands, 262-265, 282-283
    databases, 227-228
    operators, 394-396
removing duplicates, 126
REMSPECIAL( ) function, 412
REPLICATE( ) function, 412
Report headers, 170
report writer, 160-161, 164
Report Writer screen, 31

reporting
  data, 30-33
  databases, 194
  fields, 100
reports, 26, 161
  browse tables, 162
  columnar, 162-164
  creating databases, 168-175
  custom
    creating, 166
    placing fields, 197-198
  enhancing in sets, 237-240
  input forms, 161
  letters, 162
  mailing labels, 162
  memo fields, 209
  preprocessing, 178
  previewing, 182
  printing, 182-183
  Quick Setup, 165-166
  refining, 194-195
  saving, 182
  statistical, 220
  subgrouping, 189
Required field rule, 150
restricting access, 51, 162,
  351-352, 440-441
resynching files, 129
retrieving
  data
    linked, 254-255
    refining, 133
  records, 103
RIGHT() function, 412
ROUND() function, 412
{RPL} command, 387
RTOD() function, 412
RTRIM() function, 412
rules, field, 18, 143
  calculating, 18-21
  checking, 22, 23
  creating, 18-19, 144, 300-301
  creating expressions, 398
  dates, 402
  saving, 21
Runtime Module utility
  creating applications, 418
  installing, 418-420

S

save As command, 194
saved searches, 133
  creating, 130
saving
  field rules, 21
  memo fields, 74
  memos, 67
  reports, 182
  variables between sessions, 371

scrambling files, 258
{SCREENFREEZE} command, 387
{SCREENOFF} command, 353, 387-388
{SCREENON} command, 388
screens, 46-48
  Calculated fields, 29
  color
    Version 1, 293-294
    Version 2, 295-296
  context-sensitive help, 48
  Crosstab Description, 282
  customizing, 27-28
  help, 350
  input, 299-300
  Range Settings, 23
  Report Writer, 31
  settings, default, 48-50
  splitting, 182
  Summarization Selection, 136
  template, 342-343
script commands
  {ABORT}, 379
  {ALLOWKEYS}, 392
  {BEEP}, 379
  {CANCEL}, 379
  {CASE}, 379-380
  {CLEAR}, 380
  {DEBUGOFF}, 380
  {DEBUGON}, 380
  {ENDAPP}, 381
  {EXEC}, 381-382
  {EXECCLR}, 381
  {GOTO}, 382
  {IF}, 382
  {LOOP}, 382-383
  {MAINMENU}, 383
  {NOCLEAR}, 383
  {ONERROR}, 383
  {ONESCAPE}, 383-384
  {ONKEY}, 384
  {ONMAIN}, 384
  {PAUSE}, 385
  {PLAY}, 385-386
  {PROMPT}, 386
  {READ} command, 387
  {RPL}, 387
  {SCREENFREEZE}, 387
  {SCREENOFF}, 353, 387-388
  {SCREENON}, 388
  {SET}, 360-361, 388
  {SHOW}, 388-389
  {TONE}, 389
  {TOOLEND}, 389
  {TRIGKEYS}, 389-390
  {VSAVE}, 370, 390-391
  {WAITKEY}, 391
  {WAITSCRN}, 391-392
  {WAITUNTIL}, 392
  {WRITE}, 354, 391

script libraries, 376-377
script variables, 359-360
   carrying data between records, 363
   setting, 360-361
   system, 360
SCRIPTED.EXE utility, 424-427
scripting languages, 430
scripts, 331, 349, 355-356, 431
   automating with exclamation points
     (!), 370-371
   comparing with applications, 315-316
   creating dialog boxes with menu
     structures, 363-365
   dialog, 308
     creating, 316-318
   editing, 424-427
   field statistics variables, 375-376
   for accounts receivable, 374
   for automatic file execution, 369-370
   hotkey, 357
   keystroke, 308, 426
     creating, 318-319
   libraries, 428-429
   locating, 357-358
   networks, 442
   open database, 356
   paths, 373-374
   playing from Tools menus, 358-359
   quick, 357
   saving variables between sessions,
    371
   shortcuts, 300
   single, 426
   solving real-life problems with, 377
   start up, 356
   steps for using, 356
   Tools, 319-320, 357, 361-363
   trigger, 326-327, 357, 365-366
     passing data between files,
      327-328
   tying into menu systems,
    374-375
Scripts menu, 41
Search and replace command, 99-101
Search command, 99-101
searches, 130-131
   defining, 133-134
   one-time, 133
   ranges, 131-132
   saved, 133
     creating, 130
selecting
   fields, 20
   printers, 183
{SET} command, 360-361, 388
set pieces, 121-123
sets, 39, 58, 89, 228
   browse tables, 97
     creating, 247-249
   copying, 256-258
   creating, 228-233, 247, 251-256
   data entry, 249-250
   documenting with A4DOC, 420-424
   enhancing reports, 237-240

   fields rules, 252
   fine-tuning with link parameters, 233
   forms, 247-249
   summarizing data, 277-282
   zooming files, 234-235
setting up unique indexes, 125
settings, default
   networks, 441
   screen, 48-50
SHARE command, 443
shortcuts, script, 300
{SHOW} command, 388-389
SIGN( ) function, 412
SIN( ) function, 413
single scripts, 426
single step enters settings, 50
sizing
   mailing labels, 203
   windows, 175-176
Skip Entry field rule, 150
software, integrated, 37
sort orders, 114-115
SOUNDEX( ) function, 413
SPACE( ) function, 413
spacing menus, 344-345
splitting screens, 182
spreadsheet format, 68
spreadsheets, importing, 286
SQRT( ) function, 413
start up scripts, 356
starting Alpha Four, 13-14
startup command, 367
startup directories, 368
statements
   AND, 134, 138
   IF, 217, 400-401
     cascading, 401
     nested, 94, 401
   OR, 134, 138
   true, 94
statistical reports, 220
statistics, field, 219
storing expressions, 395
STR( ) function, 134, 403, 413
strings
   data, 95
   find, 425
stripping desktops, 427
structure, application, 335-337
STUFF( ) function, 413
styling menus, 344-345
Sub-menu command, 346
subapplications, 351
subgrouping, 114, 301-302
   files, 121-130
   reports, 189
subgroups, 208-209, 213
SUBSTR( ) function, 414
Subtract command, 262-265, 272-273,
   282-283
Summarization Selection screen, 136
Summarize command, 136,
   262-264
summarizing data without reports, 219

summary
    databases, 136-137, 197,
        221-223
    fields, 173-175, 196-197
    creating, 195
    numeric fields, 198
    records, 240-243
support files, 194
suppressed blank lines, 173
swap mode settings, 50
sWitch command, 237, 250
switches, 351
    application startup, 369
switching
    applications, 350-352
    compared to zooming, 236-237
syntax, 394
    functions, 394
    SCRIPTED.EXE utility, 424
SYSTEM database, 207-208
system script variables, 360
system variables, 323

T

table format, 68
Table mode, 133
    creating expressions, 397
tables, 54
    browse, 26, 90-92
        color, 92-94
        data entry, 96-97
        default, 74-76
        defining, 79-82
        editing, 79-82
        reports, 162
        sets, 97
    lookup, 151-152
TAN() function, 414
templates, 147
    screens, 342-343
terminate, stay resident (TSR), 39
terminology, database, 54
text
    deleting, 87
    fields, 95-96
    justification, 176
    moving, 87
text blocks
    copying, 74
    deleting, 74
    inserting, 74
    marking, 74
TIME() function, 414
Timeslips billing system, 377
titles, column, 171-172
{TONE} command, 389
{TOOLEND} command, 389
Tools Box, 316
Tools menus, 358-359
tools script, 319-320, 357, 361-363
Top/Bottom margins command, 217
TOSECONDS() function, 414

TOTIME() function, 414
transaction
    databases, 194
    files, 262
transactions, 240-243
TRANSFORM() function, 414
trigger
    events, 326-327, 365-366
    scripts, 326-327, 357, 365-366
        passing data between files,
            327-328
    variables, 366
{TRIGKEYS} command, 389
Trim command, 207
TRIM() function, 396, 414
true statements, 94
TSR (terminate, stay resident), 39

U

.UDN files, 372-373
UNABLE TO WRITE PRINTER DRIVER FILE
    error code, 455
Undelete record command, 102
uninterruptible power supply (UPS), 449
unique
    data, 176
    indexes, 125
unsuppressible blank lines, 171
Update an index command, 129, 441
updates, global, 253
updating
    fields, globally, 139-141
    indexes, 129
UPPER() function, 414
UPS (uninterruptible power supply), 449
user access, restricting, 162
user-defined variables, 323
user-entered fields, 85, 144-146
utilities
    A4DOC, 420-424
    A4LIB.EXE, 428-430
    Runtime Module, 418-420
    SCRIPTED.EXE, 425-427
        syntax, 425
utilities should lock settings, 50

V

VAL() function, 415
Value data, 176
Value default mode, 148
variables, 323-324
    creating, 325-326
    defining, 324-325
    field statistics, 375-376
    passing, 453
    saving between sessions, 371
    script, 359-360
        carrying data between records,
            363
        setting, 360-361
        system, 360

setting filters with, 378
system, 323
trigger, 366
unsettable, 378
user-defined, 323
viewing, 326
View mode
    entering data, 71-72
    input forms, 76
viewing
    multiple records, 89
    records, 23, 74
    spreadsheet format, 68
    table format, 68
    variables, 326
visual links, 240
{VRESTORE} command, 389-390
{VSAVE} command, 370, 390-391

W

W_COUNT() function, 415
W_UPPER() function, 415
{WAITFOR} command, 392
{WAITKEY} command, 391
{WAITSCRN} command, 391
{WAITUNTIL} command, 392
WARNING: UNEXPECTED END OF FILE
  error code, 458
wildcards, 257
Window On command, 48
windows, 46-48
    activating, 48
    Expression, 21
    sizing, 175-176
word processors, 218
WORD() function, 415
WordPerfect, exporting data to, 286
wordwrapped fields, 90
{WRITE} command, 354, 391
WRITE ERROR error code, 457

Y

YEAR() function, 415

Z

Zap command, 441
ZBLANK() function, 415
zeroes, averaging, 198-199
Zoom command, 97, 234-237
ZOOM STACK FULL ERROR error code, 457
zooming
    compared to switching,
      236-237
    files, 234-235

Free Catalog!

Mail us this registration form today, and we'll send you a free catalog featuring Que's complete line of best-selling books.

Name of Book _____

Name _____

Title _____

Phone ( ) _____

Company _____

Address _____

City _____

State _____ ZIP _____

Please check the appropriate answers:

1. Where did you buy your Que book?
   - ☐ Bookstore (name: _____)
   - ☐ Computer store (name: _____)
   - ☐ Catalog (name: _____)
   - ☐ Direct from Que
   - ☐ Other: _____

2. How many computer books do you buy a year?
   - ☐ 1 or less
   - ☐ 2-5
   - ☐ 6-10
   - ☐ More than 10

3. How many Que books do you own?
   - ☐ 1
   - ☐ 2-5
   - ☐ 6-10
   - ☐ More than 10

4. How long have you been using this software?
   - ☐ Less than 6 months
   - ☐ 6 months to 1 year
   - ☐ 1-3 years
   - ☐ More than 3 years

5. What influenced your purchase of this Que book?
   - ☐ Personal recommendation
   - ☐ Advertisement
   - ☐ In-store display
   - ☐ Price
   - ☐ Que catalog
   - ☐ Que mailing
   - ☐ Que's reputation
   - ☐ Other: _____

6. How would you rate the overall content of the book?
   - ☐ Very good
   - ☐ Good
   - ☐ Satisfactory
   - ☐ Poor

7. What do you like *best* about this Que book?
   _____
   _____

8. What do you like *least* about this Que book?
   _____
   _____

9. Did you buy this book with your personal funds?
   - ☐ Yes   ☐ No

10. Please feel free to list any other comments you may have about this Que book.
    _____
    _____
    _____

⌐Que

Order Your Que Books Today!

Name _____

Title _____

Company _____

City _____

State _____ ZIP _____

Phone No. ( ) _____

Method of Payment:

Check ☐ (Please enclose in envelope.)

Charge My: VISA ☐   MasterCard ☐

American Express ☐

Charge # _____

Expiration Date _____

Order No.	Title	Qty.	Price	Total

You can **FAX** your order to **1-317-573-2583**. Or call **1-800-428-5331, ext. ORDR** to order direct.

Please add $2.50 per title for shipping and handling.

Subtotal _____

Shipping & Handling _____

Total _____

⌐Que

BUSINESS REPLY MAIL

First Class Permit No. 9918   Indianapolis, IN

Postage will be paid by addressee

11711 N. College
Carmel, IN 46032

||.|..|.||.||..||....||..|.||.||.|.|.|.|..||....||.|.||

BUSINESS REPLY MAIL

First Class Permit No. 9918   Indianapolis, IN

Postage will be paid by addressee

11711 N. College
Carmel, IN 46032

||.|..|.||.||..||....||..|.||.||.|.|.|.|..||....||.|.||